D1577890

RHETORIC & DIALECTIC

IN THE TIME OF GALILEO

RHETORIC &

DIALECTIC IN THE

TIME OF GALILEO

Jean Dietz Moss and William A. Wallace

The Catholic University of America Press

Washington, D.C.

The paper used in this publication meets the minimum requirements of
American National Standards for Information Science—Permanence of
Paper for Printed Library materials, ansi z39.48-1984.

∞

LIBRARY OF CONGRESS CATALOGING-IN-PUBLICATION DATA
Moss, Jean Dietz.
    Rhetoric and dialectic in the time of Galileo / by Jean Dietz Moss
and William A. Wallace.
        p. cm.
    Includes bibliographical references and index.
    ISBN 0-8132-1331-2 (alk. paper)
        1. European literature—Renaissance, 1450–1600—History and criti-
cism. 2. Rhetoric, Renaissance. I. Wallace, William A. II. Title.
    PN721 .M67 2003
    808'.009'024—dc21

                                                2002009752

Contents

Preface

This book had its origin in courses the authors taught in a collaboration that extended over a period of more than fifteen years. The courses, offered to graduate students at The Catholic University of America in the School of Philosophy and in the Rhetoric Program of the Department of English, were centered on the period of the emergent scientific revolution. Because of the interdisciplinary nature of the content, we hope that this distillation may be of interest to other scholars and students in the fields of philosophy, Medieval and Renaissance studies, rhetoric, and the history of science.

The introduction of this work, "The Disciplinary Scene," situates the authors' plea for a broader understanding of the nature of rhetoric and dialectic during the late Renaissance in Northern Italy. The discussion focuses on the teaching and practice of the arts of persuasion in Galileo's time and place and relates earlier reforms of the *studia humanitatis* to it. The authors chose to focus on the Galileo scene because concepts of argumentation and proof figure so prominently in the famous trial of Galileo, and because the pedagogues whose writings are translated in the book crossed Galileo's path in important ways. It was at the trial in 1633 that Galileo was faulted for his misuse of the privilege given him to publish a dialogue on the Copernican issue. The style of argumentation assumed to be appropriate to the subject by the Church authorities and that actually used by Galileo became a pivotal issue. The deeper issues of what he believed and what he tried to prove were alleged to be revealed by what he wrote. While we do not attempt to rehearse here the details of this crisis in science and faith, we do try to clarify the methods of argumentation manifested in the trial, which should then reflect back upon the scientific principles at stake.

Current readings of the period tend to treat humanist reforms of the traditional liberal arts as universally welcomed, overlooking disciplinary concepts that continued to dominate the practice of philosophical argument into the eighteenth century. This study seeks to show that these concepts did not languish, but instead were infused with new energy through fresh translations and commentaries on Aristotelian logic and rhetoric and by the application of scholastic method to classical rhetorical works revived in the Renaissance. The humanist movement, thus, did not everywhere cast off its scholastic heritage so much as combine it with recovery of the classics, particularly in the influential writings of scholars in the Northern Italian cities of Rome and Padua, from which the translations emanate.

The translations themselves provide evidence for our claims and establish the linkage of Aristotelian thought with the dilemma of Galileo. They make available in English substantial excerpts from published writings of two scholars of the late Renaissance, Ludovico Carbone and Antonio Riccobono. Their writings emanate from two influential institutions of the time. The first, the Collegio Romano, was established at Rome by the Jesuits in 1551. Carbone was a student there during the second decade of its foundation, where he became so impressed by its professors that he attempted to make their teachings known through his many publications on logic, rhetoric, theology, and sacred oratory. The extensive influence of the Jesuit *ratio studiorum* adopted by the Order's colleges throughout the scholarly world makes Carbone's contribution of particular importance to the history of the arts of communication during the period. Likewise, Paduan Aristotelianism was equally important to late Renaissance thought. Riccobono represents the Paduan school in his writings on rhetoric. His innovative translation of Aristotle's rhetoric and his commentaries on the work offer insights as to the application of rhetoric to a variety of subjects beyond those considered proper to it.

Each of the translations is preceded by an introduction to the work, which places the text in relation to thought of the period. The order of the translations offered and a brief description of their content is as follows:

Section One. Ludovico Carbone's *Introductio in logicam*
   This work summarizes Jesuit teachings on the essentials of logic, its nature, and kinds, and treats Aristotelian concepts of human nature and the operations of the intellect.

Section Two. Carbone's *Tabulae rhetoricae,* a guide to Cipriano Soarez's *De arte rhetorica*
   Here Carbone orders and capsulizes the perennially popular text by the Spanish Jesuit, a work used in Jesuit schools throughout the world into the eighteenth century.

Section Three. Carbone's *De arte dicendi*
   This companion volume to the *Tabulae* offers disputations on definitions, principles, and parts of rhetoric.

Section Four. Antonio Riccobono on Aristotle's *Rhetoric*
   Three essays written by Riccobono comment on Aristotle's *Rhetoric,* which he had also translated into Latin.

Section Five. Carbone's *De oratoria et dialectica inventione*

This work offers a glimpse of an unusual advanced course in which invention in logic and in rhetoric are described. It compares the aims and methods of the two arts.

Section Six. Carbone's *Divinus orator*

Carbone offers this text for the use of preachers, claiming that it is the first of such books to take its principles and illustrative materials entirely from Sacred Scripture. It contains his most refined and sophisticated treatment of rhetoric developed in relation to human nature and ordered to the aims of preaching.

Both of us have contributed to the completion of this study. The introductory essay is chiefly the work of Moss and the translations are by Wallace. Both have contributed introductions to the translations, Wallace to Carbone's logic and Riccobono's essays and Moss to the rhetorical texts. The ideas, however, in the interpretations of history and texts are impossible to allocate definitively, as each has benefitted by hearing the other during the many classes we have team taught and in our extracurricular discussions.

Introduction

The Disciplinary Scene

Galileo and Argumentation

The setting for this book is Northern Italy in the late sixteenth and early seventeenth centuries, a time when arguments were more than entertaining verbal duels, where they might mean death or imprisonment for the orator or the author. Here is where Giordano Bruno and Tommaso Campanella expressed their opinions too rashly for those who possessed the power to determine what might be argued in a public forum. The punishment for their trespasses was severe. And it is the same time and space where Galileo Galilei learned the folly of speaking too strongly on one side of the question.

In this study the focus is on the twin arts of argumentation, rhetoric and dialectic, as these were taught and practiced in the late Renaissance. Dialectic had been the approved means of exploring problems in the realm of the speculative sciences since the late Middle Ages. In that period the provinces of the two arts were clearly demarcated, but in the Renaissance the boundaries were debated and overturned by humanists in Italy and Northern Europe, of whom the most influential were Northern Protestants. Those contestants and the shifting boundaries in the arts created part of the background against which Galileo's problem with the Church must be viewed.

The art of rhetoric was taught everywhere in the schools and its concepts were found in many a manual. But no rules for its application to this scene are inscribed. The concept of appropriateness, *aptus, to prepon,* decorum, was abstractly recommended, but the author had to calculate the elements critical to the moment. Life might depend on the assessment or on whether the argument deserved to be heard despite the risks. Galileo knew the risks; well-placed friends had told him. Nevertheless he argued, cajoled, and ridiculed. He skewered the refutations of Copernicanism voiced by his powerful opponents, but in the long run he failed to win them over. His arguments were not persuasive for those who mattered most. Why?

Galileo's *Dialogue on the Two Chief World Systems* provides some answers, but these must be considered only partial answers because ultimately the truth lies hidden in the human psyche—the emotions and the motives of Pope Urban VIII, the Qualifiers of the Holy Office, others who were Galileo's enemies, and Galileo himself. The surface objection to Galileo's arguments was that he *claimed* to present scientific (i.e., dialectical) arguments on both sides, but he actually presented only one side fairly, ridiculing the other.[1]

1. The report of the commission appointed by Pope Urban VIII to review the *Dialogue*

The intent of our book is not to rehearse the case of Galileo in its entirety, although we shall revisit it briefly. Rather, our purpose is to present what lay in the background of those charges against him, to look closely at what the acknowledged forms of rhetorical and scientific arguments were in the period. One of the barriers to our modern comprehension of the injustices done to Galileo and, by extension, to the practice of argumentation of the time is a lack of familiarity with the disciplines taken for granted in the charges against him. So much attention in recent scholarship has been given to style, the part of rhetoric that first captivates the modern eye, that the art resident in the sinews of the arguments has often been overlooked. Where attention has been directed to argumentation, it generally lingers over early humanist reforms, not noticing that in some geographical regions these reforms were absorbed and reworked within a much older heritage. That heritage, clarified and augmented, continued to furnish the essential concepts and principles for the arts of reasoning, particularly in areas with a strong Roman Catholic allegiance such as that of Northern Italy in the mid-sixteenth century.

The effect of the recovery of Cicero's letters and lost works and the finding of Quintilian's treatise on rhetorical education has been well documented by many scholars in the history of rhetoric throughout the twentieth century. On the other hand, only a few have described the continuing importance of Aristotle.[2] It is true that late scholastic extensions of his logic became an easy target for the frustrations of budding humanist scholars who labored over elaborate *insolubilia*. Polemics against dialectic were received with high approval, and are so even today.[3] But nevertheless

---

appears in *Le Opere di Galileo Galilei*, ed. Antonio Favaro 20 vols. in 21 (Florence: Giunti Barbèra, 1890–1909, rpt. 1968), 19:327.102–3. Stillman Drake translates the major findings in his translation and edition of Galileo's *Dialogue Concerning the Two Chief World Systems* (Berkeley: University of California, 1967) 477. Moss discusses the charges at length in *Novelties in the Heavens: Rhetoric and Science in the Copernican Controversy* (Chicago: University of Chicago Press, 1993), chapter nine; Maurice Finnochiaro translates the opinions of the opponents of Galileo in *The Galileo Affair* (Berkeley: University of California Press, 1989), chapter nine. Annibale Fantoli discusses the problems with Galileo's advocacy in *Galileo for Copernicanism and for the Church*; George V. Coyne, trans. (Studi Galileiani, vol. 3; Vatican City: Vatican Observatory Foundation, 1996, 2d ed.), chapter three.

2. Paul Oskar Kristeller was the first to draw attention to the importance of Aristotle to the Renaissance in *Renaissance Thought I* (New York: Harper & Row, Harper Torchbooks, 1961); more recently Larry Green describes the Renaissance appropriation in "The Reception of Aristotle's Rhetoric in the Renaissance," in *Peripatetic Rhetoric After Aristotle*, edited by William W. Fortenbaugh and David C. Mirhady, Rutgers University Studies in Classical Humanities, vol. 6 (New Brunswick, New Jersey: Transaction, 1994), 320–48. The translation history of Aristotle's *Rhetoric* is carefully treated by Paul D. Brandes, *A History of Aristotle's Rhetoric with a Bibliography of Early Printings* (Metuchen, New Jersey and London: The Scarecrow Press, 1989).

3. Petrarch vented his frustration in a letter to Tommasso Caloria of March 12, ca. 1335, *Epistola de rebus familiaribus et variae*, edited by J. Fracasetti. 3 vols. (Florence: 1859–63), I, 7 [6]; English

the general terminology and concepts of reasoning he outlined in the *Organon* guided the protocols of serious scholarship in Italy during the Renaissance and far beyond.

To help to fill in the background more fully, this work offers translations from Northern Italian works on the arts of rhetoric and dialectic by two authors whose thought was influential in Galileo's day. One may wonder how translations from only two authors' works can support the claims we have made regarding the importance of this neglected classical strain in the history of the period. The reason is that the writings of Ludovico Carbone and Antonio Riccobono emanate from a much broader provenance and provide the clearest and most coherent account of that background. In addition, the two authors also had close connections to Galileo. The linkage between Carbone and Galileo was engendered by their mutual interest in the teachings of scholars at the Jesuit College of Rome. Carbone was a student at that College in the late 1550s and early 1560s. The University of Padua was the site of Galileo's contact with Riccobono. He was already an authority on rhetoric at that university when Galileo wrote to him in 1588, apparently to seek his help in gaining a position as professor of mathematics there. Riccobono had given the funeral oration for Giuseppe Moletti, whose chair Galileo wished to have, and the professor seems to have taken an interest in Galileo's suit.[4]

These two important schools illustrate the prevalence of Aristotelianism within the Humanistic current, and they issue from two places of particular importance to Galileo: Rome and Padua. In Rome the Collegio Romano carried on the scholastic tradition while at the same time endeavoring to incorporate a humanistic regard for classical texts. Instituted by Ignatius Loyola in 1551, the College was especially noted for its teachers of mathematics, logic, and natural philosophy.

Study of the humanities was prefaced by immersion in the *De arte rhetorica* (1562) of the Spanish Jesuit Cipriano Soarez, one of the most perennially popular texts in rhetorical history. Soarez's disciple Peter Perpinian came to the College to teach rhetoric.[5] Apparently, Perpinian was

---

translation by Hans Nachod in *The Renaissance Philosophy of Man*, edited by Ernst Cassirer, Paul Oskar Kristeller, and John Herman Randall, Jr. (Chicago: University of Chicago Press, 1983), 134–39. Valla's reservations are treated at length by Peter Mack in *Renaissance Argument* (Leiden: E. J. Brill, 1993), 31–50ff. Cesare Vasoli treats Valla's views on dialectics in *La dialettica e retorica dell'Umanesimo* (Milano: Feltrinelli,1968), 41–77. Neal Gilbert points out that while the early humanists criticized dialectics as taught by the "Terminists," many of them thought it important to students' education, "The Italian Humanists and Disputation," in *Renaissance Essays in Honor of Hans Baron*, edited by A. Molho and J. A. Tedeschi (Florence: Sansoni, 1971), 203–26.

4. Wallace discusses the links between Galileo and Riccobono in "Antonio Riccobono: The Teaching of Rhetoric in 16th-Century Padua," *Rhetoric and Pedagogy*, edited by Winifred Bryan Horner and Michael Leff (Mahwah, NJ: Lawrence Erlbaum Associates, 1995), 149–70.

5. Lawrence J. Flynn, S.J., provides a facsimile of the Latin text, a translation, an introduction,

in turn the mentor of Ludovico Carbone. On becoming a pedagogue himself, Carbone capsulized Soarez's rhetoric in a set of tables: *Tabulae rhetoricae Cypriani Soarii* (1589).[6] An English rendering of these tables is included in the second section of the translations. Carbone later became well known for his many books on rhetoric. He also sought to convey Jesuit teachings on logic in another work, *Introductio in logicam,* according to his own testimony and that of a discomforted Jesuit professor at the Collegio, Paolo della Valle, who thought Carbone had borrowed too much from his logic without sufficient acknowledgment.[7] Since the Aristotelian logic conveyed by Carbone's text is propaedeutic to the rhetorical texts that follow it, excerpts from his *Introductio in logicam* are included in the first section of the translations.

The influence of the *ratio studiorum* drawn up for Jesuit schools was extensive. Not only was it adopted by other schools of the Order throughout Europe, Asia, and the New World, it became the model for curricula for other institutions as well. Rhetoric was also a subject highly valued by the Jesuits, as Carbone's textbooks derived from their courses illustrates.

Padua was the site of an Aristotelian school of philosophy, which had been presided over by Jacopo Zabarella (1533–1589) at the University of Padua shortly before Galileo arrived there in 1592. Galileo knew of Zabarella's work, and he seems also to have been acquainted with the rhetorical teachings of Riccobono. Whether consciously or not, he used Riccobono's terminology in describing his rhetorical intent in the *Dialogue.*[8] Both Riccobono and Zabarella shared an interest in argumentation, although they differed on the nuances of rhetoric's scope and its subservience to dialectic.[9] The Paduan approach to rhetoric evinced in the

---

and a commentary in his "The 'De Arte Rhetorica' (1568)," 2 parts, diss. University of Florida (Ann Arbor: University Microfilms, 1955, Doctoral Dissertation Series, No. 16,926). Flynn notes that the text was reprinted 134 times from its first edition in 1562 to 1735. He also provides a summary of the careers of Soarez and Perpinian, who both started teaching in Jesuit schools in Portugal. Moss treats rhetorical instruction there in "The Rhetoric Course at the Collegio Romano In the Latter Half of the Sixteenth Century," *Rhetorica* 4 no. 2 (Spring, 1986), 137–51, but this discussion should be supplemented by the extensive study of Renaissance rhetoric by Marc Fumaroli *L'Âge de l'Éloquence: Rhétorique et "res literaria" de la Renaissance au seuil de l'époque classique* (Geneva: Librairie Droz, 1980). On the contribution of Carbone and the Collegio Romano at the time of our focus, see 175–86.

6. Creating *tabulae* for Soarez's text was not unusual. Since the book was often used in more than one course, its repetition meant that a summary of its definitions, principles and rules was found to be quite useful. These took various forms. From 1574 to 1836, 28 *tabulae,* 35 *compendia,* and 10 *methodus* based on the text were published.

7. Wallace notes this in his discussion of Della Valla's logic in *Galileo and His Sources: The Heritage of the Collegio Romano in Galileo's Science* (Princeton: Princeton University Press, 1984), 19. Moss discusses Carbone's treatises on rhetoric in "The Rhetoric Course at the Collegio Romano," 137–51.

8. The point is discussed briefly below, and in Moss, *Novelties in the Heavens,* 10–11.

9. Wallace, "Antonio Riccobono," 149–70.

writings of Riccobono's predecessors Hermolao Barbaro, Carlo Sigonio, and Marc Antonio Mureto culminated in the sophisticated, nuanced work of Riccobono. He taught the humanities at the university from 1571 to his death in 1599, gaining wide respect for the erudition displayed in his translation of and essays on Aristotle's *Rhetoric*. An account of his work and translations of these essays are included in section four.

The remaining translations are of other works of the prolific Carbone. As a group they convey something of the richness and breadth of the Northern Italian blend of scholastic-humanistic teachings on rhetoric. Carbone seems to have been a popular author, judging from Della Valle's statement that he was well known and from the fact that many editions of his work can still be found in various libraries in Europe and some in the United States. In his *De arte dicendi* (1589), a portion of which is translated in section three, Carbone defines the nature of rhetoric and describes its parts in a text meant for beginning students. More advanced students were treated to a full exposition of invention in *De oratoria et dialectica inventione* (1589), which Carbone customarily refers to as his *De inventione,* of which a substantial excerpt is translated in section five. Here, Carbone discusses the essence of both rhetorical and dialectical invention, taking into account ancient and contemporary texts. The final translation in section six excerpts what must be regarded as his master work, *Divinus orator* (1595). There he combines his knowledge of rhetoric with theology to give the reader a complete course in rhetoric as applied to preaching on sacred texts. He draws his rhetorical principles from the divine orators—prophets, apostles, and Jesus—to provide a sanctified handbook for the timorous.

Carbone's writings show that Aristotelian logic taught at the Collegio was undergirded by an understanding of rhetoric as defined by Quintilian: "the good man speaking well." This Ciceronian-Quintilianesque view of rhetoric combined scholastic thought and method with humanistic erudition. That meant in the case of rhetoric that logical argumentation was central to the training of "the good man," for "speaking well" required a thorough knowledge of Aristotelian logic in addition to mastery of the stylistic repertoire.

Returning to Galileo and his connection to the Collegio Romano, we know that he studied manuscript lecture notes on Aristotelian dialectic and demonstration by its Jesuit professors. He evidently did so during 1588 or 1589, about the same time that Carbone probably availed himself of those treatises in preparing his works for publication. Among the lecture notes, which were regularly deposited in the Collegio's library, Galileo copied out a treatise on demonstration contained in a series of lectures by Della Valle. Wallace has argued that Galileo studied these texts to acquire a thorough knowledge of Aristotelian logic, probably in anticipation of gaining a teaching position at the University of Pisa.[10] We know also that he was acquainted with some of the Collegio's leading figures, that he revered the wisdom of Christopher Clavius, its prominent mathematician, and that he later challenged the authority of Clavius's successor Orazio Grassi, who had published a humanistic disputation on the comets. That Galileo may have had contact with Carbone also during his visits to the Collegio may be conjectured, though we have no proof of this. We know only that both men were influenced by the same logical texts, as the introduction and the excerpts from Carbone's *Logic* in section one make clear. Further details of Carbone's life and work may be found there as well.

Galileo, like most educated men of his time, was well trained in rhetoric as well as logic. He studied both in his years at Vallombrosa before entering the University of Pisa in 1581. An illustrious faculty of humanists taught at Pisa in the period: Francesco Robortello and Ciriaco Strozzi before Galileo's arrival, and Pietro Angelio Bargeo and Aldo Manucci during his stay. We can be sure that Galileo was thoroughly initiated there into the *studia humanitatis*. A passage from Isocrates which he translated into Latin is preserved in his collected works.[11] That he was a master of style and its application to argument is illustrated in many of his writings, but that he also understood distinctions in types of argument is not generally noted. His *Dialogue* contains various allusions to specific qualities of demonstrative, dialectical, and rhetorical discourse.[12] These distinctions became the fulcrum in the charges of the evaluators in Galileo's trial, who claimed that he attempted to persuade his readers of the superiority of the Copernican system. And ironically, because he was such a master of the arts, he could play with these modes in his *Dialogue*. On the other hand, the authorities of the Church during Galileo's trial in 1633 took quite seriously the traditional hierarchical distinctions that separated the certain knowledge of scientific demonstration from the probable reasoning of dialectic and the seemingly probable discourse of rhetoric.

Since the beginning of the Renaissance the disciplines of dialectic and rhetoric had been subject to revision by the humanists; thus for many in the academic world the content of the two arts was neither fixed nor indisputable. It was in fact a time of experimentation, of reconfiguration, as

10. Wallace has revealed the source of Galileo's expertise in logic in *Galileo and His Sources,* 16–23. Moss notes the coincidence of Carbone's and Galileo's study of the Collegio Romano materials in *Novelties in the Heavens,* 6.

11. *Opere,* IX, 283–84. For further details about his education and his use of rhetoric in his writings see Moss, "The Interplay of Science and Rhetoric in Seventeenth Century Italy, *Rhetorica* 7, no. 1 (Winter 1989). Details of the tenure of professors are found in the *Rotulus almi studii* in the Archivio di Stato of Pisa.

12. See the discussion in Moss, *Novelties in the Heavens,* chapter nine, especially 275–76.

the historical background that follows makes clear. Nevertheless, there were core elements of each art that could be invoked to challenge an opponent's intent.

Conservatism, religious and philosophical, appears to have motivated the Church to seek to hold the intellectual hard line against innovators. One might speculate as to whether the professors of rhetoric and philosophy whose books are described here were also motivated by their religious beliefs to adopt the positions they did. Oddly enough, the philosophical distinctions contained in the works translated are essential to understanding the intellectual milieu leading to the tragic denouement of the trial.

As is well known, the acceptable methodology for debate about scientific issues in Galileo's day was scholastic dialectic and demonstration. Logic furnished the format for the investigation and proof of arguments. Of course, "science" then referred to certainty, the knowledge of necessary truths arrived at in theology or any of the disciplines traditionally classified under philosophy: mathematics, natural philosophy, or metaphysics.[13] Certainty was most often illustrated by a demonstrative syllogism having both material and formal validity. Such demonstrations were not easy to formulate. Generally they were achieved only after a thorough review of sense evidence, principles, causes, and opposing opinions. When an argument seemed no longer merely probable and firm premises could be posited, a conclusion could be shown to follow necessarily. Demonstrations in natural philosophy were the most difficult to establish because physical evidence could be recalcitrant or deceptive or because a mixture of proofs from different philosophical fields could be required, for example, the application of mathematics to physics. Galileo was a pioneer in combining such proofs. Theoretically, rhetoric had no part to play in scientific demonstration or in dialectical debate.

In Galileo's day only an expert in a discipline would attempt to propose a demonstration. If a speaker aired a scientific subject before an educated public and claimed to have a demonstration, even though all of the auditors might not have the specialized training in the subject to thoroughly understand it, all knew that the claim was meant to be taken seriously. A demonstration was supposed to embody truth. If its premises were certain; that ended debate.

On the other hand, when an expert could suggest only likely causes, even those that seemed to be exceedingly probable, he could claim only a probable or dialectical conclusion. Listeners to such arguments knew that such conclusions ranged from the strongly probable to the seemingly probable.

13. For a brief exposition of this term's meaning in the Renaissance, see W. A. Wallace, "Science," *Encyclopedia of the Renaissance,* 5: 427–29.

The trial of Galileo came about because Church authorities believed that in his *Dialogue* of 1632, Galileo had trespassed against the edict of 1616 not to hold or teach the Copernican system as true, since that system contradicted passages in the Scriptures. Although Galileo had been warned in 1616 by Cardinal Robert Bellarmine to obey the edict, he had reason to believe in 1624 that the new pope, Urban VIII, with whom he had had several conversations, might be lenient. The astronomer seems to have thought that if he treated the Copernican system as debatable and did not claim for it a more credible explanation for the movement of the planets than the Ptolemaic system, this would be acceptable to the pope.

Nevertheless, Galileo ventured further when he proposed to Urban in 1624 an "ingenious" demonstration of the earth's movement and its revolution around the sun based on the ebb and flow of the tides. The pope countered with the caveat that God in his infinite power could cause the tides to occur by some other means. After all, he said, despite proofs such as these, we still cannot know for certain the work of God's hands.[14] He thought that Galileo should confine himself to mathematical arguments in the book, since these would "save" (explain) the appearances but not rise to the level of absolute proof.

But to Galileo the Copernican question was no longer merely academic. He believed that he had found sufficient support in sensory evidence for strong arguments in favor of the Copernican hypothesis; moreover, he might have thought that the movement of the tides actually provided a demonstration. In order to appear to be impartial, however, he included signals in the *Dialogue* that could be interpreted to mean that he was merely intrigued by the issue and wished to pose artful arguments on either side. Thus, the frontispiece of the book described the contents as "presenting a congress of conversations over four days about the two Chief Systems of the World, Ptolemaic and Copernican," and, in smaller type, declares it as "proposing indeterminately philosophical and natural arguments as much on the one, as on the other side."

In the *Dialogue* Galileo brilliantly laced his dialectical arguments and demonstration with rhetoric, using luminous examples, convincing enthymemes, and rhetorical figures such as ridicule, irony, analogy, metaphor, metonymy, prosopopoeia, and more. He clarified and amplified his arguments so that no perceptive, intelligent person could but agree with Salviati, the stand-in for Galileo, that Copernicus was right. Only a stubborn, conservative peripatetic like Simplicio, Salviati's opponent, could still follow Ptolemy. Yet, at the end of the work, in case he should be seen

14. Giorgio Santillano presents convincing evidence that this was the point at which Urban expressed this view: *The Crime of Galileo* (Chicago: University of Chicago Press, 1955), chapter 8.

as arguing for the certainty of his proof, Galileo used Simplicio to recite Urban VIII's belief, that after all is said and done, we cannot know for certain the causes God has ordained for moving the tides.

The readers of the work included not only adepts of natural philosophy and mathematics, but also theologians, members of religious orders, princes of the secular and spiritual realms, humble clerics, and educated laymen. The convinced Ptolemaicists among them found their views given short shrift, the sillier arguments supportive of their side mockingly displayed, the weightier ones dismissed or ignored. Tycho Brahe's alternative view of the system of the world was not even mentioned. And Kepler's theory that the moon pulled the tides was treated by Galileo as occult nonsense, unworthy of Kepler's great mind.

Despite the clever, persuasive, and often amusing arguments, people opposed to the mobile earth theory thought that Galileo had not offered convincing physical proof that the earth moves; his argument from the tides seemed an unlikely story. After all, our senses declare that the earth is stable. Direct experimental evidence had to wait for two more centuries.

The pope, greatly annoyed at Galileo's treatment of his serious reservations and incensed at having his opposing argument expressed by Simplicio (a name with the connotation of simpleton), called for an evaluation of the book's contents and the author's intentions. Weary and ill, Galileo was forced to leave his home in Florence and travel to Rome by litter.

At his second interrogation by the papal commission of cardinal inquisitors appointed by the pope, Galileo came to admit that on rereading his work as requested, he found that it did indeed offer strong arguments for "the false side." But he added that he had only yielded to "[t]he natural gratification everyone feels for his own subtleties and for showing himself to be cleverer than the average man, by finding ingenious and apparent considerations of probability even in favor of false propositions." He quoted Cicero, "'I am more desirous of glory than is suitable'—if I had to write out the same arguments now, there is no doubt I would weaken them in such a way that they could not appear to exhibit a force which they really and essentially lack. My error then was, and I confess it, one of vain ambition, pure ignorance, and inadvertence."[15]

While we wince today at his tragic humiliation, the quotation reveals Galileo's awareness of the power of the rhetorician to shape arguments to his purpose. His humble confession did not soften the heart of the pope nor those of most of his inquisitors. The report of the commission found

---

15. "The Second Deposition" of Galileo , 30 April 1633 in Maurice A. Finnochiaro, *The Galileo Affair*, 278. Finnochiaro translates the documents of the trial and provides a valuable commentary.

Galileo "vehemently suspected of heresy." The cardinals did not believe his testimony to the effect that he had not "held or believed a doctrine contrary to the divine and Holy Scripture" after the edict of 1616 was handed down. Despite the edict's having prohibited advocacy of the Copernican thesis, he "dared to treat of it, defend it, and show it as probable."[16] Yet Galileo's apologia persuaded three of the ten inquisitors not to sign the sentencing report. One of these was the pope's own nephew, Cardinal Francesco Barberini.[17]

The Church hewed to the line of disciplinary distinctions. While the *Dialogue* may have been modeled on the popular Ciceronian dialogues, it was not merely an intellectual entertainment. It treated on the rhetorical stage a topic of natural philosophy and astronomy, presenting physical evidence through dialectical and putatively demonstrative arguments so persuasively that average readers could not discount their weight. These were not equally probable arguments on both sides of the controversy. Rather, the Copernican arguments were crafted as highly probable, and even certain, thereby inclining readers wholly to one side. Galileo's supporters could not help but delight in his ingenuity. But his critics saw the rhetorical presentation as a deceitful ploy, designed to evade censure and ensnare the unwitting. It was a dangerous work, they believed, masking as harmless and even-handed.

Traditional Rhetoric and Dialectic

Rhetoric was central to the humanist revision of the medieval liberal arts and even to reforms in the political and cultural practices of Italian cities, as Salvatore Camporeale has argued, building on the famous study of Renaissance humanism by Jacob Burckhardt.[18] During the High Middle Ages rhetoric had been considerably less significant. Grammar and logic far outshown it in the interests of educators and philosophers.

In the *trivium,* rhetoric was preceded by grammar, which included not only grammar instruction but the analysis of literary texts and graduated composition exercises. The teachings of the grammarian flowed naturally into the studies of rhetoric; indeed, separating the two at the more advanced stages of grammar had always created some tension when different teachers taught the subjects. On the other hand, logic had at times in the

16. "The Sentence," pronounced 22 June 1633 by the Inquisitors, translated by Finnochiaro in *The Galileo Affair,* 290.

17. Finnochiaro relates these details, *The Galileo Affair,* 38–39.

18. Salvatore Camporeale, "Lorenzo Valla: The Transcending of Philosophy through Rhetoric,' *Romance Notes* 30 (3), 269–84. For Burckhardt's interpretation of the Renaissance, see "Jakob Burckhardt," *Encycloopedia of the Renaissance,* 5: 288–91.

Middle Ages been placed before rhetoric in the *trivium*, in line with the thinking that in order to argue well one needed training in logical reasoning. But because grammar and rhetoric had companionable concerns, such as word choice, syntax, the arrangement of parts of compositions, and the figures of speech, and because logic was the indispensable tool for the nobler speculations of philosophy, the more appropriate alignment seemed to be the one prevailing at the beginning of the Renaissance, namely, grammar, rhetoric, logic.

In this book we focus mainly on argumentation in rhetoric and in logic (or dialectic) as presented to students after the first flush of humanism had passed and absorbed into the more traditional curricula of schools and universities like the Jesuit college in Rome and the University of Padua. Of the parts of rhetoric, we are most concerned with invention—the creative pulse and formulator of argument and the part of the art closest to dialectic. The other classical canons of rhetoric—arrangement, style, memory and delivery—are sketched out succinctly in the *Tabulae rhetoricae,* Carbone's guidebook to *De arte rhetorica* of Cipriano Soarez, found here in the second section of the translations. Readers who regret the neglect of style, generally the center of books on Renaissance rhetoric, will find succinct summaries of the elements of style in the *Tabulae.* In so limiting our attention in this volume, we hope with the help of the texts translated here to illuminate those aspects of late Renaissance argument that have been least noted. By this focus we do not intend to minimize style and "things literary" in this "Age of Eloquence," described so brilliantly in the work of Marc Fumaroli, but to turn the spotlight to another important aspect of that eloquence.[19]

To place in perspective the translations that form the bulk of the book, we rehearse briefly the historical and philosophical context of these works and outline the nature of dialectic and the canon of rhetorical invention as they are presented in these texts. We have kept our account and interpretation to a minimum, urging readers to study the texts, which speak so well for themselves. Readers familiar with the history of rhetoric and logic in the Renaissance may wish to skip over the reprise.

Aristotelian Invention in Dialectic and the Demonstrative Process

Students were generally introduced to argumentation by both teachers of logic and teachers of rhetoric during the High Middle Ages and at the start of the Renaissance. A more advanced version of argument was taught

19. The focus of Fumaroli, *L'Âge de l'Éloquence.*

in the medieval universities as a part of Aristotelian philosophy. Given the resulting redundancies it is no wonder that pedagogues during the revival of the classics wanted to revise the *trivium*. Their revisions centered on the teaching of invention, the first step in the development of arguments.

Before the curricular revisions, study of argumentation began with a treatment of inferential reasoning. Under "dialectic" in philosophy and "invention" in rhetoric, students learned exploratory techniques for discovering arguments that could be held against any and all objections. Students were taught to examine thoroughly arguments pro and con so that they could see both sides of a controversy (*in utramque partem disserere*). Since this was considered to be an essential art for an investigator of philosophical questions or for any actor on the civic stage, ancient scholars had devoted considerable thought to the process. Humanist reformers aimed to streamline invention and make it more efficacious for the needs of the time.

Since "dialectic" today has taken on different meanings, to clarify our own here we should note that we refer to the Aristotelian dialectic of the High Middle Ages, which originated from the methods employed by Socrates and Plato.[20] The result was a method of investigation and debate that Aristotle thought could be used in any subject matter. Unlike "demonstration," the method of science (*scientia*) or certain knowledge, which Aristotle also described, dialectical reasoning was to be used in a realm of uncertainty wherein reputable opinion (*endoxa*) must supply the premises.[21]

At the beginning of his treatment of dialectic in the *Topics*, Aristotle notes that dialectic can be useful for several purposes: "training the intellect, conversation, and for use in the philosophical sciences." In the last instance, inquirers would weigh the most reputable opinions so as to arrive at basic principles in a science.[22]

Aristotle thought that his summary of these strategies of inquiry, topics or *topoi* in the Greek, simply systematized a natural reasoning process. In his view topics could provide the middle terms for arguments. From the High Middle Ages onward, when the corpus of lost writings of Aristotle was recovered through Arabic and Greek translations and commentaries, dialectical topics were employed by scholars to attack issues in perplexing matters of natural philosophy, theology, and metaphysics.

The concepts and strategies of Aristotle's dialectic had been further

---

20. See D. W. Hamlyn, "Aristotle on Dialectic," *Philosophy* 65: 254 (Oct. 1970), 465–500, esp. 465–67. Hamlyn cites the opinions of Gilbert Ryle, G. E. L. Owen, and Martha Nussbaum on the relation of Aristotle's dialectic to his mentors'.

21. Aristotle, *Topica*, translated by E. S. Forster (Loeb Classical Library, Cambridge: Harvard University Press, 1960), I.1 100a–100b.

22. Aristotle, *Topica*, I.2, 101a.

developed by the peripatetic Themistius, adapted by Cicero, clarified by Porphyry, resystematized in the early Middle Ages by Boethius, and further clarified in the High Middle Ages by the commentaries of Albert the Great.[23] Peter of Spain added increasingly abstract considerations of semantics and syntactics, introducing syncategorematic terms applied to suppositions, relative terms, extensions, and exponibles. His "termininist" followers expanded the speculations of logic to take up *insolubilia,* insoluble problems in logic, grammar, and natural philosophy. These late medieval developments moved logic further away from practical problems or issues encountered in the disciplines.

In the Renaissance, humanists attempted to reform the curriculum to make it more responsive to human concerns. Carbone's *Introductio in logicam* (1597) follows the Jesuit approach of retaining useful elements of the logic of the High Middle Ages while incorporating humanist erudition. In harmony with contemporary interests also, in his logic he first describes the nature of the human soul and its powers, before discussing the methods of reasoning set forth in the Aristotelian corpus. For Carbone and many other scholars in the Renaissance, knowledge of the powers of the human soul, known today as philosophical psychology, was necessary to understanding the processes of perception, conceptualization, reasoning, judgment, and persuasion. A diagram of Carbone's view of the soul is included in the introduction to the translation.

The dialectical topics, described at length in Carbone's book on invention (excerpted in section five), were conceived as ways of answering questions. Questions (*problema*) stimulated the process of invention in dialectic and in rhetoric. When explaining the origin of Aristotle's *Topics,* Robin Smith suggests that the philosopher intended the work as a guide to help students engage more skillfully in the kind of debate that must have been practiced in Plato's Academy and in his own Lyceum.[24] The dialectical disputation of that time included a questioner and an answerer. According to Aristotle, a question should address a controversial issue for which the answer differs from what most people think or what authorities have thought. The question was proposed by the arguer, who drew out the answer held by his opponent with its supportive arguments. The questioner then proceeded to refute these and, finally, to propose his answer to the question with buttressing arguments. Arguments to be refuted were usually presented first so as to introduce principles on which the question-

23. See Albert the Great's commentaries on the *Organon* in is *Omnia Opera,* edited by Auguste Borgnet, 38 vols. (Paris: Vivès, 1890–99), vols. 1 and 2.

24. The context is carefully analyzed in the introduction to *Aristotle "Topics": Books I and VIII with excerpts from related texts,* translated with a Commentary by Robin Smith (Oxford: Clarendon Press, 1997).

er could then base his case. A similar format was followed in the more elaborate disputations of the scholastics, where a determiner decided whose was the most convincing argument. Such disputations continued to be the approved method of examination for students in many European universities into the nineteenth century.

But as Aristotle announces in the passage quoted above, the *Topics* should also be of aid in the investigations of philosophy. Albert the Great, whose commentary on the *Topics* influenced teaching on dialectic far into the Renaissance, elaborates, saying that dialectic provides a method of topical reasoning about the unknown. It considers common aspects of things and weighs relationships, enabling the reasoner to derive principles that yield a dialectical syllogism. He speaks of two kinds of dialectic, one for teaching *(docens)* and one for use *(utens)*. Teaching imparts the method, and use applies the topics in pursuit of knowledge. The topics allow one to syllogize using probable inferences about any problem proposed. Albert mentions various kinds of syllogisms, noting that the syllogism itself is simply the work of reason.[25]

The topical lines of investigation, which every schoolboy learned, were four: genus, species (or definition), property, and accident. These topics were explained to them as follows: if one comes upon something unknown, one attempts to place it in a class *(genus);* discerns how it differs from other things in that class *(species);* sees what elements always accompany it *(property);* and notes what may or may not accompany it *(accident).* Each of the four, termed a topic (Lat. *locus*), becomes an angle of investigation or a mode of inference that leads to finding a principle or a cause. Carbone explains that the topics are called predicables because they are used to predicate something about something else. And apart from these, subsidiary topics, such as relationship, cause, and effect, might suggest themselves in the course of the investigation. The principle or cause found by means of these topical probes could then furnish the middle term for the major and minor premises of a syllogism, the basic logical pattern underlying verbal debate.

In this same work Carbone also addresses Aristotle's addendum to his treatise on dialectic entitled the *Sophistical Refutations.* The essentials of Aristotle's discussion of fallacious reasoning survive today in modern textbooks, even though his teachings on dialectic in the preliminary books have disappeared.

Dialectical argument by its very nature could offer only conjectural premises and probable conclusions. Yet these could be very persuasive, as

---

25. An analysis and translation of parts of Albert's treatise is found in William A. Wallace, "Albert the Great's Inventive Logic: His Exposition of the Topics of Aristotle," *American Catholic Philosophical Quarterly* 70 (1996): 1–39.

they were when mathematicians such as Copernicus and Galileo argued that the heliocentric system was the best explanation for the movement of the heavenly bodies. On the other hand, as we have observed, conservative theologians and philosophers demanded certain proof before giving up their own sense-based views. Proof for them could be furnished only by "necessary" demonstrations, that is, arguments whose premises and conclusions were seen as certain. Certainty alone could yield the perfect knowledge of the sciences. Such demonstrations, Aristotle explains in the *Organon,* must be sound in both form and matter or content.

The significance of necessary demonstration is explained in the introduction to Carbone's logic and in that text itself, so we need not linger over its requirements here. We might note, however, that furnishing such demonstrations became increasingly difficult in natural philosophy—which was equated with "science" until the nineteenth century—as research moved into areas where only probabilities could be entertained. In the realm of the very large, the makeup of the universe, or of the very small, the micro world, probable knowledge was the best attainable. During the period of early modern science, the context of our study, dialectic began to assume a greater and greater role. Its sister art, rhetoric, complicit in the act of claiming and framing, expanded its horizons as well.

Invention in Rhetoric

Of the five parts of traditional rhetoric only style claimed more attention in the Renaissance than the invention of arguments. The insights of Aristotle on rhetorical invention were contained in his *Rhetoric,* a work that captured the interest of many Renaissance scholars, eliciting new translations and commentaries. Riccobono's own translation and his commentaries on the text, presented in the form of essays, illuminate many of the difficulties in that work. The main issues discussed in the period were the nature of rhetoric, its relation to dialectic, its *genera,* and its distinctive topics and proofs. All of these, we might note, are among the issues that continue to evoke discussion today.[26]

The implications of the first sentence of the *Rhetoric,* in which Aristotle declares that rhetoric is an *antistrophe* of dialectic, has repeatedly invited explication.[27] Most often the term has been taken to mean "counterpart,"

---

26. New volumes of essays on these topics emerge almost yearly. The most recent are collected in the following: David J. Furley and Alexander Nehamas, *Aristotle's "Rhetoric": Philosophical Essays* (Princeton: Princeton University Press, 1994); Amelie Oksenberg Rorty, ed. *Essays on Aristotle's "Rhetoric"* (Berkeley: University of California Press, 1996); and Alan G. Gross and Arthur E. Walzer, eds., *Rereading Aristotle's "Rhetoric"* (Carbondale: Southern Illinois University Press, 2000).

27. Larry Green takes up the various interpretations of the term in "Aristotelian Rhetoric, Dialectic, and the Tradition of *Antistrophos*," *Rhetorica* 8.1 (Winter 1990): 1–27.

eliciting discussion of similarities in the arts. But other views also were voiced. Riccobono airs a variety of opinions in his first essay-commentary and refers readers to the *Topics,* where Aristotle explains that the term has the same meaning as "similarity" or *isostrophe.* Similarities in the two arts are brought out in a number of places in the *Rhetoric,* chief among these being that both argue from opinion about probabilities and signs. Both can avail themselves of topics to generate arguments on all subjects. Riccobono points out that rhetoric is dissimilar in that it generally treats civic issues, whereas dialectic treats all matters, and that rhetoric voices only probabilities that promise to persuade, whereas dialectic introduces all probabilities. Then too, the format of the two types of discourse differ—question and answer is proper for dialectic, continuous speech for rhetoric.

Riccobono excels in explaining the "artistic" rhetorical proofs of the *Rhetoric:* the familiar triptych, *ethos, pathos,* and *logos,* and the ready-made "inartistic" proofs such as testimony and contracts. He treats the role of the emotions in rhetoric in his essay *On the Nature of Rhetoric,* arguing against the view of the philosopher Zabarella, who held that according to Aristotle *logos* alone was a licit topic for use in rhetoric. Riccobono devotes an entire essay to *logos* or demonstration and another to *ethos* or character. In the first, "On the nature of oratorical demonstration," he takes up at length the enthymeme and the example, the topics as founts of the proofs expressed in the enthymeme and example, and the kinds of arguments suited to the three genera (deliberative, forensic, and epideictic) of rhetoric. In the second, "On the nature of the oration of character," he departs from the usual treatment, addressing not only the character of the speaker but also that of the audience and the speech. Throughout the essays he cites Aristotle along with ancient and contemporary scholars.

Carbone, like Riccobono, throws much light on the topics in his *De inventione,* whose alternate title is *De locis communibus* (On common topics). Carbone observes that in his *Rhetoric* Aristotle listed the rhetorical topics in rather haphazard fashion, beginning in the first book with the most common lines of argument *(koine),* namely, past fact and future fact, the more and the less, the possible and the impossible. Then, in Book 2 of that work, Aristotle identifies twenty-eight common topics, among them: opposites, conjugates, relative terms, comparison, definition, and division. Oddly enough, Carbone omits Aristotle's list, although he gives those of Cicero, Boethius, and Agricola.

Carbone also takes up a second variety of topics, the special or proper topics, which are explained by Aristotle in the *Rhetoric* as matters that are proper to the various sciences. In the *De inventione,* published in 1589, Carbone mentions that these include definitions and principles of a science; then, in his *Divinus orator,* published in 1595, he illustrates them at considerable length. The special topics are not mentioned as such in the *Topics* of Aristotle. Since the *Topics* is thought to be an earlier work, perhaps the special topics were the result of further reflection. But, as noted above, in the initial discussion of the use of the topics there, Aristotle does mention that they could aid in arriving at the principles or special topics of a particular science.

The Aristotelian rhetorical topics were augmented by later teachers of the sophistic tradition and relayed by Cicero in his *De inventione*. The Ciceronian version was lovingly examined by Renaissance rhetoricians and their students, who could then turn to Cicero's newly recovered speeches to identify how he actually used them. Surprisingly, in view of the peripatetic nature of his logic text, Carbone's approach to rhetoric followed Cicero, as seen in his *De arte dicendi*, published in 1589, and that of his *De inventione*, published in the same year. These two works compose, respectively, sections three and five of the translations.

One other important strategy of invention that Renaissance authors carried over into their own texts was *status*. Cipriano Soarez treated this in his *De arte rhetoricae* and Carbone developed it further in the *Tabulae* (section two) and again in the disputations contained in the *De arte dicendi*, which he appended to the *Tabulae*. The purpose of *status* was to enable forensic orators to arrive at the crux of a case, but it served other kinds of rhetoric as well. Its technique, ascribed to Hermagoras, explicated first by Hermogenes and then by Cicero and Quintilian, applied four questions to the subject matter at hand to determine the point on which the issue turned. The first questioned the fact of the matter, "Is it?" (*An sit?*); the second asked for its definition, "What is it?" (*Quid sit?*); the third sought to discern its quality, "What kind of thing is it?" (*Quale sit?*); and the fourth questioned the court's jurisdiction, "Should it be in another court?" (*Translativa?*). The technique enabled the arguer to focus on an issue and to turn aside any arguments not to the point.

Such training could account for the perspicuity with which authors like Galileo attacked an issue and then used the topics to amplify the argument *ad infinitum* so as to leave the opponent literally speechless. An observer of Galileo in action reported with delight on the manner in which he neatly epitomized his opponent's arguments, amplified them, then turned them upside down, destroying the case with withering irony.[28]

Galileo's use of both Ciceronian and Aristotelian topics is obvious in his published writings. For example, the preface to his widely popular *Sidereal Messenger* contains a fulsome exploitation of the Ciceronian epideictic or ceremonial topics for amplifying praise of his desired patron, Cosimo

28. Moss, *Novelties in the Heavens*, 298.

de' Medici II. The young man's descent, education, actions, wealth, character, and even astrological portents are limned in an imaginative expansion of the template of external circumstances. Then, Galileo asks why he should use only "probable arguments" to forecast his lasting fame, when he could "deduce and demonstrate it from all but necessary reason?"[29] Other writings such as his *Letters on Sunspots* discuss in Aristotelian fashion the probable substance, genus, and *differentiae* of the sunspots, taking up similarities and differences to other known celestial phenomena. The same *techne* of dialectical topics is employed often in the *Dialogue*, as is the disputational format in which opposing opinions are destroyed first.[30] Whether Galileo consciously turned to a checklist of topics to amplify or situate his reading of sense evidence, one may readily doubt; that he was programmed to do so by his earlier education and cultural practice may surely be credited, especially given the pervasiveness of their use. Fernand Hallyn, in a recent essay on the disparagement of rhetoric in Galileo's and Descartes's writings, notes that Galileo says in *The Assayer* that he delighted in disputations when young but at present dislikes it because it tends to mire the disputants in "'an ocean of distinctions, of syllogisms and other terms of logic.'"[31] Nevertheless, despite his protestations, Galileo shows that he found the techniques quite useful.

Aristotle's conception of topics as prompts for the mind, based on the natural process of inquiry, was expanded by later teachers of rhetoric to include stock opinions *(loci communes)*, what today we refer to as commonplaces. Cicero's *De inventione* contains some of these. It notes common opinions useful in argument, for example, that punishment for injustice will come in the next life; that philosophers are atheists; that one should or should not put trust in rumors; that evil doers should not be pitied. These could readily become set pieces, as did Cicero's collection of tried and true ways of beginning a case, of replying to objections, and of de-

29. Citing and quoting from the dedicatory letter of Galileo in *Sidereus nuncius or The Sidereal Messenger of Galileo Galilei,* translated by Albert Van Helden (Chicago: University of Chicago Press, 1989), 32–33.

30. See the discussion throughout the chapters on Galileo's arguments in Moss, *Novelties in the Heavens.*

31. Fernand Hallyn argues in "Dialectic et rhétorique devant la 'nouvelle science' du VIIe siecle" that Galileo and Descartes sought to rid science of rhetoric and the commonplaces. He discusses Galileo's attitudes in the text of the *Dialogue,* where the three kinds of rhetoric are deplored for use in the "new science". But the instances Hallyn cites are commonplaces or texts that Simplicio uses from Aristotle to refute Copernican arguments. Hallyn does not understand topics as "probes" nor does he see that Galileo is beating Simplicio with the stick of pedantry. The essay is in *Histoire de la rhétorique dans l'Europe moderne 1450–1950,* published under the direction of Marc Fumaroli (Paris: Presses universitaires de France, 1999), 601–28. The passage in *The Assayer* is quoted from the French translation of C. Chauviré (Paris: Les Belles Lettres, 1980), 153. The English translation is Moss's.

fending the seemingly indefensible. The variety of understandings of the term *loci communes* is treated extensively at the end of the first book of Carbone's *On Invention*.

The Prefatory *Organon*

Before turning to the influence of humanism on the twin arts of argumentation in the Renaissance, we should note that knowledge of the books of the *Organon* that precede the *Topics* was presumed in the discussions of invention by both Carbone and Riccobono. Carbone's *Introduction to Logic,* which summarizes all of the *Organon,* also brings students up to date concerning contemporary commentaries. He explains that the first of Aristotle's logical treatises, entitled *Categories,* treats ten modes of existence, the types of being one observes in the universe. Substance, the underlying substratum of everything that exists, although unseen by the observer, is presupposed in the nine other aspects of being that can be discerned. These are quantity, quality, relation, place, time, position, possessing or having, acting, and being acted upon. The ten categories are not merely logical entities existing in the mind, as are the "predicables" (genus, species, etc.). Rather, they exist outside the mind as modes of being. They are called "predicaments" (*predicamenta,* the Latin equivalent of the Greek *kategoriai*), to indicate their ontological or epistemic status.

In *De inventione* Carbone combined his knowledge of philosophy and rhetoric to create even more topics based on the predicaments, which he saw as the foundation of the predicables or dialectical topics. Carbone follows Albert the Great here, noting that all of the predicables can be located in one or another category. As may be seen in section five of the translations, Carbone turned the predicables loose upon predicaments to expand the possibilities of inferential forms, for example, in considering "accident" (a dialectical *topos*) in relation to place and time.

Carbone turns next to *On Interpretation,* where Aristotle takes up propositions and what enables one to judge them true or false. Along with judgment Carbone discusses reasoning, describing the proper forms of the syllogism treated in the *Prior Analytics* and its material content treated in the companion treatise, the *Posterior Analytics.* He explains that knowledge of both the formal and the material aspects of reasoning is necessary to create a demonstrative syllogism. Dialectical reasoning as presented in the *Topics* follows, along with a treatment of the fallacies.

Although Carbone does not take this position, some peripatetic philosophers would include the *Rhetoric* in their discussions of the *Organon* because of its concern with probable reasoning. Likewise, the *Poetics* was often classed by peripatetics with the logical treatises because of Aristotle's contention that poetry is concerned with universal truths plausibly

presented in a particular context.[32] The closeness of rhetoric to philosophy and of rhetoric to poetics is manifest in the scholastic view of a continuum of truth, wherein certain truth first shades into probable truth,
then into persuasive truth, and finally into the plausible truth of poetics.

Unfamiliar to most scholars today is the matter addressed in the last
book of Carbone's *Logic,* Book 6. Extrapolated from the *Organon* and compiled from Aristotle's *De anima* and others of his texts, this book treats the
psychology and epistemology of reasoning. Carbone is adept at explaining
the difficult terminology involved in characterizing the three operations
of the human intellect as it conceives, judges, and reasons. Readers may
find the diagrams supplied in the introduction of section one of the translations helpful for explicating his text.

Rhetoric and Dialectic Reappraised

Having examined the kind of rhetoric and dialectic which our authors
preserved, let us step back and place them in the broader scene of the humanist revolution. The authors were writing more than a century after the
humanists of the mid-fourteenth and early fifteenth centuries had recovered the seminal classics of rhetoric: Cicero's orations and letters, his ma-
ture books on rhetoric, the complete *De institutione oratoria* of Quintilian,
and the writings of Seneca and Tacitus. By the late Renaissance rhetoric
had already reclaimed the position of prominence it had had in the Augustan age. The Roman rhetorical heritage had been enhanced by the recovery of Greek and Byzantine works, Aristotle's *Rhetoric,* and the texts of
Hermogenes and Dionysius of Halicarnasus. These writings, conceived
for practical use, were to gain impetus through George of Trebizond's emphasis on the salience of rhetorical argument to civic life.

Practical rhetoric had received a boost also from the new men of humanistic learning who gained prominence in public affairs. This was particularly true in Florence and in the papal court. Coluccio Salutati,
Leonardo Bruni, and Poggio Bracciolini during the early Renaissance
were all chancellors of Florence and secretaries in the papal chancery.
Lorenzo Valla, who sought to elevate rhetoric at the expense of dialectic,
was likewise a papal secretary as well as a teacher of rhetoric in Rome in
this period.[33] These active political men were captivated by the role they
saw rhetoric had played in affairs of state in the ancient world.

The very popular rhetoric text of Cypriano Soarez adopted throughout

32. This was the view of Arab philosophers, and it was taken up by Albert the Great and
Thomas Aquinas.
33. Kennedy, *Classical Rhetoric,* 226–27.

Jesuit colleges, for which Carbone provides a guide and commentary, illustrates in its five-part rhetoric the effect of the recovery of the classics of the Augustan Age. Soarez based his work primarily on Cicero and Quintilian, with an occasional nod to Aristotle. In *De arte rhetorica* (1562) he includes generous quotations and paraphrases of the Romans' treatment of the art to elucidate principles and elements of the art. His is an eclectic summation of all that Soarez thought students should know about rhetoric before reading Greek and Roman classics.

The Revival of Aristotle's *Rhetoric*

Incredible as it now seems, a wave of interest in Aristotle's *Rhetoric* among humanists was responsible for numerous printings of that work from 1477 to 1599. Nineteen of these were in Greek, seventy-two in Latin, and eleven in both Greek and Latin. In 1475 Trebizond became the first Humanist to translate and publish Aristotle's *Rhetoric,* and in the next century twenty-seven Latin editions were published.[34]

Aristotle's *Rhetoric* had become known to scholars in the West during the High Middle Ages through the translation of William of Moerbeke. The work became part of the university curriculum, but it was seen as rounding out logic in its treatment of probable reasoning and valued for its insights on moral philosophy. It does not seem to have influenced the teaching of rhetoric in the grammar schools. Thomas Aquinas, using Moerbeke's translation, pointed out the similarities between dialectic, rhetoric, and poetics in his foreword to the *Posterior Analytics.* Basing his analysis on Aristotle's treatises devoted to these arts, he classified their reasoning processes as investigative only, unable to conclude with necessity. But for him dialectical reasoning comes nearest to demonstration in that its reasoning inclines wholly to one side of an argument, whereas rhetoric produces only a suspicion that one side is best. Poetics uses representation to offer a conjectural truth. Sophistic reasoning, Aquinas says, fails to reach truth because of a defective principle in its premises.[35]

Riccobono's translation of Aristotle's *Rhetoric* benefitted greatly from Moerbeke's, as the introduction to section four demonstrates. Riccobono's explanation of the difference between dialectic and rhetoric as the difference between the probable and the persuasible was clearly based on Moerbeke. Galileo was to use the Latin term *"persuasibile"* in the preface to

---

34. Brandes, *A History of Aristotle's Rhetoric,* 74–79.

35. William A. Wallace, "Thomas Aquinas on Dialectics and Rhetoric," in *A Straight Path: Studies in Medieval Philosophy and Culture.* A Festschrift in honor of Arthur Hyman. Ruth Link-Salinger, editor (Washington, D.C.: The Catholic University of America Press, 1988), 244–54. Reprinted in Wallace, *Galileo, the Jesuits and the Medieval Aristotle* (Hampshire, Great Britain: Variorum, 1991), Essay 13.

the *Dialogue* (a work written in Italian), where he speaks of "the probability" (*probabilità*) of his speculations regarding the ocean tides that make it "persuasible" (*persuasibile*) that the earth moves.[36]

While Riccobono was decidedly sympathetic to Aristotle, the response to the Philosopher's authority in the earlier Renaissance varied considerably. Trebizond was a rather passionate advocate of Aristotle's originality in his conception of rhetoric, and in this he opposed the opinion of his contemporary Cardinal Bessarion, who saw Plato as the source and Aristotle as merely elaborating upon the guidelines for an ethical rhetoric set out in the *Phaedrus*.[37] The argument of Bessarion has merit, for any reader of both can see the elaboration by Aristotle. In the twentieth century Solmsen has argued convincingly for the same position.[38] But since Aristotle never claimed originality, except in regard to the emphasis he placed on the centrality of logical argument to justice and for the enthymeme as the chief engine of rhetorical argument, the point of the conflict seems moot. Nevertheless, as Green points out, the controversy was bitter in the Renaissance.[39]

Two angles of concern are evident in the debate between Bessarion and Trebizond. For his part, Trebizond emphasizes Aristotle's contribution to the rhetorical art in general, viewing him as a precursor to Cicero and the Roman approach to rhetoric where invention and style figure most prominently. Bessarion, on the other hand, emphasized the ethical elements as they relate to moral philosophy and beyond that to theology. As Green notes, in the background was a theological battle begun at the Council of Florence in 1439 over which of the two Greek philosophers offered a philosophy more compatible with Christian theology.

The issue of whether the pagan Aristotle was a fitting intellectual guide in philosophy remained controversial even in Galileo's day, although the Jesuits by then had pledged their members to embrace Aristotle in philosophy. The Dominican Tommaso Campanella, however, argued that Aristotelianism should be rejected altogether because Aristotle was a pagan and, moreover, was dogmatic in his views regarding the heavens. He cites

---

36. The preface, "Al discreto lettore," the title of which has been variously translated as "To the Discerning Reader," by Stillman Drake and "To the Judicious Reader" in Thomas Salusbury's edition of 1661 (appearing in his *Mathematical Collections and Translations*, 2 vols.), illustrates the ambiguities of the piece. Most commentators think it was placed there by Galileo to placate the Church through its treatment of the work as a fictive, rhetorical dialogue not to be taken too seriously. The "persuasibile" saps the "ingenious fantasy" (*una fantasia ingegnosa*) of the tides of its force as a demonstration. I have used the Italian of the original *Dialogue* in *Le opere*, vol. 7, 29–31.

37. Larry Green, "The Reception of Aristotle's *Rhetoric*," 323, notes 10, 12.

38. Friedrich Solmsen, "The Aristotelian Tradition in Ancient Rhetoric," *American Journal of Philology* 62 (1941): 35–50, cited by Green in "The Reception of Aristotle's *Rhetoric*," 325 n. 22.

39. Green, "The Reception of Aristotle's *Rhetoric*," 324–28.

Aquinas against Aristotle! Plato's paganism did not trouble him, probably because Campanella was Augustinian in his philosophy and because Augustine had accomplished for Plato and Neoplatonism what Aquinas had for Aristotle.[40]

Trebizond's view of Aristotle as a forebear of Cicero was echoed by Danielo Barbaro, who claimed that each of the three books of the *Rhetoric* serve in turn to promote the Ciceronian aims of rhetoric: to teach, to move, and to please.[41] His claim is well supported by the content of the *Rhetoric*: book one treats the causes and methods of persuasion, book two, the emotions and the *topoi,* and book three, style and the organization of an oration.

Carbone seems oblivious to such conflict over Aristotle's teachings. In his text on invention he is close to Trebizond when he emphasizes the argumentative components of both Aristotle's *Rhetoric* and Cicero's writings. Yet in his *Divinus orator* he takes a Bessarion-like view, drawing on Aristotle's *De anima* and the *Rhetoric* to offer preachers methods of stirring the emotions to prompt moral actions. Francesco Benci, a Jesuit who taught in Florence near the end of the sixteenth century, similarly takes Bessarion's approach, finding Aristotle's view supportive of Christian morality. Taking an ameliorative position, at the University of Padua Zabarella sees both Aristotle and Plato as committed to ethical ends for rhetoric.[42]

Aristotelianism, then, did not cease to interest scholars or to be a point of contention in the later part of the Renaissance. Not only was it a target for many humanists who detested the scholastic curriculum because of its formalistic pedantry, but it was to figure in the revolt of Protestants against whatever was characteristic of Catholic thought. It is not a geographical accident that Peter Ramus's attacks on Aristotle and his revision of the curriculum (see below) were embraced enthusiastically by Northern Protestant countries and yet rejected in Italy.

Reformulations of the Curriculum

Reforms of the *trivium* begun in the early Renaissance moved away from the formal fashioning of pupils, which too often aimed merely at

40. Bernardino M. Bonansea describes Campanella's views on Galileo in *Tommaso Campanella: Renaissance Pioneer of Modern Thought.* (Washington: The Catholic University of America Press, 1969), 160. The text of Campanella's defense of Galileo is found in Thomas Campanella, O.P., *A Defense of Galileo, the Mathematician from Florence,* translated, with an introduction and notes, by Richard J. Blackwell (Notre Dame, Ind.: University of Notre Dame Press, 1994). Moss has treated Campanella's defense of Galileo and his condemnation of Aristotle in it, *Novelties in the Heavens,* 158–61.

41. Green, "The Reception of Aristotle's *Rhetoric,*" 335.

42. Green, "The Reception of Aristotle's *Rhetoric,*" 334–36.

proficiency in grammatical and rhetorical exercises and skill in empty scholastic disputations. Scholars, instead, urged practice in expression for ends that would be useful in the world outside the classroom.

The new practical and aesthetic concerns eliminated formal study of logic from the new curriculum, but this did not mean that interest in dialectic was dead. Many humanists were like Petrarch, who inveighed against scholastic preoccupation with logic and yet recommended it as an essential elementary study.[43] But logic needed to be revised, if only to remind teachers and students that as an instrument it should be used to attack issues and problems of the day, not simply universal questions or language puzzles. Some reformers embedded whatever dialectic had to offer within the study of rhetoric, thus preserving useful techniques of verbal combat. Others accorded the investigative and creative parts of rhetoric to dialectic, winnowing both inventional arts to produce one highly teachable subject.

But to Carbone and Riccobono both dialectical and rhetorical invention were necessary, given the difference in subject matter and aims of the two arts. Riccobono takes for granted the unaltered character of the two, while Carbone often addresses what he saw as the misconceptions of his contemporaries, occasionally naming names.

Lorenzo Valla. Valla was one of the first to weaken allegiance to the scholastic curriculum. Attacking scholastic logic passionately, he declared the Aristotelian-Boethian system mad, complex, and impractical, expressed in barbarous language, and completely self-absorbed. His *Repastinatio dialecticae et philosophiae* (1439) ridiculed Aristotle's metaphysics and the logic resting upon it. Parts of the old system he thought, however, could be revamped, given simpler terminology, and turned to new uses. The categories or predicaments described by Aristotle he reduced to three: substance, quality and action. For him, such concepts as essence, quiddity, and truth could be understood much more easily if people could simply see that what Aristotle was trying to point out was the existence of "things." Things are substantial. In a thing (*res*) we perceive substance, its qualities, and activity. So Aristotle was needlessly complex. In addition Valla revamped the predicables, which he saw as the components of a definition, the answer to the question 'what is it?' The topics of genus, species, property and accident supply the answers. The important thing is to show how these tools of logic can be used to answer questions of the moment and how the answers can be given in ordinary language, not in philosophical jargon.[44]

43. Neal Gilbert notes this in "The Italian Humanists and Disputation," 203–26.

44. Peter Mack has analyzed Renaissance reforms with particular attention to Valla and Agricola in *Renaissance Argument.* He also discusses Valla's views on the metaphysical underpinnings of Aristotle's logic, 38–49.

The disciplinary distinctions between dialectic and rhetoric were unimportant in Valla's creation of a practical argumentation. For him, the tools of dialectic were meant to serve rhetorical purposes. Two kinds of invention are not needed, he declared. The ordinary language of rhetorical argumentation was to be preferred to the precious, specialized terms of scholastic philosophy.[45] Yet, as Peter Mack points out, the language Valla had in mind was classical Latin, that of Quintilian, adapted to contemporary concerns.[46]

Valla thought too that the categorical syllogism as the model form of argument was far too confining. He would expand argument to emphasize alternative forms: the hypothetical and extended syllogism, sorites, the epichireme, the dilemma, the enthymeme, and the example.[47] He wanted to open up the rigidity of formal considerations in argument to take in the power of individual words, to point to further development of thought.

Valla believed that his reform of logic not only was applicable to language usage but would benefit theology as well. Theologians would be much better served by a rhetorical conception of language and argumentation than they were by scholastic dialectic. Charles Trinkaus points out that indeed Valla's views on rhetoric's relation to theology were influential in this pre-reformation period and cites as evidence Valla's famous *Encomium of St. Thomas Aquinas,* which Salvatore Camporeale has analyzed brilliantly. In it Valla extolls Thomas's piety but not his philosophy. Camporeale explains that for Valla eloquence is more necessary to belief than are the artificial edifices of reason.[48] Victoria Kahn argues similarly that Valla grasped that rhetoric influences the will to assent to faith. Human reason alone cannot do this. The will and divine grace are the most important elements for grasping the truths of revelation.[49]

Perhaps Carbone owes something to Valla in the similar stress he places on emotional appeals for moving auditors in *Divinus orator.* Of course Carbone did not mention Valla specifically, for he obviously did not embrace his philosophical reductions nor his excoriations of Aristotle.

---

45. Salvatore Camporeale shows that for Valla ordinary language was language developed in a social context and meaningful to those employing and listening to it, *Lorenzo Valla: Umanesimo e Teologia* (Florence: Istituto Nazionale di Studi sul Rinascimento, 1972), 101–8; 149–52.

46. Mack, *Renaissance Argument,* 57.

47. Mack, *Renaissance Argument,* 84–88.

48. Charles Trinkaus, "Italian Humanism and Scholastic Theology," in *Renaissance Humanism: Foundations, Forms and Legacy,* edited by Albert Rabill, Jr. (Philadelphia: University of Pennsylvania, Press, 1988): 327–348, 338–339; Reprinted with same pagination in Charles Trinkaus, *Renaissance Transformations of Late Medieval Thought.* Variorum Collected Studies Series (Brookfield, Vt.: Ashgate, 1999). Trinkaus refers readers to the discussion of dialectic and rhetoric in Gianni Zippel's edition of Lorenzo Valla's *Repastinatio dialecticae et philosophiae* (Padua, 1982).

49. Trinkaus notes the contribution of Victoria Kahn, "The Rhetoric of Faith and the Use of Usage in Lorenzo Valla's *De libero arbitrio,*" *Journal of Medieval and Renaissance Studies* 13 (1983), 91–109.

Valla's iconoclasm was probably an impediment to the further development and refinement of his new approach to dialectic and rhetoric, for there is little evidence of his reform of logic extending beyond his circle.[50] But the efforts of another humanist with similar practical aims, one who was disinclined to consider the metaphysical underpinnings, provided a more systematic method that attracted a greater following, especially in Northern Europe.

Rudolph Agricola. Agricola's *De inventione dialectica* (1515) also sought to save what he thought was indispensable in logic, reform it, and make it more serviceable to students. For Agricola, however, dialectic, not rhetoric, was the important discipline, the reasoning part of the creative process. Rhetoric was simply the embellishment added to thought to make it appealing to an audience. He reversed Valla's picture of discourse and made rhetoric serve dialectic. While he did not renounce Aristotle's metaphysical basis for the topics, he did not discuss this foundation in detail.

Dialectic, Agricola declares, is "the faculty of discoursing." As such it takes under its wings all "convincing" or serious discourse. The intent of such discourse for Agricola is to teach. *De inventione dialectica* in his eyes contains the key to intelligent, articulate communication. He notes that the art is divided into two parts: invention and judgment, but his work treats only invention, postponing judgment for a later book, which, unfortunately, he never got around to writing. But he thinks of judgment in the Aristotelian sense as the evaluation of the correctness and the validity of reasoning. The first part of his text discusses the basic tools of reasoning, the topics; the second treats application of the topics in expatiating "the question" or the matter. The third part is concerned with the creation of effects, moving the emotions and pleasing through ornamentation, and with arrangement.

Carbone evidently respected the work of Agricola, for he includes a summary of his topics and references him repeatedly in his books, although he did not always agree with him. The weight Carbone gives to such things as the question, causes and effect, and ornamentation seems to reflect Agricola's influence, if not Carbone's desire to incorporate popular elements from Agricola's program.

The differences between Agricola's approach and that of Carbone and Riccobono are significant for the differences between the "northern" and "southern" views of rhetoric, dialectic, and science we aim to unfold in this book. Thus, a closer look at Agricola's writings and recent scholarship concerning them seems merited at this point.

As a humanist, Agricola embraced Cicero's articulation of rhetoric's

---

50. Mack, *Renaissance Argument*, 144–46.

aims: to teach, to move, and to please, but these are, in the eyes of this Renaissance scholar, the aims of all serious communication. To teach is foremost; to move and to please an audience are ordered to the first aim. To teach, one first of all needs to think about the matter to be imparted. The tools of thinking are the topics.

Agricola's conception of the use of the topics in all kinds of discourse, however, expands their area of applicability beyond the Aristotelian conception. Walter Ong observes that Agricola's contention that one logic, dialectic, suffices for all discourse actually originated in the thirteenth-century *Summulae logicales* of Peter of Spain. Peter's teachings were to absorb or side-track many terminist scholars in the fourteenth and fifteenth centuries and bring on a strong reaction against dialectic. Ong sees Peter's work as the inspiration for the reforms of both Agricola and Ramus. The medieval scholar was the first to claim that dialectic was the "art of arts and the science of sciences." Ignoring Aristotle's discussions of demonstration as the foundation of science, Peter proposed dialectic as sufficient for all reasoning. This modification of the traditional view that reasoning takes different forms in different subject matter appears frequently in the Renaissance.[51]

Mack casts further light on the problem when he points out that Agricola uses the term *probabilis* in a wider sense than does Aristotle in treating the probable reasoning of dialectic and rhetoric. Agricola's meaning shifts as he writes at one place that dialectic is "speaking convincingly *(probabiliter)*" and that "*probabile* will mean whatever can be said as suitably as possible *(quam aptissime)* for creating belief, according to the situation of the matter proposed."[52] In this sense he seems to use the word "*probabile*" simply in the sense of a persuasive proof in an argument. But in another passage Agricola clearly means to extend probable to include scientific proof. Mack translates, "But if we say that the provable *(probabile)* is not only what can be said ambiguously and on both sides, but that the more certain anything is the more provable it is, and that what is undoubted would seem to be the most provable of all, then all arts of every kind will be made up of provable things."[53]

But perhaps a better translation of Agricola's "*probabile*" might be the "probable," which would refer to the datum of the argument, or even the "credible," which would point to the effect of the proof on the audience. The "provable" would imply incontrovertible argument, whereas Agricola seems to be saying that certainty is simply the reigning *opinion* regarding

---

51. Walter J. Ong, *Ramus, Method, and the Decay of Dialogue* (Cambridge: Harvard University Press, 1958, 1983), 60, 101–3.

52. Mack, *Renaissance Argument*, 170, translating Agricola's *De inventione dialectica*, 192.

53. Mack, *Renaissance Argument*, 171, citing Agricola's *De inventione dialectica*, 207.

what is probable. Nevertheless, Mack is surely right in seeing that this extensive application of *probabile* is key to Agricola's notion that all serious discourse, including that of the sciences, is dialectical. Furthermore, in Agricola's hands the differences between the probable argumentation of rhetoric and that of dialectic have disappeared as well. The point is one that Riccobono will clarify in his use of the "persuasible" to differentiate rhetoric's resoning from the probable.

Turning now to the topics, which are central to Agricola's conception of the art of dialectic,[54] we can begin to understand why he sees them as the means of creating discourse on any subject. He has searched the various compendia of topics in Aristotle, Cicero, Boethius, and Quintilian to come up with what he thought to be the most basic and fecund set. Much as Boethius had, he sorts these under two general heads, internal and external, and an intermediate group. Internal topics relate to the substance of a thing, whereas external topics relate to what is outside the substance. Internal topics conduce to an understanding of a thing's nature, what is "partly in the substance of the thing," as Carbone in his work on invention transmits it.[55] These internal topics contain the familiar predicables— definition, genus, species, property—to which Agricola adds wholes, parts, and conjugates. In an intermediate position are topics that disclose what may be surrounding the substance: adjacents, actions, subjects. Mack remarks that these last are new topics that Agricola may have drawn from Valla's three categories.[56] The external topics include efficient and final causes, effects, and things destined; applied things, such as place, time, connections, and contingencies; accidents, of which there are five subdivisions, i.e., pronouncements about it, its name, comparisons, similars and dissimilars, repugnants, that is, opposites, and differences.

This extensive checklist would seem to be capable of turning up a vast number of possible arguments, and as such is ordered to a consideration of universal subjects in full accord with Agricola's view of invention as a teaching engine. He presumes the metaphysical ground of the categories in seeing substance as the basis of the topics; all things would depend upon it. Agricola's topics are not ordered to the three kinds of rhetoric but possess the flexibility of dialectical topics in their applicability to any subject. Absent are Aristotle's three most common topics, the *koine* of the *Rhetoric,* focused on kairotic qualities: the possible or the impossible, the more and the less, past fact or future fact. Absent also are the inartistic proofs, such as documents and witnesses. Since Agricola proposes that one inventional system is sufficient, his dialectical topics are pressed into

---

54. The context is carefully analyzed in the introduction to *Aristotle "Topics": Books I and VIII*.
55. Ludovico Carbone, *De inventione,* 81.
56. Mack, *Renaissance Argument,* 150.

rhetorical service. They are meant to be used also for particular cases for particular audiences, as Agricola explains in the third book when he takes up moving and pleasing.

To the reader of the period, used to the myriad applications of Cicero's commonplaces of person and action and the richer development of these in the *Rhetorica ad Herennium,* Agricola would seem to offer meager assistance to the orator and the poet. For natural philosophers, too, he had his limitations. Although dialectical invention as Agricola conceived it might aid in the teaching of logic to school boys, it would fail to convey the aims of scientific reasoning; neither would it cultivate respect for the truths of its deliberations. His invention, however, does preserve the predicate types of Aristotle's *Topics,* intensifying and elaborating on these. As such, his dialectic would foster the utility noted by Aristotle for intellectual training and ordinary conversation. Perhaps it would be useful also for arriving at first principles or causes in philosophical questions, as Aristotle suggests, although Agricola does not promise that.[57] Yet, for philosophers of his day, because he does not explain the categories of being, nor make explicit the relation of the predicables to them, nor develop a doctrine about what is needed to make a proposition indubitable, the relation of his dialectic to the sciences is not clear.

Carbone, unlike Agricola, follows the enumeration and order given in Cicero's *Topics* when listing the topics in his own text on invention. In this he echoes Soarez. But Carbone goes beyond all three when he shows in detail how the topics are applied by both rhetoricians and dialecticians.

Essential to successful use of the topics, Agricola explains, is gaining an understanding of what a question is and how to pose one. His teachings on this score may be seen as additional refinements of the Greek and Roman rhetorical teachings on *status.* Carbone's treatment of the question throws into bold relief the difficulties engendered in Agricola's attempt to reformulate parts of traditional logic while retaining parts of it untouched. For Carbone, questions arise first of all from the phenomena of nature (with which the *Categories* is concerned) and man's attempts to reason about them (the subject of the rest of the *Organon).*

Carbone follows Aristotle in distinguishing between "questions" or "problems" (Gr. *problemata*) and propositions in his treatment of dialectic. He calls questions and problems subjects for reasoning on both sides (what we would call issues) and propositions the bases of arguments made on one side alone.[58] Furthermore, Carbone clearly treats the differences between the solutions to problems gained by dialectic and those gained by demonstrative reasoning.

57. Aristotle, *Topica* I.2.101a. Aristotle describes dialectic's usefulness here.
58. Aristotle, *Topica* I.4, 101b.

But in Agricola the problem and the proposition are conflated and become the question. In conflating them he mingles rhetorical, dialectical, and scientific questions, all of which yield to the topics and supply matter sufficient to convince. By treating all of these as subject to the conjectural reasoning of dialectic, Agricola, while perhaps not meaning to, weakens the claims of the sciences.

As noted above, Agricola sees dialectic as applicable to all kinds of discourse, which he divides into exposition and argument. Exposition he defines as "a statement which only explains the opinion of a speaker, without doing anything to convince the hearer."[59] Mack suggests that this is the first treatment of exposition to come down to us, and he thinks that it originates in the discussion of the *narratio* in the anonymous *Rhetorica ad Herennium,* where the author explains that this part of the oration recounts what probably happened or did not happen in a case.[60]

Carbone credits Agricola with noting that sentences and speeches can be either expository or argumentative. In chapter eleven of book one of *De inventione* (translated in section five), he follows Agricola when he says that exposition, unlike argument, implies an audience not disposed to differ with what is said, whereas argument attempts to induce belief. He further comments that each can be used by the other—exposition can include an argument and argument an exposition. But Carbone does not seize the opportunity to go on and take up the forms of exposition that Agricola treats.

Exposition, as Agricola sees it, includes three major types: poetry, designed to please an audience; history, whose intent is to explain things, give an account of words and deeds; and oratory, philosophy, and textbooks, all of which attempt to create belief in what is presented.[61]

One of Agricola's most creative pedagogical innovations is his discussion in book three of the uses of dialectic. It is true that in the *Topics,* book eight, Aristotle is also concerned with the uses of dialectics, which he divides into two: opposing or refuting arguments (*dialectica obviata*) and practice in debate (*dialectica exercitativa*). Agricola, however, provides exercises in analysis, illustrating these with examples from classical texts. He suggests that students first develop practice in finding the *medium* (in Aristotle, the middle term) so as to gain a deeper understanding of the sinews of reasoning, which make an argument logical. While Agricola resists the idea of predication as Aristotle describes it, he nevertheless retains the structure of the syllogism in his exercises. He explains that the middle links the major and minor terms but does not occur in the conclusion. It is this middle that is furnished by the *topos* of the argument. That can be de-

---

59. Mack, *Renaissance Argument* 190, citing *De inventione.* pp. 1–2.
60. Mack, *Renaissance Argument,* 190–91.
61. Mack, *Renaissance Argument,* 195.

termined by running through the list. After having become proficient in discerning the *topos,* students are asked to find the question being argued, a more difficult task when it is embedded in a lengthy discussion of a subject.

Rhetoric comes into Agricola's picture of discourse when he takes up pleasing and moving the audience in the third book. Rhetorical discourse he shows as always framed in relation to an audience. Style figures large in this book, amplification being accorded three chapters.

On the direct influence of Agricola's writings Mack disagrees with Ong, finding it not as widespread or lasting as Ong thought it to be. Mack claims, however, that the secondary influence of Agricola passed on through Erasmus was profound. He suggests that Erasmus's *De copia* may owe some of its principles and techniques to Agricola's *De inventione dialectica.* Nevertheless, it was Erasmus who made invention pleasurable, while Agricola made it reasonable.[62] Although Carbone devoted lavish attention to copious style, he did not cite Erasmus, nor approach that subject in a similar way. Since works of Erasmus were on the Index of Prohibited Books by Carbone's day, this omission is not surprising.

For Agricola, as for Valla before him, usefulness was the first consideration in the reforms of the curriculum he introduced, usefulness for the teacher in explaining dialectic and for the pupil who would go on to apply these methods in everyday life. But Mack, unlike Cesare Vasoli and Lisa Jardine, sees little dependence of Agricola on Valla. He agrees, however, that the two Renaissance pedagogues had a common goal of "reuniting logic with real language."[63]

Although Agricola was most influential in Northern Europe, particularly in the Low Countries, Germany, France, and England, he had some impact on Italy as well. Soarez, however, does not cite him at all, nor, for that matter, any other Renaissance author. Carbone, as we have seen, responds to him both positively and negatively. Although he gives an account of Agricola's topics and addresses similar issues, at the same time he distances himself from his global claims for dialectic.

Peter Ramus. It was in France at the University of Paris that Johannes Sturm conveyed Agricola's teachings to the young Peter Ramus, who was to modify and carry the spirit of reform far beyond anything Agricola had dreamed. We give little attention to Ramus because his writings relate so little to the account of Northern Italian dialectic and rhetoric described in

---

62. Mack, *Renaissance Argument,* 309–11.

63. Mack, *Renaissance Argument,* 245. John Monfasani also finds little dependence of Agricola on Valla, "Lorenzo Valla and Rudolf Agricola," *Journal of the History of Philosophy* 28 (1990), 181–99, cited in Mack.

the rest of the book. Ramus's views on the classics of rhetoric, however, are of passing interest for the contrast his withering critiques of Aristotle, Cicero and Quintilian provide to the writings of previous authors. Ramus sees the trivial arts that emanated from their classical teachings as redundant, in great need of pruning and realignment. In his reformulation of the curriculum, dialectic, or logic, is given the arts of invention, arrangement, and memory; style and delivery, on the other hand, are allotted to rhetoric. His handling of the constituents of the arts proceeds from the outside in, moving to apportion these in the manner of an accountant who has little interest in the philosophical context.

In his *Dialectique* (1555) Ramus defines dialectic as "the art of discoursing well" and he divides it as did Agricola into two parts—invention and judgment. His treatment of invention also devotes attention to the question as the focus of reasoning and discoursing. He follows Agricola in avoiding discussion of predication and conceives of middle terms as binding the "'major part'" and "'minor part'" of reasoning. Invention, via the topics, supplies the cement, the middle term. The topics are not based in the concept of substance as in Agricola, for Ramus rejects the categories and thinks of topics simply as arguments—they are there waiting in the well-filled storehouse of the mind. With Ramus these become fillers, not stimuli to the development of thought.

Ramus's list of topics as they appear in an English translation of 1632 by Robert Fage comprises five major arguments, from which nine others follow. The major ones are causes, effects, subjects, adjuncts, "disagreeings"; the nine "derived arguments" are genus, form, name, notations, conjugates, testimonies, contraries, distributions, and definitions.[64]

After invention finds the arguments appropriate to a question, judgment goes to work in ordering their collocation or arrangement. Ramus was to revise his discussion of this part several times, but in its final form judgment has three steps. The first "collocation" includes types of reasoning: induction, the syllogism, the enthymeme, and the example. He describes these in his own idiosyncratic way. The next step is what will become "method," the arrangement of the whole discourse. This, he explains, is obtained by following the principles of definition and division. In a later edition Ramus notes a twofold method, that of teaching and of prudence. The method of teaching is to proceed from the universal or general principles to the particular parts, while the method of prudence takes into considerations rhetorical elements: the audience, circumstances, and occasion. Some people may be ignorant or opposed to learning what we may teach.[65]

64. Ong, *Ramus*, 183.   65. Ong, *Ramus*, 245–47.

The third step of judgment makes possible a Platonic ascent to the divine light that illumines the realm of ideas. This step seems to be taken by surveying what one has written, revising, eliminating what is unsuitable, seeing the whole as a movement from grammar, through rhetoric to dialectic, which guides the products of God's creation.

As Ong remarks, Ramus has included a Platonic conception of dialectic because he saw that this was missing in the scholastic system.[66] The insertion of an idealistic "method," as Ramus describes it, makes the system more spiritual than the *Organon* of Aristotle and ranges Ramus on the side of the Platonists in the ongoing battle against pagan Aristotelianism. Not surprisingly, though, this nebulous part of Ramus's system was dropped in his revision of the *Dialectic*.[67]

Ramus, like Agricola, provides exercises in the third part of his dialectic, adding them to the sections on invention and judgment. He explains that exercise or use (*usus*) takes three forms: interpretation (*interpretatio*), writing (*scriptio*), and speaking (*dictio*). The first of these resembles Agricola's directive asking students to analyze the text with the "natural" light of reason. They were first to find the question, note the arguments and their middle terms, remove the ambiguities and amplifications, and reduce the arguments found to the one main syllogism underlying the whole. The next step, writing (later "genesis" by Ramus—"synthesis" by his followers), encouraged students to reassemble the pieces of the analysis and create a new work. This for Ramus and his followers constituted imitation. Cicero thus could serve as a model for Ramus's students, but he would be systematized and corrected, in a sense, not followed slavishly.[68]

Some historians of science have credited Ramus's method as stimulating the rise of modern science. Norman E. Nelson provides a withering refutation of a view popular after the publication of Perry Miller's *The New England Mind,* that Ramus's logic proved "friendly" to the new science, as Miller put it.[69] Far from aiding the rise of the new science, Nelson argues, Ramus produced confusion with his "essentially dogmatic and aprioristic" methodology. The reformer did not replace the *Posterior Analytics.* He merely rejected the inductive syllogism "as a means of discovering truth, confined it to the expository function of clarifying doubtful propositions, and left truth to be grasped at all stages of discourse . . . simply by the clear assent of the 'natural reason.' In effect, all knowledge is intuitive."[70]

66. Ong, *Ramus,* 189.   67. Ong, *Ramus,* 190.

68. Ong, *Ramus,* 190–93.

69. Norman E. Nelson, "Peter Ramus and the Confusion of Logic, Rhetoric, and Poetry," *Contributions in Modern Philology* 2 (April 1947), 1–22; on p. 4 Nelson quotes Miller, p. 116, in *The New England Mind* (New York: 1939).

70. Nelson, "Peter Ramus," 11.

Carbone also employs the term method, but he explains it in the first book of his logic as an Aristotelian would, making clear that it is concerned with disposition, the ordering of things following either the order of nature or the order of teaching. He states that method is compositive, divisive, or resolutive. Unlike Ramus he does not conflate method and judgment. With regard to invention, Carbone devotes an entire treatise, *De inventione,* to that subject. Although he considers the origin and nature of both dialectical and rhetorical topics, he allows the full exploitation of each for amplifying propositions in different ways depending on the subject matter. Unlike either Agricola or Ramus, Carbone respects the special requirements of demonstrative and dialectical reasoning when considering philosophical matters. He also considers judgment, but in the Aristotelian sense as examining the correct method of reasoning in regard to the syllogism and the enthymeme and in considering the truth and falsity of propositions.

In the translations that follow, Carbone's synthesis of ancient and modern elements attests to the remarkable assimilation of the two imparted to him in his years at the Jesuit college in Rome. This does not subtract from Carbone's own contribution, which was similar to that of other reformers who remodeled the learning passed on to them to fit contemporary needs as they saw them.

Where does Galileo's understanding of scientific reasoning and rhetoric fit within this pedagogical context? His own writings supply the answers. His manuscript notebook in which he described demonstration and the foreknowledge required for it follows the Jesuit lectures given at the Collegio Romano; the details are given in the introduction to section one below, concerned with Carbone's logic. Wallace has shown convincingly not only that these notes were appropriated by Galileo, but that the concepts of reasoning contained in them were incorporated into his later scientific writings.[71] Dialectical reasoning is evident in those works as well, wherever probabilities are explored and defended. Galileo also illustrates and refers to demonstration and dialectic directly in his *Dialogue on the Two Chief World Systems.* In the preface he mentions that he plans to argue showing the Copernican hypothesis to be superior, "not indeed absolutely," but to combat the arguments of the Peripatetics. At one place in the *Dialogue,* Salviati replies to a correction to his logic by Simplicio: "Logic, as it is generally understood, is the organ with which we philosophize. But just as it may be possible for a craftsman to excel in making organs and yet not know how to play them, so one might be a great logician and still be

71. William A. Wallace, *Galileo's Logic of Discovery and Proof: The Background, Content and Use of His Appropriated Treatises on Aristotle's* 'Posterior Analytics,' Boston Studies in the Philosophy of Science, vol. 137 (Dordrecht: Kluwer, 1992).

inexpert in making use of logic." The distinction implied is that between: logic as taught (*docens*) and logic in use (*utens*). Salviati goes on to argue that mathematics is required for demonstration on the subject of the heavens. Thus, for Galileo, making distinctions in the kinds of reasoning to be applied to a subject continued to be important. His approach is that of Riccobono and Carbone and not that of Agricola or Ramus.

That Galileo was an expert in the matter of rhetoric is universally acknowledged. His knowledge of the subject and his ability to mix it with other methods of proof was unique in his time. In the *Dialogue* he attacked his opponents' views using true-to-life characters with poetic ease. Above all, he thought he knew his audience and what would persuade them. He had delighted his readers, even Pope Urban VIII, with *The Assayer*. There he had taken on the Jesuit astronomer Orazio Grassi about the nature and position of the comets and demolished his arguments, though, as we now know, Grassi was more right than he.[72] Thinking that he could again display his wit and mastery of all the arts and sciences, he pressed too hard in the *Dialogue*. He forgot or underestimated the allegiance of part of his audience to the preservation of the rule that a physical, necessary demonstration must be the sole criterion for arguing that Copernicus was right. Only then could the Scriptures be reinterpreted to agree with the truth of science. Probable reasoning, even the strongest arguments of dialectic, could not substitute. The argument from the tides could not be taken seriously—not enough physical evidence was offered in the *Dialogue*. And all the persuasive artifices could not remove such obstacles. The need of the Roman Catholic Church to defend itself from Protestant inroads made it cling to the opinion of its theologians regarding the call for reinterpretation of Scripture implicit in Galileo's argument. That, coupled with the *Dialogue*'s insensitive framing of Urban VIII's caveat regarding the tidal proof, was enough to negate the persuasive force of the text. That the demand for scientific demonstration might have been unreasonable never occurred to the pope or his theologians.

Only in 1992 was the subject of the appropriateness of probable reasoning as proof in science revisited by the Roman Catholic Church. At that time John Paul II admitted that the Church had been wrong in condemning Galileo for heresy. Drawing on the findings of a special commission he appointed to study the celebrated conflict between science and religion, he noted that while it is true that Galileo did disregard the Church's demand that he treat the Copernican system hypothetically and not demonstratively, he did so because of the demands of his new science. He stipulated further that theologians should become informed about sci-

---

72. See the discussion in *Novelties in the Heavens,* chapter eight.

entific matters to understand what "can be regarded as an acquired truth, or at least as enjoying such a degree of probability that it would be imprudent and unreasonable to reject it. In this way unnecessary conflicts can be avoided."[73]

The "new science" incorporated observation, experiment, and probable reasoning. It still respected demonstration of the type described by Carbone. But in 1632 such demonstration was not yet possible in many of the astronomical matters that were addressed by Galileo, and particularly the problem of the earth's motion.[74] That had to await two more centuries of scientific investigation.

73. *L'Osservatore Romano,* English edition, no. 44:4 Nov. 1992, pp. 1–2. The statement was made in an address to the Pontifical Academy of Sciences in a context of noting the complexity of modern science. John Paul II adverted to Bellarmine's requirement, in the early seventeenth century, that Galileo actually demonstrate the earth's motion before the Church would consider revising its longstanding interpretation of Sacred Scripture. The pope admitted that this requirement is much too stringent to be enforced in the present day. If a scientific theory cannot be known to be definitively true, he said, at least it should be "seriously and solidly grounded." In fact, he went on, the purpose of the Pontifical Academy of Sciences is precisely to advise him when this criterion has now been met.

74. William A. Wallace, "Galileo's Trial and Proof of the Earth's Motion," *Catholic Dossier* 1.2 (1995), 7–13. See also note 13 above.

Renaissance Texts
in Translation

Ludovico Carbone's
Introduction to Logic

INTRODUCTIONIS IN LOGICAM

Sive

TOTIUS LOGICAE COMPENDIJ ABSOLUTISSIMI LIBRI SEX

In quibus non solum quae ab Aristotele de re Logica scripta sunt, sed etiam quae ab aliis addita fuere, brevi facilique ratione continentur.

Quibus accessit Catalogus locupletissimus Auctorum, qui de rebus ad logicam pertinentibus, vel in libros Logicos Aristotelis aliquid scripserunt

Auctore

LUDOVICO CARBONE

A COSTACCIARO

Academico Parthenio, et sacrae Theologiae in almo Gymnasio Perusino olim publico Magistro

CUM PRIVILEGIIS

VENETIIS, MDXCVII

Apud Io. Baptistam, et Io. Bernardum Sessam.

SIX BOOKS OF AN INTRODUCTION TO LOGIC

or a

COMPLETE COMPENDIUM OF ALL OF LOGIC

*in which not only what Aristotle has written on Logic,
but also what others have added to it,
is summarized briefly and simply*

*To which is added a complete catalogue of Authors,
who have written on matters pertaining to Logic
or have commented on the logical works of Aristotle*

by

LUDOVICUS CARBONE

OF COSTACCIARO

*of the Parthenian Academy, Some time Master of Sacred Theology
in the Gymnasium at Perugia*

WITH PRIVILEGES

VENICE, 1597

With the Firm of John Baptist and John Bernard Sessa

Ludovico Carbone and Jesuit
Teachings on Logic

Carbone, the Jesuits, and Galileo

As indicated in the introductory essay, Ludovico Carbone was well acquainted with Jesuit teachings on logic and published a number of logical works himself, several of which are now known to have been plagiarized from Jesuit sources. The most important of these works is Carbone's *Introductio in logicam sive totius logicae compendii absolutissimi libri sex* (Introduction to logic, or six books containing a complete compendium of all of logic), published at Venice in 1597, portions of which are translated in this section. Parts of this work are already found in one of Carbone's earlier works published at Venice in 1588 and entitled *Introductio in dialecticam Aristotelis per Magistrum Franciscum Toletum Sacerdotem Societatis Iesu, Philosophiae in Romano Societatis Collegio Professorem* (Introduction to Aristotle's dialectic by Master Franciscus Toletus, Priest of the Society of Jesus, Professor of Philosophy in the Society's Roman College). This Carbone proposed as an introduction to the famous logic text of Franciscus Toletus, a Jesuit priest, whose *Introductio in dialecticam Aristotelis* (Introduction to Aristotle's dialectic) was first published at Rome in 1561, when Toletus was a professor at the Collegio Romano, with many editions thereafter. Then, also at Venice in 1597, Carbone came out with another book ostensibly based on Toletus's *Commentaria una cum quaestionibus in universam logicam Aristotelis* (Commentaries together with questions on all of Aristotle's logic), which was first published at Rome in 1572, likewise with many editions thereafter. Carbone entitled this his *Additamenta ad commentaria D. Francisci Toleti in Logicam Aristotelis: Praeludia in libros Priores Analyticos; Tractatio de Syllogism; de Instrumentis Sciendi; et de Praecognitionibus atque Praecognitis* (Additions to Dr. Franciscus Toletus's commentaries on Aristotle's logic: Preludes to the books of the *Prior Analytics;* Treatises on the syllogism, on instruments of Knowing, and on foreknowledges and foreknowns).

Detective work by one of the editors of this volume, extending over many years, has revealed that the author of all of these works was not Carbone, nor was their basic source the logic texts of Toletus.[1] Rather, Car-

---

1. This discovery was first reported in William A. Wallace, *Galileo and His Sources: The Heritage of the Collegio Romano in Galileo's Science* (Princeton: Princeton University Press, 1984), pp. 10–23 and *passim.* Fuller details are given in what follows.

bone's works were actually based on the teaching notes of the Italian Jesuit Paulus Vallius (Paolo della Valle, 1561–1622), who taught the logic course at the Collegio Romano in the academic year 1587–1588. There his name is listed in the *rotulus* of professors as Paulus Valla—an unfortunate entry causing his name to be noted in the early literature as Valla rather than Vallius.[2] Moreover, this detective work was not done in the context of Jesuit logic, but rather in attempts to locate the source of one of Galileo's early notebooks whose provenance has lain hidden for over four hundred years. This is the Galileo manuscript now listed as MS Gal. 47 in the Galileo collection conserved in the Biblioteca Nazionale Centrale in Florence, entitled "Dialettica" by the curator who bound it centuries ago.[3] Surprisingly, the manuscript, written in 1588 or 1589 and in Galileo's own hand, was appropriated from the very set of notes that Carbone plagiarized from Vallius. The plagiarism was detected by Vallius himself, who published his entire logic course in two folio volumes of over 700 pages each in the year of his death. In the prefaces of both these volumes, whose title is *Logica Pauli Vallii Romani ex Societate Iesu, duobus tomis distinctis* (The Logic of Paulus Vallius, a Roman Jesuit, in two different volumes); Lyons: Sumptibus Ludovici Prost haeredibus Rouille, 1622, Vallius points to portions of the logic course he taught at the Collegio Romano many years before, specifically in 1587–1588, that were later published by Carbone under his own name and without acknowledging their source.[4]

This situation obviously has profound implications for a work entitled "Rhetoric and Dialectic in the Time of Galileo." In Galileo's time all of

---

2. In Wallace's publications up to 1988 the name of this author is given as Valla, following the listing in the *rotulus* of the Collegio. In an article published in that year, "Randall *Redivivus*: Galileo and the Paduan Aristotelians" (*Journal of the History of Ideas*, 49: 133–149), Wallace changed the spelling to Vallius. This was done at the suggestion of Paul Oskar Kristeller, who counseled against using the first spelling because of the possibility of confusing Vallius with Lorenzo Valla or others of the Valla family. By that time, of course, it was known that Vallius had published his logic course in 1622 under the correct spelling of his name.

3. This manuscript was never transcribed by the editor of Galileo's works, Antonio Favaro, and thus does not appear in the National Edition of his writings, *Le opere di Galileo Galilei*, 20 vols. in 21 (Florence: G. Barbèra, 1890–1909, repr. 1968). The Latin text was finally transcribed by William F. Edwards in 1967, and then, after Wallace's discovery of the source from which it was appropriated, was published in 1988, four hundred years after it was written. This appeared in the Saggi e Testi Series (No. 22) sponsored jointly by the University of Padua and Columbia University. The full title is *Galileo Galilei, Tractatio de praecognitionibus et praecognitis and Tractatio de demonstratione, transcribed from the Latin autograph by William F. Edwards, with an introduction, notes, and commentary by William A. Wallace* (Padua: Editrice Antenore, 1988). The Latin text has been translated into English and is now available in William A. Wallace, ed. and tr., *Galileo's Logical Treatises*. A Translation, with Notes and Commentary, of His Appropriated Latin Questions on Aristotle's *Posterior Analytics*, Boston Studies in the Philosophy of Science, Vol. 138 (Dordrecht/Boston/London: Kluwer Academic Publishers, 1992).

4. Translations of portions of these forewords will be found in *Galileo and His Sources*, pp. 18–19, and in *Galileo's Logical Treatises*, pp. 9–11.

logic was frequently treated under the scope of dialectic, although more properly the term should be applied to the part of logic that deals with dialectical or probable reasoning. Galileo himself had studied logic as a youth in the monastery of Vallombrosa, and then at the University of Pisa, where he was a student from 1581 to 1585. Later, in 1587, when he became seriously interested in demonstrative proof, he consulted with Christopher Clavius, the famous Jesuit mathematician, who was teaching at the Collegio Romano along with Vallius. Apparently Clavius put Galileo in touch with this logic professor, who made his logic course available to Galileo. Galileo then not only studied Vallius's notes, but, seeing how superior they were to the instruction he had earlier received in logic at the University of Pisa, copied out large portions for his own use. When the results of this appropriation from Vallius are studied in detail, along with the use Galileo made of that teaching in his later investigations, one can reconstruct the logic of discovery and proof that lay behind his life-long contributions to modern science.[5]

Galileo's views on demonstration are not of key importance for this study. It should be noted, however, that Aristotle's teaching on demonstration, that is, on what is required for true and certain reasoning, is essential for understanding his teachings on the two weaker forms, probable reasoning (i.e., dialectic) and persuasive reasoning (i.e., rhetoric). Now Carbone, as should be clear from the Introduction of this volume and the later sections, was an expert on rhetoric in his own right. But there seems little doubt that his knowledge of logic and particularly of dialectic derives from Vallius and possibly other Jesuit sources.[6] For purposes of this study, therefore, we will not be far wrong in regarding Jesuit logic, Galileo's logic, and Carbone's logic as basically the same body of knowledge.

Ludovico Carbone (1545–1597)

Ludovico Carbone was born at Costaciaro, near Urbino, in 1545, as attested by a document in the Archivo della Curia Patriarcale in Venice, which identifies him as a doctor of both philosophy and theology.[7] His

---

5. This theme is developed at length in Wallace's companion volume to *Galileo's Logical Treatises* entitled *Galileo's Logic of Discovery and Proof, The Background, Content, and Use of His Appropriated Treatises on Aristotle's Posterior Analytics,* Boston Studies in the Philosophy of Science, Vol. 137 (Dordrecht/Boston/London: Kluwer Academic Publishers, 1992). The same theme runs through Wallace's essay, "Galileo's Pisan Studies in Science and Philosophy," in *The Cambridge Companion to Galileo,* ed. Peter Machamer (Cambridge: Cambridge University Press, 1998), pp. 27–52.

6. Vallius mentions that Carbone had published materials from Jesuits other than himself similarly without acknowledging his source. See *Galileo and His Sources,* p. 18.

7. The document, which is a profession of faith, is dated 25 October 1587 and states that at that time Carbone was 42 years of age. It also attests that he taught philosophy and theology, had

date of death is not documented, but in the card file of the Vatican Library he is listed as a priest who died in 1597. He was a prodigious author and published extensively in philosophy and theology, as well as in logic, rhetoric, and the spiritual life.[8] He was taught by Jesuits at the Collegio Romano in the late 1550s or early 1560s, where he was a member of one of their sodalities, the Congregatio Beatae Mariae Annuntiatae, but was not himself a Jesuit. He claims to have studied logic under Franciscus Toletus, who taught the logic course at the Collegio in 1559–1560.

Early in his career Carbone prepared a study guide for a popular compendium of rhetoric by the Portuguese Jesuit Cipriano Soarez entitled *De arte rhetorica*, which is translated in the next section. Carbone claims to have seen this work in manuscript. It was first published in 1562 and then reprinted some 134 times down to 1735. In the preface to his guide Carbone praises his professors at the Collegio for the content of their lectures and the manner in which they instructed their students. He wrote then that he was actively preparing ten more works that would benefit not only his own students but those who attend Jesuit schools. It is possible that some of these are based on *reportationes* of lectures on rhetoric given at the Collegio. Since these are of Jesuit authorship, this would corroborate a charge made by Vallius that Carbone had stolen not only his writings but also those of other Jesuits. Fairly recently a manuscript has been uncovered containing Carbone's notes on Aristotle's *De caelo* and *De generatione* that bear affinity to Jesuit lectures on Aristotle and also to Galileo's MS Gal. 46.[9] By present-day standards one might regard these works as plagiarized. Such a charge, however, should be alleviated in light of the piety he exhibits towards his mentors and his own expressed concern to further their teachings.

Summing up the evidence now available with regard to Carbone, we

---

lectured publicly at Perugia, and was then at the Seminario di San Marco in Venice. The authors thank Paul Grendler for communicating this information to them.

8. There is no complete list of Carbone's publications, but the following is a working list compiled by the authors from entries in the card files of the Vatican Library and other libraries in Europe and the U.S.: *De pacificatione*, Florence, 1583; *Interior homo vel de suiipsius cognitione*, Venice, 1585; *Vir iustus*, Venice, 1585; *De amore et concordia fraterna*, Venice, 1586; *Compendium absolutissimum. . . [?]*, Venice, 1587; *Fons vitae et sapientiae*, Venice, 1588; *Introductio in dialecticam Toleti*, Venice, 1588; *Introductio in sacram theologiam sex comprehensa libris*, Venice, 1589; *Tabulae rhetoricae Cipriani Soarii*, Venice, 1589; *De arte dicendi duo libri*, Venice, 1589; *De dispositione oratoria, disputationes xxx*, Venice, 1590; *De praeceptis Ecclesiae opusculum utilissimum*, Venice, 1590; *De elocutione oratoria*, Venice, 1592; *De octo partium orationis constructione libellus*, Venice, 1592; *De caussis eloquentiae libri iiii*, Venice, 1593; *Divinus orator, vel De rhetorica divina libris septem*, Venice, 1595; *Introductio ad catechismum sive doctrinam Christianum*, Venice, 1596; *Della Ammaestramento de' Figliuoli nella Dottrina Christiana*, Venice, 1596; *Introductionis in logicam . . . libri sex*, Venice, 1597; *Additamenta ad commentaria D. Francisci Toleti in Logicam Aristotelis*, Venice, 1597; *Introductionis in universam phiosophiae libri quatuor*, Venice, 1599; *Summa summarum casuum conscientiae*, Venice, 1606.

9. See Jean D. Moss, "Ludovico Carbone's Commentary on Aristotle's *De caelo*," in *Nature and Scientific Method, Essays in Honor of William A. Wallace*, ed. Daniel O. Dahlstrom (Washington, D.C.: The Catholic University of America Press, 1990), pp. 169–92.

may gather that: (1) he had studied philosophy at the Collegio prior to 1562, probably beginning in 1559 under Toletus; (2) he taught an introduction to Toletus's dialectic in Rome in 1588 and possibly at the Collegio, where Vallius had taught a similar introduction in late 1587; (3) in 1588 he published some preludes to, and tables for, Toletus's introduction to dialectic, adumbrating materials that would later appear in his own introduction to logic of 1597, now known to be based on Vallius's lectures; (4) he published in 1589 a guide and tables to Soarez's rhetoric, at which time he stated that he was preparing ten more works related in some way to Jesuit teachings; (5) he wrote out in 1594 manuscript notes on the *De caelo* and *De generatione* based on Jesuit materials, possibly one of the ten works then under preparation; (6) he published in 1597 and under his own name the *Introductio in logicam,* appropriating Vallius's similar introduction from the latter's lectures given in 1587; (7) in 1597 he likewise published under his own name an *Additamenta* to Toletus's *Logic,* similarly appropriating materials in it from Vallius's logic course; and (8) in 1599 an *Introductio in universam philosophiam* was published under his name (posthumously), containing a treatise *De scientia* alleged by Vallius to be based on his own logic course.

On the matter of Carbone's possible contribution to all of these reworked treatises, it seems that his part was mainly that of a pedagogue—ordering the materials so that their connections could be readily seen and supplying apt illustrations to make them intelligible. His writing style was direct but elegant, not flowery but explicit, and replete with pertinent illustrations from the classics. Apart from Vallius's prefaces, therefore, and on the bases of Carbone's style and his own testimony, it seems reasonable to attribute the basic content of the *Additamenta* and the appropriated treatises in the *Introductio in logicam* and the *Introductio in universam philosophiam* to Vallius's lectures of 1587–1588. The stylistic and pedagogical innovations in them, on the other hand, would seem to be the result of Carbone's work in 1597 for the *Additamenta* and for the two introductions, one to logic and the other to the whole of philosophy.

Selections from the *Introductio in logicam*

The *Introductio in logicam* is made up of six books, not all of which are relevant to our enterprise. The first book provides a general introduction to the nature of logic and its work, and this is translated in its entirety. The next three books are devoted to predicables and categories, propositions, and syllogisms respectively—materials usually treated in courses on formal logic—and these are skipped, no selections being given from them here. The fifth book, however, is devoted to material logic (now referred to by some as epistemic or content logic), and the first twenty chapters of this book are translated. It is here that distinctions are drawn between demonstrative or scientific reasoning, dialectical or probable reasoning, and sophistical or fallacious reasoning. The portion dealing with probable reasoning is the best overview of the subject matter of dialectic in this volume. The sixth book, finally, is devoted to the operations of the intellect and various kinds of intentionality, and the first eight chapters of this book are translated. They provide a more advanced treatment of the materials covered briefly in the fourth chapter of the first book, which gives a condensed exposition of the "Powers of the Human Soul" and how they interact in the knowing process. Their operation may be explained through the use of two diagrams that are displayed in what follows.

The translation is given in idiomatic English and stays close to the text. Carbone documents his exposition with glosses in the margins; these have been removed from the text and are presented as endnotes that follow the translation.

Powers of the Human Soul

Figure 1 summarizes Carbone's account of the soul's powers and how they are the source of human activities, as explained in the first book.[10] Underlying the diagram is the Aristotelian claim that the various organs of the human body are matched by different powers or capacities of the human soul that enliven or activate the operations of the different organs. So, just as the body has integral or quantitative parts, which we recognize as its organs, so the soul has "power parts," that is, matching abilities or capacities that empower or inform the organs to perform their proper functions. The basic life functions of a human being are those of the vegetative powers, shown at the bottom of Figure 1; the sensitive powers, the four powers directly above the vegetative powers; and the intellective powers, on the right of the sensitive powers.

The vegetative powers, according to Carbone, are three in number: the generative power, which is needed for producing offspring; the augmentative power, which accounts for growth; and the nutritive power, which controls the process of nourishment. These powers are proper to the vegetative soul and they are the only powers found in plants. They are also found, however, in sensitive and intellective souls, where they are required for the production and conservation in being of animals and humans. They do not produce knowledge, however, and so are not directly involved in the knowing process [9].[11]

---

10. This drawing is based on a similar figure on p. 41 of *Galileo's Logic of Discovery and Proof.* The following explanation is adapted from that on pp. 40–42 of the same work, which explains how the powers function in more detail.

11. Numbers in square brackets here refer to the page numbers of Carbone's *Introductio in logicam,* which are inserted at appropriate places in the English translation of the work that follows.

Powers of the Human Soul

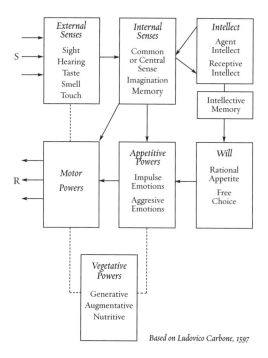

Based on Ludovico Carbone, 1597

FIGURE I

In view of the fact that the animal soul includes also the powers of the plant soul, the five powers on the left of Figure I can be seen to account for all animal activity. In our day we may also interpret the schema along the lines of a stimulus-response model, as intimated by the letters "S" and "R" shown at its left—a notation that was not known to Carbone. When sense impressions from an object stimulate an animal's sense organs, they transmit impulses to the internal senses, where they register an image or percept. The image perceived may initiate a motor response directly, to perform what modern psychologists call an autonomic function. In this case, shown by a diagonal line with an arrow going from the internal senses to the motor powers, the animal reacts by moving spontaneously. Alternatively, the percept may arouse a response in the animal's appetitive powers, shown by lines with arrows going down from the internal senses to the appetitive powers and then left across from the appetitive powers to the motor powers. In this case the percept provokes an emotional reaction that in turn can stimulate movements of various kinds [10–11].

All of the aforementioned powers are prerequisite to understanding knowing activity in humans. This takes place on a higher plane than knowing in brute animals, in view of the unique status of humans as rational animals endowed with free will. Although Carbone does not discuss the human will and its operations in this place, we show the will in Figure 1 on the right of the appetitive powers. This enables us to complete the S-R circuit for a distinctively human act, to be explained presently. Carbone's major interest in this section is in the intellect, shown directly above the will. For him the intellect is made up of two components, an agent or active intellect and a receptive or passive intellect, and it is also complemented by an intellective memory that is shown directly below it. The intellect is thus the highest cognitive power in humans and it is served by the two preparatory sets of cognitive powers, the external and the internal senses [12–13].

The external senses send their species to the internal senses directly, but the internal senses do not in turn affect the intellect directly. In Carbone's theory of knowledge a marked difference separates the percept generated in the internal senses from the concept that is formed in the intellect. The percept is a concrete and singular image that is a representation of a particular individual object perceived. As opposed to this, the concept is abstract and universal, and as such is capable of being applied to any and all similar objects perceptible in sense experience. The universalizing process whereby the concept is produced is triggered by a natural light that comes from the agent or active intellect, which is shown in Figure 1 by the line with an arrow coming from the agent intellect to the internal senses. This natural light illuminates the percept, as it were, and abstracts from it its intelligible content. The result is an 'immaterial species,' as Carbone calls it, that acts on the receptive or passive intellect, as shown by the line with an arrow returning from the internal senses to the intellect. In so acting, the immaterial species causes the receptive intellect to give birth to the concept, with its abstract and universal features. (The concept or *conceptum* is called such because it is 'conceived' in the receptive intellect, on the analogy of the way in which an offspring is conceived in a womb.) All of this takes place naturally, in Carbone's view, just as do breathing and sensing and imagining. And once conceptualization of this type has taken place, the mind spontaneously goes about combining and separating its concepts first to form judgments and then to engage in discursive or syllogistic reasoning so as to attain the truth about the external world [13–14].

In a completely human act all seven of the boxes shown in Figure 1 above the box for the vegetative powers are involved. A much simplified sketch of the operation of the sets of powers involved would be the following. As already explained, stimuli external to the human body, indicated by

the "S" at the upper left of Figure 1, act on the organs of the external senses and produce a variety of sensations in the box labeled 'external senses.'
From here the various sensations are passed on to the box labeled 'internal
senses,' where they are unified into concrete and individual percepts corresponding to the different individual objects perceived. The agent or active intellect in the upper part of the 'intellect' box then illuminates these
percepts and abstracts from them their contents or meanings, which are
expressed as concepts in the receptive intellect in the lower part of the 'intellect' box. Concepts are also stored in the box for 'intellective memory'
for future reference. More immediately, they prompt the will, shown in
the box directly below the intellective memory, to begin the process of reacting to the knowledge now received. The will chooses to act or not act
on that knowledge and then moves the emotions, shown in the box to the
left of the will labeled 'appetitive powers,' to the appropriate activity or
activities. Finally, the emotions in turn activate the 'motor powers' in the
box to their left, and a reaction, indicated by the "R" below the "S" on the
left of Figure 1, is produced.

The entire process as thus explained is labeled a 'human act' because it
is an operation that is distinctive of human beings, who as rational animals
are capable of reacting knowingly and willingly to the stimuli they receive.
Although humans can react to stimuli 'humanly' in this sense, it is not
necessary that they do so. As can be seen from Figure 1, it is possible for a
reaction to short-circuit the path through the intellect and the will and
make use of only the four boxes to the left of those for man's higher faculties. The S-R path would go first from the external senses to the internal
senses, and then, through an activation that the appetite powers would receive from the internal senses, pass on an emotive response to the motive
powers. The act thus produced would be labeled an 'act of man,' as opposed to a 'human act,' because, although produced by a human being, it
would not be produced intellectually and willingly, and thus not in a way
that is distinctively human.

First and Second Intentions

The account of concept formation just given is concerned with knowledge of external objects, that is, of things known in the real world, what
are referred to as 'real beings.' As a consequence, the concepts of such beings formed in the way diagramed in Figure 1 may be referred to as 'real
concepts.' In chapter two of the first book Carbone explains that the subject matter with which logic is concerned is not real beings, but rather
with what, by way of opposition, are called 'beings of reason' *(entia rationis)*.
He does not explain in any detail how the concepts relating to this type of
being are formed, but merely supplies a number of examples of such con-

cepts from which the reader can form an intuitive idea of their nature. He promises, however, to treat this matter more fully later [3–6].

The place where he does so is in chapters five through eight of the sixth book under the general topic of intentionality [251–272], a substantial portion of which is translated in this section. The relationships between concepts and intentions are diagrammed in Figure 2 below, which builds on the materials already presented in Figure 1 and establishes the connection between the two figures. Before explaining Figure 2, however, we first summarize the contents of Carbone's exposition in these chapters so as to acquaint the reader with his terminology on intentionality.

Carbone begins with the notion of 'intention,' which he says means a tending toward, or a tendency to, an object. Then, since the powers by which humans know or desire objects tend toward those objects, the word 'intention' can be used to explain the operations of various human powers, and particularly the intellect and the will.

As applied to the will, he goes on, intention sometimes means the act of the will by which it tends to the good, and this is the same as willing it or grasping it. Sometimes, however, it means not the will's act but the thing to which that act tends, as when we say that the intention of the teacher is to help the pupil learn. Thus the word refers properly to the act of the will, improperly or by metonymy to what is intended by the will [251].

When transferred to the intellect, the term intention has similar references, but these become more complicated. The complication arises from the intellect's ability to reflect on its own activity and so form concepts relating to mental entities rather than to entities in the real world. To handle this difficulty Carbone proposes two distinctions: one divides intentions into two types, 'formal' and 'material,' with material understood in the sense of 'objective'; the other divides intentions into 'first' and 'second,' with first applied to unreflective concepts of the real world and second applied to concepts formed in the mind when reflecting on concepts already formed unreflectively. Combining the two one may speak of 'first intentions,' which have both a formal and an objective aspect, the first the acts by which they are formed and the second the objects with which the acts are concerned, and 'second intentions,' which likewise have both a formal and an objective aspect, the first the acts by which they too are formed and the second the objects with which these acts are concerned [252–253].

On this accounting, things that are said to exist objectively in the intellect are two in kind. One kind comprises things that exist outside the intellect and independently of it—as man or lion. Such things when known are said to exist objectively in the intellect, and the concepts we form of them are referred to as 'first intentions' and 'real concepts.' The other kind are things that do not exist apart from the intellect's operation, and thus they are said to exist because they are known, and as known they are referred to as 'second intentions' and 'beings of reason' [254–255].

In Carbone's epistemology the human intellect has the basic ability to know and understand objects of sense experience. These objects are real and have natures, and as known their natures become first intentions. The natures are real and they exist in the objects whose natures they are. As simply existent they are not intentions, but as known they are objective first intentions. A lion has a nature, and this is whatever it is that makes it be what it is; the objective first intention whereby it is known is a concept, the concept of lion, and this is its nature as known. Because the lion's nature is real, the concept whereby it is grasped may be called a real concept. But here one has to be careful, for the concept may be looked at in two ways, either as the act of conceptualizing (the formal concept) or as what is conceptualized (the objective concept). The formal concept is real only in the sense that the psychological act of conceptualizing is a real act in the one knowing. The objective concept is real in another sense, for as a first intention it is in the lion also, since it is the nature of the lion as known. In virtue of its being a lion, the knower can say that he knows the lion as a real, extramental, or mind-independent being.

The situation with respect to second intentions is otherwise, as may be made clear through a simple example. Having the real concepts of 'lion' and 'zoo' one may make the judgment expressed in the sentence 'The lion is in the zoo.' That sentence can prompt further acts of the intellect wherein 'lion' and 'zoo' give rise to additional concepts such as 'subject' and 'predicate.' Thus, reflecting on the sentence 'The lion is in the zoo' one may make additional judgments such as "'The lion' is the subject of the sentence and 'in the zoo' is its predicate." Here the concepts of 'subject' and 'predicate' are second intentions. In this order too it is possible to differentiate between formal and objective intentions. There is the formal second intention, the act of conceptualizing 'subject' and 'predicate,' and an objective second intention, what is conceptualized in that act, namely, the type of being that is denominated a subject or a predicate. Logic is the discipline that works with beings of this type. Unlike real beings they exist only in a mind such as one considering the judgment that the lion is in the zoo. In this sense they are mind-dependent, whereas real beings may be said to be mind-independent.

By way of summary, we present in Figure 2 a diagram that builds on Figure 1 to show how first-second and formal-material intentions may be related to the powers of the soul already discussed.[12] Of the various powers of

---

12. This drawing is based on a similar figure on p. 55 of *Galileo's Logic of Discovery and Proof.* The accompanying discussion is based on pp. 53–56 of the same work.

Intentions of Intellect and Will

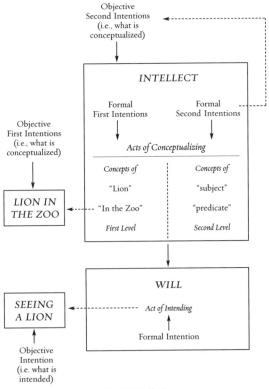

FIGURE 2

the soul in Figure 1 only the intellect and the will are shown here, the other powers being blocked out. The contents of the intellect box are now those of the portion of the intellect box in Figure 1 designated the receptive intellect, since this is where concepts are generated through the action of the agent intellect on the percepts of sense experience. In view of the fact that intentions can be seen as acts of the will more readily than as acts of the intellect, the lower part of the figure, showing the will and its object, should be considered first. The diagram assumes that a person is intent on going to a zoo to see a lion: if so, the intention formed has both a formal and an objective aspect. The formal intention is the 'act of intending' in the will, the objective intention is simply 'what is intended,' namely, seeing a lion. These formal and objective aspects then have parallels in the operation of the intellect whereby the person knows the lion when seen, as follows.

Assuming that the person senses a lion at the zoo through a percept, the lion is grasped intellectually through a concept, which in turn is signified by a word or term, 'lion.' (One way of understanding intention as applied to a concept is to see it as what the person 'intends' when using the word that is the sign of the concept.) Consider then the content on the left side of the intellect box, that showing the level of first intentions. In knowing the lion in the zoo as presented by the senses, the person knowing it conceptualizes both the lion and its location, represented there by the words 'lion' and 'in the zoo.' Their corresponding concepts are formal first intentions; their correlates, which are conceptualized, are objective first intentions. These correspond to the formal and objective intentions in the will shown directly below them in the diagram. On their basis the person can formulate the proposition 'The lion is in the zoo.' Although the proposition is formed in the intellect, it is a statement about the real world. The lion, its location, and the joining of the two are all mind-independent entities.

Consider, as opposed to this, the content on the right side of the intellect box, that showing the level of second intentions. After forming first intentions of the lion and its location, the knower can form additional concepts, represented in the box by the words 'subject' and 'predicate.' The acts of conceptualizing subject and predicate, similarly represented there by the words 'subject' and 'predicate,' are formal second intentions; their correlates, which are conceptualized, are objective second intentions, namely, 'lion' seen as a subject and its location seen as a predicate in the proposition 'The lion is in the zoo.' Now the person can form additional propositions, "'The lion' is a subject" and "The phrase 'in the zoo' is a predicate." These are not statements about the real world; rather they are statements about a statement and so involve entities that are mind-dependent or simply 'beings of reason.' Such second level concepts are logical entities, and these are the objects of consideration in the science of logic.[13]

What has been said about 'subject' and 'predicate' may now be extended to all of the technical terms used in sciences related to logic such as grammar, dialectic, sophistic, and rhetoric. They are 'beings of reason,' all formed in the mind as one reflects on one's thought or modes of discourse. They enable a person not only to organize thought and discourse, but also to develop rules to regulate their composition and expression, and so facilitate their comprehension by those to whom they might be addressed.

---

13. A fuller elaboration of this exposition will be found in William A. Wallace, *The Modeling of Nature: Philosophy of Science and Philosophy of Nature in Synthesis* (Washington, D.C.: The Catholic University of America Press, 1996), pp. 100–156. The diagrams on pp. 134, 143, and 145 are similar to those referred to above in *Galileo's Logic of Discovery and Proof.*

BOOK ONE

In which the nature of logic and its causes and attributes are explained

Chap. I. On the names of logic

[1] In every art and discipline that is treated rationally one should begin with knowledge of its name, as reason demonstrates and the authority of wise men confirms.[1] Since therefore our course provides a kind of way and path to correctly understanding all other disciplines, we shall dwell briefly on its various names, for reason demands that we do this first. Therefore our faculty, like the doorway to all others, received three special titles among the Greeks, namely, *Dialectica, Logica,* and *Organum,* which the Latins took as their own.

The first cultivators of this art among the Greeks called it *Dialectica,* from the word *dialegesthe,* [2] which means variously to use a word, to have words interrelated, to decide, or to argue, but not to reason, as some think, or to discourse.[2] Properly speaking *disserere* means to scatter seed in different directions, and by translation, to do the same with words.[3] The Latins thus used *disertrix, disputatrix,* and *disceptatrix,* and, as some say, *disertura* and *disputatura,* after our use of terms like *agricultura* and *literatura.*

Logica, or *Logice,* has been said to be from *apo tu logu,* but it is called *Logos* among the Greeks. This nearly always means reason, mind, speech, oration, word, definition, mode or proportion, computation, book, fame, or opinion.[4] Here it is taken in its first signification as the Latin *Logica.*[5] This designates a rational faculty, either because it directs reason and teaches a doctrine of reasoning correctly, or because it treats beings of reason, things of a certain type that follow from reason, as explained more fully below. Logic is thus not said principally from 'word' or from 'oration,' as if it were a sermonic or oratorical faculty, because of itself it does not treat such subject matters.

Organum, Lat. for instrument, is so called because it is like an instrument for acquiring sciences, or like an instrumental art that treats instruments of knowing that are necessary in other sciences. For this reason, as some point out, Aristotle entitled his books concerning this art the *Organon.*[6] That is why it is also sometimes called 'modes of knowing,' because it teaches ways of acquiring knowledge.[7] . . .

Chap. 2. On the nature of logic, or on its matter and form

[3] Since, as Aristotle teaches in various places,[8] one has perfect knowledge of the nature of any thing only when one understands its causes, we first explain its causes to give some idea of its nature. To do this, however, we provide some notations required as foreknowledge.

First, the causes of things are enumerated as four: matter, form, agent, and end.[9] Matter is that from which something is made, as a house from stones, a table from wood; thus stones are the matter of the house and wood of the table. Form is that which, together with the matter, makes up the whole, determines it to be a certain kind, and distinguishes it from others, as the human soul man and whiteness the white thing. But form is twofold: one internal, which is said to be essential, such as the sensitive soul that is the form of an animal; the other accidental, something apart from the thing's nature, such as whiteness in snow, heat in water. The efficient agent is what produces a thing or with which a process begins, as the sun is the cause of the day, the teacher of the lesson, and fire of burning. The end is that for the sake of which something is done, as the goal of war is peace, of learning science, of man eternal life. The two prior causes are called intrinsic because they are within the thing, make it up intrinsically, and so produce its nature; the two posterior are called extrinsic because they are outside the thing effected.

In any art the matter is that with which the art is concerned, [4] what it explains and treats and proposes to be known; this is said to be its subject and object, as proper speech is the matter of grammar. But there is a twofold matter, one remote, which the art presupposes, as the art of building wood in the forest, the other proximate, which the art treats directly and in which it induces a form, as the wood that is worked on by the artisan.

Moreover, to explain what the subject matter of logic is, it should be noted that the human intellect, which is the power by which we know, has three operations:[10] one, by which it apprehends something simple, as when it conceives and understands 'man'; another, by which it joins one thing to another by affirming or denying, as when it affirms that 'man is an animal' or denies that 'man is a stone'; and a third, when from one thing known it gathers another by reasoning, as, 'man is an animal, therefore he has sense knowledge.' By nature alone we perform these three operations imperfectly, and so we require an art to direct and perfect them. This art is logic, which is a teaching by which we apprehend, compose, and reason correctly; on this account it is said to be a faculty of knowing correctly. And since nothing can be directed without a rule, logic explains matters that are like rules for directing the aforementioned operations. These are called instruments of knowing or beings of reason, about which we make a few remarks here and treat more fully later.[11]

'Being,' a participle from the substantive 'to be,' signifies that which *is,* as running signifies the one who runs. It is either something outside the intellect in things themselves, as man, heaven, fire, and things of that type, and these are called real beings, that is, things outside their causes, actually produced, and existents; or it is another type, things that are said to exist differently because they are products of the intellect [5] and cannot exist without the intellect. These are things that are fabricated by the intellect, such as a gold mountain and a chimera. They are not said of things except as they are conceived, and so are said to be in the intellect the way in which things seen are said to be in the eye seeing. To things existing in the intellect, therefore, there come modifications and denominations, or relations, by which they are extrinsically denominated, as 'man' considered by the intellect separately and apart from individual men is said to be a 'universal' because of its relation to inferiors, in which it exists and from which it is abstracted. It is said to be a 'predicable' since it is predicated of them and is attributed to them; and it is said to be a 'species' as it is referred to individuals. Similarly, 'animal' is said to be a 'genus' because of the way it is related to 'species,' which is a subject of which 'genus' is predicated as a superior category. These terms and others like them, denominations and relations that come to things as they are conceived by the intellect, are said to be 'beings of reason' *(entia rationis),* as coming to things extrinsically through the work of reason. This is the way in which a wall is said to be 'seen' when perceived by the eye, or 'to the right' by its relationship to things in that direction. The beings of reason that are considered by the logician are those that come to things as they are apprehended, composed, and joined to others, and so direct the operations of the intellect. From this rough explanation one can gather some idea of logic's subject matter.

As to the proximate matter of logic, some say that it is the three operations of the intellect that are directed by logic; others say that it is beings of reason, or a being of reason as it is an instrument directing the same operations, or some kind of instrument, such as an argumentation and a syllogism. As to the [6] remote matter, this is things that logic presupposes. These are first intentions on which beings of reason are based, and which themselves are called second intentions because they are known in the second place. That suffices for the object of logic; now we turn to its form.

Logic is a habit of the intellect by which we know things. Every habit of this kind is either an art, which is a correct plan for doing something, or a science, which is certain knowledge of the truth. It is also either practical, if it is concerned with action, or speculative, if it consists in knowledge alone. Briefly, logic is more a science than an art, and more speculative than practical. It does not do any work in the proper sense, nor does it produce anything, nor is it ordered to action.

From the two causes of logic and from what has been said, it is possible to gather what logic is. It may be described as follows. Logic is a habit that directs the operations of the mind; or, it is a science of beings of reason as they are directive of the intellect's operations. Or, it is a faculty that treats of the method by which things that are obscure are manifested by defining, things that are confused are discerned by distinguishing, and truths are confirmed and errors refuted by arguing.[12]

Chap. 3. On the efficient cause and the end of logic

As to its efficient cause, if we are speaking of natural logic, this is a natural power with which the minds of men are endowed by nature and by which, without being taught, they exercise the three operations of the intellect readily.[13] The ultimate source of this power [7] is God himself, so that humans might proximately have the first notions and sources of this art which have been handed down to them for its perfection.[14] The person who was the first developer of, or the first writer on, this art is not known. It is generally agreed, however, that Aristotle was not its first inventor, since before him there were others who wrote about logic and passed on its precepts, so that we might learn these from Aristotle himself.[15]

Otherwise, this much can be said about Aristotle, and it is the judgment of the sources now extant, that he reduced this art to a system that could be more easily passed on, if we are speaking of matters that pertain to its substance. There are other things that he omitted and which were later taken from others, as from Porphyry the explanation of the five universals, from Boethius the teaching on definition, division, and hypothetical syllogisms, from Gilbert Porretanus the treatment of six of the categories, and yet other matters that were added without difficulty to what was already known. Granted, therefore, that Aristotle was not its inventor, nonetheless he can be rightfully be regarded as its perfecter because he perfected what pertains to its substance. His books can be read and he himself may be taken as its teacher, even though what he wrote may be taught in simpler and clearer fashion.

With regard to the goal of this art, briefly its end is knowledge of modes of knowing through which the operations of the intellect are directed so that subsequently objects can be known with facility and without error. Thus logic is a certain art or faculty by which the intellect, reflecting on itself, teaches and directs itself so that, so informed, it might come to learn other sciences. And from the aforementioned causes of logic, [8] we may offer a more complete definition of this discipline, as follows.

Logic is a rational science, acquired by the light of the intellect and by study, that prepares the mind for operations that are suited to attaining knowledge correctly. It is said to be a 'science' because it is a certain and evident habit of mind, by which element of its definition is indicated its category, both genus and form. It is said to be 'rational' to demonstrate its object, either its matter, namely, beings of reason or intellectual operations, or the subject in which it is present, namely, human reason. It is said to be 'by the light of the intellect' etc., to manifest its efficient cause. The remaining terms indicate its effect or its final cause. And what we have thus far treated about the nature of logic will become clearer from what we say in the sequel.

Chap. 4. On impediments to knowing things and how they come to be known or enter into our knowledge

So that we may better understand what has just been said about the nature of logic, and also what is taught in philosophy generally, it is desirable to set down a few fundamentals. When philosophers first began to investigate the nature of things, they discovered that there were certain impediments that had to be overcome if students were to learn expeditiously and not fall into error. Among others there are the following impediments.

First, students do not understand how we can come to knowledge of things outside ourselves, with what [9] powers or ways of knowing we do so, since they make no distinction between sense and intellect. Another impediment: the great multitude and confusion of things and the general obscurity of their natures. A last impediment: the defective ways of human knowing, and lack of knowledge of the methods whereby we come to grasp those natures. These obstacles to knowing are pervasive, and we hope to remove them in our treatment. First we focus on the operations of the intellect, since logic is concerned with directing these operations, as we have already stated. In doing so we will explain how the intellect comes to a knowledge of external reality and how things known enter into our minds.

To begin simply, we note that man is a composite of body and soul, and that he has certain powers or faculties, some on the part of his body and others on the part of his soul, which enable him to perform operations that are distinctively human. There are three kinds of soul:[16] one is said to be vegetative, with which things nourish and grow, as do plants and trees; another is said to be sensitive, which endows things with sense knowledge, as found in brute animals; and yet another is intellective, found only in man, whereby he knows and understands.

The vegetative soul has three principal powers: the generative, whereby progeny are produced; the augmentative, wherefrom growth results; and the nutritive, which nourishes. These powers do not produce knowledge but are useful only for producing and conserving organisms in existence, and thus we omit them here. All things that have this type of soul, however, are designated as living.

[10] The powers or senses of the sensitive soul are of two types, external and internal. There are five external senses:[17] sight, whose power is in the eye, the organ of seeing, whose object is what it perceives, a colored or bright object; hearing, whose organ is the ear and whose object is sound; smell, whose organ is the nose and whose object, odors; taste, whose organ is the tongue and whose object, flavors; and touch, whose organ is flesh and nerves and whose object, things affected by heat, cold, wet, and dry. An animal perceives with these powers by sensing things outside itself, and they are the avenues, one might say, through which objects enter the soul, as we will now explain.

To produce an act of sensation, for example vision, three things are required: the power of sight in its organ, as the power of seeing in the eye; an object to be perceived, as a colored object; and the union of the object with the power, since there cannot be action if the agent and the thing acted upon are not conjoined.

But, one might ask, how can it be that an object remote from the eye is united with it? This union is effected by a certain species,[18] a similitude or representation of the thing seen, which is diffused through the air and comes to the eye, just as the rays of the sun on leaving the sun are diffused in every direction. When the eye receives these species and are affected by them, it sees. That such species and their similitudes that come into our senses are to be granted is based solidly on experience. For when a man wishes to see his face, he takes a mirror, which like any transparent object receives a species. This cannot pass through the mirror because of its backing, and so is reflected to the eye. When the eye receives the species, the man sees himself. For seeing, therefore, what is needed is an organ that is properly affected, an object, and its species, [11] which, when received, produces the act of seeing. And what we have said of the eye and sight applies similarly to hearing, which perceives sounds, and smell, which perceives odors, and the other senses. So these external senses, just like doors or custodians, receive species of external objects and transmit them to other senses that are internal, which we now consider. These similitudes of things, something like images, are called sensible species because through them things attainable by the senses come to be perceived.

Three internal senses are commonly enumerated:[19] the central or common sense, the imagination, and the memory. These have their seats in three parts of the brain that are like three cellules, one in the anterior part, another in the middle, and a third in the posterior. The central sense, which is situated in the first part, receives and perceives the species that come from all the external senses, on which account it is called the common sense. The species it perceives it unifies and transmits to the imagination. From this species the imagination forms an image [also called a percept], which it retains and whereby it knows things that are absent from it. It also associates a notion of good or harmful with the percepts of things perceived. This power apprehends and judges things, and stores its notes and species of them in the memory. The memory, finally, is situated in the last part of the brain. It has the power of conserving all species transmitted by the imagination, and on this account becomes a kind of storehouse of information.[20]

Apart from these internal senses there are also appetitive powers in animals. These are divided into an impulse or concupiscible power, concerned with sensible goods that have no difficulty associated with them, and an aggressive or irascible power, concerned with difficult sensible goods. From these appetitive powers arise various emotions, such as love, hope, desire, fear, desperation, etc. Apart from these two powers there is also a motive power, which enables an animal to move from one place to another.[12] This suffices for the powers of the sensitive soul, which are necessary accessories for coming to a knowledge of external reality. Now we have to treat of the intellectual powers of the soul.

The proper form of man is a rational soul, created by God and infused into man's body. . . This is an immaterial and incorruptible form, more perfect than the other two types of soul, and containing within itself all the powers of the others.[21] Thus it gives a human being the powers of vegetating, of sensing, and of reasoning. Its powers are enumerated as three: the will, which seeks the good and whose object is all things under the aspect of their goodness; the intellect, by which man knows and understands and whose object is all things under the aspect of their truth; and the intellective memory, which conserves a record of things past. In what follows we consider only the intellect, whose operations are directed by logic.

The intellect, as is commonly taught, is twofold: an agent intellect and a receptive or passive or possible intellect. The agent intellect, acting on the percepts formed by the imagination, produces by its own natural light immaterial species of things whereby they can be known under their universal aspects and without the singular conditions found in sensible species.[22] These species are impressed on the receptive intellect and there produce, or give birth to, or conceive, the concept, which is the end result of the activity of intellective knowing.

It should be noted that the agent and receptive intellects are not really two in number; they are one and the same intellect, but are called by different names because of the different operations attributed to them. Why the agent intellect is necessary [13] as a cause to produce a new species arises from the fact that the phantasm or percept, the image presented to the intellect by the imagination, is material and so cannot move the intellect, which is immaterial. So there is need for immaterial species, which are called intelligible species, through which things can be represented without matter and in their universal aspects.

When the receptive intellect receives a simple intelligible species and produces a single concept, its operation is referred to as simple apprehension. When, on the other hand, it receives two species and forms two concepts, it can join the two together and attribute one to the other, by composing or affirming, as it might with the concepts of man and animal in the proposition, 'man is an animal.' Or it can divide the two and deny one of the other, as it might with the concepts of man and stone in the proposition 'man is not a stone.' This is the second operation of the intellect, also referred to as judgment. Finally, when the intellect joins one proposition to another and produces from it yet a third proposition, this is the third operation of the intellect, called discourse or reasoning, as in the syllogism 'an animal is sentient; man is an animal; therefore man is sentient.' These then are the three operations of the intellect—apprehension, composition, and reasoning—and logic directs these operations when it teaches how to perform all of these operations correctly. The nature of these operations is explained more fully in a later book.[23]

But from what has been said one can gather how things that are outside us enter our minds and how our intellects acquire knowledge of things. Things themselves emit their similitudes to the external senses, as a colored object sends its species to the eye. The eye transmits this to the central sense, which sends it to the imagination, which forms images and percepts of things even when they are absent. The agent intellect produces intelligible species from the imagination, and these are received [14] in the possible intellect just as sensible species are received in the eye. In receiving them the intellect apprehends. Then it composes things apprehended, either affirming or denying one of the other. From matters affirmed it discourses to new conclusions, and thus new knowledge is acquired through various acts. And when this is done frequently, different habits, and ultimately sciences, of various subject matters are acquired.

Chap. 5. On the work and instruments of logic

The arts are nothing more than habits of knowing or doing things correctly. They were excogitated to this end, namely, that we may perform perfectly operations that we perform imperfectly by nature. They have their ends, their matter, their work, and instruments with which they attain the ends.[24] Having already explained the matter and the end of logic, it remains for us to say something of its work and instruments.

The work in any art, as we gather from Cicero,[25] is what the artificer must carry out to attain his end. Since the end of logic is to direct the operations of the intellect, the logician's work is to supply the precepts or the instruments with which intellectual operations can be directed correctly.

Instruments of this kind are five in number: definition, division, proposition, argumentation, and method.[26] Definition is an expression whereby the nature of a thing is clearly manifested, as rational animal, which manifests the nature of man; and by this instrument the first operation of the intellect is directed. Division is an expression in which a whole is separated into its parts, as animal into rational and irrational, [15] one part of man the body, another the soul. This serves the second operation particularly, though it can assist other operations as well. Proposition is an expression in which one thing is affirmed or denied of another, as risibility of man, and by this the second operation is directed.[27] Argumentation is an expression in which one thing is noted as following from another, as 'The sun has risen, therefore it is day,' and this directs the third operation. Method is the proper arrangement for treating any matter, and this is necessary for directing operations of any kind. And so, before we proceed to the direction of the operations themselves, to be undertaken in the following books, we should treat of logic as an instrument common to all of them.

Chap. 6. On the usefulness and necessity of logic

To show the utility and necessity of logic, it may suffice to propose the argument that Epictetus, a most serious philosopher, once used.[28] When asked by his students to show this, he asked them in turn if they wanted him to give the reasons why. They said that they did. Then he inquired whether the reasons should be true or false, and again, whether they should be probable or evident. True and evident, was their reply. Then the master asked them how they would be able to know whether the reasons he gives them are true and evident if they had not already studied logic, since it is logic's task to teach how to tell the true from the false.[29] They agreed with that response. So, if without logic one cannot have this knowledge, logic must be necessary. [16]

With regard to logic's usefulness, logic awakens one from sleepiness in a remarkable way, it sharpens dullness of mind, it removes rust, as it were, and polishes and refurbishes the mind's operations. It offers a brief and easy path to the sciences and makes it ready for them. It makes clear the obscure, it removes the doubtful, it confirms the true, and it disproves the false.[30] Finally it is of great value in speaking, in business dealings, in disputations, in the market, in public life, and in education.

These utilities also bear witness to logic's necessity. If we cannot know anything with certainty except through the correct and sure use of the three operations of the intellect, and if we also need other sciences, even more do we need the instrument needed for their acquisition. Then, if things have to be known to acquire a science, so also the way in which we must know them is requisite if we are to be said to know scientifically, and for this logic is again necessary. So useful and necessary ought logic to be regarded that we should waste no time in learning it. In that way we will attain as soon as possible the goals that impel us to study it.

Chap. 7. On the division of logic and its parts

Although logic can be divided in many ways, we will be content here with one basic division. Logic can conveniently be divided according to the three operations that it directs. In the first of these the first operation is directed, and this is contained in Aristotle's book *On the Categories.* In the second, the second operation, and this in the books *On Interpretation.* In the third, the third operation, and this in the remaining [17] books. And since the third part is concerned with the syllogism, in it two things are considered, its form and its matter, and the matter in turn is threefold: necessary, probable, and sophistic. The form of the syllogism is treated in the two books of the *Prior Analytics.* The necessary syllogism is treated in the two remaining books, i.e., the *Posterior Analytics;* the probable syllogism, in the eight books of the *Topics;* and the sophistic, in the two books of the *Sophistical Elenchis.* From this division is apparent the number and ordering of the books of Aristotle's logic. (It may be noted that the books of the topics are more a part of dialectics than they are a part of logic, for dialectics, strictly speaking, is a faculty different from logic.)

Another division, somewhat new and actually improper, is that into logic teaching (*docens*) and logic using (*utens*). 'Logic teaching' is that which treats the precepts of the discipline and the operations of the intellect it directs in teaching, whereas 'logic using' is the same discipline as it is applied for use in other sciences. So much for the division of logic.

Chap. 8. On the nature, kinds, and uses of method

'Method' is a Greek word that has the same meaning in Latin, that is, a brief and compendious way; translated, it signifies a simple arrangement or manner of treating a science in orderly fashion,[31] although sometimes it is applied to the arts as well as the sciences. The way to investigate any matter is twofold: [18] one way is that which nature uses in effecting things when it proceeds from principles to things that are composed of principles, as from parts to a whole and from causes to effects, and this way is called the order of nature (*ordo naturae*). Another way is used in understanding things, when we proceed from what is more known to us to what is unknown to us, as from effects to causes, from a whole to its parts or principles, and from sensibles to things that can be perceived only by the intellect, and this way is called the order of doctrine (*ordo doctrinae*). We usually employ this in teaching and also when we first present things whose knowledge is required for understanding what follows. From these considerations one can readily grasp the nature of method.

Method, therefore, is the disposition of matters to be treated in any discipline in an orderly fashion that is appropriate to the nature of the thing or to its understanding and appeal to an audience. It is said to be a disposition because it consists in an ordering or arranging according to which one thing is to be posited or said before or after another. And because this order is ascertained from the matters that are being treated or from those who are teaching them or being taught, the phrase is added: 'to its understanding and appeal to an audience.'

Method, then, is threefold: the first way is said to be compositive and is used in almost all the arts, where one progresses from the smallest parts and from first principles to the larger parts and to the whole, as when the grammarian progresses from letters to syllables, to words, and to sentences. The second way is said to be divisive, in which a whole is first described in general fashion, then by its larger parts, then by its smaller, until one comes to its first principles, as when, treating of an animal, one first explains it as a whole and then treats its parts and principles; this method is also spoken of as resolutive. Related to this [19] is the definitive method, when something is first defined and then the parts of the definition are explained; in this way the complete nature of the matter being treated is exposed. The third way is the resolutive, as when the end or purpose of a thing being explained has been proposed, we first explain the end itself and then we treat those things that are required for its attainment, as Aristotle does in the *Ethics*.

When therefore one wishes to write with a method, that is, in orderly fashion, one should see what method is appropriate for the matter and the persons being addressed; and, if nothing prevents doing so, one should always begin with things that are more known and more common;[32] one should use division, which best illustrates method at work provided it not be too lengthy and involved; one should propose what one wishes to say and summarize it in an epilogue, noting there what still remains to be done. Method teaches easily and briefly, it aids the memory, and it clarifies the obscure. But that is enough for method and for this book, in which we have treated briefly the nature of logic, of which we have disputed more fully and accurately elsewhere and which will be easily grasped by one who has understood these few preliminaries.

END OF THE FIRST BOOK

BOOK FIVE

*In which the three kinds of syllogism are treated,
demonstrative, dialectical, and sophistic, along with
dialectical and sophistic topics*

[Demonstration and Science]

Chap. 1. The demonstrative syllogism

[165] We have established above that the syllogism is composed of form
and matter. Its form consists of three terms and two premises arranged
artificially according to quantity and quality. Its matter are the things that
are signified by these terms and propositions, and it is threefold. The first
is necessary matter, with which a type of syllogism is constructed from
which a conclusion is drawn necessarily, on which account it is called a
demonstration. The second is probable matter, from which a syllogism
that concludes probably is made, and it is called dialectical or topical.[33]
The third is false matter, from which a captious or deceptive syllogism is
constructed. Others propose a fourfold matter: necessary and what seems
to be necessary, from which a demonstration is made; provable and what
seems to be provable, from which a pseudographic syllogism, that is, a
falsely ascribed demonstration, is made; the third, dialectical; and the
fourth, sophistical, which [166] imitates the dialectical but falsely. The
first generates science, the second error, the third opinion, and the fourth
deception. We propose to write briefly of the three kinds of syllogism, and
particularly when treating demonstration, the teaching of which is much
more difficult and requires greater detail than would be expected in an introductory course.

Science, which is universally taken to be the effect of demonstration, is
nothing more than certain and indubitable knowledge of a particular
thing.[34] This can be had in two ways: first from an effect that is known to
the senses and from which one comes to knowledge of the cause, as from
the fact that human beings are capable of wonder one proves that they are
rational, since wonder arises from reason; second, through a cause, when

from the knowledge of a cause one arrives at knowledge of an effect that is traceable to that cause, as when one proves that human beings are capable of wonder because they are rational.[35] When we prove something in the first way we have the type of demonstration that is called *quia* demonstration, or better, that something is, and it is called such because it proves that something exists. When we prove something in the other way we have another type of demonstration that is called *propter quid* demonstration, because through it we know the cause on account of which something exists. The former takes an effect for its middle term, the latter is made through a proximate cause. When we know through a cause that is remote, the demonstration is only *quia*, as, for example, proving that a wall does not breathe because it is not an animal, for in that case the proximate cause of its not breathing is that it does not have lungs.[36] The second type is called demonstration in a qualified way, the first, demonstration that is unqualified.

Demonstration taken universally is defined in this way: demonstration is a syllogism that is productive of science.[37] It is said to be a syllogism, because it is one of the species of syllogism; it is said to be productive of science to distinguish it from other species of syllogism through which one does not acquire science. Demonstration *quia* is a [167] syllogism that is productive of science through an effect, or, what is the same, it is a syllogism through which we know scientifically that something exists, as, for example, when we prove that a lunar eclipse exists through the interposition of the earth between the sun and the moon. Demonstration *propter quid,* which Aristotle sometimes calls a *philosophema,* that is, the reasoning proper to a philosopher, is a syllogism by which we know something through its proper cause. It is said to prove through a proper cause to distinguish it from a demonstration *quia.*[38] Or it may be defined in this way: a demonstration *propter quid* is a syllogism composed of necessary propositions that contain the proper cause of the conclusion.[39] The latter definition is given through a genus and a material cause, for there are twelve conditions that Aristotle assigns to a perfect demonstration. These are that it must proceed from causes, from firsts, immediates, truths, priors, more knowns, necessaries, universals, essentials, commensurates, propers, and eternals. All of these can be reduced to two: that it proceed from causes and from necessaries, as does the following demonstration. 'Every rational being is capable of laughter; every human being is a rational being; therefore, every human being is capable of laughter.' Thus three things are to be found in a demonstration: a subject; a property to be proved of the subject; and a middle term, which must be a cause through which the property belongs to the subject, as in the example just given.

From this one can gather that scientific knowing is knowledge of something through a cause.[40] This is through necessary propositions, as has been said, which are said *per se* or essentially,[41] and in particular those in which a definition or a part of a definition is said of the subject, or in which the subject is put in the definition, i.e., when a proper passion is predicated of its immediate subject, as being able to sense, of an animal, or being able to bark, of a dog.

And since all of our knowledge arises from preexistent knowledge, before any [168] demonstration can be made some things have to be foreknown.[42] These foreknowledges are three in number: principles; the subject of the question or proposition to be proved; and the property that is to be proved. The questions that can be proved are likewise three: whether something is; what kind it is; and why is it so.[43] Note that the question 'what is it' is answered not by demonstration but by definition.

Principles are either common to all the sciences, as is this, 'It is impossible for something to be and not be at the same time'; or to many sciences, such as this, common to all the mathematical disciplines, 'Equals taken from equals the results are equal'; or to one science, as is this, 'Nature exists,' which is proper to natural philosophy.[44]

Before a demonstration can be made the following must be foreknown: of principles, that they are, i.e., that they are true; of the term predicated, what it is, i.e., what it means; and of the subject, both that it is, i.e., that it exists, and what it is, i.e., its nominal definition.[45]

And since no demonstration is had without a middle term or argument, we should briefly discuss what is meant by the middle of a demonstration. An argument or the middle of a demonstration is something necessary that is found and gives rise to indubitable knowledge through a necessary connection between the extremes [i.e., between the subject and the predicate]. Three *topoi* are assigned for this middle: those of definition, causes, and effects. If the middle is taken from a definition and a proximate cause, the demonstration is *propter quid*. If it is taken from an effect or from a remote cause, the demonstration is *quia* or *quod*.[46] Which cause the demonstrator uses depends on his subject matter. The natural philosopher demonstrates through all four causes; the metaphysician through the same but excepting the material cause; and the moral philosopher particularly through the final cause.

Finally, a perfect demonstration is made in the first mode of the first figure of the syllogism, from which one concludes with a universal affirmative proposition.[47] The reason for this is that an affirmative demonstration [169] is superior to a negative, and one that concludes directly is superior to one that leads to an impossibility.

The proper effect of a demonstrative syllogism is science. Science, taken strictly, is certain and evident knowledge of something necessary through its causes. By being 'certain' science differs from opinion, which is knowledge of something that is not certain because of fear of the contrary. By being 'evident,' science differs from divine faith, which, although most certain, is not evident; it also differs in this way from human faith. The type of knowledge called 'faith,' strictly speaking, is based on the authority of its source. Science is said to be of 'something necessary' because there can be no science of mutable things, as are singulars, and of beings that are merely accidental.[48] It is said to be 'through its causes' because when something is known to be necessary but not through its causes, such knowledge does not deserve being called science.

From this definition three conditions are found to be required of science: it must be of something necessary, it must be through causes, and it must be certain and evident. But there are two kinds of cause. One is a cause of knowing, as is anything that, when known, leads to knowledge of something else, as is knowledge of an effect through which comes knowledge of a cause. The other is a cause of being, as is that from which a thing is made and by which it is constituted, as are matter and form, which are also causes of knowing *a priori*.

From what has been said we can gather the kinds of cause that are used in science. That form is such a cause is apparent from the definition given above. Matter is science's subject, and it has the principal conditions that it be necessary, universal, real, and essential, that is, not merely an accidental aggregate; and it must be a unity either univocally or analogically, whose principles, parts, properties, and kinds are treated in the science. From this a science takes its unity, distinction, nobility, and order, such that one type is superior, called 'subalternating,' another inferior, called 'subalternated.'[49] The [170] subject of an inferior science must be contained under the subject of a superior science, to which it adds an accidental condition that it cannot be a property flowing from the thing's essence. An example is the numbering of sounds in the science of music, which is contained under the science of arithmetic.

From all of this we can gather the requirements for anything to be said to be knowable scientifically, namely, it must be one, essential, necessary, and universal. The proximate end of a science is knowledge of its subject, its remote end, knowledge of God. The proximate efficient cause of a science is the intellect, which, by reasoning from first principles that are known in themselves, comes to knowledge of things previously unknown. From this various other habits of mind are produced, namely, wisdom, science, prudence, and art, which all derive from knowledge of first principles.[50] These matters, like all the other things that are mentioned summarily in this chapter, are treated more fully elsewhere.[51] This suffices for our discussion of the demonstrative syllogism.

[Dialectic and Probable Reasoning]

Chap. 2. On the probable or dialectical syllogism

[170] The dialectical syllogism, as we have said, is one composed of probable propositions. These are thought to be probable because they seem to be verisimilar and worthy of acceptance, that is, they can be regarded as true. Of these there are various kinds.

The first are those that are admitted by all, e.g., that parents love their children, that people want a bargain.[52] Others are agreed on for the most part, e.g., that people prefer to be rich rather than poor. Others are admitted by the well informed, and of these, some by all, e.g., that the good in itself is preferable to the useful;[53] some for the most part, e.g., that the universe is one, that happiness lies in virtue alone. Yet others, by the best informed, that the universe [171] had a beginning, as Plato thought, or that sight is achieved by the reception of species, as Aristotelians taught.[54] For this reason matters that go contrary to the opinion of all are not enumerated among probables, e.g., that anything can come to be from anything else; that any one thing contains all others; that all things are one. Also included among probables are those propositions that can be deduced from probables.

A syllogism that is composed of probable propositions, or of a probable proposition and a necessary proposition, or of necessary propositions that are regarded as probable, is said to be dialectical. It is sometimes referred to as an *epicheirema* or an *aggressio* [i.e., attack] because it is well adapted to attacking an adversary.[55]

We use this type of syllogism for explicating probable questions, which are also referred to as problems, either part of which can be disputed with probability.[56] Again, they are said to be theorems, as worthy of consideration when not yet explored. On this account, just as the one who demonstrates accepts only one proposition, which he takes as true, since the truth alone can be demonstrated,[57] so the dialectician, who argues on both sides, takes up either side. In so doing he has to interrogate the person with whom he is arguing, because the side for which he argues either is not necessary or does not seem to be so. Thus, when one side has been conceded by his respondent, he may argue: Is it true that one ought to seek after riches? This question is said to be a dialectical proposition: just as it serves as an interrogation for the questioner, so it is an assumption for the reasoner. A dialectical proposition, then, is a probable interrogation that questions something that is regarded as true by all people or at least by the majority. A dialectical question, on the other hand, is a problem about which all or many people take neither side, or common people take a position opposite that of the well-informed, or the well-informed opposite that of the majority, or even differ on it among themselves.

[172] Since in a question one asks whether a predicate goes with a subject, the cause of which is being sought after, there are different kinds of questions for different predicates. These Aristotle reduced to four:[58] questions of definition, of property, of genus, and of accident. Any others can be reduced to these. Such questions may be asked in two ways: either explicitly, when one inquires, e.g., "Is virtue the genus of justice"? or implicitly, when one investigates a problem, e.g., "Is justice a virtue?" Again, "Is man alone capable of laughter?" or alternatively, "Is man capable of laughter?" As proposed in the first way, this is a question of property. As proposed in the second way the question is one of simple inherence or of accident, taking accident in the sense of any qualification attributed to a subject.[59] The general question of a differentia said of a lower species is reducible to a question of genus, as, e.g., "Is having sense knowledge a differentia man has in common with other animals?" So likewise is the question of species with respect to individuals, as "Was Christ a true man?" Now let us say something about the argument or the middle term of the topical syllogism.

Chap. 3. On the dialectical middle, or the topic, and how many there are

Since human teaching makes use of opinion no less than it makes use of science, and since many more things are held by opinion than are held by science, those who wish to be concerned with the knowledge of things should be well informed about topical places or probable arguments. For this reason we intend to treat it in detail here, though not to the full extent possible. What motivates us to do so [173] is the great utility beginners can gain in argument from knowing the topics. This tract is generally skipped in the schools, either because it is thought to be separate from logic, as indeed it is, or because it is thought to be easy and not very necessary. In my judgment, however, nothing is more suitable for an educated man than to be prepared with this doctrine to argue knowledgeably and to persuade subtly on either side of a proposed topic, as we have taught in more depth elsewhere.[60]

A dialectical middle, or argument, is something probable invented to induce belief.[61] It is conjoined verisimilarly either to both extremes of a question or with one or the other so as to gain an assent to what is to be proved, though without absolute necessity. In this the dialectical argument differs from the demonstrative, since the latter joins its extremes necessarily and thus generates a perfect and indubitable assent. The former is regarded as joining its extremes only probably. On this account the demonstrative argument can become a dialectical argument if one does not advert to its necessity, for matters that are necessary may be regarded as probable, as frequently happens in the judgment of the many. So it is that the teaching on the invention of the dialectical middle can also serve for discovering necessary middles.[62] This is the reason why Aristotle, when treating of the invention of the demonstrative middle in the second book of the *Posterior Analytics*, refers back to the teaching contained in the *Topics*. In the books of the *Topics* he occasionally mentions that the treatment of topics is common to both the dialectician and the philosopher, that is, to the one arguing probably and to the one arguing demonstratively.[63]

This argument or middle term is commonly named from the translation of the Greek *topos* or the Latin *locus*, and the books that treat of the invention of topics are called the *Topics* or, in Latin, the *Loci* (places), although strictly speaking 'topic' [174] designates the argument itself more than its seat or where the argument may be found. So it is that a topic is generally defined as the seat of an argument or the place from which it can be obtained, for when topics are known arguments are easily discovered.[64] Aristotle spoke of this not only as a place but metaphorically as an element, because, although simple, it becomes the origin of many arguments, as will become clear in what follows.

There are two kinds of topics, the first of which is said to be a maximal topic and the second a maximal differentia.[65] A maximal topic is a common and self-evident proposition whose truth is invoked to support a number of arguments. That is, it is a proposition that is self-evident and does not require proof, whether it is a necessary proposition, as "When a cause is posited its effect is also posited," or a probable one, as "Mothers love their children." From its truth arguments get their force; thus, "The sun has risen, therefore it is day" gets its force from "When a cause is posited its effect is also posited." For this reason some maximal topics can be put in an argument, as can this, "The good is to be loved," whereas others cannot, as the following, "When equals are subtracted from equals the results are equal." The latter is not put in an argument but is presupposed to it. Such statements are called maximal, either because of their great amplitude, in the sense that they contain many other propositions under them, as do theses (or positions) that contain many hypotheses (or suppositions) under them, or because they are over others that are minimal and so are broader in extent.[66]

A maximal differentia is a topic wherein maximal topics of various orders differ among themselves; thus the topic of definition, through which maximal topics contained under it differ from other maximal topics contained under the topic of causes, which in turn is another locus for a maximal differentia. Or, as others define it, a maximal differentia is a receptacle for several maximal topics; an example would be the topic of definition, which embraces many maximal topics, as will become clear in their explication. Indeed, [175] both in the *Topics* and in the *Rhetoric* Aristotle treated the earlier topics of genus so diligently, enumerating the various maximal topics for different subject matters, that it would seem that nothing further could be added to them. But he did not do the same for the later topics.[67] As a consequence those who followed him, while treating them not in the same way but broadly or more compactly, did so more fully and more artfully, for it was not difficult to add additional discoveries. And indeed this later manner, as prior and more common or as briefer, is better suited to the art. When we speak of the prior ordering of topics we usually say "The topic is from definition, from causes, and so forth," whereas when we speak of the later ordering we say "The topic of definition and of causes."

Chap. 4. The definition and division of maximal differentiae

In this treatment of topics, which pertains to their number, there is great diversity among authors, some enumerating more, others less. This diversity can also be discerned in their division, as we taught in the first book of our *On Invention*.[68] In this context, following certain traces there, for reasons of brevity we will divide and enumerate them differently from the way done previously.

Some topics are artificial, and these are either intrinsic, taken from the matter being disputed about, or extrinsic, or lacking in art, taken from without.[69] Intrinsic topics signify either the thing from which the argument is sought or things that are conjoined with it or disjoined from it. In the first ordering are contained the topics of definition, description, and etymology. In the second are the topics of conjugates, parts, [176] wholes, causes, effects, antecedents, consequents, things coming before, things accompanying, and things coming after. In the third are the topics of similars, greaters, lessers, equals, dissimilars, opposites, and repugnants. Extrinsic topics are listed as many by certain authors but we shall posit only one, that of authority, and this can be subdivided in the same way as are the other topics enumerated above.

For all these topics a twofold consideration is possible, one common, when it is considered generally and not as applied to a particular subject matter, the other proper, when accommodated to a determinate matter of a particular art, as when the topic of definition is confined to nature, morality, rhetoric, or any other art. For each art and science has its own proper principles that cannot be used licitly in another discipline.

The explanation of common topics pertains to dialectics, which also has proper topics relating to its own subject matter. These are the topics of definition, genus, species, description, property, and of other things pertaining to dialectics. It also has other topics that are used to give definitive answers to the four dialectical questions, namely, questions of genus, definition, property, and accident.[70] From this it follows that one part of dialectics must explain the common topics used in other sciences, another part topics that are proper to dialectics. We shall take up common topics first and then proper topics.

Chap. 5. The topics of definition, description, and etymology

In treating individual topics three things need to be explained: the topic itself, the mode of arguing from it, [177] and its use. We treat the first two only briefly, and the third we omit entirely since we have treated it fully elsewhere.[71] Since we have stated above the nature and kinds of definition, in this topic we treat only the mode of arguing from it. Here let us advert to something we shall use in exposing all the topics. When we are seeking a proof we should look at the extremes, the subject and the attribute of the question, and then adduce arguments on the part of each extreme and do so either by affirming or denying. Just as we can prove something of the thing defined from its definition, so we can prove something of the definition from the thing defined; but the second way of proceeding is not as common as the first—although those who hold the first will also hold the second.

Now to the various modes of arguing. Let the following question be proposed to be proved: Is rhetoric an art or is it artless? The affirmative part of this I can prove as follows. From the definition of the attribute, in this way: rhetoric is a correct procedure for doing something; therefore it is an art.[72] From the definition of the subject: a doctrine for speaking well is an art; therefore rhetoric is an art. From the definition of both: rhetoric is a doctrine for speaking well and also a correct procedure for doing something; and anything of this kind is an art; therefore rhetoric is an art. The negative part can be proved as follows. Rhetoric is not an inept way of doing something; therefore it is not artless. Or, a doctrine for speaking well is not artless; therefore it is not an inept way of doing something. Or one can take the contrary of rhetoric, namely, the inability to speak, and argue as follows: the inability to speak is not a procedure for doing something correctly; therefore it is not an art.

Here we can use the topic of differentia, which is constitutive of a species, and from it argue in the same way. Thus, from his being rational one can prove other attributes of man. The common topics or the maximal propositions of this topic are the following. Anything of which the definition can or cannot be said applies also to the thing defined; [178] whatever can or cannot be said of the definition applies also to the thing defined.

From description we may argue with the same modes as from definition, since it makes use of the same maximal topics, simply substituting description for definition.[73] Thus one can offer proofs about dialectics from the following description: it is an instrument for investigating the true and the false.

The topic of property is also reducible to this topic. For example, one may prove that courage is a virtue because it is praiseworthy on its own merits, this being a property of virtues; or that a surface is a quantity because it is divisible, divisibility being a property of quantities.

Related to this is the topic of etymology, that is, the derivation of the term, for this has the same modes of argument and the same common topics.[74] One can dispute correctly from this topic if one can reduce it to something already known, as frequently happens in the case of common names, which are usually drawn from some property of the things named. Examples are king, canonist, Christian, consul, procurator, tutor, monk, and so on.

Here note also the topic referred to as transumption, which uses a term that is more known in order to offer a proof about something designated by an obscure word.[75] An example: one wishing to prove that magic is not to be looked down upon because wisdom is not to be looked down upon, since magic refers to a teaching or wisdom about hidden things. Some would say that they are speaking of transumption when they argue from a term accepted in a metaphorical sense to some associated property. Examples: 'One ought to flee from a roaring lion; therefore, flee from the devil'; or, 'Christ is a lion, therefore a king.'[76]

Chap. 6. The topic of conjugates

[179] Among the topics of the second order first place goes to the topic of conjugates.[77] Conjugates are nouns or verbs or adverbs that are taken from inflected forms or various changes in a root source, as, from wisdom, wise and wisely. And since in conjugates one ought to attend more to the meaning of the term than to its ending or similarity with another, their going together should not be abandoned if their terms do not, provided that their meanings coincide. An example would be harmful and detrimental, even though they are not joined to the same term, as is the case with being endowed with virtue and living virtuously. This topic, though

sometimes used, is done so rarely, since conjugates should be known equally or in the same way.

One can argue from this topic in two ways: first, by affirming: 'Wisdom is praiseworthy; therefore to act wisely is also.' Second, by negating: 'Wisdom is not to be despised; therefore neither are wise men.' Here there are two common topics: The first, what goes with one conjugate goes with the others; the second, what does not go with one conjugate does not go with the others. 'If injustice is displeasing, why is acting unjustly not displeasing?'

Here one must be careful not to be deceived into taking one conjugate for another, as to take *officere* (detrimental) as a conjugate of *officium* (service), or *somniculosus* (drowsy) as a conjugate of *somnium* (dream), which is associated with sleeping. Again, one should avoid equivocation of terms. One would argue poorly if one were to say: 'Since we are humans, we must be concerned only with *humana* (human affairs),' because in this statement *humana* in the consequent does not designate things that pertain to humans but rather transitory and perishable things, as differentiated from the heavenly and eternal.[78] [180] Finally, one must see to it that the attributes of conjugates are assigned properly, that is, one should see whether the predicates correspond correctly to the individual subjects. The following argument is invalid: 'Courage is a virtue; therefore one who acts courageously acts virtuously or zealously,' since one can attack with courage under evil circumstances.[79] Yet the following argument is valid: 'He acts courageously; therefore he acts virtuously.' Likewise the following is invalid: 'Doctrine (teaching) is the same as discipline (learning); therefore whoever teaches learns.' On the other hand, one might argue: 'Wherever teaching is present, learning is also present.'

So, when one treats of topics, that is, the materials of arguments or middles as ordered to conclusions, one should attend to the sense of the antecedents and derive conclusions appropriate to them, considering the fact that the consequences whereby these things are conjoined are not formal but material—a fact that many texts that treat of this topic do not take into account.

Chap. 7. The topic of wholes and of parts

[180] Since these two topics are interrelated, they may be treated together. In as many ways as a thing can be said to be a whole a thing can also be said to be a part. A thing is said to be a whole in the following ways.[80]

In signification 'whole' is a term with many meanings: either an integral quantified whole, as a whole human body; or an essential physical whole, composed of matter and form, or an essential metaphysical whole, composed of a genus and difference; or a universal whole, as a term in some way common, [181] as animal, virtue, substance. Under these some add a quantitative whole or one in quantity, and that is the same as a universal whole, that is, a term that is common under a general signification, as 'all animals,' which includes parts that are quantitatively distinct, the individuals contained in that multitude. Similar to these are other wholes: a whole in place, as indicated by the verb 'everywhere,' whose parts are 'here,' 'there'; a whole in time, as indicated by the adverb 'always,' whose parts are 'today,' 'now,' 'tomorrow'; and a whole in mode, that is, a universal without addition, as 'man, white,' whose part is the same as a universal with addition, as 'just man,' 'one with white teeth,' etc. The fact that something is added need not take away or diminish the meaning of the whole, as so the term 'whole' can be applied to an entire aggregate.

Although whole and part can be taken in many ways, for uses in argument wholes in signification and metaphysical wholes are generally omitted. And since, for purposes of concluding, practically the same meaning can be given to the integral whole and the essential physical whole composed of matter and form, from the viewpoint of ways of arguing what is said of the one may be understood of the other. For this reason arguments are taken from this twofold whole or kind of part: from an integral whole and from a universal whole, the latter indicating something common to everything contained under it. A whole of multitude, place, and time is reducible to an integral whole, and so is a quantitative whole by reason of its parts; a whole in mode is reducible to a universal whole.

With respect to the integral whole the following is to be noted. In it there are some parts that are necessary, without which [182] the whole cannot be constituted, as a head in man and a roof and walls in a house; there are other parts that are not necessary for its constitution but are required for its perfection, as a hand and fingers in man. From the latter, arguments can be drawn for proving or refuting a thing's perfection. Again, the integral whole does not consist of parts considered in any way whatever, or in any way of counting them, but of parts constituted in a particular order. This is obvious in a city, which is made up of many individuals in a subordinated order, and this is true also of an army and a house. These matters explained, it will be easy to comprehend the ways of arguing from these two topics, which we shall treat together.

First, from an affirmation of a whole to all of its parts together and taken singularly, as, if a house, then a roof, walls, and a foundation.[81] Second, from all the necessary parts to the whole, as, if constituted from a head, trunk, and other necessary members, then a man. Third, from the negation of a whole to a negation of all the parts taken disjunctively; as, there is no house, then either a foundation, or walls, or a roof is lacking. Fourth, from the negation of a necessary part to a negation of the whole; as, there is no roof, then no house either. In the same ways one may argue from other wholes, to recall which we say: if God is everywhere and always, then he is in the temple at this moment; if an angel is in heaven, then not nowhere; in heaven, then not everywhere. Note here that a particular time and place can be regarded as a type of whole, as sometime, with respect to this or that time; somewhere, with respect to this or that place, in which cases the same modes of arguing apply. These forms of arguing are contained under two common topics: if all the integral parts are posited, the whole is posited, and vice versa; if any [183] integral part is taken away, the whole is taken away, and vice versa. In the same ways one may argue from a perfect whole and perfecting parts, from which one may not argue to an integral whole by negating.

One may argue from a universal whole and subjective parts in these ways. First, by affirming on the part of the predicate: from a whole to individual parts disjunctively; as, man is an animal, therefore rational or irrational. Second, by affirming on the part of the subject: the animal is rational, therefore a man; irrational, then a brute. Third, by negating on the part of the predicate, from a whole to the individual parts: a stone is not an animal, therefore neither man nor brute. Fourth, by negating on the part of the subject, to the parts disjunctively: as, the animal is not lacking reason, therefore a man; it is lacking reason, therefore a brute. One may argue from parts to a whole in all these ways, examples for which are easy to find. One may also argue in the same ways from a whole in mode, but when we proceed from a whole, the whole is take with universality, when we proceed from a part, the whole is taken particularly: thus, God wishes no one to be damned, therefore not even foreigners; God wishes the ungodly man to be damned, therefore he wishes a man to be damned. Here note also that a whole is said to be particular with respect to singulars: as, some man, with respect to this or that man. Since the indefinite is a certain kind of whole, the same modes of arguing hold for it.

The common topics are these:[82] any subjective part being posited, the whole is posited, and vice versa; all of the subjective parts taken way, the whole is taken away, and vice versa; the whole being posited, etc.

Finally, to remove sophisms that might come up in the use of this topic note that this pronouncement, 'Whatever comes with (*convenit*) the whole also comes with the part,' is to be understood of those [184] predicates that can be common to both. For, if they were proper to the parts, they could not be affirmed of the whole; as, if it were to be said that body and soul are principles of natural things, so also is man; or, man is not an animal, because body and soul are not animals.

Chap. 8. The topic of material cause and of its effect

What causes are and how many kinds there are we have covered elsewhere.[83] Thus we presuppose these matters for this topic and, for individual causes, we treat only details that are necessary for understanding the various modes of argumentation.

Beginning with matter, we may say that matter is divided into anything from which something is made, as a statue from wood; anything in which something is present as in a subject, as the shape of the statue is in the wood; and anything that is the object of an activity or that an agent treats, as speech being the matter of grammar and action the matter of the praise of virtue, since every praise of virtue is an action of some sort. Again, matter is twofold: one kind is permanent, which by its nature remains in the effect, the way in which stones are the matter of a house and wool of clothing; another is not permanent, the way in which flour is the matter of bread. Yet again, matter is twofold: one kind is proximate, as is that from which a thing is made or is worked on by an artificer; another kind is remote, as the wood in the forest which the carpenter puts in place. Note here that with this topic we prove that a thing exists or not, or can exist and come to be, and also the attributes of causes from their effects, as will be seen in the examples.

[185] The following arguments are taken from the material cause. First, from the positing of the cause the effect can be proved; for example, there are wood, stones, and cement, therefore a house can come to be. This mode does not conclude absolutely, since apart from the matter other causes are necessary. Second, by negating, from permanent matter with a simple verb, as, there is no steel, therefore no sword; with a transient verb, from a past time to a present effect, there was no flour, therefore no bread. This is also valid in the present tense if the verb designates an operation: there is no flour, thus no bread. The common places or maxims: a material cause posited, the effect can be; if permanent matter is taken away, no effect. Third, from the effect of a permanent material cause by affirming, but not by negating; thus, there is a table, therefore wood, not the other way round. In the case of transient matter, it follows only if the cause has preceded; thus, there is oxymel, therefore there was vinegar and honey. Finally, from the attributes of the matter and the effect, as, the wood is dry, therefore it can be burned. Man is made of elements, therefore he is exposed to corruption; lead is heavy, therefore it contains much matter; dialectic is not the same as logic, therefore its matter is different.

Here some put arguments taken from the nature of the places in which things are or are born; as, fish live in water, therefore they are moist; he was born in Africa, therefore he is black and of shorter life.

Chap. 9. The topic of formal cause and of its effect

Form is threefold: the first is essential, and this constitutes a thing in a determinate species and is the source of the thing's properties [186], as man's properties flowing from his soul; the second is accidental, and this is every accident in relation to its subject, as whiteness with respect to a white object, shape with respect to a stone; the third is external, as is the exemplary cause, which provides a similitude for making something, as the idea of a house in the mind of an architect. Reducible to this cause is anything that informs by receiving something from another, the way in which molten objects are made in casting operations.

From this topic, apart from other common forms of argument there is this additional one, that from the nature of the form one may argue to the condition of the matter—since form is the cause not only of the composite but also of the matter—to anything the form prescribes for a certain matter that it informs, or that it treats, or with which it is concerned. We may argue from form by affirming and by negating to prove that a thing exists, that it is such and so, that it acts in such a way, or that any attribute or function belongs to it, as will be clear in these examples. The soul is already in the body, then it is already human; the soul has left the body, now it is not a man but a cadaver. Whiteness is in the body, so the body is white. The soul is that by which we live, sense, and understand,[84] therefore the body that it informs must have various distinct organs; the soul is eternal and it desires to be united with a body, therefore at one time it will be joined to it. The soul is immortal, thus it is different from things subject to corruption. A dog cannot laugh or does not laugh, thus it lacks a soul capable of reason. Theology is a doctrine with a definite subject matter, therefore theologians do not discourse about physical things or in a physical manner. Dialectic is not a science,[85] therefore those who treat it as a science pervert it, for from an art (which is an accidental form) it is licit to deduce the art's functions. The soul is an intelligent form, [187] therefore man is intelligent. The wood is round, therefore it can be rolled. Man is made in the image of God, therefore he is rightly made.

Examples from the effect of form: a sponge senses, therefore it has a sensitive soul; the heavens revolve easily, therefore they are round; brutes have properties and men have different properties, therefore they have different forms; the characters are unequal, therefore their [print] types are also. This man loves his enemies, therefore he also loves God; he lives respectably, therefore he was born of respectable parents, or, vice versa, he came from a respectable family, therefore he lives respectably.

Maxims of this topic: a form being posited, the thing itself is posited along with its properties and attributes. A form being removed, the thing and its proper effects and attributions are removed. If a formal effect is posited or removed, the form itself is posited or removed.

Some reduce the topic from conjugates to this topic, since conjugation arises from form. One can also reduce to it the topic Aristotle calls *ab inesse et denominari* (from being in and being denominated), because a thing is denominated from its form.[86] But, for a good argument to be taken from this topic, the form must not be only in part, as whiteness in teeth, or only for a time, as red in the face, or only in a remiss state, as heat in [luke-warm] water. Nor can the form be attributed in any way whatever, since action is in the recipient, and it is not attributed to the agent but to the action itself, and place is not attributed to the thing located but rather to the locating.

Finally, some reduce this topic to apposition, for, if a thing is such and so because of the apposition of another thing, it seems that if the other thing is more so it should be able to be denominated similarly.[87] An argument from this topic: water is heated by fire, therefore fire is hotter; he loves his enemy for love of God, therefore he loves God more.

Chap. 10. The topics of efficient cause, of generation, and of use

[188] An efficient cause is that from which an operation first proceeds. One kind is necessary, as is that from which an effect follows necessarily, since it cannot arise from any other cause—in this way the sun is the cause of day. Another kind is sufficient, which can produce the effect by itself even though the effect can be produced by another cause—in this way the taking of poison is the cause of death and fire is the cause of heat. Again, of effective causes some are principal, as is God in every kind of operation, or in a certain area, as an architect in things built or a king in ruling.[88] Others are auxiliary, which serve the principal cause, as tradesmen for the architect and natural causes for God, the Author of Nature. To these may be reduced instrumental causes, consulting causes, those that remove impediments, and others that attend the production of the effect in any way. Finally, some causes are conserving, others destroying. Again, some efficient causes cause actually, designating a cause that brings an effect or an operation into actual existence, as the one building or the one reading; others designate a cause that is such only potentially and do not designate the effect or the action, as a builder or a reader.

This topic provides many ways of arguing. The first mode is from a necessary and solitary cause, affirming or negating: the earth came between the sun and the moon, therefore an eclipse; the earth did not, therefore no eclipse.[89] Christ has risen, therefore we too will rise. From an effect to its cause: it is day, therefore the sun has risen; it is not day, therefore the sun has not yet risen; fish do not breathe, therefore they have no lungs. Common [189] topics: if a necessary and solitary cause is posited or removed, the effect is posited or removed. If the effect of such a cause is posited or removed, the cause is posited or removed.

The second mode is from a sufficient cause by affirming and from its effect by denying: as, he took poison, therefore he died; he did not die, therefore he did not take poison. The common topics: a sufficient cause posited, the effect is posited; the effect removed, the cause too is removed. The third mode is from a cause actually causing. We may argue by affirming and denying, but on the part of the effect a verb should be added specifying the action; as, he is reading, therefore there is a lesson; there is a lesson, therefore he is reading. Fourth mode: from a potential cause, for proving that the effect can come to be, by affirming, but by positing all the requirements; as, he is a builder, therefore he can make a building; the building is made, therefore he was a builder. Common topics for these arguments anyone can easily formulate. From a conserving cause one may argue in this way: fishes swim in water and live there for a long while; they are out of water, so they are unable to live. This city is free from discord, so it is conserved; the kingdom is divided against itself, so it falls.

We may frequently argue from nature and from the attributes of an efficient cause by affirming it or by negating its effects; as, this universe was made by an all-powerful creator, therefore it is perfect; nature does nothing in vain,[90] therefore there are no groundless effects in nature; the student studies under an ignorant teacher, so he does not come out educated.

Reducible to this topic is the topic from generation and corruption, which others treat separately, since generation and corruption are particular effects of efficient causes.[91] This place has these common topics taken from the quality of the causes: if the generation of something is good, so it is good; from any attribute, other things similar are to be understood; as being beautiful [190] and similar attributes. . . .

Chap. 11. The topic of final cause and of its effect

The end, which is that for the sake of which something is done, is said to be the reason for the means and for the other causes. Matter cannot be perfected without form, and form cannot come into existence without an efficient cause, and an efficient cause is not moved to [191] action without some end being proposed. Hence it is that both causes and means are proved from the end, but the means more frequently than the causes. For the existence and quality of ends we use this topic and these maxims: whose end is good is himself good; whose end is bad is himself bad. Here the end is taken as end *per se,* that is, that for which the thing was constituted and to which its nature refers.

Since three things are involved in the formality of end,[92] the thing that is the end and on whose account the thing comes to be; the thing or the person for which it is the end or the thing tends to the end; and the grasping or possession of the end, three kinds of end are assigned: *quod, cui,* and *quo.* For example, the end *quod* [what] for the miser is money; the end *cui* [for which] is himself; and the end *quo* [by which] is the possession and retention of money. So, by reason of the first, the miser is said to work for money; by reason of the second, to work for himself, or rather for others, since the miser denies to himself what he takes from others;[93] by reason of the third, to have his heart in riches, to contemplate money in the bank,[94] while he ignores the value of money, which offers one use.

These are modes of arguing from the end: first, God is better than riches, therefore it is better to hope in God than in riches; knowledge of natural things is good, therefore it is good to apply oneself to the study of nature; profit is unseemly, therefore to study for the sake of profit is unseemly, and those who do so are called cobblers *(certones);* from the formality of end to the formality of its causes: a sword should cut, therefore it should be made of steel; therefore it should be sharp; a house should protect a man from the elements, therefore it should be made of stone or other solid material;[95] front teeth should cut and molars should [192] grind, therefore both should be made of hard material, but the former should be sharp, the latter flat. Third, from desire of the end and for its quality, to the use and quality of the means: Do you wish to enter into eternal life? Then obey the commandments.[96] Do you wish your son to be well educated? Then try to obtain the best teacher. On this, see what Horace wrote.[97] Finally, from the end should be removed all means that are extraneous and unsuitable to its attainment. Do you wish to see God?[98] Take care that your heart does not dwell on things that are unclean. You strive after wisdom? Have leisure in your life.

From effects, the following arguments may be sought.[99] Someone seeks occasions for calumniating a friend, therefore avoid him. Cement holds stones together, therefore use both for building.

In sum, to conclude this topic of causes, one may reduce all the modes of arguing to the following three.[100] A cause in potency and an effect in potency may be together, or they may not, presupposing everything that is necessary. A cause in act and an effect in act may be together, or they may not and were not, although the full existence of the effect cannot be inferred, only its coming to be, as usually happens with some efficient causes and the final cause. This topic differs from the foregoing because in the foregoing the cause is taken as producing an effect whereas in this topic the cause is taken absolutely, as it exists in nature. Finally, if the agents of something are good or bad, it itself is good or bad; if things that do away with it are good, it is bad, and the opposite also, if they are bad, it is good.[101] All of these statements make sense from the foregoing. And from what has been said it can readily be understood how broad this last topic of causes can be.

Chap. 12. The topics of antecedents and of consequents

[193] In this context we take antecedents and consequents to mean things that necessarily precede or follow the matter that is called into question. Thus if one were to ask whether a woman has borne a child and then were to investigate the things that necessarily precede birth and that follow after it; from these one could construct an argument.

There are two kinds of antecedents and consequents: the first is what precedes or follows in the order of attribution, the way man precedes animal, or in the order of time, the way the taking of poison precedes a death that results necessarily from drinking it; the second is anything that necessarily results if something else is given, the way the blossoming of fruit comes before its eating and the foundation of a building before the walls. Here the animal and the death are consequences of the first kind, the fruit and the walls of the second. Antecedents of the first kind differ from those of the second in that the first precede or follow in an absolute way, the latter only suppositionally *(ex suppositione)*. Again, there are two kinds of antecedents and consequents; some are recursive, that is, convertible, the way dead people have a testator and the testator executes a will; others are not, as to be just and to be virtuous, to give birth and to conceive.

Some reject this topic[102] because the arguments that are drawn from it can be reduced to other topics or because there is need for an antecedent and a consequent in every topic and argument. Those who do so do not understand how the terms [194] antecedent and consequent are to be understood, and how arguments drawn from them can be reduced to another topic, as will be apparent from a few examples.

Examples of antecedents of the kind of absolute attribution: 'He is a son, therefore an heir; courage is desirable in itself, therefore it should be sought; laziness is not in accord with reason, thus it is not a virtue; his throat was cut, therefore he died.' If antecedents and consequents are reciprocating, one may go from the denial of the antecedent to the denial of the consequent and from the placing of the consequent to the placing of the antecedent. Thus: 'He is not infused with charity, therefore he does not love God above all things; he loves God above all things, therefore he is endowed with charity; he does not love God above all things, therefore he is lacking in charity.' The common topics on which the foregoing arguments are based are these: placing the antecedent necessarily involves placing the consequent; removing the consequent necessarily involves removing the antecedent.[103]

Examples of antecedent and consequents of the second kind: 'She did not conceive, therefore she did not give birth; she gave birth, therefore she conceived; a building is to be built, therefore foundations must be laid; foundations have not been laid, therefore there will be no building; he was not an adolescent, therefore neither will he be an adult; he is an adult, therefore he was an adolescent; he went bankrupt, therefore he had wealth; he had no wealth, therefore he did not go bankrupt; he wants to attain beatitude, therefore he should believe in God and act virtuously.'[104] The maxims: removing the antecedent involves removing the consequent; placing the consequent involves placing the antecedent.

Chap. 13. The topics of adjuncts and of circumstances

[195] This topic differs from the previous one in that arguments from adjuncts do not conclude necessarily, as can those from antecedents and consequents, as will be apparent from the examples to be given.

Of adjuncts or connected things some are antecedent,[105] as are things that come before an event; if a homicide has occurred, antecedents are character, education, provocation, readying of arms, as well as concomitants, such as opportunity, place, time, and other factors that usually accompany an event. Other things are consequent, as a weapon with blood on it, a pale countenance, flight, public rumor, and similars. This topic is not so much dialectical as it is rhetorical. Although adjuncts conclude nothing necessarily, nonetheless they conduce to great probability if they are of frequent occurrence. . . .

Chap. 14. The topic of similars and of dissimilars

[196] By similars in this context we mean things that share a common quality, or quantity, or essence, or that agree in some proportion, as two whites, two equal bodies, two species of virtues or of animals, tranquillity

of the sea and of the heart, the mind in relation to the soul as the eye in relation to the body.[106] For white is similar to white, man to man, by reason of form, and mind is similar to the eye by reason of proportion and analogy. And although this topic brings much to teaching and to illustrating obscure matters, one cannot deny, as some do,[107] that it has probative force, as experience teaches, since unwilling adversaries are often attracted by similars. . . .

Chap. 15. The topic of things compared

[198] Arguments that are taken from the topics explained thus far are taken from part of a question, that is, from a predicate, from a definition or description or from causes of a subject, or from other attributes already explained. Now we come to topics from which arguments are taken that pertain to an entire question or conclusion.

Things that have greater probability are said to be greater than things to be proved or concluded; those that have lesser probability are said to be lesser; and those that have equal probability are said to be equal. One argues from greaters only by negating, as follows: 'He could not overcome a single obstacle, therefore he cannot overcome many; he could not learn grammar, therefore [199] he cannot learn logic'; If you do not perceive what falls under the senses, much less will you grasp things attained by the intelligence'; If you are not solicitous for yourself now, who will be solicitous for you in the future?' The common topic: If what seems more probable is not the case now, what seems less probable will not be the case in the future. . . .

Chap. 16. The topic of opposites

[200] The kinds of opposites, as we have taught in the second book, are four: some are relatives, as husband and wife; others are contraries, as hot and cold; others privative, as blind and having sight; and others contradictory, as the man is good, the man is not good.

This topic has two maximal propositions. [201] First, if one opposite is affirmed of something, the other is denied, e.g., 'If Peter is the father of Francis, he is not his son; if it is cold, it is not hot'; 'If he sees, then he is not blind,' 'If something is good, then it is not non good.' But from the fact that one thing is denied it is not necessary that the opposite be affirmed; as, if he is not a teacher, it does not follow that he is a student; if it is not beautiful, it does not follow that it is repulsive, for there are some contraries that have other intermediaries. Second, if one of two opposites follows from another of two opposites, the other of the first opposite will follow from the other of the second; if this does not follow, then neither does that. In opposites that are relatives, if a relative of major comparison is said of the father, and a relative of minor comparison is said of the son, then if the second is not the case, then neither is the first. In the case of contraries, if virtue is to be praised, then vice is to be condemned; and if the latter is not to be condemned, then neither is the former to be praised. In the case of contradictories, animal and non animal, man and non man: If every man is an animal, every non animal will be a non man, for if it is not the case that every non animal would be a non man, neither would every man be an animal. . . .

Chap. 17. The topics of repugnants, of differents, and of disparates

[203] Repugnants are things that, while not being opposites, cannot be affirmed of the same subject; thus all opposites are repugnants but not all repugnants are opposites. Examples: man and beast, stone and wood, substance and accident, to love and to hate, to help or not to help, spirit and bone, to be a parent and to neglect offspring. There are also various species or genera of disparate things, i.e., things that universally negate each other, as 'No man is a stone, thus no stone is a man,'

From this topic one may argue only by affirming, in this manner. It is a man, therefore not a beast; it is a body, therefore not a spirit; he loves, therefore he does not vituperate; he serves the world, therefore not God. Such arguments make use of one maxim: what agrees with one repugnant does not agree with the other, or with the rest. The following axiom also applies to this topic: if repugnants are immediate, under one genus to which the other does not pertain, or the rest apart from the one, that must apply to the rest.[108] Under this axiom is contained the topic from division, which has the following use: if, having enumerated the members dividing a particular subject, one is affirmed, the other or the rest are denied. If, however, the other or the rest are denied, with one exception, that must be affirmed. Examples: the plant lives, and it does not have an intelligent or a sentient soul, therefore a vegetative soul; there is one lightest element and this is fire; therefore it is not air, water, or earth; he loves perishables, therefore not eternals.

Chap. 18. The topic of authority

[204] There is only one external topic, that from which arguments not from art are drawn, the topic from authority or testimony.

Authority is twofold: one kind is divine, which cannot be false, and so it provides arguments that are most certain; the other is human, and this requires two things—knowledge of matters had from science or experience, and virtue or probity. The former is required so that a man knows what he is talking about, the latter so that he speak truthfully about what he knows. Otherwise truth itself sometimes speaks directly without any guarantee of its probity, as occurs in proverbs taken from the common usage of mankind, since few individuals are good. Some have authority from use alone,[109] as in grammar the meanings of words and phrases, and in the republic many ceremonies. Sometimes human authority is most certain, as when one believes on authority alone that the French exist; sometimes it is firm but not completely certain; sometimes it is unreliable on account of the diversity and the reasoning of those whose authority is invoked.[110]

This topic has two maximal propositions; the first is: In the use of words follow common usage, for this, as Horace said, provides the norm for speaking.[111] For this reason if a person were to offer a greeting or were to advise men from common custom, one should confide in his authority. The second is: In offering judgments about things, faith should be placed in one who is expert in his art; thus, Plato said that souls are immortal, therefore they are free from corruption.[112] So one should speak with the many and judge with the few; and in judging matters the judgment of the wise should be followed. Appeal should be made to things that conserve strength and restore health. [205] What these are we confirm from the judgments of physicians.

One argues from this topic by affirming and negating, in the following way: 'Astronomers say that the sun is many times larger than the earth; thus they are to be believed.'[113] 'Astronomers hold that the heavens are not square in shape; therefore they are not square.' The examples show how one should argue from authority by negation. One should not argue in this way: 'Plato does not say it, therefore it is not so,' because, just as from nothing nothing comes, so nothing can be concluded by arguing from a negation.

There are also extrinsic topics that are referred to as non-artificial, as reputations, witnesses, prejudices, tables, tortures, and oaths. Since these are proper to rhetoric we do not treat them here. Thus much of this topic and the tract on topics.

There should follow now a treatment of topics that deal with the comparative question, which Aristotle analyzes in his *Topics*, but because these are of more use to the orator than to the dialectician, we omit them also. Those interested should consult Aristotle and our work on oratorical and dialectical invention.[114]

Also in this place one might treat of topics that are proper to dialectic whereby dialectical questions are answered,[115] as is the question of genus, of definition, etc. We skip these also because from what we have already said about genus, definition, and common topics one can gather whatever is required for answering such questions;[116] again, because their explanation would be long and involved, and thus should be postponed to another place. There remains, however, that we write something of the correct use of topics, concerning which we have already treated generally in our book on invention.

Chap. 19. On the proper use of dialectic and of the teaching on topics

[206] Anyone who wishes to use the art of dialectics and the teaching on dialectical topics correctly should take note of my animadversions, advert to them, and then put them to use, as follows:

First, one should know the number, nature, and distinction of topics and their modes of argument.

Second, one should put them to use[117] in such a way that he knows them thoroughly and sees them as placed before his very eyes. One should do so with such diligence that he need not turn back to individual rules as necessity requires or simply to recall them. They should present themselves to him spontaneously without being recalled.

Third, when something is proposed to be proved, one should examine the subject and the attribute of the question. For each, one should look into the term, the definition, the denomination, the parts, the causes, the effects, the antecedents, the consequents, the adjuncts, the similars, the dissimilars, and the repugnants. From these, various arguments can be drawn, and these will offer him a vast supply for disputation.

Fourth, one should beware lest out of vain contentiousness he attempt to draw arguments from any topic whatever for proving any question whatever, since not every topic will be suitable to proving it. Some things do not have causes, parts, opposites, etc., that can offer a topic or source for arguments.

Fifth, if one wishes to dispute more fully, more topics should be present and one should take additional arguments from them. In this way he will not only prove his point but also [207] amplify it by an abundance of arguments. Again, one can adorn it by figures that can be sought from those topics.

Sixth, one should realize that topical places do not contain things themselves but are only notes that indicate where they are hidden. Therefore, when there is a paucity of arguments the doctrine of proper topics should be reexamined; those who do not attend to this will learn dialectics in vain. The person who wishes to become a perfect dialectician, that is, an artist who is able to discourse with probability on any matter proposed, should prepare himself by hearing, reading, and even writing out the teaching on proper topics.

Seventh, in acquiring knowledge of proper topics one should go to the special arts or to the matters that are treated in the special arts, and in this way he will prepare from them common topics for himself. First he should learn the proper meanings of ambiguous words and terms of that art; then he should perceive the first principles on which the entire teaching depends. After that he should learn the subject matter universally, its parts, causes, and properties. After that he should go to the species. He should do this in physics, metaphysics, and ethics, and in other arts and in all of learning. Only a person who has filled his mind with the doctrine of common and proper topics can be called a true dialectician. How the topics that have been found should be used when he moves on to disputing or to writing we will explain with the admonitions that follow.

Eighth, the rule for locating and using topics is to be observed fully, since the art of arranging arguments is no less important than the art of discovering them, and this includes everything that is necessary for explaining any subject matter.

Order, however, is twofold, one kind of nature, the other of doctrine. (The order of time, which serves the needs of history, [208] does not pertain to our project.) The order of nature is one that we see nature observe in its operations, and this again is twofold: the order of generation, which proceeds from the more to the less perfect and from causes to their effects; and the order of perfection or of intention, when we proceed from effects to causes. Within the order of generation are contained composition and division. We use composition when we move from the integral parts to the whole, division when we descend from superiors to inferiors. Resolution and collection are contained under the order of perfection: we use resolution when we go from the entire whole to its integral parts and from effects to causes, collection when we ascend from inferiors to superiors. In the order of perfection are also contained what are called axioms (*dignitates*), when the process is from the more worthy to the less worthy. The order of doctrine is one that proceeds from things that are required for the understanding of persons or things, as when we treat first things that contribute to the knowledge of what follows, and, to the degree possible, proceed from the easier to the more difficult. Usually this process is followed in the order of generation or that of perfection or both together. On the other hand, when things treated are equally known or equally perfect or easy, we may use whatever order we judge suitable. These matters are clarified in our treatment of method in the first book.

Ninth, the orders of composition and division should be followed in teaching, so as to follow nature to the degree possible. This order of teaching Aristotle uses in various places[118] when he proceeds from parts to whole, and from the more common to the less common. [209] Mathematicians observe this order when they construct one demonstration after another. Resolution and collection are employed equally in invention; on this account one should go from manifest sensibles and singulars to universals. Resolution was used by Aristotle in the first book of the *Prior Analytics*,[119] where he resolved the syllogism into the proposition and the proposition into terms. He also used it in the *De animalibus*, when from their history he proceeds to their parts.[120] Collection delighted Socrates, who, since he professed to know nothing, held to the order that is appropriate for those willing to learn. Aristotle taught that this order was to be followed in discovering the principles of the sciences. When, however, disparate matters are to be treated, or those unequal in perfection and dignity, the order of perfection should be retained and one should begin from the more known.

Tenth, when an entire matter is to be explained by us, it is usually correct to proceed in the following order: treat the name, existence, nature, cause on account of which it is, its effect or function, its parts, species, similars, and contraries. Or, the whole treatise might be reduced to the four questions: is it, what is it, what kind is it, and why is it [of this kind], that is, by what causes the thing is effected or acquired.[121] Alternatively, if we are to treat of a virtue, its necessity should be demonstrated, then its object and its subject, from which its nature will be made apparent; then its conditions and properties, how it may be compared to other things, and in what way impediments to it may be removed.

Eleventh, when any simple conclusion, question, or opinion is to be confirmed by argument, the arguments should be set up in this order: the stronger principle and the weaker middle [210] should be put together, and the strongest argument should be put in the last place.[122]

Twelfth, if something is to be confuted by discourse, it is proper to use a threefold method.[123] First, the truth should be confirmed, and from the truth thus known the errors of others should be refuted; second, the opinions of others should be referred to and refuted, and what is to be held should be stated afterwards; third, the arguments in favor of each side should be advanced, along with opinions, and then the truth should be explicated and proved; and lastly arguments to the contrary should be refuted. Practically all schools now follow this order, and Aristotle approves it at the beginning of the third book of the *Metaphysics*.

In asserting opinions and arguments he should refrain from citing light-weight and empty-headed writers, as well as those concerned with minutiae.

Thirteenth, what has been said about the methods to be followed in arguing or in writing should not to be taken as inviolable rules. When the circumstances of the matter being treated persuade otherwise, one may depart reasonably from the prescribed formulas. What should move us in so doing is the fear that by always following the same path we may fall into complacency and fastidiousness. Other things that one might wish to know about the doctrine of topics and dialectic may be read in our *On Invention*. We now turn to the final part of this book.

[Sophistics or Fallacious Reasoning]

Chap. 20. The sophistic syllogism, and those who are called sophists

Of the three kinds of syllogism based on their matter, the third [211] is that by which we are induced to error and deception. This is to be learned not in order to use it, but rather that we may beware of it. Thus we treat of it to the same end that physicians treat of poisons.

Just as there are two kinds of good syllogism, one that generates science and the other opinion, so there are two kinds of useless or bad syllogism. The first of these is the syllogism that presents itself as a true species of demonstration but in reality is not a demonstration, as when principles are taken as true when in fact they are false. From this arises the type of syllogism that is called a pseudograph, that is to say, a false description. This occurs when the principles and axioms of an art or science are taken in a sense broader than they ought, and when taken in this sense are regarded as true and necessary, whereas actually they are not. For example, 'All good is to be loved for itself' is true only of the unadulterated good; 'From nothing nothing comes' is false, unless it is understood to occur in a process of generation; 'All semicircles are equal' is not true, unless understood of parts of the same circle. But this type of syllogism is of rare occurrence.

Second is the kind of bad syllogism that mimicks the probable syllogism and attempts to do so falsely, when in trying to deduce probable conclusions from probable premises it actually deduces false conclusions. On this account it is usually called a captious, or insidious, or sophistical syllogism, or a sophism. Those who use it do not actually know but wish to appear to know by offering captious arguments. So they are called sophists, that is, vain displayers of wisdom. At one time that term had a good meaning and meant the same thing as being wise.[124] Afterwards philosophers changed its meaning to designate those who philosophize wrongly and do not attain the truth or the true wisdom that is sought, but rather a vain [212] type of wisdom. . . .

[LISTING OF FALLACIES, TO THE END
OF THE FIFTH BOOK]

BOOK SIX

In which are treated the operations of the intellect, 'beings of reason' (entia rationis), universals, and the distinction of the sciences

Chap. 1. Things to be treated in this book

[241] What we have treated in the previous books would seem sufficient for attaining the end we initially proposed. Nonetheless, what we have added like a corollary in this last book should prove very useful, and indeed, if one thinks about it, may even be necessary for avoiding errors in our thought processes.

Since, therefore, the entire work of logic has been situated in directing the operations of the intellect, and these operations are directed solely by beings of reason, one has to understand the nature and power of beings of reason to perform such operations properly. That is what we propose to explain in this book. And because beings of reason arise especially from considering things universally, something should be added about the nature of universals, a topic that logicians cannot ignore. Again, since all of these matters and even the [242] entire content of logic is directed to the acquisition of the sciences, something should be said about the division and varieties of the sciences, and this is added at the end.

Thus this book is divided into four parts, which, for instruction purposes, are divided into various chapters. The first three cover the operations of the intellect, their natures and various characteristics. Although the mind's operations properly pertain to natural philosophy,[125] the logician needs to understand and explain them in his own way, since no one can direct something of whose nature he is ignorant, as should be obvious.

Chap. 2. What are the operations of the human intellect?

So that we may propose our instruction on this matter in clear and perspicuous fashion we preface our treatment with a series of propositions.

First proposition. Some knowledge of the intellect's operations, at least rough knowledge, is necessary for logical work. This is apparent from what we have just said in the first chapter, for what the logician is to direct, and how, cannot be understood without having some knowledge of how the mind operates. This may be confirmed from knowledge of the categories, which logicians require, whose application involve him with the use of second intentions and beings of reason. Just as he must know the categories, he must understand the mind's operations, and also [243] these beings of reason by which the operations are directed.

Second proposition. The operations of the intellect by which we come to knowledge of things are three in number. I say 'by which we come to knowledge of things,' because words are concerned with these and through them we know things.[126] Other operations are attributed to the intellect, such as decision and speech, but we say nothing about them because they do not pertain to our project. But there are operations that we do treat, and these are three: simple apprehension; composition or division, which are called affirmation and negation; and discourse or reasoning. What these are we explain in the following chapter.

That these operations are three in number follows from these considerations. First, from the common opinion of logicians and philosophers, who assign these names and functions to them, and there is no reason why we should depart from that practice. Then, from our own experience, for each one can note oneself following these operations when one knows. Finally, the operations themselves can be discerned from human speech, since as Aristotle teaches,[127] words are signs of concepts or passions that are in the soul. Sometimes we pronounce one word, or more, but separated, as when we say 'man, animal'; sometimes two are joined and connected by a link, as when we affirm or negate one thing of another; or finally, sometimes we pass from one expression or composite term to another, as when we say 'man is an animal, therefore he senses.' The first way of speaking is a sign of the first operation, that is, of simple apprehension; the second, of composition; the third, of argumentation.

[244] These three are operations of the intellect that philosophers refer to as receptive or possible, that is, the intellect that, upon receiving intelligible species, perceives things themselves, as explained in the first book.[128]

But against what has just been said one might oppose the authority of Aristotle,[129] who in some places seems to acknowledge only two operations, the first and the second.[130] The response: when Aristotle mentions these two operations he does not exclude the third. And when he says that sometimes the intellect is true and sometimes it is neither true nor false, here he is referring to simple apprehension, while insinuating that in the other two operations there is truth and falsity.

Again, contrary to the assigned number, one might object that the second and third are not different operations, for both consist in a type of composition, for just as the second composes simple notions or concepts, so the third composes two sentences or propositions; therefore there are only two, apprehension and composition. Response; it is true that both consist in a certain composition; nonetheless, since one composition is specifically different from the other, the two operations are themselves different. Again, even if one were to concede that they are not different in species, it is sufficient if the two differ by their accidents, since they have different modes and forms of composing—which it would not be prudent to deny. Thus they are assigned a different way of directing by the logician, and they direct in distinct ways.

Chap. 3. What is the nature of the three operations of the intellect?

As to what we propose to teach in the second place, we note the following propositions. [245]

First proposition: The first operation of the intellect is the simple conception of a thing, or a notion whereby we conceive a thing alone without affirming or denying anything of it. This operation is called simple conception, not because by it we apprehend simple things alone (for we also apprehend composed things, as white man, rational animal), but because it lacks composition, that is, affirmation or negation, and on this account it is not said to be true or false.

Second proposition: The second operation is a kind of judgment by which we judge that one thing goes with or does not go with another by affirming or negating.[131] On this account it is called affirmation or negation and composition or division: composition affirms, division denies, because the former attributes something, the latter removes something.

Third proposition: The third operation is the deduction of one thing from another; or it is a judgment wherein we judge that one thing truly follows from another; as, if we posit that a plant grows, we deduce from this that it is alive.

Fourth proposition: The operation of the intellect or all intellectual knowledge takes its origin from the senses. Hence the adage: nothing in the intellect that was not first in the senses.[132] Sensitive knowledge is the first knowing in man, and intellective knowledge comes next.[133] The process is as follows: the senses are affected by external things, which are principles of our knowledge through sensible species, and these arrive in the imagination, and from them phantasms are formed, and from these the agent intellect elicits immaterial species, and when affected by these the

intellect produces its concepts. This is the first operation, and then come the others.

Fifth proposition: As to why the intellect exercises its first operation, two reasons may be assigned. The first is taken from the senses, [246], for just as the senses provide simple species, so they show also that either one thing is found in another or it is not. Thus they provide the occasion for the intellect either to affirm one thing of another by its judgment or to deny it. Second is the natural light of the intellect, whereby we conceive the thing and also recognize that something goes with it or not. For example, in conceiving a whole the intellect apprehends it as composed of parts; by its own light it then understands that the whole is greater than each part; as a result it affirms that the whole is greater than its part. From this one can gather how the intellect also produces the third operation. This consists in reasoning, a power of the human mind by which, from one thing known and understood, it can arrive at something previously unknown. For example, when the intellect knows something to be good, it immediately infers that it is desirable; again, when it knows that someone is running, it immediately gathers that he is moving.

Sixth proposition: There is a certain intrinsic ordering among the three operations, such that the second depends necessarily on the first, and the third on the second. For one cannot compose without things being apprehended, nor can one reason without their being composed.

But in this place there may be a doubt concerning what was said about the nature of the first operation, namely, that there is no truth or falsity in it, because every affirmation is either true or false; but there is an affirmation in the first operation; therefore, truth and falsity. The minor proposition follows from Aristotle saying that negation is subsequent to affirmation; but the second operation contains negation; therefore affirmation precedes it in the first. I explain: if someone through the first operation conceives a crow, he immediately can formulate this negative proposition through the second, 'The crow is not white.' Therefore before this negative [247] in the second there precedes an affirmative in the first, and so also truth.

To this objection one may respond by negating the minor proposition, which taken strictly is not true. One must therefore make a distinction as follows: that the affirmation precedes the negation may be taken in two ways; one way actually, if the affirmation proposition was expressly made; another way potentially, that is, if it were understood as if it were actually made. With this distinction I say that Aristotle's statement should be understood as an affirmation taken in the second way. Thus, when the intellect says that the crow is not white, it supposes that an affirmative, though tacit, has already preceded the statement potentially.

Chap. 4. The qualities of the three operations

Of the three chapters proposed for explaining the operations of the intellect there remains the third, in which the virtues and vices of these operations are made clear, so that, these being known, they can be better directed and emended. On this matter we add the following propositions.

First proposition: The three operations of the intellect, by their very nature, can be exercised well or poorly. Hence it happens that they have various strengths and weaknesses, and on this account they need arts whereby their defects can be corrected.

Second proposition: The perfections and defects of the operations derive from two sources: the objects with which they are concerned and their manner of acting. Perfection arises in an operation from the object when the whole and integral object is perceived; defect, when the whole is not perceived [248] or one thing is taken for another. Such defect is called ignorance. From the manner of proceeding the intellect acts well when it is concerned with its object in proper and orderly fashion. Since this can occur in various ways there are various perfections and defects that arise on this score. The perfections are clarity, rectitude, and truth; to these are opposed the defects of ignorance, obscurity, obliquity, and falsity.

Third proposition: Ignorance can be found in all the operations of the intellect. That this is so in the second and third operations is obvious, but there can be doubt concerning the first. Yet ignorance can occur even in the first operation: for example, when uninformed individuals do not have proper concepts of particular things, such as rare animals, plants, and similar objects. For this reason there can be ignorance in the first operation with regard to the totality of being.

Fourth proposition: The second defect, obscurity, can be found in all operations. This vice is contracted when one does not have a proper concept for a thing, as when conceiving things that are separated from matter, such as angels; when conceiving things that are very small; and when conceiving things that are very remote from the senses, with respect to which our eyes are like those of an owl to the light of the sun.

Fifth proposition: The third defect, which is obliquity or lack of rectitude, is contracted when one does not apprehend a thing correctly, as when one grasps its genus as a differentia or a superior as an inferior. And since the fourth defect, falsity, cannot be grasped properly if one does not understand the concept of truth, [249] we now add some propositions relating to truth.

Sixth proposition: Truth is twofold; one truth is like a common property that runs through all entities, for a thing is true to the extent that it is in conformity with its principles, and this is truth on the part of the thing, and this is not our concern here.[134] Another is truth that is found in the intellect, and the latter is nothing more than the conformity of the intellect with the thing known.[135] The falsity opposed to this type of truth is simply lack of conformity of the intellect with the thing known.

Seventh proposition: Truth that is in the intellect is twofold, active and passive. Active truth follows the judgment of the intellect and so it depends on the intellect. If the intellect judges that an animal is alive, this is said to be active truth because it follows from a judgment of an affirming intellect. Passive truth is conformity between the intellect and the thing as it is in the intellect (and also outside the intellect), but without the judgment of the intellect. If a man is presented to someone and the person conceives 'rational animal,' this conformity or agreement between the concept of the mind and the man is said to be passive truth. This also can be in the senses, which are said to be true if they receive a true species. To both types of truth there is opposed its falsity. Whence active falsity is the lack of conformity between the intellect and the thing known that follows on the judgment of the intellect. Passive falsity, on the other hand, is the lack of conformity between the thing and the intellect that does not arise from the judgment of the intellect. Passive truth and falsity are found only in the first operation of the intellect, because this operation alone is exercised without the effort of reason, since the intellect is related passively to such apprehension.

Last proposition: Active truth and falsity occur in the second and third operations of the intellect, but not in the same way and so this requires further discrimination. [250] The reason for this is that in producing these two operations the intellect concurs with its own judgment and assent. We say 'further discrimination,' for in the second operation there is only one truth and falsity, whereas in the second both truth and falsity are twofold. In the third operation there is one truth in the proposition, another in the form of the argument; the first is taken from the matter, the second from the form of reasoning. In the following syllogism both truths are found: 'Every animal senses; every man is an animal; therefore every man senses,' because both propositions in the antecedent are true and the form or the illation is proper. Indeed, the truth or form that is discerned in the illation is better said to be correct and the falsity that is opposed to it incorrect. On this account we speak of correct or incorrect consequence and not true or false consequence. To this twofold truth is opposed a twofold falsity, one on the part of the proposition and the other on the part of the form, as is apparent in the following syllogism: 'All learned individuals are good; all logicians are good; therefore all logicians are learned.' Here there is a falsity on the part of the matter, because it is not true that all learned individuals and all logicians are good, and on the part of the form, since the reasoning is in the second figure with two affirmative premises. Therefore the foregoing are said to be active truths and falsities because the intellect makes them, with its own judgment, and does so correctly or not.

From what has been said one can readily understand the work of the logician, namely, to provide precepts in terms of which one can tell truth from falsity, for it is his function to discern the true from the false so as to preserve the former and avoid the latter. This concludes the first matter we have proposed to treat; now we turn to the second.

Chap. 5. The term intention and whence it derives its various meanings

[251] Having explained the nature of the three operations of the intellect, we now treat of the entities by which the operations are directed, that is, beings of reason or second intentions. These are two names for the same thing, as will be shown later. We begin with 'intention,' and. since this is a somewhat ambiguous term, we first consider where it comes from and what it means.[136]

Intention is an expression composed of 'in' and 'tention,' the second of which is not a word, though it takes its origin from 'tending.' If we look to its signification, intention designates a tending toward, or a tendency to, something. Since the powers by which we know or desire anything tend toward their objects, the word intention can be used to explain the operations of both the intellect and the will. As applied to the will, intention sometimes means the act of the will by which it tends to the good, and it is the same as willing it or grasping it; sometimes it means the thing itself to which the will tends, as when we say that the intention of the teacher is to help the pupil learn. Thus the word refers properly to the act, improperly, by metonymy, to the thing intended. In its second reference the will's intention is divided into good and bad, and it is this kind of intention that concerns moral philosophers and theologians. When the term [252] is transferred to the intellect it also takes on a variety of meanings.

First and properly, an intention designates the knowledge or the act of knowing whereby the intellect is brought to bear on the thing known. Secondly and improperly, it is used for the thing known; and because a thing is known through a species that is a kind of similitude of the object known, the species of things known are also called intentions. Thus it is that the species of sensible things that are perceived by the senses are called intentions, as the species of a colored object is called its intention. Finally, intention is taken to mean a type of relation that accrues to the thing known precisely as it is the terminus of intellection. This type of relation is either to the intellect that understands or to the object known, as is seen in the relationship of genus to species. From the fact that the intellect considers, for example, human nature universally, there arises in it a kind of relation to the intellect whereby human nature is said to be known and understood, and another kind of relation to the inferiors from which it is abstracted, on which account human nature is denominated a species, a universal, a predicate, and so on.

In this work the term intention is taken specifically in this last signification, for to treat of intention in its other meanings pertains to other treatises. So by the word intention logicians mean certain relationships or extrinsic denominations that come to things as they are understood and so exist objectively in the intellect, as, for example, genus, species, predicate, subject, antecedent, and like terms.

Note here that intention, when taken for the object on which the intellect bears, includes two things: one is quasi material, and it is the real nature as understood, which is denominated from the relation coming from without, [253] such as the human nature that is said to be a species; the other is quasi formal, and it is the relationship from which the thing known takes its denomination, as the relationship of human nature to individuals, on which account it is called a species as opposed to an individual. Another example may be taken from something concrete, such as a white body, which refers materially to the body, formally to its whiteness; here species refers materially to the real nature, formally to the relationship. The latter is referred to as a second intention just as the nature is said to be a first intention, the second formal and the first material, as will be explained in the next chapter.

Chap. 6. Kinds of intention in general

Intention generally taken is divided into formal and material. The formal intention is the act that tends toward the object known; the material intention, also called the objective intention, is the object toward which the act tends. Each is again twofold, first and second. The first formal intention is the act in which the intellect first bears on the thing known, that is, in which the thing is first known as an object. The second formal intention is the second or reflex act in which the intellect knows objective second intentions, namely, the relationships that follow on things as first known. The first material or objective intention is the object itself, first known, as it exists on the part of the thing that the intellect first attains, as man, lion, heaven, etc., on which account it is said to be first. The second material or objective intention is the relationship that comes to the thing known precisely as it is in the intellect, and on which the intellect bears secondarily; on this account it is said to be second, as something intended and known in the second place. Things therefore considered in themselves and first known are said to be first intentions; relationships that are attributed to things and that follow after them are said to be second intentions, as things known in the second place. The first can be said to be things known primarily; the second things known secondarily. Both kinds of intention agree in this, that neither is said to be an intention except insofar as it is known and terminates an act of intellection in such a way that it implies a relationship to a knowing intellect.

First and second intentions differ from each other in various ways. First, because the first are named first intentions, that is, a type of imposition that signifies things as they are in themselves and considered simply, without any relationship to an intellect, as 'human nature' when designated by the term 'man.' The second are named second intentions, that is, a type of imposition that signifies things as they exist objectively in the intellect, as 'human nature' when designated by the term 'species.' Secondly, they differ because the first intention exists on the part of the object and is the real thing itself, either a substance or an accident, and so subsisting by itself or inhering in another. A second intention, on the other hand, does not exist on the part of the thing, nor does it subsist by itself or inhere in another as in a subject, since it exists objectively in the intellect alone. Thus, in considering it the intellect bears directly on it, and when the intellect is not considering it, it has no existence whatever.

On this account things that are said to exist objectively in the intellect are two in kind: one kind are things that exist outside the intellect and independently of it—as man or lion. Such things when known are said to exist objectively in the intellect because its act terminates in them, just as a thing when seen is said to exist in the eye, because the object seen terminates the act of vision. The other kind are things that do not exist apart from the intellect's operation, and thus they are said to exist because they are known, and of this kind are second intentions and beings of reason. Yet again there are other things that are said to exist both objectively and subjectively in the intellect, and these are thoughts and intellectual operations when these are recognized by us. As recognized, they too terminate an act [255] of knowing and so they exist objectively in the intellect, but as actions that are immanent within the intellect they exist in it subjectively and as an accident in a subject. Whence if a person contemplates his own knowledge act, that act can be said to be in the intellect in two ways, both objectively and subjectively, as just explained.

Chap. 7. The kinds of first and second intentions

There are three kinds of first intentions. In the first category are contained things that exist in nature without any relation to the intellect, as man, lion, heaven. The second category are things that do not exist in nature but that have existence only through the intellect. Because these are signified by the same terms as first intentions as if they existed in nature, they are said to be first intentions; examples would be a chimera, a gold mountain, and other objects the intellect fashions from what it discerns in things. The third category consists of things that are not themselves real, although they designate the negation or the privation of something real, such as blindness and darkness, which formally include a privation in one way or another. A man is not said to be blind because the intellect knows his blindness, and yet the man is really blind. The blindness is not something in itself, but rather the privation of something. And granted that merely fictitious entities and privations are sometimes called second intentions and beings of reason, this is not proper terminology, because they are known as if they did exist in nature. They are not the consequence of something known previously by the intellect, and they are not mere relations of reason; on this account they are more properly first intentions. Things in the second category are sometimes said to be beings of reason, because they are conceived [256] by the reason and do not exist in reality. Those in the third category, although not existing in reality, are said to exist because reason apprehends them, and thus they are known as if they were something. That suffices for the kinds of first intention; now on to the second.

The first division of second intentions is that some are immediate, as coming to things directly, as to be an object, to be known, to be abstracted; others come to things mediately through the first kind, as to be universal, to be indifferent to many, because these come to a thing previously abstracted from singulars; yet others follow from the second kind, as to be a species, a genus, a supreme genus, or a lowest genus, which are associated with a nature that is both known and universal. On this basis there can be various degrees of second intention.

The second division of second intentions is that some are associated with every kind of being, as to be predicable, subjectable, universal, particular. Others are associated only with beings in the various categories, as to be a genus or a species. Yet others are associated only with certain categories, as to be a person, to signify *hoc aliquid,* not to be predicable of a subject, which are found only with substances; or to be a proper accident, or a common accident, to exist in a subject, to be concrete, which are attributable only to predicamental accidents.

The third division is that some signify a kind of privation, as to be abstract, to be one in species or in number; others designate a kind of relationship, either to the intellect, as to be known, to be intelligible, or to some other attribution precisely as known, as to be a genus with respect to a species, to be a predicate with respect to a subject.

The fourth division: some are associated with things as they are in the first operation of the intellect; here are found all intentions that are simply apprehended, [257] such as things considered in the predicables and in the categories, as to be universal, to be a genus above a species, below it, etc. Others are attributed to things that are in the second operation, as to be an affirmation or a negation, to be true, to be false, etc. Yet others are attributed to things that are in the third operation, as to be an antecedent, a consequent, a major or a minor extreme, etc.

The fifth division of second intentions is that some are contraries, as are all those that cannot be attributed to the same thing under the same consideration, as to be a highest genus, a lowest species, to be universal and particular, a predicate and a subject; others can be attributed to the same thing, as to be universal, to be a genus; yet others are necessarily associated with only one thing, as to be singular, to be individual, to be a highest genus, to be the highest thing in a genus.

Finally, second intentions can be divided according to the diversification of the arts, whence some are grammatical intentions, as are a proper noun, or an appellative, primitive, or derivative noun; others are rhetorical, as to be a member, a period, an exordium, a proposition; and yet others are logical. Grammatical second intentions can be different in the various languages that are proper to nations, but logical intentions are the same for all, since they are associated with the same things.

Chap. 8. The nature of first and second intentions

It should not be difficult from what has been said to understand the nature of intentions, which we propose to explain in this chapter, since it has been partly explained above. [258] So as to clarify the subject still further, we here consider the matter and the form of different intentions.

From what has been said one can gather that there are four kinds of intentions: two are objective, and these are called objective concepts; and two are formal; and both kinds are divided into first and second. Objective intentions are things that are known, formal intentions are acts of knowing; the former exist only objectively in the intellect, the latter also subjectively. The matter of first objective intentions is all things that can be known by the intellect in any way whatever, either directly or indirectly; these include universals, singulars, positives, privations, and negations, as these are conceived under the aspect of being something real *(sub aliquo reali)* that can be the terminus of an intellectual power. None of these is said to be an objective intention except insofar as it terminates an act of intellection and as it is known. Hence it follows that things considered in themselves and as they exist outside the mind are not said to be intentions. The form of a first objective intention is the relationship that arises in the thing known toward the first formal intention, that is, toward the first act of the intellect, and on the basis of this relation the thing is said to be known and understood. On this account the thing known is like the matter that is denominated, and the relation of reason is like the form that is denominating.

The material of a second objective intention is the nature or the thing already known; its formality is the relationship that comes to things in virtue of the rational aspect that arises in them as they exist objectively in the intellect and in relation to other things known. For example, the relationship of genus is the form by which a generic nature existing in the intellect is referred to a species, and a relationship of species is the form through which a specific nature is named a species; and the same can be said of other relationships whereby a subject, predicate, etc., are denominated. On the other hand, the material of a formal intention, [259] that is, the act of understanding itself, is the act itself as a kind of operation of the intellect; its formality is the relationship of the act of understanding to the thing understood whereby it is denominated a first or second formal intention. These things presupposed, it is a simple matter to describe all the aforesaid intentions.

A formal intention is the act of the intellect that tends toward any object. A first formal intention is the act of the intellect, or the knowledge or concept by which the first intention is known. A second formal intention is the second act of the intellect by which second intentions are known; some call this a reflex act, but improperly. A first objective intention is a real nature as it is first known by the intellect. A second objective intention is a relation of reason which is consequent on things known as they are known secondarily by the intellect. Or, it is a relation of reason by which first intentions are extrinsically denominated precisely as they exist objectively in the intellect.

GLOSSES AND ENDNOTES

1. Cic. lib. 1 *Offic.*; Aristotle, 1 *Poster.* cap. 1; Socrat.
2. Mars. Fic.
3. M. Var.
4. Bud. in com.
5. Senec.
6. Diog. Laer.
7. 2 *Meta.* t. 15
8. 1 *Physic.* tex. 1; 1 *Poster.* tex. 5
9. 2 *Physic.*

10. Aristot.

11. [In Book 6, chaps. 5 through 8; see below.]

12. Tolet.

13. Arist. lib. *Rheto.* cap. 1

14. Cice. lib. *de leg.*

15. Lib. 2 *Elenc.* Bessar.

16. Aristo. 2 *De ani.*

17. Aristo. 2 *De ani.*

18. Libr. 3 & 7 *Phys.*, Arist. lib. *De ani.* 2

19. Arist. lib. 2 *De ani.*

20. Arist. lib. *De mem.*

21. Aristo. 2 *De ani.*

22. 3 *De ani.*

23. [Book 6. Chaps. 1–4; see below.]

24. Aristo. in *Post.*

25. Lib. 1 *De inv.*

26. 1 *Meta.* tex. 48, 2 *Poster.* tex. 5; Plato in *Phaed.*, Cicer. *De fin.*

27. Porph. in *Proem.*

28. Arian.

29. Plato, *Republic*; Augustine, 3 *Contra Academicos*

30. Lovanienses, *In Topicam Aristoteleis*; Aristotle, Lib. 1 *Topicorum*, c. 2.

31. 1 *Physic.* tex. 1

32. 1 *Physic.* tex. 2

33. 1 *Top.* 1, and 8 *Top.* c. 4

34. 1 *Poster.* t. 30

35. 1 *Poster.* t. 30

36. Arist. *loc. cit.*

37. 1 *Poster.* t. 5

38. Lib. 8, *Topic.* 4

39. 1 *Poster.* t. 5 et seq.

40. 1 *Poster.* t. 5

41. 1 *Poster.* t. 9

42. 1 *Poster.* t. 2

43. 2 *Poster.* t. 1

44. 1 *Poster.* tex. 24

45. 1 *Poster.* t. 2

46. 1 *Poster.* tex. 30

47. 1 *Poster.* t. 31

48. 1 *Poster.* tex. 42

49. Lib. 2 *De anima*, t. 1

50. Aristotle, 6 *Eth.*

51. [In Book 6, below.]

52. 1 *Top.* 1

53. Cic. *De offic.*

54. Aristo. 1 *Phys.*

55. 8 *Top.*

56. 1 *Top.* 3 & 9

57. 1 *Poster.* t. 5

58. 1 *Top.* 3

59. 1 *Top.* t. 5; 2 *Top.* 2 & 4, *Top.* 1 & 7, *Top.* 3

60. Lib. 1 *De inv. orat.*

61. Cic. in *Part.*

62. 2 *Poster.* 14

63. Libr. 8 *Topic.*, in initio

64. Boet. 1 *De diff. Top.*

65. Boet. loc. cit.

66. Boet.

67. Cice. in *Top.*

68. Cicer., Them., Agric.

69. Arist. lib. 1 *Rhet.* c. 2, Cic. in *Part.*

70. 1 *Top.* 7

71. Libr. *De inv.* lib. 1, c. ult.

72. 2 *Top.* 2, loc. 3

73. 6 *Top.* 3, Boet. libr. 2 *De diff. top.*

74. 2 *Top.*, loc. 18

75. 2 *Top.* c. 2, loc. 8, Io. Bap. Porta

76. Caesar., Burid., Io. Fab.

77. 2 *Top.* 3, loc. 19, Cic. 2 *De orat.*

78. Arist. 10 *Eth.* c. 7 & 1 *Meta.* c. 2

79. Aristo. 2 *Eth.* c. 4

80. Boet. 2 *De diff. top.*

81. 2 *Top.* 2, loco cit.

82. 2 *Top.* 2, loc. 10 & 11, & c. 4.

83. Lib. 1 supra [See also *De inventione*, lib. 3]

84. Lib. 2 *de Anima*

85. 1 *Rhet.*

86. 2 *Top.* 1

87. 2 *Top.* 4, loc. 34

88. 2 *Phys.* 2

89. Aristo. *De resp.* 1 & 6

90. Libr. 2 *Phys.* & 1 *Polit.*

91. 2 *Topic.* 2, loc. 31

92. Aristotel. 2 *Physic.* D. Tho. 1.2.

93. Senec.

94. Horat.

95. 2 *Phys.*

96. Matt. 18.

97. *Qui cupit optatam cursu contingere metam, / Multa tulit, fecitque, puer, sudavit, et alsit. / Abstinuit Venere, et Baccho, extimuitque magistrum.*

98. Matt. 5.

99. Prov. 18.

100. 2 *Phys.* 3

101. 2 *Top.* 3 loc. 31

102 Agric.

103. 2 *Top.* 2, loc. 13

104. Lib. 2 *Poster.* c. 12

105. Cic. in *Top.*

106. 1 *Topic.* 14

107. Rodol. [Agricola], lib. 1, c. 26.

108. Arist. 2 *Top.* loc. 19.

109. Horat.

110. Cic. lib. 1 *De natu. deor.*

111. 2 *Top.* 2, loc. 5, *In poet.*

112. Cic. *Tusc.* 1

113. Aristo. 1 *De cael.*

114. [See the excerpt from *De inventione,* p. 79 of the translated text.]

115. Lib. 4

116. Perion. in sua *Dial.*

117. Cicer. lib. 2 *Orat.*

118. 2 *Phys.* 2, *De gener. anim.* c. 3

119. Cap. 33

120. Lib. *De mun. ad Alex.,* Libr. 2 *Poster.* c. 18, Libr. 1 *Met.* c. 1

121. Libr. 2 *Poster.* c. 1

122. Cic. in *Orat.*

123. Arist. 3 *Phys.* c. 2, Aristo. 1 *Phys.* in tract. de prin., 1 *De ani.,* Aristo. 4 *Physic.* in tract. de loco, vac. temp.

124. Plat. in *Sophista*

125. Lib. 3 *De anima.* [In the present day we refer to this part of natural philosophy as psychology.]

126. D. Thomas, 1.2.

127. 1 *de Inter.* c. 1.

128. [See the excerpt from Chap. 4, supra.]

129. 3 *De anima.*

130. 2 *Periherm.* c. 1.

131. Aristotle, lib. 1 *de Inter.* c. 4.

132. Aristotle [?]

133. Cicer. *In Lucul.*

134. [The reference here is to what is called ontological truth.]

135. [The reference here is to what is called epistemological truth.]

136. [The attention of the reader is again directed to the introduction of this section, pp. 53–57, which provides preliminary notes about first and second intentions. See also Figure 2 on p. 56, which diagrams relationships among the various types of intentions here being discussed.]

Cipriano Soarez's
Art of Rhetoric

TABULAE
RHETORICAE
CYPRIANI SOARII

Sacerdotis e Societate Iesu

QUIBUS ACCESSERUNT DUO LIBRI

DE ARTE DICENDI

in quorum uno de Rhetoricae natura et caussis;
in altero vero de partibus copiose
accurateque disputatur

Auctore Ludovico Carbone a Costaciaro, Academico
Parthenio et Sacrae Theologiae
in Almo Gymnasio Perusino
olim publico professore

CUM PRIVILEGIO

VENETIIS, MDLXXXIX

Ex Officina Damiani Zenarij

THE TABLES OF
RHETORIC
OF CYPRIAN SOAREZ
Priest of the Society of Jesus

TO WHICH HAVE BEEN ADDED
TWO BOOKS ON

THE ART OF SPEAKING

in one of which the nature and causes of rhetoric,
in the other its parts,
are fully and accurately discussed

by Ludovico Carbone of Costaciaro
of the Parthenian Academy
Some time Professor of Sacred Theology
in the University of Perugia

WITH PRIVILEGE

VENICE, 1589

From the Press of Damian Zenario

Carbone's Tables of Cypriano Soarez's Art of Rhetoric

The Tables of Rhetoric was devised by Ludovico Carbone as a précis of the perennially popular text of Cypriano Soarez, *De arte rhetoricae* (1562). An overview of the content of Soarez's text itself is provided by the Latin table of contents and the English translation that follows this introduction. The popularity of the work was due to the fact that Soarez offered a complete introduction to classical rhetoric replete with definitions, principles, and illustrations taken, often verbatim, from the writings of Aristotle, Cicero, Quintilian and numerous literary works. As such, it lent itself easily to abbreviations that could then be amplified at will by instructors.

Summaries of Soarez's text appeared almost immediately following its publication. Carbone had an advantage in preparing his précis in that he experienced first-hand the application of the teachings of Soarez when he was a pupil at the Jesuit's Roman College in the decade after its founding in 1551. His introduction to the *Tables* makes clear his opinion that Soarez's text is the best of its kind because of "its fullness of doctrine, the ease of its method, its brevity, and its clarity." He explains that he devised *The Tables* as a study guide for his students, something he habitually did in his courses.

Cypriano Soarez

Born in Ocaña, Spain in 1524, Soarez early decided to become a priest and later to join the Society of Jesus. He did so in Coimbra at the age of twenty-five. Lawrence Flynn, S.J., whose doctoral dissertation provides the text and English translation of the humanist's *De arte rhetoricae,* has also collated the sparse information on Soarez's life.[1] Flynn explains that Soarez followed the practice of many Spaniards in traveling to Portugal to join the more flourishing province of the Order. He was ordained there and taught there for almost thirty years before returning to Spain in 1580, where he remained until his death in 1593. Surprisingly, Soarez came from a family of *neo-conversos,* as did Juan Luis Vives. Even though their roots were not Christian, many offspring of Jewish ancestry were admitted to the Society and had distinguished careers.

In 1553 Soarez began his career teaching rhetoric in the Jesuit's new College of Saint Anthony in Lisbon, where he soon gained a reputation for successful teaching. His superior reported that "'the learning, zeal, and interest of Father Soarez' were responsible for a good portion of the success of the five hundred and forty students in the Lisbon school."[2] As was

---

1. "The 'De Arte Rhetoric' (1568) by Cyprian Soarez, S.J.: A Translation with Introduction and Notes." 2 vols. (Ann Arbor: University Microfilms, 1955), 1:59.
2. Flynn, 1:61.

expected of Jesuit pedagogues, he taught other subjects as well—Latin (which he detested teaching), Sacred Scripture, and theology. He was soon appointed Prefect of Studies at the College of Saint Anthony. Despite the demands of these duties, he found time to introduce gifted students to Greek and Latin literature and even to introduce them to the Arabic language. This was the beginning of the Jesuit academies, the literary-debating societies developed and guided by faculty.

Two years after his teaching career began, Soarez was transferred to the illustrious Royal College of Coimbra. King John III had wanted the College to equal the University of Paris in the quality of its teachers, but too many students preferred Paris to Coimbra for their studies and careers, depriving the College of new faculty. The King was also quite concerned about religious unity and orthodoxy. For that reason he applied to Ignatius Loyola for assistance in staffing the College with members of the Order. None could be spared from Rome but fortunately the Portuguese colleges could supply a limited number. Along with Soarez, Peter John Perpinian was recruited to teach the humanities in Coimbra, and Emmanuel Alvarez, grammar. This was a felicitous conjunction, as Alvarez was to write a grammar that became even more popular than Soarez's rhetoric, and Perpinian was already highly appreciated for his eloquence.

In 1560 Soarez was awarded a Master of Arts degree, by King John III, for his seven years of successful teaching of rhetoric. A year later, when he was made Prefect of Studies, Alvarez was appointed Rector of the College.

Eager to perfect the teaching curriculum of the Order's colleges, the Jesuit superiors, not surprisingly, asked Soarez to write an introductory experimental text on rhetoric to prepare students for the study of the ancient texts read in the humanities course. He set to work around 1560 and the first edition was printed in Coimbra in 1562. Soarez's knowledge of the rhetoric texts of Aristotle, Cicero, and Quintilian is evident in the book. Although Aristotle receives fewer direct references than Cicero and Quintilian, the manner in which Soarez introduces concepts of the art is thoroughly Aristotelian. Cicero is most frequently cited, not only his rhetorical writings, but also his philosophical works and orations. In addition liberal selections from other classical authors appear, particularly Horace, Livy, Ovid, Sallust, and Virgil. Flynn argues that Soarez's work is original in its aim and range of teachings, despite the claim of Georgius Majansius in 1744 that Soarez modeled his text after Antonius Nebrissensis' *Artis Rhetoricae compendiosa Coaptatio* (1515). That Soarez learned rhetoric from the disciples of Nebrissensis and knew the text, Flynn admits, but he argues that his acquaintance with it would only have spurred him on to give an adequate treatment of the classical teachings, which the former brief work neglected.[3]

3. Flynn, 1:66; a detailed analysis of Soarez's of classical sources in included, 1:29–31. According to Flynn other Renaissance sources do not appear to have had a direct influence, 1:32–37.

Soon after completing his book, Soarez left off teaching rhetoric and began to teach courses in natural philosophy, theology, and Sacred Scripture. A few years afterwards he was awarded the degree of Doctor of Sacred Theology by the Jesuit College of Evora. At some later point he was named Rector of the College of Evora, and in 1570, became rector of the College of Braga.[4]

Little is known of the rest of his life beyond the fact that in 1586 he was appointed to a committee to critique the *Ratio Studiorum* of that year. He died in Placentia in 1593.

Perpinian and the Revision of *The Art of Rhetoric*

Because of his reputation as a stylist, Perpinian was asked by his superiors to revise Soarez's *Rhetoric* for wider distribution. This was an excellent choice, for Perpinian had worked closely with Soarez when they were both teaching in Lisbon and later in Coimbra. Thus, he knew first-hand Soarez's intentions for the text.

Perpinian was indeed a remarkable man, an orator acclaimed for his "Ciceronian purity simplicity and power,"[5] a first-rate scholar, pedagogue, and theologian. While in Coimbra, Perpinian was asked to deliver the funeral oration for the King's brother and later was appointed court preacher to the Queen.

In the Fall of 1561 Perpinian was summoned to Rome to teach rhetoric in the Collegio Romano. At the exercises celebrating the reopening of classes Perpinian delivered a memorable oration, *"De Arte Rhetorica Discenda,"* to inaugurate his rhetoric lectures. On the same occasion the following year his oration *"De Officio Christiani Doctoris"* before ten cardinals and two ambassadors was highly praised. That year Perpinian gained attention for his introduction of public repetitions in rhetoric, the sort usually held in philosophy.[6] Such practices seem to have made a deep impression on Ludovico Carbone, who used the disputation form to define and distinguish rhetorical principles.

In 1566 Perpinian was given the responsibility of defending the Order and orthodoxy from the attacks made against the opening of Clermont as a Jesuit college in Paris. Foremost among his Calvinist opponents was Peter Ramus, whose revisions in the discipline of rhetoric Perpinian deplored. Eventually the Jesuits prevailed and Perpinian delivered an oration at the opening of the new college. Only a few days later, having been in ill health for several months, Perpinian died. He was but thirty-six years of age.

Jesuit schools served as the major conduit for Soarez's *Rhetoric*; it ap-

4. Flynn, 1:67–69.

5. Flynn, 1:73, citing Allan P. Farrell, *The Jesuit Code of liberal Education. Development and Scope of the Ratio Studiorum* (Milwaukee, 1938),113.

6. Flynn, 1:75–76, citing Farrell, 66–67.

peared on the *Ratio Studiorum* for the Order, which after 100 years of the Order's founding covered 444 schools, and by 1739, 669, not including the 176 seminaries that were also bound by the *Ratio*'s regulations. The work no doubt had a wider influence as well, since Jesuit schools were a model of educational innovation and the work was such a convenient compendium of classical rhetoric. Even English rhetorical manuals were influenced by the work, although Jesuits entered England at risk of their lives. Thomas Vicars, Thomas Farnaby, and John Holmes credit Soarez explicitly among others as sources for their rhetorics.[7]

The Text of the Second Edition

The best printing of Perpinian's revision of 1565 Flynn thought to be that of 1568. This he selected for his English translation.[8] Judging from careful comparison of the original with the second version, Flynn found that Perpinian's emendations were not major: smoothed transitions, sharpened distinctions, restyling of some sentences and amplification of explanations. He also added a brief chapter on imitation and clarified some of Soarez's definitions.

The first edition of the work also seems to have had its devotees, as many printings of these continued to appear even after the second edition was published.[9]

Carbone's *Tabulae* or guide to Soarez's book contains the revisions described by Flynn, showing that Carbone availed himself of the revised version. One of these definitions is pertinent to the translation of Carbone's guide that follows. In the original version, Soarez had defined rhetoric simply as *ars dicendi* (the art of speaking); following Quintilian's conception, Perpinian replaced the definition: "*Rhetorica est vel ars, vel doctrina benedicendi* (Rhetoric is the art or doctrine of speaking well)." Carbone was to repeat the definition in his *Tabulae*, but in the volume of disputations annexed to that work, *De arte dicendi, libri duo* (1589), he went on to disagree with Quintilian that rhetoric is a moral virtue.

Carbone writes that he had read Soarez's book "before it saw the light of day."[10] The statement must refer to the second edition. Born in 1547, Carbone would probably have been completing his studies in the humanities at the Collegio Romano, while Perpinian was working on his revisions of the *Art of Rhetoric*. Perhaps Carbone's zeal for dispensing the rhetorical knowledge he claims to have gained at the College was inspired by Perpinian's charismatic example.

The popularity of Soarez's work is undisputed. While Flynn was unable to survey all of the texts to determine which of the editions was more popular—the original or the revised—when both are taken together, Flynn re-

---

7. Flynn, 1:44–45, 50–54.
9. Flynn, 1:68.

8. Flynn, 1:65–67, 92.
10. *Tabulae*, English translation, 1.

ports, they "had at least one hundred and thirty-four printings in forty-five different European cities, over a period of one hundred and seventy-three years."[11]

Summaries and Guides

Almost immediately, condensations and outlines of Soarez's *Rhetoric* appeared, 207 according to Flynn. These have an even longer history than the book itself, the last one being printed in 1836. These took different forms: condensation; question and answer, *summa*; and *tabulae,* a sentence outline of the work. *Tabulae* were especially popular since they furnished teacher and student with the essential principles and definitions. Teachers could then illustrate these with appropriate classical texts. A published version of this type, termed *methodus,* combined the *tabulae* with expanded explanations and many examples. The *tabulae* received twenty-eight re-prints in thirteen cities, the compendium, thirty-five in nineteen cities, and the methodus, ten in three cities.[12]

Carbone's *Tabulae* probably was not seen by Flynn, for it does not fit the description of the one example he did examine. That contained but "bare rules and definitions . . . without the framework of transitions and explanatory passages.[13] The work of Carbone, on the other hand, could be used as a manual or handbook on the order of the rhetoric handbooks familiar to teachers of college English classes in the United States. It follows exactly the chapters of Soarez's text as revised by Perpinian. For each chapter Carbone transmits the essence of the content, eliminating the illustrations from the classics provided by Soarez. He is precise without being cryptic, expressing each point with scholastic clarity and grace.

Carbone must have intended his *Tabulae* for the instruction of students either in a higher level of the grammar course or in the humanities class that followed. The grammar course would require about four years of study, the humanities, two years, corresponding to the years spent by students in our high schools and the first year of college. The introduction to rhetoric would prepare students for more extensive study of rhetoric in the final stage of the revised trivium. Logic, formerly part of the trivium, was deferred until the student began his three-year study of philosophy. *De arte dicendi,* the commentary published with the *Tabulae,* Carbone probably expected to be read by more advanced students either in the rhetoric class or in one of the literary academies of extracurricular study the Jesuits had developed and encouraged.[14]

---

11. Flynn, 1:37.   12. Flynn, 1:38–44.

13. Flynn, 1:38. Flynn notes that 28 reprints of *tabulae* from 13 cities were published as compared with 35 reprints of compendiums from 19 cities and 10 *methodus* from 3 cities, 1:42–43.

14. The development of the studia humanitatis within the scholastic framework of the Jesuit Ratio Studiorum and the function of academies is discussed at length by Flynn, 1:16–29.

CYPRIANUS SOARIUS
DE ARTE RHETORICA

Latin

CYPRIAN SOAREZ
THE ART OF RHETORIC

English

THE FIRST BOOK

[1r] Chap. 1. The meaning of rhetoric, its function, and purpose

Rhetoric's definition: It is the art or teaching of speaking well.

> An art consists in precepts and thoughts that aim at a single goal and never mislead.
>
> Since some speak poorly, one should note what enables others to speak better, and from these the art is formed.
>
> Speaking well means to speak the best opinions with carefully chosen words.

Its function: to speak properly for persuasion.

Its purpose: to persuade by speech.

[1v] Chap. 2. The excellence and utility of eloquence

Eloquence is excellent because it has always flourished and held sway among free people;

> because nothing is more agreeable to the understanding and the ear than embellished speech and thought;
>
> and because nothing is more impressive and moving than a speaker who is able to change men's minds.

It is useful because it furnishes advice on matters of great importance;

> because it stirs up an indifferent populace, subdues an unruly one, and converts a greedy one;
>
> because it urges people to goodness and calls them back from error;
>
> and because it praises the good, censures the evil, and consoles those in sorrow.

Therefore, eloquence must not be abused, and the greater its power the more must it be joined with integrity and discretion.

Chap. 3. The material of rhetoric

The material of an art is that with which it is concerned, as medicine with diseases and wounds;

> its subject matter is usually contained within specific bounds, except for dialectics and rhetoric, which are not limited in this way.

Whence the material of rhetoric is any subject that can fall under discussion and any inquiry that is proposed.

Chap. 4. The question or the inquiry

One type of inquiry is general or infinite, called in Latin a *propositum* or in Greek a *thesis,* as when one asks if [2r] philosophy should be studied;

Another is fixed and definite, called a *controversia* or a *causa* in Latin or an *hypothesis* in Greek, when the inquiry is limited to particular persons, places, times, and dealings, as "Was Socrates justly condemned by the Athenians?"

There are two types of *propositum,* one concerned with knowing, whose end is science, as "Is the sun larger than the earth?" The other is concerned with actions or with doing things, as "What must one do to promote friendship?" These may also be transferred to particular cases or causes.

There are three genera of causes: those of judgment (as in a court trial), deliberation, and embellishment.

Chap. 5. Embellishment, deliberation, and judgment

Embellishment has two divisions, praise and blame. The time may be present or past. The end in view is honor or dishonor. The effect sought is pleasure in the audience.

Deliberation embraces persuasion or dissuasion, and the time is future. The end in view is utility or harm. The effect sought is hope or fear in those deliberating.

Judgment embraces prosecution and defense, and its time is the past. The end in view is to punish or not. The effect sought is severity or clemency in the judge.

Chap. 6. How an *hypothesis* is to be reduced to a *thesis*

A *consultatio* or a general inquiry is in some way part of a cause or a limited inquiry, because it is contained within it; [2v] for example, "Should Aristotle's philosophy be studied?" contains within it the general inquiry "Should philosophy be studied?"

Whence the matter of a dispute should be transferred to a general inquiry, unless it is concerned with a fact, which is usually settled by inference (*coniectura*). The reasons:

Because there is more freedom in debating a general class rather
than a particular;

what is established generally can be transferred to particulars;

what has to be examined in the general case must also be
examined in the particular;

whence, an outstanding orator always deflects a debate away
from particular persons and times.

Chap. 7. The elements or parts of rhetoric

The elements or parts of rhetoric are five in number:

Invention is the thinking out of valid or very probable arguments
that make a cause capable of proof.

Arrangement is the orderly disposition of the arguments found
by invention.

Expression or elocution means the adjusting of words to make
them suitable for stating ideas.

Memory is the mind's firm grasp of matters and words to be
used.

Delivery or pronunciation is the control of voice and body
suitable to the materials being communicated.

(Note that judgment is not a sixth part of rhetoric but is intermingled
with the first three elements, because without judgment there can
be neither invention, nor arrangement, nor expression.)

[3r] Chap. 8. Means for achieving eloquence: first, natural ability

Eloquence is achieved by means of natural ability, art, practice, and
imitation.

Natural ability offers,

on the part of the mind, quick operations that are keen in
inventing, fertile in explanation and embellishment, and firm
and lasting in memory;

on the part of the body, a strong constitution, a pleasing voice,
readiness of tongue, and a proper conformation of the mouth
and the body as a unit.

These gifts of nature can be improved and polished by art. Whence,
those who are lacking in natural talent need not be discouraged
from the study of oratory, for even mediocrity in speaking has
brought renown to many.

Chap. 9. Art

Art itself has originated from the study of nature, that is, from natural eloquence. On this account, eloquence does not come from the art, but rather the art from eloquence. Of itself, the art alone cannot produce eloquence, for if so, since everyone can study the art everyone should be able to be eloquent, and this is not the case.

Art therefore perfects natural abilities when it:

> affords reminders that guide us in achieving the goal intended;
> makes us confident that what we achieve by nature, study, and practice is right;
> restrains us from speaking on the spur of the moment, and encourages us always to be prepared.

In such matters art is a more reliable guide than nature.

[3v] Chap. 10. Practice

The effect of practice is to perfect and preserve a natural ability that art has polished.

Its utility is that without it there can be nothing exceptional and nothing perfect, and certainly not eloquence.

The way to practice:

> 1. those things should be practiced that best serve the orator;
> 2. it is true that men become speakers by speaking, but it is also true that by speaking poorly one very easily becomes a poor speaker;
> 3. time should therefore be taken for reflection so as to speak with better preparation and more accuracy; and
> 4. the most important advise is to write, for the pen is the best teacher of eloquence.

There are three kinds of practice:

> one is speaking itself,
> another is activities and drills of the voice,
> and a third is memorizing.

Chap. 11. Imitation

The usefulness of imitation is that without it no one can make satisfactory progress.

The way to imitate:

propose the most excellent model and study it carefully;
pursue it in all its details with great diligence;
apply it by frequent and extended practice and especially by
   written composition.

There are two kinds of imitation:

one is imitation of orators, of which we are here speaking;
the other is imitation of actors, by exercises that remove
   shortcomings in performance.

[4r] Chap. 12. Invention

There are two duties of the orator:

one is to discover arguments that effect persuasion,
the other is to arouse feelings by amplifying elements found in
   cases, and these are four in kind: distress, fear, pleasure, and
   desire. These latter are concerned either with evil, as it is
   present or imminent, or with good, as it is present or future.
   Thus:
   Distress is newly-formed apprehension of present evil.
   Pleasure is newly-formed expectation of present good.
   Fear is apprehension of threatening evil.
   Desire is expectation of future good.

But the apprehensions or expectations in all four are only feeble
   affirmations.

Chap. 13. The meaning of invention, argument, and argumentation

Invention means thinking out an argument.

An argument is a probability invented to ground confidence or belief.

Faith is a strong expectation induced by an argument.

An argumentation is the unfolding of an argument; this is done with
   more display by orators than by dialecticians.

Argumentations are taken from topics.
A topic is the location of an argument or a sign that reminds us
   of what we ought to investigate in the question proposed.

Chap. 14. The kinds of arguments

Some arguments are inherent in the subject being treated and so are
   said to be intrinsic; for example, to say that eloquence should be
   desired because it is the art of speaking well.

[4v] Other arguments are said to be extrinsic because they are remote from the subject; for example, to argue the same proposition on the ground that Aristotle says so.

Chap. 15. The number of topics

There are sixteen topics from which intrinsic proofs are derived. Some come from definition; others from enumeration of parts; others from etymology; others are called conjugates; some come from genus, species, resemblance, difference, contraries, adjuncts, antecedents, consequents, repugnants, causes, and effects; from comparison with others that are greater, equal, or less [see chaps. 16–28].

There are six types of extrinsic proofs: previous judgments, public opinion, evidence under torture, records, oaths, and witnesses [see chaps. 29–30].

Chap. 16. Definition

A definition explains the nature of what it defines; for example, rhetoric is a teaching of how to speak well.

To formulate a definition,

1. find something common between the thing to be defined and other things, for example, "teaching" in the definition of rhetoric;
2. find something wherein the thing to be defined differs from other things, for example, "how to speak well" in the same definition;
3. an orator give definitions more fully than does a dialectician and employs analogies from other fields.

[5r] Definition is necessary for the orator in order to make clear the subject being inquired about.

An argument can be based on a definition. For example, should you wish to prove that civil law is useful, define it in this way: Civil law provides a knowledge of equity; but a knowledge of equity is useful; therefore civil law is useful.

Chap. 17. Enumeration of parts

The enumeration of parts is the distribution of any genus or whole into the various elements that make it up; thus virtue or good living has four parts: justice, prudence, fortitude, and temperance.

An argument from the enumeration of parts must consider all the parts and not omit any.

Thus, should you wish to prove that cleverness is not a virtue, argue thus: Cleverness is neither justice, nor prudence, nor fortitude, not temperance; therefore neither is it a virtue.

Chap. 18. Etymology

Etymology, in Latin *notatio,* investigates the origin of words.

It is often employed by orators and poets. An example: A consul is one who has regard for his native land; therefore Piso is not a consul, for he is overthrowing it.

Chap. 19. Conjugates

Conjugates are terms that are derived from the same family, that is, from a single stem but having different grammatical forms, as wise, wisely, wisdom.

An argument taken from this topic: Since my entire case was consular and senatorial, I need the help of consul and senate. Similarly: Highest praise should be given to loyalty, therefore also to one who acts loyally.

[5v] Chap. 20. Genus and species

A genus is a grouping of things that are alike in some respect, but differ specifically in two or more ways.

The parts of which a genus are composed are called species. For example, virtue is a genus and its species are prudence, justice, temperance, and fortitude. Whence:

> A species is a part subjected to a genus.
> An argument taken from a genus would be: "All merit of virtue consists in action; therefore, all merit of prudence consists in action."
> An argument from species would be: "Whatever is justice is certainly a virtue."

Chap. 21. Resemblance and difference

Resemblance is a sharing, between things that are unlike, of elements in which they are alike.

An argument taken from resemblance would be: "Just as the sick person does not perceive the flavor of food, so the greedy person has no taste for generosity."

An argument taken from difference would be: "If barbarians live only for the day, our plans ought to be for eternity."

Chap. 22. Contraries

There are four kinds of contraries: opposites, privatives, comparatives, and negatives.

Opposites are found in the same category but at different extremities; thus: war and peace, virtue and vice.

Arguments: "War is destructive; therefore one should pursue peace." "If virtue should be sought, let us run away from vice."

[6r] Privatives consist in a state and the absence of the state; thus: life and death; light and darkness.

An argument: "Those who would not restore life to a man if they had the power to do so are not avengers of his death."

Comparatives are things that are related within the same genus; thus: given and received, officer and soldier.

Arguments: "If there is value in what is received, so also in what is given." "If to learn is noble, so also is to teach."

Negatives are things that are contrary to their opposites in every respect; thus: this is so, that is not.

An argument: "He is honest; therefore, he is not dishonest."

Chap. 23. Adjuncts or collateral circumstances

Adjuncts are things that are connected to an object in some circumstantial way; examples: place, time, clothing, conversation, a blush, pallor, and so on.

They cover a very wide field, since they include things that relate to the soul, such as virtue and life, and also to the body, such as beauty, ugliness, etc.

Arguments: "He was seen in the evening armed with a sword, therefore he is the killer." "This man has unparalleled character and constancy, therefore he will not break a treaty."

Chap. 24. Antecedents and consequents

Antecedents are events that precede things that follow in such a way that they are necessarily tied to them; in this way they [6v] differ from adjuncts. For example: "The sun has risen; therefore, it is daytime."

Consequents are things that inevitably follow from something posited. Examples: "It is daytime; therefore, the sun has risen." "He received a heavy wound, as is seen from the scar."

Chap. 25. Repugnants

Repugnants are opposites for which no fixed rule or norm serves to differentiate between them; in this way they differ from contraries and differents. For example, to love and to hurt, injure, and abuse are repugnants, whereas to love and to hate are contraries.

An argument: "He loves him, therefore he does not inveigh against him or abuse him."

Chap. 26. Causes

A cause by its own power produces that of which it is the cause; thus, fire, of heat; indigestion, of sickness.

There are four kinds of cause: the final cause or purpose, the efficient cause or agent, the form or formal cause, and the matter or material cause.

The final cause or purpose is that for the sake of which something is done, as happiness for man.

An argument: Man is destined for contemplation; therefore, not for food alone.

The efficient cause is that by whose agency something exists; thus, the sun causes day.

An argument: old age lacks drinking parties; therefore, also drunkenness.

The form is the nature and distinctive character of a thing that makes it be what it is and differentiates it from other things; thus, the rational soul is the form of man.

An argument: The souls of men are immortal; therefore, they should strive for eternal happiness.

Matter is that from which a thing is made and which remains in it; as the bronze of a statue.

An argument: Man's body is mortal; therefore his soul is withdrawn from it at death.

[7r] Chap. 27. Effects

Effects are what take their origin from causes, as the day from the sun.

There are as many kinds of effects as there are of causes, since each cause has its own effect.

Effects are known through their causes, since each cause points to its effect; for example, war is the effect of peace in the sense that the purpose of war is to attain peace; day is an effect of the sun; man is an effect of body and soul being conjoined.

> Arguments: Virtue produces respect; therefore, it should be practiced. Sensuality causes disgrace; therefore, it should be shunned.

Chap. 28. Comparison

Comparison is treated in three ways, as things compared may be greater, less, and equal.

The topic from comparison of the greater: what is not found in the greater is not found in the less. An example: "If famous citizens were not stained with the blood of Saturninus and others, but were even honored, neither will the slayer of Cataline, this murderer of citizens, fall into disrepute."

The topic from comparison of the less: what is found in the less is also found in the greater. An example: "To cut men's throats robbers rise at night; do you not rouse yourself to serve your own needs?"

The topic from comparison of equals involves neither superiority nor subordination. For example: "If it is not licit to command a ship for the Mamertine allies, neither is it licit to do so for the Tauromenian allies."

Chap. 29. Extrinsic arguments

Extrinsic arguments, or those that are said to be inartistic, are called such not because they lack art but because they do not arise from the art of the orator.

[7v] Those that Cicero included under the term testimony, Quintilian divided into previous judgments, public opinion, etc.

Although of themselves these are inartistic, it often takes all the power of oratory to disparage and refute them.

Orators of the past treated them as they pertained directly to court trials; in the present day, trials have been transferred from the care of orators to that of lawyers, and this should be taken into account when reading classical orators.

Chap. 30. Decisions of previous courts and witnesses

Decisions of previous courts fall into three categories:

The first involves matters that at some time or other were decided for similar cases, and these are more properly called precedents;

the second involves decisions that pertain to the case itself and also involves a precedent, as the senate's decision against Milo; and

the third involves a decision pronounced in the same case.

With regard to witnesses, orators in the past spoke both for witnesses and against them, as is apparent in the orations *Pro Flacco*. Today, the different character of trials makes this work unnecessary.

Chap. 31. The use and advantage of topics

One who hopes to achieve distinction in speaking should have topics ready and at command.

Once a subject has been proposed for discussion, one should diligently search over all the topics from which arguments may be taken.

All this is easily done by one who examines the topics carefully and applies them with diligence.

[8r] Chap. 32. Method of using arguments

One should not use a collection of arguments without discrimination, not only in selecting them but also in making judgments about them.

Decisive proofs do not always or in all cases come from the same sources.

Now and then frivolous or irrelevant or useless arguments arise from topics; therefore use discretion in selecting them.

Some topics have value for convincing an audience and arousing their emotions. But since it is difficult, even for those familiar with topics, to draw from them what will effectively move the emotions, this subject will now be treated separately.

Chap. 33. The emotions

An orator is most effective in arousing the minds of men, and he does this by amplification.

Amplification is a weightier kind of assertion that gains credence in the course of speaking by arousing the emotions.

This is accomplished by the kinds of language used and by the facts offered; the language to be employed will be taken up when we deal with the rules for expression [Bk. III].

The amplification of facts is taken from the same topics as are used to secure credence: cumulative definition, frequent summing up of logical consequences [as follows]:

Chaps. 33 to 39. Topics from which amplifications are taken

Amplifications are taken from:

cumulative definition, when a subject is defined in a variety of ways; for example, "History is the witness of the ages, the sum of truth, the soul of memory, the moderator of life."

summing up of logical consequences, when many consequences are added together;

contrast between opposites; for example, "But who can bear this—that cowards should lie in wait for brave men, fools for the wise, the drunken for the sober, sluggards for the watchful?"

[8v] conflict of dissimilars and of contrary statements; for example, in the second *Philippics,* "O unhappy dwelling, with what an ill-matched owner"; or, "Would you call the same man honest and a rascal, most distinguished and a reprobate?"

cumulative causes and their consequences, when many causes and many effects are grouped together.

resemblance and example, when similarities are noted repeatedly and examples added together.

Chap. 40. Things that should be used for amplifying

If the case allows, things considered highly important should be used for amplifying:

those important by nature, for example, divine and heavenly
objects, things whose causes are mysterious, and wonders of
the earth and the universe;

those important by custom, what men think especially
advantageous or disadvantageous; these are of three types, for
men are motivated by: love, for example, of God, country, and
parents; or by affection, for example, towards brothers, wives,
and dependents; or by the honor due to virtue, especially that
of justice and liberality;

all of these serve as admonitions to preserve them when in
danger of being lost, or, when lost, to regain them.

Chap. 41. The rule for amplification

In amplification too much explanation is to be avoided, for carefulness
always operates on a limited scale, whereas this topic calls for
treatment on a grand scale;

whence there is need for discretion in deciding what kind of expansion
to use in each case. [9r] Thus:

1. in cases involving ornamental style, employ topics that arouse
   expectancy, wonder, and delight;
2. in exhortations, enumerations and examples of good and bad
   deeds are most effective;
3. in trials, things that arouse anger are effective for the
   prosecutor; those that arouse compassion are effective for the
   defendant; but at times a prosecutor can excite compassion
   and the defendant anger.

Chaps. 42–48. The reason for proposing certain rules of invention appropriate for the kinds of causes; the excellence of embellishment

Even though invention as a whole extends to every speech, nonetheless
separate rules may be given for each type of cause.

The rules for embellishment: this is a wide and diversified field, used
to praise not only men but also other living beings and things
without a vital principle;

no other style of oratory can be a more copious source of
speaking or more serviceable to governments;

it is more appropriately designed for gently directing the
movements of the soul than for persuading or convincing, for
the proper function of praise is to amplify and adorn.

Deriving praise from the past (ch. 43);

> preceding a man's birth will be his country, parents, and ancestors;

[9v] Deriving praise from the subject's lifetime (ch. 44):

> from external circumstances, for instance, education, resources, riches, power, and neighbors,
>> if he possessed these, for using them well, not proudly, etc.
>> if he did not possess them or lost them, for showing wisdom in being without them;
> from qualities of his body, for its beauty as a sign of his virtue, less for his strength and health except as these also are the result of virtue;
> from qualities of his soul, his character and virtues, first those of knowledge and learning (ch. 45):
>> for his prudence, which is knowledge of things we should seek and of things to avoid;
>> for his wisdom, which is knowledge of things human and divine;
>> for his scientific knowledge, whose companions are dialectics and oratory, and to these should be added all the noble arts;
> then second, from his virtue that consists in conduct (ch. 46):
>> for his justice, for giving to each his due;
>> for his fortitude or courage, for his endurance of hard work and undertaking dangerous tasks;
>> for his temperance, for controlling his passions; and
>> for his possessing modesty, the guardian of all other virtues.

[10r] Deriving praise from the topic of virtue (ch. 47): since individual virtues have their own definite duties and functions, to each form a special praise is due, for example:

> for deeds involving toil and great danger, undertaken without profit and reward;
> for bearing mishaps wisely and preserving honor in trying situations;
> for achievements of outstanding importance, foremost in originality, or unique in their class;
> for deeds that bear comparison with those of other men of distinction.

Deriving praise from the period after death (ch. 48):

> for the way he died;
> for what happened after his death:

    for honors conferred posthumously;
    for rewards bestowed for virtue;
    for further gestures that have won the approval of men;
    for the accomplishments of children, cities founded, works
       of art, etc.

Chap. 49. Praise of cities

Cities are praised for:

    their founders;
    their antiquity;
    their illustrious citizens and their deeds; and
    their geographical position and fortifications.

Chap. 50. Deliberation or deliberative speaking

Traditional rules for embellishment are useful for expressing an opinion, for the subject of praise in one case becomes the subject of exhortation in another.

In deliberation the purpose is honor, to which everything is directed in giving advice.

[10v] Three points should be considered when exhorting or dissuading:

    the subject for deliberation;
    those involved in the deliberation; and
    the one doing the exhorting [as follows:]

Chap. 51. The subject of deliberation

Either it is certain that the subject of deliberation can come into being, and then there can be doubt as to the proper time and manner;

Or it is uncertain, and then we should first show that even if it can come to be it ought not, and then that it cannot come to be.

The elements of exhortation as a whole are three:

    we should show that what we exhort can be accomplished, and easily, for things that are difficult should be considered as if impossible;
    we should show that it is morally good; and
    that it is advantageous, and also important, and from this its necessity will be apparent.

Chap. 52. Those who deliberate

The minds of those who deliberate differ from one another, whether they are groups or individuals:

> if groups, it is important whether they are the senate or the people, Romans or Gauls;
>
> if individuals, there is a difference whether Cato, Cicero, or Caesar deliberates.

Next we have to consider the sex, rank, age, and particularly the character of the deliberator(s).

There are basically two classes of men:

> the one, the unlearned and unpolished, always prefers expediency to honor;
>
> the other, the cultivated class, places honor above all else.

Chap. 53. The first element in exhortation

Nobility would arouse a marvelous longing were it seen by the eye, but for mankind it requires careful encouragement to be sought after:

[11r] it is easy to exhort a noble man to noble deeds, but to make virtue prevail among evil men:

> we should not upbraid them openly, but rather we should move them by
>> praise and public approval,
>> showing subsequent advantage, and
>> holding up fear of evil, for many are more influenced by fear of evil than by hope of good.
>
> Sometimes, rather than seeking the noble, people are better moved by a sense of duty:
>> the duty to maintain unity in society precedes one's duty of acquiring knowledge or skill;
>> within society itself there are various priorities in matters of duty: first to God, second to country, third to parents, and so on.

Chap. 54. Utility

Those who persuade should inquire whether the object of their persuasion is easy, great, pleasant, and free from danger; those who dissuade, whether it is difficult, trifling, unpleasant, and dangerous; all of these considerations also bear on the subject of utility.

When utility comes in conflict with honor or integrity:

> the champion of utility will relate the advantages of peace, wealth, power, and benefits whose value can be measured by usefulness, and also, the disadvantages of their opposites;
>
> one who urges to nobility will present examples of glorious achievements, even those that involved danger, and the immortal glory of posterity; he will also argue that praise engenders utility and that utility is invariably joined to nobility.

[11v] Exercises in defending utility against nobility should be promoted in schools, for one must know what injustice is if one is to preserve justice.

Chap. 55. The exhorter

Exhorting or dissuading is the task of a person who is wise, has integrity, and argues fluently; thus he can forecast intelligently, prove authoritatively, and speak persuasively.

If a person is famous, from a distinguished family, of an age and worth that arouses expectation, he must be careful that what he says is not out of harmony with himself as a speaker.

If he does not possess these benefits, he will have to adopt a more humble manner, for what is called liberty in some is called license in others; prestige suffices for some, but reason itself scarcely manages to safeguard others.

Chap. 56. Certain points to be carried out in deliberative speaking

The essential point in giving counsel is to have knowledge of the commonwealth.

But for persuasive speaking one should have probable knowledge of the character of the community; since this often changes, it frequently calls for a change in the style of speaking.

In the senate, speaking should be marked by less display, for it is a wise body, and the floor must be yielded to others; any suspicion of cleverness and exhibition must be avoided.

Discourse before a public assembly demands power, weight, and variety, [12r] and the chief part of the speech must be directed toward arousing the emotions.

For purposes of persuasion, the effect of recent examples is greatest because they are more familiar; so also is the effect of ancient ones because they are more venerable.

Nothing need be said about the exhortation to be used in court trials, for the different procedure now in use renders this of slight necessity. Rules can be gathered, however, from the topics already discussed and from what will be said below concerning the divisions of speech.

THE END OF THE TABLES OF

THE FIRST BOOK

THE SECOND BOOK

Chap. 1. Arrangement

Arrangement is very necessary for an orator, for it is nothing other than the instruction of a commander to his army lest it be confused and disorganized.

Arrangement is the division, into an order, of materials that have been discovered.

It is almost the same in a general inquiry [12v] as the one explained for the topics.

In a particular inquiry the same considerations that relate to the arousing of the emotions should be applied.

Thus we make use of four elements of speech: exordium, narration, confirmation, and peroration.

Exordium and peroration move the emotions; narration and confirmation are useful for explaining.

Chap. 2. The exordium

The exordium is the part of a speech that aptly disposes a hearer's mind for the rest of the speech.

It is best done in three ways, namely, by making the hearer well-disposed, attentive, and docile or reflective.

A speech will be heard favorably if the speaker first procures goodwill with his own person and from his auditors and his adversaries. This he accomplishes:

by narrating personal merits, positions, and virtues and by ascribing the opposite qualities to his opponents.

To be heard attentively he should present facts that are important, or necessary, or of advantage to the parties before whom the matter will be discussed.

To be heard reflectively he should set forth what he will be speaking about, lay out its main points, and define them briefly.

Chap. 3. The kinds of cases

The different kinds of cases may be variously ordered, but they are five in number: noble, doubtful or uncertain, involved, lowly, and unusual.

A noble case is one suitable enough in itself for winning over the hearers.

A doubtful or uncertain case requires an audience that is well-disposed.

An involved case calls for a receptive audience.

A lowly case has need of an attentive audience.

[13r] An unusual case is contrary to the expectation of men, and this also includes the shameful, both of which call for expedients such as insinuation.

> Insinuation steals into the mind of the hearers unawares. It should be used:
>> if the case or the client's character is questionable, and either the one or the other might come to his aid;
>> if the hearers have been won over by one's opponents or if they are weary:
>> in the event of weariness one should attempt to rejuvenate the auditors: by the hope that one will be brief, by offering a glimpse of arguments that will frustrate one's opponents, and by the timely use of wit.

Chap. 4. The nature of exordium

A good exordium should be:

> accurate and exact;
> pointed in expression and making use of aphorisms;
> and proper for the type of case involved.

It should be derived from those topics that moderately stimulate and delight the hearer, for these are what is most expected in an exordium.

Chap. 5. Faults of exordiums

The most obvious flaws in an exordium are seven in number. It may be:

> ambivalent, when it can be adapted equally well to either side of a case;
> common, when it can be applied to a number of different cases;
> interchangeable, when, with only slight variation, it can be spoken by the opponent;

lengthy, when formed with more words and ideas than are needed;

disjointed, when it is not derived from the case itself or is not connected to the speech like a limb to a body;

[13v] irrelevant, when it accomplishes something different from what the nature of the case requires;

contrary-to-rule, when it achieves none of the aims for which the rules on exordiums have been given.

Chap. 6. Remarks concerning the exordium for forensic speaking

In this genus, care should be taken to draw exordiums from the very heart of the case.

Praising and winning over the judge should be done in such a way as to benefit the case.

When pleading for distinguished men, insist on a consideration of rank; for the lowly, insist on justice; for those who have been wronged, insist on severity; for the unfortunate, dwell on mercy.

Sometimes fear must be removed, sometimes it should be brought to bear.

One should be careful not to introduce anxiety in the introduction.

The exordium need not always be used, for in noble kinds of cases, even in brief and ordinary ones, it can be omitted.

Chap. 7. The exordium in embellishment and deliberation

In these genera exordiums are particularly free and they can be constructed from material remote from or only bordering on the subject.

Often there should be no exordium, or only a short one, since the speaker comes to the judge not as a petitioner but as an exhorter or promoter.

When he employs an exordium, he should:

disclose what he intends to say, the points on which he is going to talk, and what he wishes to obtain; and

urge the audience to hear him while he speaks briefly.

Chap. 8. Narrative

Narrative is an exposition of information and a sort of basis and foundation for producing belief.

[14r] It should possess three qualities; it must be concise, clear, and credible.

To be concise it should be composed of simple words;
each point should be mentioned only once;
anything not needed for understanding or benefit should be removed; but
conciseness need not lack adornment, though this should be unlearned.
To be clear it should be recounted in simple words;
the proper time-sequence should be observed; and
there should be no break in continuity.
To be credible it should be accurate with respect to persons, periods, and places;
the cause of each act and happening should be mentioned;
the evidence offered should be consonant with popular opinion, authority, law, custom, and pious observance;
the honesty of the one narrating should be apparent; and
his integrity, trustworthiness of his statements, and reliability should be indicated.
These qualities will render the hearer understanding, mindful, and believing.

The narrative should also be attractive and charming, and will be so if it contains:

surprises, suspense, a mixture of emotions, conversations of people, and exhibitions of grief, rage, joy, desire, and so on.

Chap. 9. The use of narrative

In trials there is no need for narrative if the subject is well known or if the opponent has offered a narrative.

In embellishment there will be no narrative that necessarily follows the exordium, but one may be used to recount facts that are to be used.

In deliberation there is no narrative because narration [14v] deals with past events; however, many points relating to the deliberation may be reported incidentally.

Surely, private deliberation never needs narrative.

In public meetings a narrative that explains the arrangement of the
subject matter is often necessary.

Chap. 10. Confirmation

Confirmation is the process during which we furnish the chief support
for a case by weakening our opponent's case and strengthening our
own.

By their nature confirmation and refutation are connected both in
treatment and in usefulness.

All hope of victory and the pattern of persuasion depend on this part
of a speech, since in it we confirm our own arguments and destroy
those of our opponent.

We shall be able to do both if we are thoroughly knowledgeable about
the constitution of the case or its status.

Chap. 11. The meaning of status

Status is an inquiry that grows out of the first conflict of the causes or
cases.

> For example, if the charge of the prosecutor is that the defendant
> has conspired with Cataline, the reply to the charge is that he
> has not conspired; from this interchange arises the inquiry.

The inquiry is usually called the issue or the status.

> It is said to be the status because the first conflict of the case is
> there, or because in it the case comes to rest.

Chap. 12. The types of status

There are three inquiries in every dispute, namely, Does the subject
exist? What is it? What kind is it? and thus [15r] there are three
kinds of status:

Does the subject exist? Did Clodius plot against Milo or not? Here
there is need of conjecture, and so this status is said to be
conjectural.

What is something and what should we call it? for instance, Was
Caesar a king or a tyrant? This status is said to be definitive.

What kind is it? wherein one inquires about a qualitative status, asking
about its utility, integrity, justice, and their opposites.

There are two divisions of qualitative status, one absolute, the
other assumptive:
> It is absolute when no extrinsic argument is brought in
> simply because the thing that was done is the right thing
> to do.
> It is assumptive when we have to bring in something
> extrinsic to prove that a thing has been done properly.

Chap. 13. Line of defense, supporting argument, and judicial examination

The line of defense is what a defendant alleges in order to destroy an
accusation against him.

A supporting argument is the reply made by an accuser to weaken a
line of defense.

From the conflict and collision of these two arises a type of inquiry
called a point of judicial examination; toward this every argument
will have to be directed, and thus it has to be sought out.

In a conjectural status there is no discussion, for one does not give an
account of what he denies has been done; [15v] in cases like this the
first inquiry and the final decision involve the same point.

Chap. 14. The status that includes the inquiry that arises concerning a written document

If the defense made in writing does not mean what the opponent
claims, it is said to be ambiguous.

Sometimes an author's intent is contrary to his writing; thus there is a
discrepancy between his writing and his intent.

Again, the writing itself may oppose what is written, as in a conflicting
document.

Yet again, the situation may arise when through reasoning something
is inferred from the document that is not in it; this is called a
process of reasoning.

These four kinds of controversy always fall within the status of quality.

Chap. 15. The management of status

After the point for judicial examination has been defined, it should be
placed before the speaker.

In this way all proofs obtained from the topics for finding arguments
   may be brought together.

With these understood and rooted in his thoughts, the speaker will see
   everything that can be said on the subject proposed.

Thus he will arrange the arguments so as to place the strongest first,
   those of a higher order at the end, those that are average in the
   middle, and those that are faulty no place at all.

Chap. 16. Argumentation

Argumentation is the unfolding or artistic polishing of a proof, and it
   has four divisions: the syllogism, induction, enthymeme, and
   example.

These are taken from the topics: one produces from them things that
   are either certain or capable of proof, or things that are doubtful or
   less capable of proof, which he sees as probable.

[16r] We hold to be certain:
   first, what is perceived by our senses, as what we see, what
      we hear, etc.;
   then, what has been confirmed by popular belief and
      opinon;
   again, we are sure of what has been decreed by law or has
      passed into custom; and
   finally, what has been proved, or anything our opponent
      does not contradict.
There are three degrees of probability:
   the first is the strongest, what is practically always the case,
      such as, that children are loved by their parents;
   next is very likely, such as, that a well person will be alive
      tomorrow; and
   the third, where there is no inconsistency, such as, that
      theft in a house was perpetrated by someone in it.

Chap. 17. Syllogistic reasoning

Syllogistic reasoning, which the Greeks call syllogism and epichireme,
   consists of:

   a proposition in which a topic is posited, and from this comes all
      the force of the reasoning;
   a confirmation of the proposition;
   an assumption through which what is to be shown from the
      proposition is posited;

approval of the assumption; and
the combination of the two, which briefly explains the
connection and what is established by the reasoning process.

Chap. 18. The number of divisions in syllogistic reasoning

It makes little difference whether syllogistic reasoning is thought to
consist of three or five parts.

A distribution into three parts, however, appears more satisfactory, in
such a way that the proposition and the assumption, with their
proofs, make up two parts.

[16v] If the proofs are taken separately, there will be five parts.

When the proposition and the assumption are known, the
reasoning is effected by mixed confirmations.
One need not always begin with the proposition, but sometimes
from the conclusion or the assumption, so as to avoid
monotony, the mother of weariness.

Chap. 19. The enthymeme

An enthymeme is an incomplete syllogism or part of a syllogism.

Whence, if one part of the reasoning process is omitted, one has an
enthymeme: for example, eloquence is an art, therefore it should be
cultivated.

The best kind of enthymeme is one that comes from incompatibles,
which some call the only enthymeme because of its excellence. An
example: "How will you find a foreigner faithful, if you have been an
enemy to your own people?"

In Latin an enthymeme is called an invention (*commentum*) or a careful
preparation (*commentatio*), which designates a twofold argumentation, because the part omitted remains buried in the mind.

Chap. 20. Induction

Induction is a form of discourse that obtains the approval of the
audience by means of undisputed facts, so that it wins assent to
doubtful statements because of their resemblance to things which
the audience has approved.

Or, induction is a form of argument that attains its objective by
making many comparisons; it is made by rhetorical questions and
responses, in this manner:

"What is the most excellent kind of fruit?" "The best, I suppose."
[17r] "And the best kind of horse?" "The fastest." And more of
the same type, and then the point of making these
comparisons: So the man of highest calibre is the one who is
particularly outstanding, not because of birth, but because of
ability.

But two things must be diligently watched:

that the things taken for comparison are of the same type, so
they are necessarily conceded; and
that the thing for which induction is being employed resembles
what was previously inferred.

Chap. 21. Example

Example is incomplete induction, or rhetorical induction.

In it, one argues from one fact to another based on their similarity.

An example: Milo ought not to be condemned for homicide, just
as Horatius was not condemned.
Example differs from enthymeme and syllogism in that in both of
these one reasons from, or concludes to, a universal, whereas in
example only a single fact is induced from another.

On this account example is regarded as a fourth kind of argumentation.

Chap. 22. Epichireme

The Greeks sometimes call epichireme an argumentation.

Sometimes it is said to be what Cicero called a reasoning process.

[17v] And sometimes it is called a condensed form of argument, all of
whose parts converge upon one proposition, as in the example:
"Does a fugitive slave accuse his master without good reason?"

If this were expanded to include all of its parts it would be a reasoning
process.

Chap. 23. Sorites

A sorites piles up in a heap and embraces many arguments, whence it
derives its name, in Latin, *acervalis.*

For example: Anything that is good is desirable; what is desirable
should be approved; what is approved is praiseworthy;
consequently, everything good is praiseworthy.
In this example, which dialecticians call from first to last, one

arrives at a conclusion by various steps and reasoning processes.

Chap. 24. Dilemma

A dilemma is a form of argument in which either of two alternatives that are granted is attacked.

> For example: "If tempers are not pacifiable, bitterness is most severe; but if they are easily calmed, good humor reigns supreme."

It is called a dilemma because it presses in such a way that it catches the opponent from either side; for this reason it is called a horned syllogism. Cicero calls it a *comprehensio.*

If it is true, it will never be refuted. If false, it can be weakened by reversing it upon the opponent or by disproving one of the alternatives.

Thus a dilemma is an incomplete syllogism that is drawn from two opposites; if one supplies the assumption [i.e., the minor premise], one arrives at a complete syllogism.

[18r] Chap. 25. Refutation

The term refutation is sometimes taken for the total action of the defense, sometimes only for the part of the speech in which the opponents assertions are invalidated, and this is properly called reproof or reprehension.

Reprehension is a process through which the opponents proof is weakened, disproved, or destroyed by argumentation.

It employs the same source as invention, for the very topics that are used to strengthen a case can serve to weaken it. This may be done in the following ways:

> by denying everything that has been assumed by the opponent; or
> by holding that his assumptions are doubtful or false rather than true and certain; or
> by showing that the results he desires do not follow from his assumptions; and finally
> by attacking his assumptions one at a time.

Chap. 26. The management of oratorical argumentation

For the management of oratorical argumentation note the following:

Sometimes an oration contains: syllogisms rounded out in a few words, obvious enthymemes, and inductions.

This understood, one should use extreme caution lest the reproof become overloaded with syllogisms and enthymemes, so as to conclude to the desired result.

On this account the reproof should employ variety and originality and be embellished with figures of speech and rhetorical ornament.

Chap. 27. The peroration

The peroration is divided into two parts, amplification and recapitulation.

With regard to amplification:

The peroration is the proper place for enlargement, although amplification can be used elsewhere, after some point has been made or refuted, [18v] but then only in shortened fashion.

Here is the proper place for opening up the flood of eloquence, to stir not only benevolent hearers but also the listless and indifferent.

To effect this all of the ideas presented in the previous book [Bk. I] on amplification are most helpful.

It is of capital importance that the speaker himself be deeply moved.

Also it helps to picture mentally images of things absent, to represent them as though present.

With regard to recapitulation:

This is sometimes necessary for one who praises, seldom for one who advises, more often for a prosecutor than for a defendant.

There are two occasions for it: one is when you distrust the memory of the audience; the other, after the main points have been repeated, to add strength to the case.

There should be repetition only of the main points, lest it seem like another speech.

What is summarized must be related with well-chosen ideas and figures, with variety rather than straight review of the facts.

In recapitulating one should avoid the childish display of feats of memory.

THE END OF THE TABLES OF

THE SECOND BOOK

THE THIRD BOOK

[19r] Chap. 1. Style of expression

This book treats of the method of expression, a method in which the orator should excel.

Both *rhetor* in Greek and *eloquens* in Latin are derived from the verb *eloquor,* "to speak out."

The power of speaking, that is, of speaking out, is found eminently in the orator alone.

"Speaking out" means telling and relating all of one's thoughts to an audience.

It is this art that is principally taught: it requires study, practice, and imitation, and in it especially does one orator excel another.

A person is said to speak well when he speaks with proof, in a matter of necessity; with charm, to elicit pleasure; and with persuasion, to attain victory.

Chap. 2. The indispensables of style

With regard to style, we should see to it that we say things:

in correct Latin, clearly—yet this is not the place for making rules for pure and clear discourse, for this aspect of style is acquired through early training; and

in language that is ornate and that it is appropriate and as pleasing as possible—which has two parts: one that it be ornate, the other that it be clear, that it influence the minds of the audience, and that it contain the most complete information possible.

[19v] Chap. 3. Embellishment

Language is embellished first by its type and then by a kind of its own peculiar savor, that is:

that it be serious, charming, learned, gracious, impressive, and refined; and

that it possess as much feeling and pathos as the subject demands.

These are not items to be aimed at individually, but rather should characterize the whole body of the speech.

We should choose the kind of speaking that:

is adapted to holding the attention of the audience, and that not only gives pleasure, but pleases without overdoing it.

But one who would speak in an embellished manner should first amass an abundance of facts and pithy sayings; for

a wealth of materials engenders wealth of words, and
if the subjects discussed are honorable, words will emerge with a splendor of their own.

Chap. 4. Embellishment of language

All discourse is constructed of words whose meaning we must understand:

one type of embellishment comes from individual words, another from words joined together;
thus we must use both: not only proper and fixed names of objects, but words that we make up and produce ourselves.

Chap. 5. Individual words

Some individual words are by nature more harmonious (*moderatio* sounds better than *modestia*), or more elevated (*optimus* compared to *bonus*), or clearer (*bos* compared to *vacca*), for, since syllables formed from the more euphonious letters are clearer, so words fashioned from such syllables are [20r] more vocal.

The more vowel sound each syllable has, the more pleasing it is.
Joining words together produces the same result as the combination of syllables: one arrangement sounds better than another.

The best individual words are considered those that have the fullest or the most agreeable sound.

Dignified words are always preferable to base words; in a learned speech there is no place for low language.
Distinct and sublime words have to be judged according to subject:

What is splendid in one situation is turgid in another; words too lowly for lofty thoughts are deemed proper for lesser ones.
These must be weighed by some trial of the ear, for in them one's particular way of speaking plays a large part.

Words a speaker may use to embellish speech possess three qualities, namely, their rareness, their newness, or their ability to transfer meaning [as follows].

Chap. 6. Rare words

Rare words are primitive and ancient, and long since have passed out of use.

Their use is freer in poetry than in oratory, because of poetic license.

Virgil made unique use of this form of ornament.

Even in an oration a poetic word lends some dignity, if used rarely and in the right place: for example, *sobolem* (progeny), *effari* (to utter), and *nuncupari* (to be announced). These can seem to make a speech more elevated and more venerable.

[20v] Chap. 7. Coined words

Coined words proceed from the speaker himself and come into being either:

> by analogy, as *syllaturit* (he wishes to be a second Sylla), *fimbriaturit* (he made a Fimbria of); or
> by imitation, as *tinnio* (tinkle), *rugio* (roar), *clangor* (noise), and similar terms; or
> by inflexion, as *bibosus* (a drinker) from *bibo* (I drink); or
> by composition, as *versutiloquus* (crafty-speaking), *expectorare* (to drive from the breast).

The Greeks had greater liberty in forming words, but sometimes we have to be daring.

And if we appear to have gone too far in innovating, we should use expressions that will disarm our critiques, as *ut ita dicam* (as I might say), *si licet dicere* (if I might say), *quodammodo* (in a way), and so on.

Chap. 8. Tropes

A trope is the successful transfer of a word or phrase from its proper meaning to another; for example, when we say *laetas segetes* (joyful crops), we change the word *laetas* from the proper meaning it has when we say men are joyful.

The tropes are eleven in number. Those formed by a single word are seven: *metaphora, synecdoche, metonymia, antonomasia, onomatopoeia,* *catechresis,*and *metalepsis.* In extended speech there are four: *allegoria, periphrasis, hyperbaton, hyperbole.*

Chap. 9. *Metaphora*

Metaphora, or in Latin *translatio,* is the transfer of a word from a place where it literally belongs to one in which the meaning is not literal, or where the tranferred meaning is better than the literal. It is done, either

from necessity, because a proper term is lacking, as in *gemmate vites* (vines sparkling like jewels), *homo durus et asper* (a hard and rough man); or

for greater clarity, [21r] as in *incensus ira* (burning hot rage), *lapsus errore* (fallen into error); or

for impressiveness and ornamentation, as in *lumen orationis* (lamp of style), *flumen eloquentiae* (river of eloquence).

The reason why we are more charmed by transferred words, even when there are proper terms, is that a metaphor is a resemblance restricted to one word, and our minds are wondrously captivated by resemblances.

There is a difference, however, between translation and resemblance, because in resemblance we compare some object to what we wish to explain, as *fecit, ut Leo* (he did it like a lion), whereas in translation we make a substitution for the object, as *homo est Leo* (the man is a lion).

Chap. 10. The kinds of *Metaphora*

There are four kinds of *metaphora:*

1. when one type of animal is substituted for another, as *hominem latrare* (e.g., one man to bark at another);
2. when inanimate qualities are assumed for other inanimates, as *concentu virtutum nihil est suavius* (nothing is sweeter than a harmony of virtues);
3. when inanimate qualities are used for animate beings, as *duo fulmina belli Scipiades* (e.g., when one calls the Scipios "two thunderbolts of war");
4. when animate things are applied to inanimate beings, as *accipiens sonitum saxi de vertice pastor* (the bewildered shepherd sits on the peak of the rock, catching the roar).

Note that a great sublimity arises in translations where we attribute a kind of emotion to inanimate objects, as in *Quid gladius in acie Pharsalica agebat, etc.* (What was your sword doing, unsheathed in the Pharsalian battle line?)

In using *metaphora* the things to avoid are the following:

1. we must avoid a lack of resemblance, as in *coeli ingentes fornices* (the high vaults of heaven);
2. we must see that a likeness is not over-extended: in place of *non Syrtim patrimonii scopulum* (the Syrtis, rock of inheritance) one should say *non Charibdim, sed voraginem bonorum* (not the Charybdis, but the abyss of his wealth);
3. the resemblance must not be too base, as *sassea verruca* (the wart is stony), or too strong for the demands of the subject, as *tempestas comessationis* (a storm of revelry), or too weak, as *commesatio tempestatis* (the revelry of a storm);
4. a repeated use of translation confuses rather than clarifies, and [21v] if continued, degenerates into allegory and enigma.

If one is afraid that the translation is too harsh, soften it by saying *ut ita dicam* (if I may say), for the translation should be restrained, and it should seem to come by invitation, not by intrusion.

Not every privilege enjoyed by poets is granted to orators; thus the speaker should not say *aves pennis remigare* (birds row with their wings), or *pastorem populi* (shepherd of the people), and so on.

Chap. 11. Synecdoche

Synecdoche or understanding is when the meaning moves:

from the part to the whole, as *ex puppi navis* (a ship from its poop deck), *ensis ex mucrone* (a sword from its point);

from one object to many, as *Romanus proelio victor* (the Romans won the battle), *hostis habet muros* (the enemy has taken the walls);

from a member of a class to the whole group, as *Sabellicus suus pro quovis* (a Sabellian boar for any boar);

from the material of which it is made to the entire object, as *pinus* (pine) for *navis* (a ship), *auro* or *aurea* (gold or golden) for *pecunia* (money), *ferro* (iron) for *gladius* (a sword); [then, in reverse order:]

from the whole to the part, as *fontem ignemque ferebat* (they brought the spring and the fire, i.e., water and some live coals);

from many to one, as *oratores visi sumus* (we are marked as orators, with Cicero here speaking of himself alone);

from a whole class to one of its parts, as *ales* (winged) for *Aquila*
(eagle);

from antecedents to consequents, as *aratra iugo referunt suspensa
iuvenci* (young bullocks bring back the plow hanging from the
yoke).

Just as *metaphora* was designed particularly for stirring the feelings and
to obtain vivid effects, so *synecdoche* was designed to add variety to
speech, but here again more freedom is allowed to poets than to
orators.

Chap. 12. *Metonymia*

Metonymia is a trope by which we understand:

effects from causes, as *dona laboratae Cereris* (the gifts of Ceres,
fashioned well), *Platonem legi* (that is, Plato from his writings);

[22r] causes from effects, as when we use *scelus* (detected
sacrilege) to designate an impious person *(scelerato); mortem
pallidam* (pale death), *timorem maestum* (melancholy fear).

the container for the contained, as *moratae urbes* (the well-
mannered ones, for cities); *seculum felix* (happy age, for
happiness), *Roma* (for the Romans).

the object possessed from the possessor, as *Ardet Ucalegon*
(Ucalegon is aflame, for Ucalegon's home);

an object from its sign, as *toga* (toga) for *pace* (peace); *fasces*
(bundle of rods, with an axe) for *magistratus* (a Roman
magistrate). Hence rhetors use the term *metonymia* for *hypallage*
[a rhetorical figure in which relations are interchanged, as "to
give wind to the fleet"].

Chap. 13. *Antonomasia*

Antonomasia, or *pronominatio* (naming for), substitutes something for a
name, as *eversor Carthaginis* (the destroyer of Carthage) for Scipio;
Romanae eloquentiae princeps (the prince of Roman rhetoric) for
Cicero.

Epitheton, or in Latin *appositum*, is not a trope, because it produces no
change. For it is always necessary that what is in apposition signify
and of itself form *antonomasia*, and *epitheton* does not do this.

Appositives are more often and more freely used by poets than by
orators as long as there is agreement with the word to which it is
applied; whence they say *dentes albi* (white teeth) and *humida vina*
(liquid wine), expressions that for orators would be redundant.

However, if an *epitheton* effects something, as in these expressions, O *abominandum scelus* (O accursed crime) or O *deformem libidinem* (O base passion), there is no redundance.

Interchanged terms help embellishment, as *cupiditas effraenata* (unbridled desire) or *insanae substructiones* (insane basements); also by annexing them to other tropes, as *turpis egestas* (ugly want), *tristis senectus* (sad old age).

Note that style, without appositives, is bare and as though unadorned, but take care that it is not over-burdened with them, for it then becomes tedious and heavy.

[22v] Chap. 14. *Onomatopoeia*

Onomatopoeia is the making of names. Among the Greeks it is one of the finest qualities of style, one hardly allowed to Latins.

Those who first constructed speech by suiting words to sounds formed many names in this way, as *mugitus* (bellowing), *sibllius* (hissing), *murmur* (murmur); but in our time this trope is to be used rarely and with great judgment, lest the frequent repetition of a strange word cause irritation.

But if one uses it skillfully and infrequently, it does embellish style.

Chap. 15. *Catechresis*

Catechresis or *abusio* consists in making use of similar and related words for the right word in this way:

"the powers of man are brief *(breves)*," "long *(longum)* deliberation," "a full-grown *(gravis)* speech" for "a long speech," "a fragmented *(minutus)* mind" for "a small mind." Thus *pyxis* (pix) is used for a small box, whatever the material of which it is made.

We misuse related words, not only in instances where there is no word for them, as when one who kills his mother is called a parricide *(parricidum)*, but even when terms are available, as "they build *(aedificant)* a horse," "they pick out *(perlegunt)* with their eyes."

There is this difference between abuse *(catechresis)* and translation *(metaphora)*: the former is less restrained and bolder, provided it is not shameless.

Chap. 16. *Metalepsis*

Metalepsis, or in Latin *transumptio,* is a change of meaning that provides a transition from one trope to another. For example, "Should I look in wonder on a few ears of corn once my kingdom?"—making a progression from corn to ears, from ears to crops, from crops to years.

This trope is very unusual and out of place.

[23r] Chap. 17. *Allegoria*

Allegoria, in Latin *inversio,* indicates one thing in words and another in meaning, and sometimes the very opposite, as in "Now is the time to unyoke the necks of our smoking steeds."

This trope finds frequent use in oratory, but generally it is intermingled with terms that are evident so as not to make continued use of allegory.

The mixed type of allegory is the most often used.

The most brilliant type is that which offers a gracious blend of *simile, allegoria,* and *metaphora.*

One must be careful to conclude with the same choice of *metaphora* with which one began, say, not starting with a "storm" and closing with a "fire."

Allegoria very frequently helps in ordinary conversation.

An *allegoria* that is too obscure is a fault that is called a riddle *(aenigma).* Poets sometimes use it, but orators never.

Chap. 18. *Ironia*

Ironia, in Latin *illusio,* manifests something not only different but contrary to the meaning and the words. This is perceived either from a speaker's tone of voice, or his role, or the nature of the situation.

Chap. 19. *Periphrasis*

Periphrasis is the expression in several words of what can be stated in fewer, even one. It is explained as circumlocution, as in the following: "It was the hour when the first rest begins for tired mortals, etc."

It is very common in poetry, and not uncommon among orators, [23v] though there more compact.

The contrary of *periphrasis* is an excess called *perisologia,* because of the fact that what does not aid, hinders.

Chap. 20. *Hyperbaton*

Hyperbaton is a disruption of the order of words either by inversion (*perversio*) or by transposition (*transiectio*). Examples of inversion: *mecum, tecum* [for *cum me, cum te*], *quibus de rebus* [for *de quibus rebus*], *maria omnia circum* [for *circum maria omnia*]. Example of transposition: *ut orationem in duas divisam esse partes* [for . . . *in duas partes divisam esse*].

Transposition of this type that does not obscure the point is very serviceable in periodic structures, to be treated later. In the period the words must build up, as they do for poetic rhythm.

Poets also separate and transpose words, as in *septem subiecta trioni* [for *subiecta septem trioni,* "lying under the seven bears"], but orators do not accept this usage.

Chap. 21. *Hyperbole*

Hyperbole is a fabricated exaggeration that can be used by increase or decrease: examples, *fulminis ocyor alis* [swifter than the wings of lightning], *vix ossibus haeret* [it scarcely clings to their bones].

But, whether exaggerating or minimizing, a certain proportion should be retained, for, though it strains our credence, it should not go beyond bounds.

Chap. 22. Embellishment in connected words

Periodic structure (*continuatio*) requires two things particularly, first, the arrangement of words (*collocatio*), then, a kind of rhythm and beauty.

Furthermore, an oration must be formed from words or sentences, which we shall discuss after the tropes; then, diction; and finally, rhythm and balance, that is, measures to be used in speech.

[24r] Chap. 23. Figures

A figure is a shaping of a discourse different from the ordinary and from that first understood.

It differs from a trope for a figure can be constructed from its own words, whereas a trope cannot; a figure depends upon a duplication of its verbs.

Often both trope and figure go together in the same sentence, as when two verbs terminate their clauses in an identical way [e.g., *alu*erunt . . . *corrobora*verunt].

Chap. 24. The kinds of figures

This is concerned with the divisions or kinds of figure.

As in the whole of discourse, so figures also are centered in words and in thoughts; thus there are two kinds, those of words and those of the mind.

A figure of speech *(verborum exornatio)* is an embellishment of words that consists in a marked polishing of language.

There is a difference between figures of speech and figures of thought: in the first the arrangement of words is lost if one changes the words, whereas the second remains the same regardless of the words one wishes to use. For example, if repetition is merged with interrogation, and the repetition is removed, the interrogation can still remain.

There is little agreement among authors concerning the number and names of figures; figures that are listed by some among those of speech are listed by others under those of thought.

We shall take a middle course and explain those on which the better authors agree.

Chap. 25. Methods of forming figures of speech

Figures of speech are chiefly formed in three ways, namely:

by addition [of the same word]: for example, "I have killed, I have killed, not Spurius Maelius"; here the verb "have killed" is repeated figuratively;

[24v] by omission: for example, "He has gone, departed, broken out, escaped"; here the conjunctions "and" are omitted;

by similarity of words: for example, "Although you do nothing for the sake of pleasing, all that you do pleases."

Chap. 26. Figures of speech formed by addition

Repetitio is a figure by which the clause is repeatedly introduced by the same word, for example: "Nothing do you do, nothing do you attempt, nothing do you think . . ."

Conversio is a figure in which discourse is repeatedly connected by means of the same word, for example: "Do you grieve . . . ? Antonius slaughtered them. Do you miss . . . ? Antonius snatched them away."

Complexio is a figure that combines the two previous figures. An example: "Who are the ones who . . . ? The Carthaginians. Who are the ones who . . . ? The Carthaginians."

Conduplicatio is a duplication of words that sometimes gives the effect of emphasis and, at other times, of humor. Words are duplicated in several ways:

> by mere repetition: "You live—and you live not to . . ."
> by beginning and ending with the same word;
> by repeating the word immediately, but in a different sentence or clause;
> by repeating a word after an interpolation;
> sometimes words in the middle can correspond to those at the beginning, or the end; and
> sometimes a whole sentence can be repeated.

Traductio is the frequent use of the same word, but with the effect of making the speech more striking, as in "He to whom nothing in life is more pleasing than life, cannot live a life of strength and excellence."

The same kind of embellishment occurs when the same word is used now in one, now in another application, as in "Why do you care so much about a thing that will bring you many cares?"

[25r] *Polyptoton,* in Latin *commutatio casuum* (exchange of cases), occurs when the same expression is put in many cases; this is done either singly or in several words, and the term case is understood of the endings of verbs that indicate tenses. Examples: "Full (*pleni*) are all books, full (*plenae*) the sayings of the wise, and full (*plena*) of examples in antiquity"; and in the same speech, the verbs *prohibuit, eripuit, aspersit.* Hence the *commutatio casuum* is not the same as *traductio.*

Synonyma is a figure in which words that have the same meaning are grouped together; for example: *Abiit, excessit, erupit, evasit.*

Not only words but also expressions that mean the same thing are piled together; for example, *perturbatio mentis, offusa caligo* [mental disorder, enveloping blindness].

Polysyndeton is a figure that abounds in conjunctions, as *tectumque, laremque, armaque.*

Gradatio repeats what has been said and dwells on several points before going on to new ones, or it is a figure that consists in gradually proceeding upward, as in "For Africanus, his diligence won power; power, renown; renown, rivals." This figure should be used sparingly, since it shows studied dexterity.

Chap. 27. Figures of speech formed by omission

These figures formed by omission are particularly desirable because of their brevity and novelty.

Synecdoche is sufficiently understood from what has already been said: for example, "No talk, except about thee."

It differs from *aposiopesis,* in which what is not spoken is either uncertain or requires a longer explanation.

Dissolutio occurs when several things are diffusely mentioned without conjunctions, either in single words or in clauses; for example, "Let Gaul be under protection of him to whose excellence, faithfulness, good-fortune she has been entrusted."

[25v] There is a single origin for *dissolutio* and *polysyndeton*; both sharpen what is said and produce an impression of vehemence. But *dissolutio* differs from *articulus*, which is the same as *incisum.*

Adjunctio is a figure in which several clauses are referred to a single word, one of which would suffice if desired; otherwise it is called *zeugma*, if the verb is placed first, or last, or in the middle; for example: "Conquered is shame by lust, boldness by fear, madness by reason."

Disiunctio occurs when each of the things we say ends with a different word; for example, "The Colophonians claim Homer as their citizen, the Chians insist he is theirs, the Salaminians claim him."

Synoikinosis brings together two different ideas; for example, "The miser misses what he has as much as what he has not."

Chap. 28. Figures of speech of the third class, formed by similarity

The third class of figures appeals to the ear and stimulates the mind by words that are similars, equals, or contraries.

Annominatio, which the Greeks call *paranomasia,* is the use of words in language that has been somewhat changed and inflected; this is done in four ways:

> by *adiectio* or addition: "Deathlessness [*immortalitatem*] he bought with death [*mortem*]."
> by *detractio* or omission: "I do not demand that you die [*immoriaris*] on your mission, just stay with it [*immorare*]."
> by *commutatio* or change: ". . . *reprimi, non comprimi . . .*" [repressed, not suppressed]
> by *metathesis* or translation: "*homini navo, an vano*" [for a man who is a worker or a shirker]

Note that this figure is trivial unless it is weighted with thought.

Similiter cadens is an ornament in which two or more words in the same grammatical construction terminate in the same inflectional ending.

> This arrangement is seen not only at the end of a sentence, but also when initial words [26r] match each other; alternatively, they may correspond at the middle or at the end or in any other fashion. For example, in the same expression: *auden*dum, *audien*dum; *proiec*tus, *para*tus; *prae*tor, *impera*tor; *audac*ia, *impuden*tia.

Similiter desinens is the similar ending of two or more thoughts, that is, when the members or parts of a speech end in the same manner; for example, "*non modum ad eius salutem extingu*endam, *sed etiam gloriam per tales viros infring*endam" [not only to bring about his ruin, but also to impair his reputation by such men].

> This last differs from the previous figure in that *similiter cadens* is only similarity of case, even though the words declined are unlike; but *similiter desinens* terminates in the same endings; also the first can be found only in words that are declinable, the second also in indeclinables, such as adverbs.

Compar, in Greek *isocolon,* is a figure in which divisions of a sentence are composed of about an equal number of syllables; for example, "*extreme hyeme apparavit, ineunte vere suscepit, media aestate confecit*" ["He made preparations in the end of winter, opened hostilities as spring began, and finished the campaign in mid-summer"].

Contrapositum or *contentio,* which the Greeks call *antitheton,* occurs when single words are contrasted to one another, and also pairs of words, as in "Passion overcomes shame, boldness fear, madness reason" and "It is not a matter of my ingenuity but of your help." Nor does the antithetical member always follow the one to which it is contrasted.

Commutatio is a figure in which two sentences that differ from one another are so arranged that the latter, which is contrary to the former, follows it. For example, "Not to eat do I live, but to live I eat."

Correctio is a figure that improves upon a word that has been employed. It occurs in two ways: either it removes the word without replacing it, as "citizen, if it is proper to call him this, . . ."; or it substitutes a word that seems more suitable, as "as every courtesy, but especially piety." There is another *correctio,* one of thought, to be treated in its proper place [see Chap. 30].

Dubitatio occurs when an orator seems to be hesitating over which of two or more things he should say, in preference to all others.

Chap. 29. The advantages and dangers of figures of speech for oratory

If one uses figures of speech sparingly and as the subject requires, he will produce a more pleasing oration. [26v] If he uses them excessively and without judgment, he will lose the charm of variety.

Thus we must take care that our figures:

are not multiplied beyond measure, and are not of the same kind; and
are not combined, or frequent.

We must understand that this concerns dignified and distinctive figures of speech, not those that are commonplace and frequent, for these do not grate on ears accustomed to them.

It is also absurd, without paying attention to the gravity of the subject and the power of thought, to waste these modes with empty words. For, since figures are, as it were, the gestures of speech, it is as ridiculous to pursue them without thought as to seek clothes without a body.

One must know what each situation, character, and time requires in a speech.

The main purpose of these figures is to delight the hearer; but when brutality and pity are the weapons of debate, who will tolerate antitheses and balanced cadences, etc., if a speaker's concern for words diminishes his appeal to the emotions of his hearers.

Chap. 30. Figures of thought

A figure of thought is an embellishment with an excellence and importance that is derived not from words but from the subject matter itself. Demosthenes excelled in this kind, and on this account he has been judged the prince of orators.

Schemata is what the Greeks call figures of thought that are important, not so much for painting with words, as for illuminating our thoughts. Also, speaking is nothing more than setting forth thoughts in a clear light by means of an idea.

Interrogatio is a figure that is used not simply for purposes of knowing but:

> for the sake of creating ill will or exciting pity; or
> to express indignation or surprise; or [27r]
> sometimes to express a sharper form of command, as "Will they not arm themselves . . . ?;
> sometimes to interrogate ourselves, as "What shall I do?"

Responsio is a figure in which one question is asked, and another answered, because it suits our purpose that way, or because it strengthens or weakens a charge against the accused; for example, "Were you beaten with cudgels? Indeed I am innocent"; "Did you kill the man? He was a robber."

Subiectio is a figure in which the speaker asks and replies to his own question, or does not wait for a reply after having asked another person. For example, "Did you need a house? But you had one."

Ante occupatio, or *praesumptio,* in Greek *prolepsis,* is a figure in which we forestall what might be objected. Presumption is also used to establish the sense of words: "that was not a punishment, but a preventing of crime." It may also take the form of a reprimand, which some call *correctio.*

Correctio is a figure which, by cancelling one notion, improves and emends it with another that appears more suitable.

Dubitatio is a figure in which we inquire where to begin, how to end, what would be the best to say, or whether anything at all should be said: "I do not know where to turn."

Communicatio is a figure in which one takes counsel from his very opponents: "And you, Labienus, what would you have done?" Or when one consults the judges: "And now, judges, I should really like to ask you . . ."

Prosopopoeia means a fictitious introduction of persons by which we may with credibility introduce conversations with our opponents, of ourselves with others, and of others among themselves.

> This form of speaking allows us to call forth even the dead. Also cities and people receive the power to speak. In such instances we may soften the figure in this way: ""For if the fatherland were to speak thus with me . . ."
> [27v] Often we can personify the ideas of fame, virtue, etc.

Apostrophe means directing our speech away from the judge, either to attack our opponents, or to turn to some type of invocation, or to bring odium upon an opponent: "O Porcian laws, Sempronian laws!"

Hypotyposis is a representation of facts made in such vivid language that it appeals to the eye rather than to the ear. This applies not only to past and present actions but even to the future or to what might have been.

Aposiopesis, or *paecisio,* or *interruptio,* displays an emotion of rage or of anxiety: "Whom I—but it is better to calm the troubled waves."

Ethopoeia is a portraying of the life and characteristics of others, an ornament especially suitable for winning over minds and arousing the emotions.

Emphasis means to draw out some concealed item from a statement or to show that more was meant than what was said: "And he lay in endless length through the cave," here giving us to understand the enormous bulk of his body.

Sustentatio is a figure by which the minds of the audience are kept suspended at length, and then something unexpected is added, or reference is made to something trivial and inoffensive.

Praeteritio, or *praetermissio,* occurs when we declare that we pass over, or know nothing about, or do not wish to say, what we then definitely talk about: "I do not complain of the decrease of revenues, nor, etc."

Licentia is a figure by which, in the presence of an audience that an orator should hold in awe or fear, he still uses his right to make a remark that is in no way offensive: "See how I stand unterrified?"

Concessio is a figure by which we pretend to admit and to submit to something even unfavorable, because of our confidence in the cause: "But never mind that. Snatch the inheritance from the relatives." Some would have the figure of *concessio* consist in words: "He may be a thief, or a profaner; still he is a good general and a successful one." And when combined with irony, the figure takes on great force: "Go, follow Italy with the winds. Seek your kingdom over the waves."

Parenthesis, or *interclusio,* is a short digression from the subject. But a longer digression, which many consider a part of the case, must not, according to some, be considered among the figures, even though Cicero admits it.

[28r] *Ironia,* which Quintilian and Cicero list among the embellishments of thought, differs from the trope termed *ironia,* in that the latter is a complete fiction of the will and is more concise and more manifest: "Strange, indeed, Gaius Caesar . . ."

Distributio occurs as a figure when something is divided into several parts, to each of which is subordinate its own classification. Or, it is a figure in which certain tasks are distributed among various things or definite persons, with no mention of subdivision.

Permissio is a figure in which we completely entrust some matter to another person and indicate that we are handing it over and resigning it to the disposition of another, or when we leave some things to the judgment of the jury, and even to that of our opponents. Some think that permission refers to deeds, concession to words.

Deprecatio, or *obsecratio,* occurs as a figure when we call upon someone for aid: "I ask it by this right hand."

Optatio is a figure that gives the significance of someone's desire: "Would that my case gave me the opportunity to proclaim this."

Execratio is a figure by which we call down evil upon someone: "May the gods destroy you!"

Epiphonema is an exclamation that is the climax of a statement or of a proof: "Such great toil was it to found the Roman race."

Exclamatio is a figure that produces a notion of a certain sorrow or indignation, through a reprimand of a person or object: "O pity me, etc."; "What an age! What principles!"

There are also other interesting devices that give our speech an
appearance of simplicity and spontaneity and make it less likely to
be viewed with distrust. For example,

> There may be a simulated repentance for something we have
> said: "But why did I introduce so respectable a character?"
>
> Or we may pretend we are searching for something to say: "What
> else is there? Have I left anything out?"
>
> Or we may even pretend ignorance: "But the sculptor of those
> pieces—who was he?"
>
> And we may store away some points in the hearers' memories
> and afterwards reclaim them.
>
> [28v] All of these devices afford the speech a number of different
> aspects. For eloquence delights in variety just as the eye is
> attracted by the sight of different objects.

Such is our teaching concerning tropes and ornaments both of speech
and of thought.

Chap. 31. The collocation of words

The collocation of words is excellent when it achieves discourse that is
connected, coherent, smooth, and evenly flowing.

For this a consideration of the order and connection of words is
necessary.

Chap. 32. Order

Order is preserved with respect to single and to connected words.

In this matter the following are to be observed:

> We must be careful that the weaker term is not subordinated to
> the stronger, so that the speech always increases in force; thus,
> do not say "profaner, and thief."
>
> There is also a natural order, and so we should rather say "day
> and night," "rising and setting," than their reverse.
>
> If an order is reversed, some words become superfluous: so
> "brothers—twins," for if "twins" precedes, there is no need to
> add "brothers."
>
> Closing a sentence with a verb is best by far, if the structure of
> the composition allows; but if this results in harshness, the
> dignity of the style is to be considered.
>
> > [29r] For, in a speech, since words are not measured in
> > metrical fashion, they can be changed from one place to
> > another in which they fit best.

Chap. 33. Connection

For a smooth and pleasing connection we should observe the following:

We should join final syllables with those that precede in such a way that they do not clash and are not too widely separated.

Those consonants clash that are themselves harsh, as "s" and "x": *Ars studiorum, rex Xerxes.*

A clashing of vowels produces an hiatus: for example, if long vowels are joined, as in *"viro optimo obtemporare"*; better that a short vowel precede a long one.

> But in this matter one should not be overly cautious, for Plato, and Demosthenes, and even Cicero tolerated a clashing of vowels.
> For hiatus is even becoming, at times, and lends a certain effect of amplitude; it also suggests a not unpleasant carelessness on the part of a man who is more attentive to his thought than to his words.
> Thus an excessive running together of vowels should be avoided, but a moderate blend, and one that fits the context, should not be condemned.

We should see that the last syllable of a preceding word is not identical with the initial one of a word that follows.

It is also a fault to have too many monosyllables in succession; likewise, a succession of short verbs and nouns should be avoided, and again of long ones, since they produce an effect of sluggishness.

Nor should there be a combination of similar cadences and similar endings, nor should verbs follow verbs in succession, nor should nouns follow nouns.

[29v] This sort of building of discourse requires extreme care, provided it is not labored, for in that case the effort would be endless and childish. A practiced pen makes this method of composition easy, as does the judgment of the ear.

Chap. 34. The form and measure of words

The unskilled speaker determines what he says by his breath more than by art. An orator, on the other hand, links his thought with words, in such a manner that there is nothing harsh, brusk, halting, or redundant in his language.

This is produced by oratorical rhythm, which makes a prose that is well-knit, and symmetrical, and smooth. [Thus we here explain the origin of rhythmical prose and its cause, nature, and use.]

Chap. 35. The origin of rhythmical prose

The inventor of rhythmical arrangement is said to have been Thrasymacus, whose writings were indeed thought to be too rhythmical.

Isocrates, on the contrary, so sensibly proportioned his entire subject matter that many consider him the author of this type of symmetry.

Aristotle and Theodectes forbid the use of verse in prose, but require rhythm, and Theophrastus is even more explicit on this subject.

The Romans at the time of Cicero were unaware of rhythm, but he laid down very careful rules for the entire subject.

Chap. 36. The reason for the discovery of rhythmical prose

The ears, or rather the mind by means of what is received in the ears, has within it a natural capacity for measuring all sound.

So, it discriminates between long and short sounds, and looks for those that are well-balanced. It senses phrases that are mutilated and, so to speak, clipped, [30r] and those that extend unreasonably, and is offended by them.

When something was accidentally said in rounded sentences, it could be noted that this phenomenon that occurred by chance had a pleasing effect, and this notation gave rise to art.

And thus, just as verse was discovered in poetry by its effect on the ear and the study of those able to judge, so also in prose, though much later, it was noted that there are certain definite movements and rhythmical cadences of words.

Chap. 37. *Incisa, membra,* and *perioda*

Incisum is an expression of thought rounded off with complete rhythm; according to most writers it is a portion of a *membrum*: "Did you lack a house? But you had one, etc."

An *incisum* is even made of a single word, such as: "*Diximus: testes dare volumus* [here the *incisum* is *Diximus*]."

Membrum is an expression of thought that is rhythmically complete, but meaningless when cut off from the body of a sentence: *O callidos homines, O rem excogitatam, O ingenia metuenda quem queso nostrum fefellit,* . . . Here the body begins when a final conclusion is joined to the three exclamations, at *quem quaeso,* etc.

Periodus: for this term Cicero uses the following: *ambitus, circuitus, comprehension, continuatio,* and *circumscriptio.*

Every rather long *circuitus* is divided by its *membra*; yet it is one thing to speak in *incisa* and *membra,* another to use *periodi.*

Speaking in *periodi* means that language is borne along from beginning to end, as if enclosed in a circle, until it comes to stop in distinctly complete, finished sentences.

We speak in *membra* when a more open discourse pauses at individual *membra.*

[30v] We speak in *incisa* when the discourse pauses at individual *incisa.*

How rhythm is to be used will be discussed a bit further on, after we have treated metrical feet by which poetry takes form and metrical prose is divided.

Chap. 38. Metrical feet

There are four feet that have two syllables: spondaic, pyrrhic, *choreus,* and *iambus,*

> A spondaic foot is made of two long syllables: *dicunt, mores.*
> A pyrrhic foot is made of two short syllables: *novus, tulit.*
> A *choreus* consists of one long and one short: *scribit, semper.*
> An *iambus* consists of one short and one long: *legunt, reos.*

There are eight feet of three syllables each, as follows:

> A *molossus* is made of three long syllables: *dicendi, conservant.*
> A *trochaeus* or *tribrachus* is made of three short: *ut, fac, mus.*
> A *dactylus* is made of a long and two shorts: *litora.*
> An *anapaestus* uses two shorts and one long: *peragunt.*
> A *bacchius* consists of one short and two longs: *amores.*
> An *antibacchius* consists of two longs and one short: *audisse.*
> A *creticus* or *amphimacrus* consists of a long, a short, and a long: *possident*
> An *amphibrachus* consists of a long, a short, and a long: *petebat.*

Cicero treats only three among the other kinds of feet, two paeons and a *dochmius:*

A paeon in the first position consists of one long and three short
syllables: *aspícite.*

A paeon in the last position embraces three shorts and a long:
facílitas.

A *dochmíus* is made of a *bacchíus* and an *íambus: perhorrescerent.*

Chap. 39. Prose rhythm

There are differences between rhythms of prose and of poetry, and
likewise, between a poem and an oration. Thus: the Greeks
designate number in prose by rhythm, but in poetry by meter.

Although rhythm and meter have metrical feet, they differ in several
respects:

Rhythms are determined by quantity of time; feet, also by
arrangement.

In regard to rhythm, it makes no difference whether dactyl or
anapest is used, since each consists of the same quantity of
time.

[31r] In verse the flow of meter is always the same, as in heroic
voice, with its dactyls and spondees; in prose nothing is
specified, except that:

All discourse that is neither halting nor uneven, but moves along
continually, is considered rhythmical, not because it consists
entirely of rhythms, but because it closely approaches them.

For this reason, it is more difficult to write prose with
rhythm than verse.

It is a serious fault if a combination of words in prose
becomes verse, and this must be carefully avoided; still,
the combination of words should close rhythmically.

[Chaps. 40–50: Specific rules for speaking in *períodus* and
membra—omitted]

[34r] Chap. 51. The three styles of speaking

It is clear that one style of speaking is needed in plain cases, another in
average, and still another in weighty ones.

Not only do different cases demand a different style of speaking,
but different divisions of a speech require a different manner
of style.

Hence something should be said about how many styles of
speaking there are, and in what cases and divisions of speech
they are to be employed.

There are three kinds of style, in each of which an accomplished orator
should be eminent:

> The first is plain, keen, and exact;
> the second is vigorous, profuse, and weighty; and
> the third falls between the two and in some way tempers them.

Since there are three functions of an orator, namely, to instruct, to
move, and to charm;

> the plain style is occupied with instructing;
> the middle style with charming; and
> the grand style with persuading.

In plain style the form of language should:

> be unshackled and free from the bonds of rhythm,
> without roaming, proceeding freely, not wandering about at will;
> one should not try to cement words together, but should
> eliminate all rhetorical ornament;
> instead, pointed, abrupt sentences should be used;
> figures of speech and of thought should be employed moderately
> and sparingly, with tropes;
> and metaphors may be rather short, but not as short as in the
> amplified manner of speaking.

[34v] A tempered style should be:

> fuller and stronger than the plain style,
> and yet more subdued than the fully amplified style yet to be
> discussed.
> All ornaments of speech combine with the tempered style, which
> possesses a great deal of smoothness;
> in it many ornaments of thought are also appropriate; and
> in it smoothness results either from a very small or a very large
> amount of energy.

A magnificent, stately, and opulent style:

> has maximum power, for now it is overwhelming, now it is
> subtle;
> here the orator will raise the dead to life, the fatherland will call
> out at times and address someone;
> here too he will elevate his style, will lift up by the power of
> hyperbole, and will play on all of the emotions.

An orator will use these three kinds of style as the situation demands,
not only with respect to the case as a whole, but to each of its parts.

> To manage and combine them he will need shrewd judgment and
> ability, so that he can determine what is needed at each point

and be able to argue the case accordingly:

> a very subdued style of speaking, such as that used in behalf of Caecina, has to be applied to plain cases;
>
> a vigorous style, like that in the trial of Rabirius, to weighty cases; and
>
> a tempered style, as was used in *Pro lege Manilia,* to cases in the middle class.

In the same manner also,

> a restrained style should be used for winning an audience;
>
> a dialectical and expository style, for instructing and proving; and
>
> the grand style, for persuading.
>
> For it is a distinguishing mark of an eloquent man that he treats less important subjects with restraint, average ones with moderation, and more important matters with grandeur.

[35r] The style should also be varied by reasons of person:

> considering the speaker and the audience, for not every authority, fate, or dignity is the same;
>
> taking into account the places and the times.
>
> In each instance we should determine the extent, mindful that too much is more displeasing than too little.
>
> So, just as wisdom is the foundation of all things, it is the foundation of style.

Chap. 52. Memory

The discoverer of the art of memory is said to be Simonides [of Chios], who, after a catastrophe, was able to identify each body for individual burial because he remembered the place where each person was.

This feat seems to have indicated that his memory was aided by impressing on his mind where each was seated.

Everyone can verify this by testing it for himself, for when we have returned to surroundings after an absence, we recall the things that were done there.

Chap. 53. Whether memory is an element of speech

Although the memory that relates to style has uses in common with that of other arts, still skillful memory (*artificiosa memoria*) is properly considered an element of oratory.

How powerful oratory can be would never be known if memory had not brought that power to its present brilliance.

It maintains an arrangement not only of things but also of words, and nearly an endless number of them, so that the patience of an audience gives out sooner than the faithfulness of memory.

Thus it is not incorrectly called a treasure-house of style.

Chap. 54. Theory of memory

The theory of memory that has been transmitted by the ancients consists of places and symbols.

Those who use this portion of their talents must observe these facts about places:

Many and extensive places can be grasped by the mind.
These are characterized by great variety and are arranged at moderate intervals;
as is seen, for example, in a rather large house or other structure.
When these are carefully fixed in the mind, [35v] one can run through them without hindrance.
Then things that are written down, or understood by reflection, must be associated with places and symbols that arouse a memory of them.
The places that have been selected should be suitably and properly noted so that they adhere permanently.

With regard to symbols:

Things written down, or thought out, should by tied to places by symbols that reawaken a memory of them.
These symbols must be associated in their proper order with their respective places.
When one has to recollect something, one will commence going over the places from the beginning and recall what is found in each one;
for the order of the places will preserve the order of the items, and the symbols will give notice of the things themselves.
Use should be made of symbols that are effective, that are sharply outlined and distinctive, so that they can encounter and quickly penetrate the mind.
The symbols must be modified from time to time according to the diversity of subjects, but the places should always be constant.

Chap. 55. The advantage of this theory of memory

Skillful memory is useful when we have to repeat many names of things in the order in which they were heard, or when different things have to be grasped in their order;

> still, when learning words of a set speech it is almost of no service, for it is useless and endless to commit symbols of individual words to memory.

If we have to memorize a rather long speech, we should do well to learn it by heart, in sections.

> To impress it on the memory more firmly, it is useful to make marks on it that can be recalled.
> It will also help to learn a passage by heart from the very paper on which it was written.
> [36r] The supreme method of memory, however, is practice and toil.
> Proof of our ability to develop the memory by nature and by work is given by many orators, for example, Themistocles, Mithridates, and Cyrus.

Chap. 56. Delivery and its value

Just as delivery seems to be derived from the voice, so gesture is derived from action.

This is a division of rhetoric which by itself exerts an influence in speaking:

> without delivery, the foremost speaker can hold no rank;
> an average one, trained in delivery, can often surpass outstanding orators.
>> When Demosthenes was asked what is most important in oratory, he gave the first, second, and third places to delivery.
> Delivery is a kind of eloquence of the body.

Delivery, however, has two elements:

> voice, which influences the ear, and
> gesture, which influences the eye.
> Through these two senses all feeling enters the soul.

Chap. 57. Voice

There are as many changes of voice as of the affections, which are particularly influenced by the voice.

For this reason, an accomplished orator will use a definite tone of voice, depending on how he wishes himself to appear moved and how he intends to influence his hearer's mind:

Rage demands a sharp, rapid, frequently broken off kind of tone.

Compassion and grief require a different one that is flexible, rich, and irregular.

Fear needs a quality that is dejected, uncertain, and disheartened.

Strength calls for a tone that is restrained, vigorous, and ready to act, with an ardor of seriousness about it.

Pleasure needs an inflection that is extensive, gentle, soft, lively, and relaxed.

Annoyance needs a quality of dignity expressed by a tone under pressure, but not seeking pity.

Excellence of voice should be sought, because it is not a part of us by nature, but the management of it lies within us.

A good orator, then, will change, modulate, and practice all intervals of tone, now and then raising and altering his voice.

[36v] Not only in different subjects but even within the same divisions, and with the same emotions, he should employ limited variations in tone, for variety, on the one hand, furnishes charm and refreshes an audience's ear, and on the other, it invigorates the speaker by his very change of effort.

Chap. 58. Gesture

Gesture should conform to the voice and, together with it, be subservient to the mind.

It should be employed in such a manner as to avoid excess. In particular:

The carriage should be erect and lofty.

There should be only slight pacing about, and not for any distance; moderate stepping forward and even then, seldom.

No irresolute bending of the neck, nor quick motion of the fingers.

The entire body should be controlled, and by manly movements:

by extending the arm in a moment of stress, withdrawing it in milder passages;

by stamping the feet when the contest is to be begun or to end.

But the key to everything is the countenance:

> With it resides the mastery of the eye, for all delivery has its roots in the soul, whose image is the countenance that has the eyes as its interpreters.
>
> This is a unique part of our body, which can produce as many meanings and variations as there are states of the soul:
>
> Facial expression is not to be varied immoderately, lest we be carried away either to absurdities or to some sort of perversity.
>
> By now and then raising and lowering the eyes, we shall indicate, at one time, an inclination of the mind, at another, a goodhumored directing of the feelings, in keeping with the style itself of the speech.

To sum up, delivery is a sort of speech of the body, by means of which it should be more in accord with the mind.

THE END OF THE TABLES OF
THE THIRD BOOK

Ludovico Carbone's
Art of Speaking

DE ARTE
DICENDI
LIBRI DUO

*In quorum uno de Rhetoricae natura et
caussis, in altero vero de partibus
copiose accurateque disputatur*

Auctore
Ludovico Carbone a Costaciaro
Academico Parthenio, et Sacrae Theologiae
in Almo Gymnasio Perusino
olim publico professore

WITH PRIVILEGE

VENETIIS, M.D.LXXXIX

Ex Officina Damiani Zenarij

TWO BOOKS
OF AN ART OF
SPEAKING

*In one of which
the Nature and Causes of Rhetoric,
in the other, its Parts,
are fully and accurately treated*

by
Ludovicus Carbone of Costiacciaro

of the Parthenian Academy
Some time Public Professor of Sacred Theology
in the Gymnasium at Perugia

WITH PRIVILEGE

VENICE, MDLXXXIX

From the Press of Damian Zenario

Ludovico Carbone on the Art of Speaking

On the Art of Speaking by Carbone may be seen as an expanded treatment of the principles or elements of rhetoric introduced by Soarez's *Art of Rhetoric*, but it has far more significance than that. It lays out the foundation for Carbone's own version of the discipline as inspired by the Jesuits at the Collegio Romano. Each of the twenty chapters of the two books will form the nucleus of other works on rhetoric, amplified, and reformulated in ingenious ways to answer contemporary markets for rhetorical practice.[1]

In the preface to the *Tables* and the *Art of Speaking,* Carbone announces that his commentary on Soarez's book will soon be followed by ten more books, over which he sweats day and night *(dies nocteque desudo).*[2] Only five of these have been found. He says that he writes these books for all students, but wishes especially "to make them available to those who attend the schools of the Fathers of the Society of Jesus, in which the rhetoric of Cyprian is generally taught." The preface goes on to describe the pedagogy of his professors and the multiple benefits gained from them. At the end of the paean Carbone says that he will soon publish *De inventione oratoria et dialectica,* and he did so in the same year (1589). The problem with Carbone's fulsome praise for his teachers is that he may have taken more than inspiration from them. Since Carbone seems to have appropriated Della Valle's logic lectures, we cannot be sure that he did not do so for his rhetoric texts as well. (See the introduction to the logic, p. 46 above.)

The two books of the *Art* are cast in the form of disputations, ten for each book. The title of the first book, "On the Nature of Rhetoric and Eloquence," describes precisely the content. The tenth disputation, translated here in its entirety, captures the essence of the questions disputed in the previous nine. Those preliminary chapters take into account argu-

---

1. The rhetoric texts that he published afterwards of which we have record are the following: *De oratoria et dialectica inventione vel de locis communibus* (Venice 1589); *De dispositione oratoria* (Venice 1590); *De octo partium orationis* (Venice 1592); *De caussis eloquentiae* (Venice 1590); *Divinus orator, vel De rhetorica divina* (Venice 1595). During that period he published two books on logic, one on philosophy, and five on theology.

2. For a detailed discussion of the first book of *De arte dicendi* see Jean D. Moss, "Ludovico Carbone on the Nature of Rhetoric," in *Rhetoric and Pedagogy: Its History, Philosophy, and Practice.* Essays in Honor of James J. Murphy, edited by Winifred Bryan Horner and Michael Leff (Mahwah, N. J.: Lawrence Erlbaum Associates, 1995) chapter 8. The second book figures in another of Moss's essays, "Antistrophic Rhetoric: Aristotelian Rhetoric in Renaissance Rome and Padua," in *Philosophy in the Sixteenth and Seventeenth Centuries: Conversations with Aristotle,* edited by Constance Blackwell and Sachiko Kusukawa (Aldershot, Hampshire: Ashgate, 1999) chapter 5.

ments advanced during the Renaissance on perennial questions concerning rhetoric. Following the dialectical method of his teachers, Carbone first poses a question, then surveys opinions on both sides, establishes principles that should figure in a conclusion, considers the best probable answer, and, finally, refutes positions opposed to his own. The range of knowledge he aims to impart is evident from the first disputation, where he introduces students to the Greek and Latin origin of the terms for rhetoric and eloquence and illustrates these with quotations from Socrates to Plutarch. In the next disputation, he prepares the ground work for the tenth in exposing the major definitions offered by classical and contemporary thinkers, including George of Trebizond and Francesco Robortello. He critiques these definitions, sometimes in withering terms.

The question of whether rhetoric can be considered a moral virtue is interesting for the distinctly modern cast of Carbone's thinking, which is reflected also in the definition offered in the last disputation. In the third, he argues against Quintilian that rhetoric is a moral virtue, holding that it is a *habitus* that pertains to reason. It enables a person to do something expeditiously and without error. Only in the sense that it is a cognitive habit can it be called a virtue or power. But it is a power to do either good or evil. He goes on to say that, as a cognitive habit, rhetoric includes the sub-habits of invention, arrangement, style, memory, and delivery. He ends the disputation noting that moral habit should not be excluded from the training of orators, for to practice rhetoric well, one needs moral virtue, and in this Quintilian was right.

The classification of rhetoric as an art occupies the fifth and sixth disputations. In the former he distinguishes between rhetoric and eloquence, arguing that rhetoric implies doctrine and eloquence, the power to apply it well. He classifies rhetoric in the following disputation as an art and not a science, says that it is not a productive art that fashions an artifact to be left behind, just as dancing and singing are not artifacts. Great orators do not always write down their speeches. Rhetoric is an art of discoursing, a rational art, and an instrumental art, which is used by politics.

In the next question concerning the content of rhetoric, Carbone surveys ancient and contemporary opinion, citing among the latter the eminent philosopher Count Iacopo Zabarella, who assigns to rhetoric only civil questions. Against him he cites Antonio Riccobono, Zabarella's colleague at the University of Padua, who takes the Aristotelian view that all subjects come under rhetoric's scope. Carbone ends this question by mentioning that Plato is also right in that rhetoric's subject is the souls of men, which he seeks to reach through persuasion.

After treating the end of rhetoric as persuasion and finding the causes of persuasion in nature, art, practice, and imitation, Carbone turns to the last disputation, in which all of the threads contained in the previous disputations are knit into his commentary on Aristotle's famous definition in the *Rhetoric*: "Rhetoric is the faculty of seeing, in any matter whatever, what is suitable for persuasion (91r)."

The second book is more prosaic in content, dealing as it does with the traditional five parts of rhetoric, but, here again, Carbone chooses perplexing implications of the questions to ignite interest even in these questions. The selection translated (the third disputation), certainly the most engaging of the book, illustrates his perspicuity. It asks "Is invention a part of rhetoric?" That question, roundly debated in the Renaissance, furnishes the central concern of our book: invention in dialectics and rhetoric and the relation of invention to demonstration. Carbone presents the opinion of opponents first, not always naming the authors but giving full explanations of their views. His own position is slowly revealed and it is, as might be expected, thoroughly Aristotelian. In his explanation of the character of rhetorical invention he cites Trebizond, Victorinus, Soarez, and refutes the views of Agricola and Ramus.

Regarding another issue important to rhetoricians of the times, whether judgment is part of rhetoric (the eighth disputation), Carbone mentions that some argue that it should be added as a sixth part, following Hermagoras. On that side scholars have placed Cicero's opinion that since dialectic has two parts—judgment and invention, rhetoric should parallel it. But Carbone notes that Quintilian opposed this view and that later writers have followed him. The most acceptable opinion rests on the principle that judgment has various meanings, as in the judgment of the true or false findings from invention and as in prudential judgment. Furthermore, it is both natural and acquired. Natural judgment is found in the senses and intellectual judgment must be trained, whether it be speculative or practical. Carbone concludes that judgment figures in all parts of eloquence and so should not be isolated as a separate part.

Carbone's exposure of the variety of opinions in the rhetorical debates of the day keeps his students apprised of current views and his conclusions channel their thinking in the directions approved by the Jesuits in their Roman College.

PREFACE TO THE READER

Wherein is explained a plan for the entire art of speaking

❧❧❧

Since the work we have undertaken to write concerning the art of speaking is much longer and more difficult than we thought at the beginning, such that it is necessary for us to take a long time to complete it, we now have decided to publish only two books. If these seem good to you, we will undertake more diligent work to finish the others. And, so that you might know what to expect in the remaining books, we propose in the present treatise the layout of the entire work and the plan we intend to follow.

Thus we divide the entire work into two parts, in the first of which we explain the power and the nature of eloquence, and in the other, everything contained in the rhetorical art. The first part will be made up of four books, of which we now give only the first and the third.

In the first book we explain in ten disputations the nature and causes of rhetoric.

In the second, we treat of the causes effecting eloquence taken separately, with disputations on whether eloquence is from nature; or from art, and what art offers; when and by whom it was invented and where it flourished; whether exercise is the cause of eloquence; on the best regimen for exercise; whether imitation is the cause of eloquence; on the best kind of imitation; certain doubts about imitation; whether rhetoric is a part of philosophy; whether it is the counterpart of dialectic, and how it is distinguished from dialectic and from other arts.

In the third, which we now publish, we treat of the five parts of rhetoric in ten disputations.

The fourth treats the offices of the orator, as follows: on the nature of the office; on the number of offices of an orator; whether teaching is an office of the orator; or moving; whether it is licit to move the emotions; or delighting; concerning jokes; whether, for teaching, the orator should be expert on all things; whether, if he is to move, he must be a good man; on the dignity, usefulness, and necessity of eloquence. And this ends the first part.

In the three following books we treat of invention, the first part of eloquence. In the fifth book, of the three kinds of causes or cases: of the division and kinds of questions; whether there are three kinds of causes; how they should be named; how all forms of speaking can be reduced to three kinds of speech; on the demonstrative kind; on the deliberative; on the judicial; which kind is the more important, and so on.

In the sixth, we treat of states; on the term *status;* on the definition of state; the kinds of state; how states arise; on the conjectural state; on the state of definition; on the state of quality; on the individual parts of this state; on the legitimate state and its parts; whether state and judication differ from each other; on the way of finding states, and so on.

In the seventh book we treat of oratorical and dialectical invention, that is, of the topics whence arguments are taken, with many chapters and a new approach; and since we will publish this book within a few days, the matters that are treated in it, which are varied and many, need not be reviewed here.

In the eighth, we treat of the disposition and parts of a speech. There we treat the following questions: on the number of parts of a speech; of the nature of the exordium; of the virtues and vices of the exordium; what kinds of exordiums there should be in each kind of case; on the nature of narration; on the parts of narration; on the virtues and vices of narration; on partition or proposition; on the use, quantity, and quality of partition; on the nature of confirmation; on the topics of confirmation; on the kinds of argumentation; on the rhetorical enthymeme; on the parts of reasoning; on amplification, polishing *(expolitio),* and illustration; on refutation and its topics; on the peroration, etc.

From the ninth to the eleventh book we treat of elocution. In the ninth, of elocution and the ornament of words in general; of the ornament of individual words; of tropes; of figures, most broadly with many chapters; of the supply of materials and words.

In the tenth, of the structure and location of words; of members and incises; of periods; of the longer period, or of spirit; of feet; of oratorical number; of the use of oratorical number; and so on.

In the eleventh book we treat of the forms or ideas of speech. Here we explain the doctrine with the following disputations based on Hermogenes: what and how many are the figures or ideas of speech; the idea of a speech said to be open; perspicuity or elegance; comeliness *(venustas)* or festivity; circumduction or magnitude; beauty; delayed oration; acute oration or acrimony; moderation, truth, and gravity; the apt form of speaking; the kinds of civil or forensic speaking, etc.

In the twelfth we treat of memory and pronunciation.

As to the rationale and method of discourse to be used in these disputations, although these can be seen in the books we have written, we explain them briefly for those not acquainted with our form of writing. In all our disputations we therefore follow the following method of writing. First, as may be needed, I explain the sense of the proposed disputation; then I offer arguments that bring the matter into doubt; afterwards I reference the opinions of authorities when they disagree; after that I will propose certain principles wherein I clarify the subject being treated; then I demonstrate with various theses what is to be rejected and what held, with supporting reasons; and finally I answer the difficulties brought against them. . . .

BOOK I.

ON THE NATURE OF RHETORIC AND ELOQUENCE IN TEN DISPUTATIONS

Tenth Disputation: An explanation and defense of Aristotle's definition, with a new description of eloquence

[90v] From what we have written about the four causes of rhetoric, one should readily be able to grasp the power and nature of eloquence. After that we shall take up the various descriptions of rhetoric covered in our second disputation and decide which are good and worthy of defense. Finally, should anyone wish to reformulate a new definition on the basis of all its causes, this can easily be extracted from what we have already taught. And since among all other definitions we have adopted the one given by Aristotle, the supreme master of definition and discourse, we now devote

a special disputation to explicating his definition and defending it against his detractors. So, Aristotle defines rhetoric as the faculty of seeing, in any thing whatever, what is suitable for persuasion.[1] Quintilian, Hermagoras, and Hermogenes all oppose this description with the following arguments.

First, the definition seems to be imperfect because all the parts of eloquence are not included in it, but only invention, and this is not proper to rhetoric. Then, this [91r] definition seems to apply not only to rhetoric but also to dialectic, which discourses with probability on any topic proposed, and so, since the definition is not convertible with the thing defined, it is seriously defective.

After that, the definition is condemned by some because it does not express any specific subject matter, such as questions relating to politics, as Hermagoras would prefer. Add to this that Quintilian is not pleased with it because it does not seem to indicate any goal for this art's persuasion.[2] Yet again, it would be preferable to say that rhetoric is an art rather than a faculty, since faculty can be taken for any habit or any power, and we have demonstrated above that rhetoric should be located among the arts.

Finally, this description goes against what Aristotle had written at the end of the first chapter,[3] where he seems to locate it among the sciences when he writes that the orator should be regarded as taking his arguments from science as well as from choice. For all these reasons some think that his definition should be regarded as less than good and so rejected, whereas others approve of it as good but still requiring proof. What is to be thought on this matter we shall explain with the following principles and theses.

First principle: Rhetoricians and orators, when defining the things with which they are concerned, are not as solicitous as are philosophers and dialecticians, nor should they be. On this account the descriptions they offer are not perfect absolutely [91v] and on every account; nonetheless they should be the same as the thing they wish to explain and differentiate from others. For this reason at one time they define through effects, at others through parts, at others through properties, at others through common attributes, and sometimes through metaphors, both affirmatively and negatively. Thus it results that among them a definition is approvable provided it includes no phrase that is repugnant to the nature being defined or puts it in the wrong place, or is opposed to the more necessary laws of correct definition. This explains why one and the same art has been defined in different ways by various writers, as documented above.[4]

Second principle: There are many ways in which dialectic and rhetoric are differentiated from all the other arts, but here we mention only one characteristic as most pertinent to our enterprise. The other arts, even while attaining to the knowledge of contraries—since, as Aristotle writes, the knowledge of contraries pertains to the same science, so the person who knows light also knows darkness, and one who knows what virtue is also knows what vice is, and one who knows health also knows illness— nonetheless no art or science ever argues on contrary sides of the same is- sue, nor does any defend opposed positions [92a] but only one or the oth- er. Thus, by way of example, medicine looks to only one goal, namely, to heal, and not to kill. But dialectic and eloquence, as Aristotle teaches, so argue on opposed sides that one side is no more proposed by them than is the other.[5] So it is not more proper to either of these arts to defend or re- ject a particular position, or to seek to prove it or not. That is why they are called *dunameis,* that is, powers or faculties, for a thing is said to be poten- tial if it can go either way. From this one can understand the importance and excellence of these two arts, for they are so expeditious and powerful that they can discern what is valid on either side and act on it. What the Greeks call *dunamin,* therefore, the Latins call force, faculty, power, and, as Quintilian says, virtue.[6]

Third principle: Aristotle's interpreters do not agree in their explana- tions of the expression *dunamis* or faculty. Some think that men are made important and worthy of honor by possessing it. But this exposition seems more applicable to men for their ambition rather than for their learning, although it is true that those who have excelled in the rhetorical art [92v] have always and everywhere gained the highest honors. Others think that these arts are called faculties by Aristotle because they can be used well or badly. The term faculty is used this way in the first book of the *Ethics* not far from its end when it is said that the blessed life is not to be located in faculties, because that life cannot be open to abuse. And since it is obvious that we can abuse rhetoric and dialectic, we thus name them faculties. But if this explanation is correct, then not only these two disciplines but also all other arts and sciences can be called faculties. Yet others, such as his disciple Alexander of Aphrodisias, offer this explanation, that Aristotle calls rhetoric and all other arts of this kind faculties because they invoke arguments that are not certain but only conjectural, and because they rest on a kind of prudence.[7] On this accounting all conjectural arts should be called faculties. The same author, in his introduction to the *Topics,* explains it in the way we have in the latter part of the second principle, namely, be- cause they take either side of one and the same issue, and this is the truer and more proper explanation. [93r] Aristotle's expositors also question the meaning of the expression 'to see' in his definition, whether it includes only invention or whether it excludes other parts, such as elocution, so that elocution becomes somewhat extrinsic to this art and so is not to be highly regarded, as seems to be insinuated in the third book.[8]

Fourth principle: Eloquence, as taught above,[9] is not one simple faculty or habit, but rather arises from the knowledge of many things in a sort of cumulative way. First there is required a sort of power conferred by nature; then knowledge of how to speak well, which is made up of five key arts—invention, arrangement, style, memory, and delivery; and finally, knowledge of all matters so that these will later be demonstrated, aided by use and practice. If all of these come together in one man they will make him able to speak copiously and ornately on any topic proposed. On this account, if one wishes to explain more fully the nature of eloquence, with a full supply of words rather than a simple and brief statement, it will be necessary to add these details, as just explained. Here one might also remember what we have taught previously, namely, that eloquence and rhetoric or the art of speaking are not completely the same and therefore they cannot be defined in one and the same way. [93v] With these principles posited, I proceed to the following theses.

First thesis: The definition of rhetoric given by Aristotle is not to be rejected in any way but is to be taken as optimal. This thesis will be proved both from the confutation of objections brought against it and from its fuller explication as contained in the following theses.

Second thesis: In this definition faculty is put in place of the genus, for it is a name common to rhetoric and dialectic, as is apparent from the principles; and if taken a bit more broadly, it is common to all the other arts. Aristotle said that it is a faculty rather than an art so that he might get closer to its genus and nature, since it is the type of art that can also be a faculty.

Third thesis: In this definition faculty is taken in the meaning explained in the second and third principles above, that is, it designates an art that is suitable for treating either side of a question. In no way satisfactory is what Maioragio says on this text, that Aristotle called rhetoric a faculty because it is not an art properly speaking, since, as stated above, it is truly and properly an art. Eustratius teaches, in his commentaries on the *Ethics,* that Aristotle uses the term art in more than one place for the same reason as we have said.[10] [94r] And Aristotle himself says the same in the first book of the *Rhetoric* that it is the 'art' of speaking well.[11]

Fourth thesis: When Aristotle says that "rhetoric is a faculty of seeing what is apt to persuade," he explains its nature through its work [*officium*], and this is how it is discerned for any art. For the end of rhetoric, as explained in the first chapter, is to persuade. For an understanding of this thesis it should be noted that Aristotle used the word *diaresai,* that is, to contemplate, and in explaining the work, the word *idein,* that is, to see and intuit.[12] Again it should be noted that in explaining the work of this art he said that the function [*munus*] of the art is to intuit the cause why men seek after an end; whence one gathers that the work of rhetoric is put there to contemplate and see the cause why the things that people say generate conviction [*fides*]. And from these considerations the teaching of this thesis is apparent.

Fifth thesis: When Aristotle put in his definition these words, "what, in any thing whatever," he indicated the matter of this art, namely, all things, as taught above in the seventh disputation. From this text it is apparent how this part of his definition should be explained.

Sixth thesis: the phrase "suitable for persuasion" [*persuasibile*], [94v] explains the end of the art, from which its work is to be gathered. From this one can see why the definition is optimal, since it tells what rhetoric is through its proximate genus, its work, its matter, and its end, all of which are put in place of a differentia.

Seventh thesis: In this definition Aristotle does not exclude the other parts of rhetoric, but omits them as already known lest his definition be too lengthy, and so he is satisfied to give the first part, which is the principle and origin of the others. So, through the expressions "to contemplate" or "to see" he wanted invention to be understood. Nor did he make use of the expression "to find" [*inveniendi*], for if he put "finding" in place of "seeing" some might misunderstand his meaning, whereas "seeing" includes the notion of "finding." That Aristotle did not wish to exclude the other parts of the definition is apparent, first from his better commentators; so Peter Victorio, M. Antonio Maioragio, Antonio Riccobono, and others.[13] Then, because Aristotle treated not only invention but also style and arrangement and delivery, he said that they were useful. And if it seems that he made little of these parts, this does not mean that he rejected them. Rather he subordinated them to invention, which is the principal part of rhetoric, [95r] for it suffices simply to mention them rather than giving them extensive treatment. Again, these parts are thought to be extrinsic if one looks to the reason why they are treated, but not if the speech [*oratio*] itself is considered, for this must be accommodated to the sense of the people. For this reason Robortello's explanation is not completely acceptable when he says that Aristotle's words do not apply to style, as Victorio holds, but only to delivery.[14]

But here a further difficulty remains, namely, why elocution is not contained in the definition. Victorio thinks that by his Greek terms *aidana*, *aidanōn* Aristotle includes the power and use of words, which pertain to elocution. Maioragio says that by the terms "seeing" and "finding" he means the finding of subjects and words, and these are treated by elocution. But Riccobono seems to have judged more accurately when he says that by the terms "seeing" and "contemplating" he includes everything that conduces to persuasion, for which the other parts are also necessary.

So from these theses, if I am not mistaken, Aristotle's definition can be easily understood and defended. Actually it does not differ much from that offered by Plato when he said that rhetoric is the faculty of persuading, that is, the power of persuading, and this [95v] refers to everything required in any way for persuasion. The definitions we have approved in our second disputation are also good definitions. And if one wishes to describe eloquence more fully one can put together the following definition from the matters just explained.

Rhetoric, or eloquence, is a natural faculty, composed of art and exercise, whereby one speaks aptly on any matter proposed, ornately and copiously, to produce popular persuasion.[15] In this description first is placed the genus of rhetoric, that is, a faculty, and the other phrases take the place of the differentia. Of these the first, "by nature, art, and exercise" explains the effective causes of eloquence; the second, "on any matter," the matter; the third, "ornately, copiously, and aptly," the work [*officium*] and the form [*forma*]; and the last, "for popular persuasion," the end. By "art," however, we mean not only the artifice of speaking, which is made up of five parts, but also all the other arts, since this faculty is not found except in a person who is skilled in the knowledge of all subjects.

From what has been noted, and from our explanation of Aristotle's definition, the arguments brought against it are easily dissolved. It should not be thought an imperfect definition, because it suffices to explain its principal part, from which the others are also understood. Nor can this definition be transferred to another discipline, [96r] as is manifest from our disputation. What is said about its matter is easily refuted, for it explains its proper matter, as is obvious from what has been said. How much in error Quintilian was when he did not approve it because it put the end in persuasion, has been covered fully above. Why he said it was a faculty rather than an art we have explained in our third thesis. To the last argument we can reply in this fashion. Of its place, which Trebizond did not translate clearly enough, the following is our opinion. Since Aristotle had said above that the consideration of *pithanon,* that is, of persuasibles, and the consideration of things that are *phainomena pithana,* that is, that seem to be persuasible, such as are those things that can be easily refuted,[16] pertain to one and the same faculty, he said that the sophist, namely, the false and captious disputer, treats of captious arguments of this kind, and not from a faculty, that is, from the very nature of the art, which recognizes both true and false arguments, but rather from the will, because he spontaneously and with the desire of inducing falsehood uses apparent arguments in order to deceive. And so the true disputer, that is, the dialectician, differs from the sophist in this, that the former recognizes fallacious arguments but does not use them, whereas the latter does. For a similar reason in rhetoric there are orators, who from their knowledge [*scientia*] are called orators [*oratores*], who know both probables and what seem to be probables but are not, but they do not [96v] use the latter; others are called orators, who use them; for in the art of speaking a different name is not imposed as it is in dialectic. So in rhetoric both are equally called 'orator,' those who recognize fallacies and use them, and those who recognize them and do not. And this is our opinion about an otherwise obscure text. And since with these ten disputations we have explained fully the nature of rhetoric, and that is what we promised to do, we here conclude this first book.

BOOK II.

ON THE PARTS OF RHETORIC
IN TEN DISPUTATIONS

Third Disputation: Is invention a part of rhetoric?

[107v] To this point we have already demonstrated that eloquence has parts; we have also taught what they are and how many there are. Now it follows that we should begin the disputation of these parts individually, since each of them has its own difficulties. Since [108r] invention holds first place among them, we give our account of it priority. And although the ancient masters of speech held for certain that invention is a part of rhetoric, certain moderns have thought otherwise; this therefore presents us an occasion of examining this question. The following arguments can be offered in favor of their opinion.

First, the authority of Cicero seems to favor this view, since he conceded the invention of topics to the dialecticians, for he wrote thus: "But Aristotle, he whom I myself most admire, proposed certain topics from which all argumentation, not only for disputation among philosophers but also those we make use of in causes [cases], is to be found."[17] And in another place he affirmed that invention is located in the acumen of dialecticians.[18]

Again, according to Aristotle rhetoric is like a certain small part and offspring and likeness of dialectic, for which reason it takes from dialectic its form of inventing and of arguing.[19] From this it happens that Cicero made invention a part of the art of discourse, that is, of dialectic,[20] for which reason it is not a part of rhetoric. And that is why Aristotle says nothing about topics that pertain to invention in his rhetorical works, nor does Hermogenes, another complete master of speech, and many others.[21]

In support of this, topics from which arguments are sought in rhetoric [108v] are completely the same as, and differ in no way from, dialectical topics, as is apparent from their enumeration and description. Therefore invention, which is totally concerned with the topics, is a proper part of dialectic. Why therefore do so many rhetoricians frustrate themselves in writing about invention, since this is taken over by the dialecticians.

Moreover, just as the orator takes matters and opinions from philosophers and from other specialists, for he does not dispute about virtues, or laws, or the republic, so he also takes the method of invention from the dialectician. Thus it happens that Gallus alone speaks about the law, but that if a question comes up about a fact, that pertains to Cicero; if a question of the law, it pertains not to Cicero but to Gallus, as if one were to say that the orator alone takes for his field voice and speech whereas the lawyer takes over the case under discussion.

Indeed, if style of expression is left to the orator and he is rid of invention, he will still retain his name, which he would not retain if he were deprived of eloquence and all the other parts one attributes to him, and for this alone he is said to be fluent and eloquent; therefore eloquence consists only in style of expression,[22] for this alone seems to pertain to the orator, that his speech be rendered with words that are ornamental and abundant. Thus it happens that Cicero, in the second discourse of *De oratore*, put to writing these words: "But what is proper to anyone, this can be judged from him by seeing what and how he teaches; for nothing can be more certain than this, [109r] that all the other arts can perform their function without eloquence, whereas without it the orator cannot justify his name. As for the others, if they are fluent, they have something from him; for unless he be instructed with copious materials, he cannot seek his supply of words elsewhere."

Moreover, all other sciences take their method of inventing and arranging from dialectic, which is the instrument of all the sciences and the arts; why not also rhetoric? For, just as it takes from dialectic its common method of reasoning, so it ought to take its method of invention.

Finally, invention is a kind of natural prudence and perspicacity, and on account of this Cicero once said that invention is more a matter of prudence than of art,[23] and in another place he wrote that it is a matter of prudence in a middle state.[24] Add to this the authority of Quintilian, saying that invention is common to us and the inexperienced and is more from nature than from art; if these things are true, it would necessarily follow that invention is not a part of eloquence acquired by art.

In this disputation I find two opinions among writers: one is that of certain moderns who, with a zeal for contradiction, have introduced a new teaching, affirming that invention is proper to dialectic alone, and thus it is useless for rhetoricians to write about invention or to prescribe rules for it, since the entire method of invention [109v] is to be sought from the dialectician. So thought Rudolf Agricola,[25] and his opinion was fully embraced by Peter Ramus and many others.

The other opinion is contrary to the first; it is what all the ancient teachers of speech constantly taught and what generally has been embraced by those who wrote rhetorics, and so this second opinion should be taken as the common one. We shall demonstrate that it ought to be retained by presenting a number of principles and theses.

In this place one may also take under discussion whether invention is a certain natural power or whether it is a faculty acquired by study and teaching. What is to be thought about this matter will be made clear when presenting the thesis.

First principle: just as there was put in the human mind by nature a certain power of discoursing, which afterwards was developed by perspicacious and ingenious men and put in the form of an art,[26] so also by the same nature there was inborn in human reason a certain power of speaking, which certain shrewd men perfected by notation and use.[27] And these two faculties have the greatest affinity to each other, what Aristotle justly termed *antistrophas,* that is, similar and reciprocal; and yet they share between them instruments and usages and many other things that are different, and, what is most important for our inquiry, can be discerned to have very different goals. For, since dialectic is totally concerned with the method and use of reason, which it [110r] directs lest it err in the knowledge of things, it has this as its goal, to which all its efforts are directed, to set forth the manner of comparing and transmitting teachings and of discoursing. Eloquence, on the other hand, looks to a different goal, that it may attract the minds of the multitude, so that it can arouse and move them to whatever it wishes. From this it results that dialectic is best suited to teaching and learning, eloquence to persuading: the former gives rise to opinion, the latter to persuasion and movement. These faculties are unable to attain such goals if they shall not have found the means whereby opinion or belief and persuasion are generated. And since those things that promote the attaining of the goal must be known and proportioned to the goal, therefore, granted that both these arts make use of invention, nonetheless their methods of invention must be different, as I will explain more fully in the second principle.

Second principle: and so it should be noted in this second place that dialectical persuasion, as we have also stated above, differs in many ways from rhetorical persuasion. The dialectician tries by discourse to generate in people's souls the type of knowledge by which they act, and this is firm and certain to the degree it can be made so by him, and comes as close as possible to science; and so he ought to invent arguments that are especially accommodated to generating such firm opinion. For by the term [110v] dialectician I here understand not only one who knows how to number and differentiate the topics and is able to teach the method of disputing with probability, but one who is able to dispute in the schools of philosophers both for and against any issue, and who holds theses that are held not by science but by opinion and probability alone. A person of this type Aristotle usually called a dialectician.[28] For just as the term rhetor at times signifies one who simply teaches precepts, but at other times one who disputes on any question in the popular mode with full and embellished speech, so a dialectician is at times said to be one who teaches the method and way of inventing arguments whereby one can dispute probably on either side of a question, but at other times one who is adorned with probable doctrine of all things, whereby he is able to dispute, as Gorgias was, on any question that might be proposed in a gathering of learned men.

On the other hand, the persuasion that is proper to the orator is one that arouses a certain faith and opinion,[29] not so much suited to the nature of a thing as to the senses of men, but clearly on the popular level, which sometimes is generated by the weakest of arguments, ones that would never be used in dialectical argument, since they offer little or nothing by way of producing belief. For sometimes to the uneducated multitude things that are not true seem more probable than those [111r] that come closer to the truth. This is possibly the reason why, in the first book on the art of speaking, Aristotle stated that eloquence is similar to the sophistic art.[30] For, just as sophistic arguments, those that are not more probable but that seem probable, are frequently used by Sophists to deceive, so the orator sometimes gives reasons that are hardly probable, provided they seem probable to the multitude, and sometimes he even uses false opinions and errors when these are conducive to persuading to what he wishes. For this reason there is a great difference between the probable that the dialectician seeks, called by the Greeks *endoxon,* and that which orators seek, called by them *pithanon.* And so, since these two common devices look to diverse goals, each of which they are unable to reach without invention, there is a different purpose behind each type of invention; for different means must be used to attain ends that are diverse or at least are viewed under a different formality. But precisely how the inventions of these disciplines differ among themselves will be explained more fully a bit later.

Third principle: by the term invention we can mean two things: first, the thinking out of an argument or of a topic or of a middle, as the dialecticians call it, for the proof of some question proposed, and on this account invention is said to be the thinking out of an argument. An argument is a probability [111v] invented to produce belief, that is, to generate firm opinion.[31] For example, if the question is proposed, "Is rhetoric an art?" to answer this question for yourself a middle term or an argument must be found whereby you produce a belief about this doubtful matter. Secondly, we can take the term invention to mean the thinking out or the inquiry into everything necessary to produce a complete speech or to argue a case, and this seems to be the way teachers of speech take it when they say that many things need to be invented by the orator. The author of *Ad Herennium* divides this into six parts:[32] exordium, narration, division, confirmation, confutation, and conclusion.

If invention is taken in the first way, it seems to be occupied only with the investigation of arguments or middles, and what this entails we shall explain more fully in our book *De inventione*. Understood in this way, a doubt arises whether invention belongs to the dialectician alone or to the orator also, and this is what concerns us in the present disputation, namely, whether the invention and explanation of topics pertains to the rhetorician. If invention is taken in the second way, without doubt it pertains to the orator, for if he cannot discover what is needed to construct a speech he will be completely unable to perform his function, for practically no art can function without invention understood in this way. And the things the orator must invent, [112r] as we may gather from Hermogenes, are somewhat as follows:[33] the question or the cause, the status of the question, the quality of the cause, topics for proving the question or *epicheiremata*, topics for amplification, exordium, the entry into narration, and narration, concerning which matters we shall write plainly and fully elsewhere.

From what has been noted, we may now gather some differences between dialectical invention and oratorical invention. First, the dialectician does not treat all of the topics that the orator is accustomed to use, for example, topics of praise and deliberation, which Aristotle covered fully in the first and second books of *De arte dicendi*; similarly, he does not treat the topics of amplification and extrinsic topics, which although called inartificial and arising extrinsically to the cause, are nonetheless explained in the art and are treated by the orator artificially, as will be told in its proper place. On this account Cicero sometimes seems to divide invention into three parts:[34] one is for proving, another is for uniting souls, yet another for moving those who hear. Second, these two techniques do not discover things that are completely the same, for the one invents things that serve to generate a firm opinion among learned men in philosophical disputation; the other, things that serve also to persuade by popular discourse. The former generates belief, the latter, what serves to move [112v] to action; the first is directed to one goal, the second, to another. Third, the orator uses a method to find, explain, and treat his topics different from what the dialectician uses. But when there are different methods of treating and explaining any matter, according to Aristotle and all philosophers,[35] different arts are thereby constituted; this is apparent in a speech, in explaining which completely different faculties are involved.

Last principle, where this part of rhetoric is to be defined. The author of *Ad Herennium* defined it as follows:[36] invention is the thinking out of things that are true or verisimilar, that render a cause probable. By things that are true, as commentators explain it,[37] he means those that are necessary and completely certain; by those that are verisimilar he means probables, which pertain especially to the art of speaking.[38] The other words in this description are added for showing the characteristics of the arguments that are discovered,[39] namely, that they demonstrate a probable conclusion, one that is verisimilar and apparently true, and that they are suited to generating opinion, and that the audience will easily believe them. Here I would hasten to warn that it is not proper for the orator, nor is this a function of his art, to make up anything false so as to produce belief.[40] A number of authors and professors of this art have fallen into this error,[41] and most egregiously Quintilian, even though he wishes that his orator be a good man. [113r]

Cicero has defined invention in almost the same way, and it is his definition that most later teachers of speech approve as a good definition. From the Ciceronian *De partitione* one can gather this description:[42] invention is the excogitation of an argument, that is, of something invented, or as dialecticians say, middle terms, with which any proposed question can be proved. It is said to be a middle term or argument because it is found by making a stir. In defining it Cicero said that it is a probability invented to produce belief;[43] an argument or invented probability, that is, an invented probable reason, not because it proves, as some explain this, nor do we say that something is credible because it makes one believe; similarly, it is not said to be probable because it is brought forth as a proof, as one author has well noted,[44] but it is said to be such because it can be believed, whether it be true, or verisimilar, or even false. Likewise, by the term belief we should understand any persuasion whatever, and especially that by which one is impelled to do something that the orator is trying to engender in the minds of his audience.

The definitions given apply to invention as it is in use; if one should wish to define it as it is a faculty, it would read as follows: invention is a faculty by which probable reasons are invented to produce belief. By reasons I mean topics and everything else that is necessary to effect persuasion. [113v] These matters being noted, I now state these theses.

First thesis: invention or finding is not so characteristic of any art that it cannot also be found in others. This thesis is to be understood of invention taken in a general way; it is most certain, since there are very many arts that have need of invention, and so in this place no proof is necessary.

Second thesis: invention is completely necessary for rhetoric, so that without it there would be no way that one could have the art. This thesis is manifest from what was said in the second disputation, and it is the common opinion of all authorities. Nor is what some say satisfactory, namely, that rhetoric invents nothing of itself but only embellishes what it takes from others, as will be made clear in the third thesis, and also from what we will say elsewhere of the teaching desired of the perfect orator. And no one, at least, will deny him the invention of words.

Third thesis: invention, as it is a faculty of inventing probable arguments for disputing in a popular way on either side of an issue, is a proper part of eloquence, and it pertains to the rhetor, who must both teach the method of inventing and himself invent. And since our total difficulty is lodged in this thesis, we shall try to strengthen it by a number of proofs. First, by the authority of all the ancient writers, [114r] who when treating of the art of rhetoric elaborated on it especially in this part. Thus Aristotle, who wrote practically everything that looks to the art of speaking, made clear the method of inventing by enthymemes, which are the sinews of a speech, and so he said little about style of expression and little or nothing about the other parts. And when defining rhetoric,[45] he said that it is the power of seeing what is persuasible in any subject matter, and seeing is the same as inventing. Again, Cicero, who entitled his books *On Invention,* as did Hermogenes also, numbered and explained the topics of invention,[46] both in *De partitione oratoria* and elsewhere. Quintilian made invention a part of eloquence,[47] and opened up the fonts of invention fully and accurately. Also modern authors, like Trebizond,[48] and others, carefully explain practically all of the topics and accommodate them to the subject matter of rhetoric. Why is it, therefore, that for no urgent reason we should recede from this common and ancient opinion? Those who do so deservedly receive the criticism of many.

But reasons add to authority, and first, if you take away from the orator the invention and treatment of topics, he will never be able to invent rightly arguments suitable to attaining his goal, if he is ignorant of the method and nature of the topics; for the topics should [114v] be especially accommodated to the cause, since they are selected so as to attain it, and they are ordered with a precise method of which dialecticians teach nothing. Moreover, if it be permitted to take away from the orator the invention of topics, it will also be permitted to take from him the invention of things and leave him nude and unarmed, with the result that he come into the forum as a rabble rouser, a noisy declaimer, and a crier. I ask you, for what reason does the orator deserve so badly of you? In what way can your orator make judgment of things taken from another, when he himself neither invented them nor knows about them? Unless you wish him to structure a speech or argue a case without any judgment! In what way will he speak of consequences and of concurrent circumstances? How will he accommodate words to things? How will he embellish with suitable words things of which he is ignorant? How will his supply of words be abundant when he is needy of things, since an abundance of words flows from the same supply of things? Indeed, if you would take away from him the invention of things, you also take away the invention of words, since, as we were just saying, the invention of words flows from the investigation of things; additionally you take away all embellishments and illuminations of sentences, since these also are taken from things themselves.

More to the point, since rhetoric is a kind of rational faculty that, as we taught in the first book, shines by reasoning, and is very different from the manner of argumentation [115r] and the topics that the dialectician uses, as we have explained above, why do you wish to take from him the invention and treatment of topics, since without these he can conclude and prove nothing? And why do these authors wish to regard this as a part of dialectic rather than of rhetoric, which is an art more inborn by nature, and earlier discovered, and more necessary for all men? And why is it, since the dialectician treats of the invention of topics, that the rhetorician should not treat of them? There is nothing against it, as we have demonstrated more than enough already. You would also take away the subject matter, namely, all things, since the dialectician is also concerned with all things. Finally, lest I urge too many arguments to the contrary, this will be made clear from the replies to the objections and seeing how false they are.

Fourth thesis: invention that is a part of eloquence is not only a faculty taken from nature but also a habitus that is perfected by art and study. With this thesis we wish to condemn the thesis of those who think that this part of eloquence is gotten mainly from nature. We propose that for acquiring eloquence a certain perspicacity and quick movements of the mind adapted to inventing are necessary, and yet we do not regard this faculty given by nature as a part of eloquence. This thesis is briefly confirmed by the following reasons. [115v]

First, if this power of inventing were to depend maximally on nature, why is it that Aristotle, Cicero, and other teachers of speech would have written so much on invention? Why would they have said that it is the most difficult of all the parts of rhetoric?[49] And why would they have developed the part of artificial eloquence? Second, the faculty of invention is found in the knowledge of topics and things, for the person who invents easily is one who possesses a knowledge of many things and knows topics and tractates thoroughly; but these notions are not acquired except by art and study; therefore the faculty of inventing is not maximally from nature. And why, lest we delay too long confirming what is manifest, is it licit to ridicule those, as some do, who think that invention is from nature alone and judgment from art alone?[50] But it is now time, since it is apparent from the thesis offered what is to be held in this difficulty, that we answer the arguments of our opponents.

[Replies to Difficulties]

To the first difficulty, we first throw up to our adversaries the authority of the same Cicero in many texts we have already cited ourselves and in various texts of his *De locorum inventione more rhetorico*. Then, when he attributes invention to the dialecticians, one ought not to think that he wishes to take away from the rhetorician this principal and most important part. He only wishes to indicate that the invention and acumen of the dialecticians—which they, because of their extensive [116r] exercises in discoursing about difficult and involved matters, are very quick at inventing—should be desired in the orator, and to carry over the dialecticians' power of disputing to the method of speaking. This we freely grant, since the person who is practiced in dialectic will be far better and felicitous in treating rhetoric and will be faster in inventing. So when Aristotle hands some topics over to them, he does not intend to despoil his own art of inventing topics, but only to teach that there is some common method of finding topics, and that it is not necessary that rhetoricians invent this, but rather that they use it in their own treatment and explanation of the topics.

From this one can easily answer the second difficulty by saying that the reason rhetoric is like a small part of dialectic is because those things that are said by dialecticians about the method of inventing and reasoning can easily be transferred to the use of rhetoric, but if these are not suitably applied by the rhetorician to his goal and his method of arguing, they will be of little benefit to him. And that we may explain this more fully, dialecticians explicate their form of argumentation very fully, but since orators are accustomed to arrange their arguments in a variety of ways, on this account they generally teach a great deal about the forms of argument that pertain to oratorical use, as we will demonstrate more fully elsewhere. Thus [116v] rhetoricians and dialecticians have a common invention, judgment, and mode of reasoning; but if this be applied to their use, their explanation and treatment are very different. To say that Aristotle said nothing about topics in his rhetoric is entirely false. Since in his day this most powerful part of rhetoric was completely neglected by other masters of speech, he pursued it fully, and indicated the fonts from which one would be able to draw enthymemes. It makes no matter that he did not repeat in his *Rhetoric* certain topics that he explained in his *Topics,* because he thought that they could easily be transposed to rhetorical usage; but he developed others that were more suited to the practice of eloquence. Hermogenes also taught much about topics, which he further reduced to their circumstances and characteristics. Add also that this author did not examine all the topics that pertain to the art of rhetoric, but he omitted many that were known in the schools and concentrated only on those that pertain to the art's use.

That the third argument leads to no conclusion is sufficiently evident from what we have noted, since there are many ways of differentiating the dialectical invention and treatment of topics from the rhetorical. These two faculties are not completely the same, nor do they invent in the same manner. The one invents things that generate opinion, the other more powerfully things that [117r] move souls; one, believables, the other, persuasibles; one, things that are admitted by the learned, the other, those that are understood by the crowd.

The fourth objection will be solved if we can assign the cause why orators do not treat things themselves but take them from philosophers and other disciplines. The reason for this is that rhetoric, as an art in its own right, teaches the method of discoursing popularly, accommodated not only to teaching but also to moving and delighting, and therefore it must treat of invention and arrangement with its own special method, for without this it cannot dispute or speak of anything. On this account it does not take this from the dialectician, as do all the other sciences that make use of dialectical invention and arrangement, but it treats of method by a right of its own. When speaking of things, however, of which he treats, it is sufficient that he take these as treated by other sciences, so that he may speak of them ornately and with a full supply of words. And yet the orator, as I have said elsewhere, should not accept this information as if he were completely ignorant of things, but should be instructed not only in voice and words but also in things, lest he wish to take on the appearance of a crier who uses words alone and be said to be an ignoramus who takes from others what to say, and neither sees nor understands what they mean or what they do. I know not what they call this kind of orator [117v] when they attribute to him words alone; perhaps they call him a rabbler, or an oarsman, or some kind of porter.

What was objected in the fifth place proves only that eloquence is especially proper to the orator, and that is also confirmed by the words cited from Cicero. But the orator would never be able to speak eloquently if he were not equipped with the faculty of inventing and did not know what he wished to embellish.

For the same reason I think that the solution of the sixth argument is sufficiently manifest from what has been said, for the method of inventing and reasoning that is used by the oratorical faculty is different from that used by the dialectical; and as for the reasoning, more will be said about this when we treat of judgment later on.

How the last argument is to be solved is explained in the last thesis. For if rhetoricians occasionally say that invention should not be too artificial, they are comparing it with style, which depends more on art, since it is much to be desired in the orator that he have a certain power of inventing easily that is given him by nature.

GLOSSES AND ENDNOTES

1. Lib. 1, cap. 2
2. Lib. 2, cap. 15
3. Lib. 1, cap. 1
4. Disp. 2
5. Lib. 1 *Rhet.*, c. 1
6. Lib. 2
7. In lib. 1 *Top.*, c. 2
8. Cap. 1
9. Disp. 3
10. Lib. 1, in cap. 2; Lib. 5
11. Lib. 1, cap. 1
12. Cap. 1
13. Petrus Victorius
14. Robertellus
15. Cic. lib. 1 *de Orat.*
16. Cic. *in Lucul.*
17. *De oratore*, lib. 2.
18. *De inventione*, lib. 1.
19. *Rhetoric*, lib. 1
20. *Topica*
21. Agricola, lib. 3, c.
22. Cicero, *De oratore*
23. *De oratore*
24. *De oratore*, 2. [The expression he uses is *prudentiae mediocris.*]
25. Lib. 2, cap. 18
26. Aristotle, *Rhetoric*, lib. 1, cap. 1
27. Cicero, *De oratore*, lib.1
28. *De anima*, lib. 1, tex. 11
29. Aristotle, *Rhetoric*, lib.1, cap. 1
30. Cap. 1
31. Cicero, in part. sub princ.
32. Lib. 1
33. Lib. *De inventione*
34. *De oratore*, lib. 2
35. Lib. 1 *Posteriorum*
36. Lib. 1
37. Franciscus Maturantius
38. Marius Victorinus
39. Ascensius
40. Franciscus Maturantius
41. Ascensius; Aulus Gellius, lib. 1, cap. 6
42. Trapezuntius, Cyprianus Soares
43. *Topica*
44. Jacobus Iod. Strab.
45. Lib. 1, cap. 2
46. *De oratore*, lib. 2
47. Lib. 3, cap. 3
48. Lib. 5
49. Cicero, *De inventione*, lib. 1
50. Gybertus Longolius

Antonio Riccobono on
Aristotle's *Rhetoric*

ARISTOTELIS
Ars Rhetorica

ab

Antonio Riccobono Rhodigino

In civitate humanitatem
in Patavino Gymnasi profitente
latine conversa

Eiusdem Riccoboni explicationum liber,
quo Aristotelis loca obscuriora declarantur,
et Rhetorica praxis explicatur
in orationibus Ciceronis pro Marcello et pro Milone,
ac oratione Demonsthenis ad epistolam Philippi
ab eodem latina facta

Aristotelis *Ars Poetica*
ab eodem latinam linguam versa

Cum eiusdem de re Comica disputatione

Cum Privilegio

VENETIIS, Apud Paulum Meiettum,
Bibliopolam Patavinum, 1579

ARISTOTLE'S
Art of Rhetoric

by

Antonio Riccobono of Rovigo

Teaching the Humanities in the City
At the Paduan Gymnasium
Converted into Latin

A book of explanations of the same Riccobono, in which
Aristotle's more obscure passages are clarified, and
Rhetorical practise explained in the orations of Cicero,
Pro Marcello and *Pro Milone,* and in the oration of
Demosthenes to the Letter of Philip,
made into Latin by the same

Aristotle's *Ars Poetica*
converted to the latin language by the same

With a Disputation of the Same *On Comedy*

With Privilege

VENICE: By Paul Meiettum
Paduan Bookseller, 1579

Riccobono as Interpreter of Aristotle's Rhetoric

The Man and His Works[1]

Antonio Riccobono was born in Rovigo, a city in the Venetian Republic close to Padua, in 1541. After completing his studies in Venice and Padua, where his professors included the eminent rhetoricians Carlo Sigonio (c. 1524–1584) and Marc Antonio Mureto (1526–1584), he was called back to his native city to teach humane letters there. This he did until 1571, when he received the *Doctor iuris* from the University of Padua. We know from a decree of the Venetian Senate that in 1571 he also was appointed to the second chair of humanities at that university—a position he was prevailed upon to accept, though he had intended to enter the legal profession because of its higher income. In the following year Riccobono succeeded to the first chair of humanities, a position he occupied until his death in 1599. An interesting folio of the *rotulus* of professors at Padua for 1592 lists his name under that of Galileo Galileo, who had just begun teaching mathematics there in that year. Whereas Galileo's assignment for the year as shown in the *rotulus* is unspecified (*ad libitum*), Riccobono's is indicated there as "interpreting" Demosthenes and Cicero's *De oratore*.[2]

Apart from his teaching, Riccobono was expert in Greek and Latin and a capable translator of one to the other. Though little known today, his translation of Aristotle's *Rhetoric* was much appreciated and often reprinted in the latter part of the sixteenth century, apparently because it was better adapted than others to the needs of students in the university.[3] At

---

1. Some of the material in this section is adapted from Wallace, "Antonio Riccobono," 149–70, which should be consulted for fuller details.

2. The contents of the folio are reprinted in Antonio Favaro, *Galileo Galilei e lo Studio di Padova*, 2 vols. (Padua: Editrice Antenore, 1966) 2:113.

3. The full title reads *Aristotelis ars rhetorica ab Antonio Riccobono Rhodigino i. c. humanitatem in Patavino gymnasio profitente latine conversa. Eiusque Riccoboni explicationum liber, quo Aristotelis loca obscuriora declarantur, et Rhetorica praxis explicatur in orationibus Ciceronis pro Marcello, et pro Milone, ac oratione Demosthenis ad epistolam Philippi ab eodem latina facta* (Venice: Apud Paulum Beiettum, Bibliopolam Patavinum, 1579). Also included in this edition is Riccobono's translation of Aristotle's *Poetics*, entitled *Aristotelis ars poetica ab eodem in latinam linquam versa. Cum eiusdem de re comica disputatione.* The last named item, the treatise on comedy, has been reprinted, with notes, in *Trattati di poetica e retorica del cinquecento*, ed. Bernard Weinberg, 4 vols., Scrittori d'Italia n. 253 (Bari: Laterza, 1972) 3:255–276, 504–7. With regard to Riccobono's *Rhetorica*, Paul D. Brandes notes that an earlier, partial edition containing only the translation of the first book was also issued (Padua: Laurentius Pasquatus, 1577). Subsequent printings of the complete edition appeared at Frankfurt in 1588, at Lyons in 1590, again at Frankfurt in 1593, at Vicenza in 1594, at Lyons at 1597, and at Avignon in 1599. See Brandes's *A History of Aristotle's Rhetoric*, 88–89, 149–51. The first complete edition of 1579 is used in what follows. It should be noted that the pagination of this edition is faulty in the latter parts that present Riccobono's essays following the translation and analyzing its contents. The first sequence begins at p. 254 and ends on p. 292; the next sequence begins at a second p. 273, which we write as 273², and continues on to p. 282², same notation.

the time printing was invented the most accurate Latin translation of the *Rhetoric* from the Greek was that of the Flemish Dominican William of Moerbeke, which dates from the second half of the thirteenth century. With the onset of the Renaissance and the humanist revival of interest in classical thought, new translations began to appear. The first in the tradition that culminates with Riccobono's work was that of George Trapezuntius (1395–c. 1473), printed at Paris between 1475 and 1477; this enjoyed some ten editions or reprintings down to 1544, when another translation appeared. This was that of Hermolao Barbaro (1454–1493), who taught at Padua, and whose version was printed at Venice and Lyons in that year; this in turn went through several editions down to 1559. Next came the translation of Antonius Maioragius,[4] who taught eloquence at Milan and whose first edition was printed there in 1550; it proved popular and effectively replaced Barbaro's version, being often reprinted down to the 1590s.

At that time the locus of activity shifted back to Padua, where new translations were prepared by Riccobono's two teachers, Sigonio and Mureto. The first of these had his translation printed in Venice and Bologna in 1565 and the second, in Rome in 1577. Mureto's work was reprinted only once, in Rome in 1585, but Sigonio's had six editions, the last at Brescia in 1584. Riccobono's partial translation made its appearance in 1577 and the full work in 1579. The latter went through six editions, the last printed at Avignon in 1599, as indicated in note 3 above.[5] When Immanuel Bekker (1785–1871) published his monumental edition of Aristotle's works in 1831, his first two volumes contained the Greek text. To this he added in a third volume the text in Latin translation, and for this he used Riccobono's translation of the *Rhetoric*, which is found in that volume.[6]

Apart from his translations of the *Rhetoric* and the *Poetics*, between 1579 and 1591 Riccobono published paraphrases of both works. Later he translated Books 3 through 5 of Aristotle's *Ethics* under the title *Ethicorum ad Nicomachum tota illa pars quae est de principiis actionum humanarum et de singulis virtutibus moralibus* (The entire part of the *Ethics to Nicomachus* concerned with the principles of human acts and the moral virtues), (Padua 1593), and later still Book 8 with the title *Doctrina de amicitia* (Teaching on friend-

---

4. This author was born in Maioraggio, a town near Milan, on 26 October 1514. He studied rhetoric and mathematics at Milan, then taught rhetoric there from 1540 to 1542. From 1543 onward he further served as professor of eloquence, doing so until his death on 4 April 1555. Like Riccobono, he was a Latin translator of Aristotle's *Rhetoric*; for a list of the editions of his translation, see Brandes, *A History of Aristotle's Rhetoric*, 142–145.

5. Brandes, *A History of Aristotle's Rhetoric*, 69–160. This work includes many plates illustrating the title pages of these and other editions.

6. On pp. 695–727; see Brandes, *A History of Aristotle's Rhetoric*, 163.

ship), (Padua 1595); his translation of all ten books then quickly followed (Frankfurt 1596). In 1596 he also published at Frankfurt an extensive comparison of Aristotle's rhetoric with that of Cicero. The year of his death, finally, saw the appearance of his extensive collation of Aristotle's *Poetics* with the works of Horace (Padua 1599), which completed a study of Horace he had begun in 1591 and aimed to show how that poet's work conformed strictly to the Aristotelian canons.[7]

Yet another side of Riccobono's career is seen in his historical writings. The first historiographer of the University of Padua, he published his *De Gymnasio Patavino commentariorum libri sex* (Six books of commentaries on the Paduan Gymnasium) in 1598. Years earlier, while still at Rovigo in 1568, he had written a treatise on history, *De historia commentarius* (A commentary on history). But among Paduans he perhaps was best known for his epideictic rhetoric, particularly for the large number of orations he delivered at the university as eulogies and on special ceremonial occasions. Among these Antonio Favaro makes extensive use of a funeral oration Riccobono preached on the death of Giuseppe Moletti (1531–1588), Galileo's predecessor in the chair of mathematics at Padua. We know from this and from his history of the university that Riccobono possessed detailed information about the curriculum in mathematics there in the latter part of the sixteenth century. Although little is available on his precise relations with Galileo, there are also indications that Riccobono was very enthusiastic about this young mathematician coming to Padua. He was in direct communication with Galileo, and conveys the impression that it was Moletti's high regard for his work that led to his being called to replace his friend who had only recently passed away.[8]

Apart from his writings and his university orations, Riccobono also was involved in political activities. Of these, the most important for this volume is his relationship with the Jesuits. This religious order, officially known as the Society of Jesus, had its canonical foundation in 1540 and very quickly had devoted itself to educational activities. The Jesuits first concentrated on the schooling of boys aged ten to sixteen, for whom they furnished a pre-university curriculum of six years duration which included Latin grammar, rhetoric, and humanities instruction. They established a

7. Most of these details will be found in Charles H. Lohr, *Latin Aristotle Commentaries II. Renaissance Authors* (Florence: Leo S. Olschki Editore, 1988) 384–386, and Weinberg, ed., *Trattati*, 3:504–505. Lohr also lists a monograph on Riccobono, C. Mazzacurati, *La Crisi della retorica umanistica nel Cinquecento (Antonio Riccobono)*, published at Naples in 1961. Additionally, Weinberg makes many references to Riccobono's teachings in his classic study, *A History of Literary Criticism in the Italian Renaissance*, 2 vols. (Chicago: The University of Chicago Press, 1961) *ad indicem*; see also citations from this work below at nn. 34, 51, 52.

8. See Antonio Favaro, *Amici e Correspondenti di Galileo*, 3 vols. (Venice: Carlo Ferrari, 1914; reprt. Florence: Libereria Editrice Salimbeni, 1983), Vol. 3, pp. 1585–1656, especially 1630–1.

school in Padua for their own members in 1542, then opened it to external students in 1552. By 1579 they had added a course in philosophy that was an immediate success, attracting eighty students. Within ten years they were offering their full three-year philosophy curriculum based on Aristotle: logic in the first year, natural philosophy in the second, and metaphysics and the *De anima* in the third. Their instruction was generally free, and quite quickly they were in open competition for students with the long established university.[9]

University students were the first to react to this development, protesting publicly against the Jesuit school in various ways. Then the faculty, notably Francesco Piccolomini and Cesare Cremonini, presented their grievances to the Venetian Senate. The basic charge was that the Jesuits were knowingly founding a rival school to draw students from the university, which by law was to be the only university in the Venetian state. Other professors attacked Jesuit teaching as superficial, not based on the text of Aristotle and his commentators, but simply on teachers' notes. A more pressing concern was the fear of lost income, since in the Jesuit school all instruction was free. The Venetian Senate reacted quickly to a fiery oration by Cremonini in support of the professors' case on December 20, 1591, and three days later ordered the Jesuits to restrict their instruction to Jesuit students only. But the decision was not unanimous, and there was much public support in favor of lifting the ban. It was at this point that Riccobono entered the fray, leading the opposition against the Jesuits, pointedly noting that they were teaching his subject, rhetoric, to a large number of students.[10] The conflict continued until 1606, when the Venetian government banished the Jesuits from the state entirely. They were not permitted to return until 1657, at which time they came back to Padua.[11]

Much of the debate during this period was really over the method of teaching Aristotelian subjects, such as rhetoric, as exemplified in Riccobono's essays contained in this section, when contrasted with the synthetic treatments offered in other sections, such as those of Cipriano Soarez and Ludovico Carbone. The Paduan professors concentrated on the text of Aristotle, and usually provided distinctive approaches to a small portion of that text and alternative commentaries on it. The result was a piecemeal exposition that focused on very small segments of Aristotle's thought. The Jesuits, on the other hand, provided integrated surveys of Aristotelian teaching in its entirety. At Padua they claimed that their men gave three hundred lectures in each major course throughout the school

9. For details, see Paul F. Grendler, *The Universities of the Italian Renaissance* (Baltimore and London: The Johns Hopkins University Press, 2002), 479–82.

10. Grendler, 482, n. 21

11. Grendler, 482, n. 22

year, two or three times the number offered by professors at the university. Beyond that, they held monthly disputations that were interdisciplinary in nature and of benefit to all their students. Far from their courses being superficial, the Jesuits claimed, it was their counterparts at the university who were failing to present an integrated philosophy program.[12]

Riccobono's Translation of the *Rhetoric*

Some idea of Riccobono's achievements as a scholar may be gained by examining in some detail his translation of Aristotle's *Rhetoric* into Latin. As a translator he was intent on using simple but uniform Latin equivalents for the technical terms of the Greek text. This is quite evident in his presentation of the topics or *loci*, a key concept in that work. Here he avoids the confusion we run into with our English renditions of "proper topics," "common topics," and "common common topics." His basic term is *locus*, but he does not apply this as broadly as we do. What we might call proper topics Riccobono calls "proper propositions" (*propositiones propriae*) or simply "forms," from the Greek *eidē*, which he renders as *forma*. These he enumerates as deliberative forms, judicial forms, and demonstrative forms. Common topics, on the other hand, he calls "common propositions" (*propositiones communes*); they are the customary four kinds: possible or impossible; past fact; future fact; and great or small. The source of these forms and common propositions is what Riccobono names "the topical faculty" (*topica facultas*); it is this faculty that yields the *loci* Aristotle enumerates in Book 2, chap. 23, of the *Rhetoric*—what Riccobono here names "dialectical topics" or *topici dialectici*. These *loci* provide the basic constituent or element (*stoicheion, elementum*) of the enthymeme, for Riccobono, and either they are "axioms" (*axiomata*) if self-evident and inducing belief (*fides*), in which case they are what Boethius called "maximal propositions" (*maximae propositiones*), or they are "rules" (*paraggelmata* or *praecepta*) associated with these that have wider application, what Boethius called "differences" (*differentiae*). A further division of *loci* are those that function in true enthymemes and those that do not, the second of which Riccobono calls "adumbrating" or apparent enthymemes.

Some have criticized Riccobono's translation of the *Rhetoric* as not being faithful to Aristotle's text.[13] A better evaluation would be that of Bernard Weinberg, who describes the principles behind Riccobono's translation of the *Poetics* in terms that suggest they were pedagogical in intent. These principles, it seems clear from what we have seen, would also apply to his translation of the *Rhetoric*. Of them Weinberg writes:

12. Grendler, 480–2
13. Brandes, *A History of Aristotle's Rhetoric*, 83, n. 29

I think that we may state thus Riccobono's principles for the translation: To achieve a Latin version simpler and more readable than those heretofore available; to adopt, by means of the translation itself, a firm stand on as many of the disputed questions of the text as possible; to render apparent the order, the parts, and the method of the original work.[14]

To achieve these objectives, Weinberg goes on, Riccobono "simplifies word order in such a way as to make it almost as simple as Italian word order; he eliminates all flourishes of style, all farfetched words, all useless attempts at variety and sonority; he adopts a uniform terminology which eliminates ambiguity and doubt."[15] This causes him to depart from precise word-for-word translation, and perhaps his Latinity suffers as a consequence, but the end result is a text that is more palatable to the Italian reader and better suited to the needs of students. His virtues as a pedagogue thus outweigh whatever defects he may have as a translator. In taking a firm stand on disputed points, for example, Riccobono risks his translation becoming a kind of interpretation of the text, but he usually informs the reader of alternate views in glosses or marginal notes. Thus he gives students a clear idea of the way he himself reads Aristotle's text, while alerting them to the possibility of other readings. Further, he breaks up the text into short, numbered sections, thus enabling students to see at a glance the order and the method behind Aristotle's presentation. All of these devices achieve for him praiseworthy instructional goals, even though they do so at the price of his forfeiting claims to elegance in translation.

The simplest way to discuss Riccobono's translation is to provide a sampling of his text. We do so by providing three sets of comparisons taken from the opening chapter of each of the three books that make up the *Rhetoric*. As we have intimated above, most Renaissance Latin translations of that work were attempts to improve the translation of William of Moerbeke, which was lauded for its accuracy in adhering to the Greek but generally proved difficult to understand. That translation was made before 1279 and, with the invention of printing, several editions were published during the Renaissance. These include editions published at Venice in 1481, 1515, and 1537, another published at Leipzig in 1499, and yet another published at Bologna in 1540. Riccobono undoubtedly used one or other of these editions as his base text, but since we have no means of deciding which one he actually used, we have relied on Bernhard Schneider's edition of Moerbeke's Latin version in the volume of *Aristoteles Latinus* published in 1978.[16]

---

14. Weinberg, *A History of Literary Criticism*, 1:584.

15. Ibid., 1:585.

16. The full title is *Aristoteles Latinus*, Vol. XXXI–2, *Rhetorica*, Translatio Anonyma sive Vetus et Translatio Guillelmi de Moerbeka, edidit Bernhardus Schneider (Leiden: E. J. Brill, 1978), 159 and ff.

In each of the selections we provide a current English translation of the passage as contained in Aristotle's text. Following this we show in parallel columns the reading of Moerbeke's translation taken from *Aristoteles Latinus*, and next to it, Riccobono's translation as given in the 1579 text. The juxtaposition of the materials in this way enables us to make a direct comparison between the texts of Moerbeke and Riccobono and to show the relationships between them. Words in Riccobono's text that are the same in Moerbeke's text we indicate in italics, whereas those that are not the same but are synonyms we show as underlined, and those that are neither the same nor synonyms we leave in roman type.

The first selection shows the opening words of the first seventeen lines of text in Book I, Chap. 1, namely, that from lines 1354a1 to 1354a17 in the Bekker Greek edition. For this we use the English translation of Hippocrates G. Apostle and Lloyd P. Gerson in their *Aristotle: Selected Works*.[17] This reads as follows:

> Rhetoric is the counterpart of dialectic; for both of them are concerned with such things which are, in a way, open to all men to know and do not come under any specific science. In view of this, all men can participate in some way in both disciplines; for to a certain extent all men try to examine the views of others and maintain their own, or to defend their own position but attack that of others. Ordinary men do this either randomly or through practice acquired from habit. So since both ways are possible, it is clear that the subject matter [of rhetoric] can be systematized; for it is possible to investigate the reason why some men meet with success, whether through practice or by chance, and all men would now agree that such success is without doubt the work of art. The current authors who compiled works on rhetoric have contributed but a small part of this art; for only persuasive techniques are subjects of the art of rhetoric, while all other matters are merely accessories. But these writers say nothing about enthymemes, which are indeed the framework of persuasion; instead, they busy themselves with matters most of which lie outside the subject. For such affections of the soul as pity, anger, and [that aroused by] slander do not deal with the subject but are directed to the judge.

The respective translations of this passage as provided by Moerbeke and Riccobono are shown below in parallel column:

MOERBEKE'S LATIN	RICCOBONO'S LATIN
Rhethorica <u>assecutiva</u> *dialectice* est; *ambe enim* de talibus quibusdam sunt *que communiter quodammodo* omnium est <u>cognoscere</u> et *nullius scientie* <u>determinate</u>; propter quod et *omnes modo quodam* <u>participant ambabus</u>; *omnes enim* usque ad	*Rhetorica* <u>convenientiam habet</u> cum *Dialectica; ambae enim* in eiusmodi rebus versantur, *quae communiter quodammodo* <u>cognoscuntur</u>, et *nullius* sunt *scientiae* <u>definitae.</u> Quamobrem etiam *omnes quodammodo* <u>ambarum</u> <u>participes</u> sunt.

17. Grinnell, Iowa: The Peripatetic Press, 1982, p. 605

aliquid *et exquirere et sustinere* <u>sermonem</u> *et defendere et accusare conantur.* <u>Multo-</u><u>rum</u> *quidem* igitur hii quidem fortuito *hec* <u>agunt,</u> hii autem *propter consuetudinem* ab *habitu; quoniam* autem *utroque modo con-tingit,* <u>palam</u> quia erit utique ipsa et dirigere; proper quod enim adipiscuntur et hii *propter consuetudinem* et hii a *casu* huius *causam* <u>considerare</u> *contingit,* tale autem *omnes* utique iam <u>confitebuntur</u> *ar-tis* <u>opus</u> esse. <u>Nunc</u> *quidem* igitur qui artes <u>sermonum componunt modicam</u> adepti sunt <u>ipsius partem;</u> persuasiones *enim* sunt *solum artificiale, alia* autem <u>adiec-tiones,</u> *hii* autem *de enthymematibus qui-dem nichil dicunt, quod* quidem *est corpus* <u>persuasionis,</u> *de* <u>extrinsecis</u> autem <u>rei</u> *plurima* negotiantur; <u>commotio</u> *enim et misericordia et ira* et <u>tales</u> <u>passiones</u> *anime non sunt de re, sed ad iudicem;* . . .

Omnes enim quadam tenus *et exquirere, et sustinere* <u>rationem,</u> *et defendere, et accusare conantur.* Ac ex imperita *quidem* hominum <u>multitudine</u> alii temere *haec* <u>faciunt:</u> alii <u>consuetudine,</u> et *habitu.* *Quoniam* vero ea *utroque modo* fieri *contingit;* <u>manifestum</u> est etiam licere eadem facere certa via, et ratione: quia contingit *caussam* <u>intueri,</u> cur finem consequantur tum qui haec faciunt *consuetudinem,* tum qui *casu.* Iamvero *omnes* <u>confessi fuerint</u> huiusmodi *esse artis* <u>munus.</u> Ac qui artes *quidem* <u>orationum</u> ad hoc usque tempus <u>composuerunt, ex-iguam ipsarum particulam</u> confecerunt. <u>Fides</u> *enim sola* continet id, quod *artificio-sum* est; *alia* vero <u>additamenti</u> sunt loco. At *hi nihil quidem de enthymematibus di-cunt,* id *quod est corpus* <u>fidei:</u> *de* iis vero, quae sunt extra rem, <u>tradunt</u> *plurima.* <u>Criminatio</u> *enim, et misericordia, et ira,* et <u>huiusmodi</u> *animi* <u>perturbationes,</u> *de re non sunt, sed ad iudicem* referuntur.

This particular passage contains 161 words in Riccobono's Latin text (ex-panded somewhat over the 149 words in Moerbeke), and of these, 65 words (or 40%) are in word-for-word agreement with Moerbeke, whereas 30 words (19%) are synonyms. The sum of these agreements is 95 words (or 59%) showing some type of dependence on Moerbeke's text. The re-maining 66 words (or 41%) are proper to Riccobono.

The second selection shows excerpts from the first seventeen lines of text in Book II, Chap. 1, namely, that from lines 1377b17 to 1378a2 in the Bekker Greek edition. For this we use the English translation of John Henry Freese in the Loeb Classical Library.[18] This reads as follows:

Such then are the materials which we must employ in exhorting and dissuading, praising and blaming, accusing and defending, and such are the opinions and propositions that are useful to produce conviction in these circumstances; for they are the subject and sources of enthymemes, which are specifically suitable to each class of speeches. But since the object of Rhetoric is judgment—for judgments are pronounced in deliberative rhetoric and judicial hearings are a judgment—it is not necessary to consider how to make the speech itself demonstrative and con-vincing, but also that the speaker should show himself to be of a certain character

18. Vol. 22, pp. 169–171.

and should know how to put the judge in a certain frame of mind. For it makes a great difference with regard to producing conviction—especially in demonstrative, and, next to this, in forensic oratory—that the speaker should show himself to be possessed of certain qualities and that his hearers should think that he is disposed in a certain way towards them; and further, that they themselves should be disposed in a certain way towards him. In deliberative oratory, it is more useful that the orator should be of a certain character, in forensic, that the hearer should be disposed in a certain way; for opinions vary, according as men love or hate, are wrathful or mild, and things appear either altogether different, or different in degree, for when a man is favorably disposed towards one on whom he is passing judgment, . . .

The respective translations of this passage as provided by Moerbeke and Riccobono are shown below in parallel column:

MOERBEKE'S LATIN	RICCOBONO'S LATIN
Ex quibus quidem igitur *oportet* et exhortari et dehortari, et *vituperare* et laudare, et *accusare* et *defendere*, et *quales sententie et propositiones utiles* ad horum persuasiones, hec sunt; *de hiis enim et ex hiis enthymemata* dicuntur, *ut* circa unumquodque est dicere propter genus sermonum. *Quoniam* autem gratia iudicii est rethorica (et enim consilia iudicant et dika iudicium est), *necesse non solum ad orationem* videre, qualiter *demonstrativa* erit et credibilis, *sed et ipsum qualem quendam et iudicem* facere; *multum enim* differt ad *fidem,* maxime *quidem in consiliis, deinde* autem et *in* litigiis, *qualem quendam apparere* et [existimare] *ad ipsos estimare habere* qualiter *ipsam, ad hec autem si et ipsi* dispositi aliqualiter existant (*apparere quidem igitur qualem quendam dicentem* utilius ad consilia est, *disponi* autem aliqualiter *auditorem ad litigia); non enim eadem videntur amantibus et* odientibus, *neque* iratis *et man-* suete *se habentibus, sed* aut *omnino altera aut secundum magnitudinem* altera; *amanti quidem enim eum de quo* facit iudicium . . .	*Ex quibus quidem* rebus oporteat tum suadere, tum dissuadere, tum vituperare, tum laudare, tum accusare, tum *defendere;* et cuiusmodi opiniones, ac *propositiones utiles sunt* ad conficiendam harum rerum fidem, *hactenus* dictum est. *De his enim, et ex his enthymemata* ducuntur, *ut* proprie in unoquoque genere loquamur. *Quoniam* vero iudicationis caussa Rhetorica est (etenim tum *consilia iudicant,* tum *iudicium* est iudicatio) *necesse est non solum ad orationem* respicere, quodmodo *demonstrativa* futura sit, et fide digna: *verum etiam oratorem, et dicentem iudicem aliquibus moribus praeditum* comparare. *Mul-tum enim* interest, primum *quidem in consiliis: deinde* vero etiam *in* iudiciis, tum si *aliquibus moribus* ornatus *appareat* orator, tum si existiment erga *ipsos* aliquo modo *eum se habere;* tum vero *si et ipsi affecti* aliquo modo *sint.* Ac *oratorem quidem quibusdam moribus praeditum apparere* consiliis prodest magis: *auditorem* vero aliquo modo *affectum esse,* iudiciis. *non enim eadem videntur amantibus, et* odeio habentibus, *neque* irascentibus, et leniter *se habentibus, sed* vel *omnino* diversa, vel *magnitudine* diversa. *Amanti enim* videtur is, *de quo* iudicationem habet, . . .

This passage contains 168 words in Riccobono's Latin text (again expanded over the 155 words in Moerbeke), and of these, 68 words (or 40%)

are in word-for-word agreement with Moerbeke, whereas 59 words (or 35%) are synonyms. The sum of these agreements is 127 words (or 75%) showing some type of dependence on Moerbeke's text. The remaining 41 words (or 24%) are proper to Riccobono.

The third and final selection shows excerpts from the first nineteen lines of text in Book III, Chap. 1, namely, that from lines 1403b6 to 1403b24 in the Bekker Greek edition. For this we again use the English translation of John Henry Freese in the Loeb Classical Library.[19] This reads as follows:

There are three things which require special attention in regard to speech: first, the sources of proofs; secondly, style; and thirdly, the arrangement of the parts of the speech. We have already spoken of proofs and stated that they are three in number, what is their nature, and why there are only three; for in all cases persuasion is the result either of the judges themselves being affected in a certain manner, or because they consider the speakers to be of a certain character, or because something has been demonstrated. We have also stated the sources from which enthymemes should be derived—some of them being special, the others general commonplaces. We have therefore next to speak of style; for it is not sufficient to know what one ought to say, but one must also know how to say it, and this largely contributes to making the speech appear of a certain character. In the first place, following the natural order, we investigated that which first presented itself—what gives things themselves their persuasiveness; in the second place, their arrangement by style; and in the third place, delivery, which is of the greatest importance, but has not yet been treated by anyone. In fact, it only made its appearance late in tragedy and rhapsody, for at first the poets themselves acted their tragedies.

The respective translations of this passage as provided by Moerbeke and Riccobono are again shown below in parallel column:

MOERBEKE'S LATIN	RICCOBONO'S LATIN
Quoniam autem *tria sunt que oportet* tractata esse *circa orationem, unum quidem ex quibus* persuasiones erunt, secundum autem *circa locutionem, tertium autem quomodo* oportet *ordinare partes orationis,* de persuasionibus *quidem dictum est,* et ex quot, quia ex tribus *sunt, et* hec que, et propter quid *tota sola (aut enim eo quod ipsi iudicantes* aliquid passi sunt, *aut eo quod* dicentes existementur quales quidam, *aut* in ostendendo persuadentur omnes), *dictum est autem et* enthymemata, unde oportet acquirere (sunt enim *hec quidem* species enthymematum, *hec autem* loci); de locutione	*Quoniam tria sunt, quae oportet* praecipere de *oratione; unum quidem, ex quibus* ipsa fides existet: alterum vero *de elocutione; tertium autem, quomodo* conveniat ordinare partes orationis, ipsa quidem fides, *dictum est,* tum ex *quot sit, quia ex tribus* existit, et haec cuiusmodi *sint,* et quamobrem *haec pauca: aut enim eo quod ipsi* aliquo modo affecti sint *iudicantes: aut eo quia* existiment cuiusdammodi *dicentes: aut* eo quod demonstratum sit, *omnes persuadentur. Dictum* vero *est* etiam, enthymemata *unde* paranda sint. Nam existunt *partim* formae *enthymematum, partim* loci. De elocu-

autem habitum *est dicere; non enim sufficit*
habere que oportet dicere, sed necesse et hec ut
oportet *dicere,* et confert *multum ad* ap-
parendum qualem quandam orationem.
Primum quidem igitur inquisitum *est secundum*
naturam quod quidem natum *est* primo, *ipse*
scilicet *res* ex quibus habent persuasibili-
tatem, secundum autem *locutioni* hec
disponi, *tertium autem* horum *quod* virtutem
quidem *habet maximam, nondum* autem ex-
positum *est, que* circa ypocrisim. Et enim *in*
tragicam et rapsodiam tarde devenit; ypocrisa-
bant *enim ipsis tragedias poete primum.*

tione vero consequens *est dicere. Non enim*
sufficit habere, quae oportet dicere: sed necesse est
etiam haec dicere, quemadmodum oportet,
valetque *multum ad* id, ut is, qui dicit,
cuiusdam modi appareat. Ac *primum quidem*
quaesitum *est secundum naturam, quod* natura
factum *est* primum, *res ipsae* unde possint
persauderi. Alterum vero, quomodo eae-
dem exponantur *elocutione. Tertium autem,*
quod vim *habet maximam,* et *nondum* tentatum
est, ea, quae pertinent ad actionem. Nam *in*
Tragicam, et Rhapsoediam sero venit. Agebant
enim ipsas Tragoedias primum *poetae.*

This passage contains 168 words in Riccobono's Latin text (expanded very slightly over the 166 words in Moerbeke), and of these 93 words (or 55%) are in word-for-word agreement with Moerbeke, whereas 51 words (or 30%) are synonyms. The sum of these agreements is 144 words (or 86%) showing some type of dependence on Moerbeke's text. The remaining 24 words (or 14%) are proper to Riccobono.

These figures show an interesting progression. As one moves from the first book to the third book of the *Rhetoric,* Riccobono's text shows more and more agreement with that of Moerbeke, moving from an initial 59% dependence at the beginning of the first book, to an 75% dependence at the beginning of the second book, to an 86% dependence at the beginning of the third book. When one averages out these figures, the average dependence in the samples taken turns out to be 73%, which is surprisingly high for a text that has been criticized for not adhering closely enough to the Greek text.

With regard to the specifics of Riccobono's translation, it may suffice to give one instance that shows his concern for students and their possible difficulty in dealing with terms to which they are unaccustomed. This occurs in the first sentence of the second chapter of Book I, where Riccobono is explaining the definition of rhetoric. There he states that rhetoric is concerned with the persuasible, which offers a convenient way of differentiating it from dialectic, which is concerned with the probable, as he explains fully in his essay on the nature of rhetoric. In Greek the persuasible is *to pithanon,* which translates into Latin as the singular *persuasibile.* This Greek term occurs three times at the end of the first chapter, first in its plural form, *ta pithana* (1355b11), and twice in the singular (1355b16); it also occurs in the definition of rhetoric at the beginning of the second chapter in the singular (1355b26). Moerbeke gives a literal word-for-word translation each time, *persuasibilia* for the plural, *persuasibile* for the singular.

Riccobono, however, expands the translation in each case, possibly because *persuasibile* is not a common term and might offer difficulty for students. For the first occurrence at 1355b11, which Moerbeke translates as *videre existentia persuasibilia circa unumquodque* (to see what persuasibles exist in any matter), Riccobono gives *videre quae in quaque re possunt apponi ad persaudendum* (to see what in any matter can be used for persuading). For the two at 1355b16, which Moerbeke translates as *haec autem quod eiusdem persuasibile videre et apparens persuasibile* (to see what are the persuasibles or apparent persuasibles of the same), Riccobono gives *haec autem eiusdem esse videre tum appositum ad persuadendum tum quod videtur appositum* (to see what is appropriate or what seems to be appropriate for persuading of the same). And for the definition of rhetoric at 1355b26, which Moerbeke translates as *Est itaque rhetorica potentia circa unumquodque considerandi contingens persuasibile* (Rhetoric therefore is the power of considering whatever happens to be persuasible in any matter), Riccobono gives *Sit ergo rhetorica facultas videndi in quaque re quod contingit esse ideoneum ad faciendam fidem* (Rhetoric is thus the faculty of seeing in any case what happens to be suitable for producing conviction). In all these instances Riccobono, one might say, is not providing accurate translations, yet they convey the sense quite clearly and cohere well with the terminology he explains fully in his essay on the nature of rhetoric.

Riccobono himself was aware that his translation differed from others that were current in his day. To explain the thinking behind his approach, he prefaces his translation with two brief pieces. The first summarizes the entire argument Aristotle develops throughout the *Rhetoric*. In explaining this, Riccobono ties the terminology he develops throughout his translation into Aristotle's basic argument. The second is a brief note "To Readers," wherein Riccobono gives specific hints on how his translation relates to the work of other translators. We provide translations of both pieces, which follow this introduction.

Our translations here, as in previous sections, are given in idiomatic English and adhere closely to the text. Riccobono supplies no documentation for his statements apart from what he gives in his exposition, but we have inserted a few explanatory notes to his second essay, which are appended to it as endnotes.

The structure of the 1579 edition of Riccobono's *Rhetoric,* which is the main source for our treatment of him in this volume, is as follows:

Dedication to Stephanus Batoreus / fol. a2–a6
The Argument of Aristotle's *Art of Rhetoric* / fol. a7–a9
To Readers / fol. b1–b7
Errata / fol. b8
Latin Translation of the *Rhetoric* / pp. 1–198

In what follows we present our English translation of the front matter of the volume plus three of the essays Riccobono appends to his translation, essays which demonstrate his skill as a commentator on Aristotle's text. The first of these essays is on the nature of rhetoric, the second on the nature of oratorical demonstration, and the third on the oration of character.

Dedication to Stephanus Batoreus of Transsylvania

[Laudatory dedication, then at a4ᵛ:]

. . . Although I profess that I owe you everything that can be offered by a most grateful soul, and since it is not in my power to grant what your great merits deserve, lest one who gives nothing be thought ungrateful when he could give but the smallest gift, after Aristotle's *Art of Rhetoric* was converted into Latin, and it was decided that it be published, I thought to dedicate it to your most famous name, so as to bring back to your memory things you had often heard from me. I did not fear that you would not have gratitude for what Aristotle, the greatest of all philosophers, wrote about the art of speaking, especially in the language that offers you the greatest delight. That almost divine author seems to be little known by many for no other cause than that he is translated obscurely, even though other very erudite men have interpreted him. I have thought to interpret him in such a way as to make his excellent and unique teaching clearer to my audience and to take on the task of interpreting—an opportunity which hardly ever occurs in the brief curriculum of those of us who dispute publicly—in this way that is more brightened up and accommodated to the studies of youth. And so I have tried to interpret the three books of Aristotle in the easiest way possible, and for greater facility to number their component parts, which are like stars in this great heaven in which all of eloquence is contained. I have tried also to explain the more obscure passages, while covering the contents of the entire work. All of these things I know will be most pleasing to you as an outstanding patron of eloquence. . .

The Argument of Aristotle's *Art of Rhetoric*

Since the art of rhetoric provides the orator with three important parts, invention, which includes proof (*fides*), style (*elocutio*), and arrangement (*partium dispositio*); and since the notion of invention includes a threefold art making use of demonstration (*demonstratio*), character (*mores*), and emotion (*affectus*); and since oratorical demonstration consists in the enthymeme and the example, and is drawn partly from propositions (*propositiones*) that are proper to each genus, partly from those that are common (*communes*), and partly from dialectical topics (*logici Topici*): Aristotle proceeds from the more proper to the more common [sic]; and therefore having treated the definition of rhetoric, and having distinguished between proof (*fides*) and enthymeme, and well supplied example, he enumerates in the first book propositions that are proper to the individual genera, which he himself calls forms (*formae*), with which anything in the deliberative genus can be proved useful or pernicious, in the demonstrative, virtuous or ugly, in the judicial, just or unjust.

In the second book are included both the common kinds of causes (*caussae*) and things that are common to all the genera. The common kinds of causes are character (*mores*), emotion (*affectus*), and some kinds of propositions, such as that of the possible or impossible, of the future or non-future, of fact or non-fact, of large or small, which seem to be found in all kinds of causes. Also common (*communes*) are the dialectical topics (*loci Topici*), which are suitable for all questions apart from those relating to the kinds of causes. Nor does Aristotle treat proper and common propositions together, because he wishes to differentiate the more proper from the less proper, and he judges character and emotion to be more proper to causes in which souls are mollified or aroused than to dialectical topics, which are of value for treating any question whatever. But he treats of character and emotion before he treats propositions that are common to the kinds of causes, because in the method of demonstration these seem to be conjoined with the dialectical topics, with which they have the greatest affinity. We, however, for reasons of facility have put all of our treatment of oratorical demonstration in one place. Thus there are two parts of the second book, one concerned with what is more proper, the other with what is more common; and on this account the treatment of character, emotion, and common propositions of causes should be read before the treatment of places (*loci*).

What is then left is to explain proof (*fides*) that is common to all, since what is proper has already been covered. Here Aristotle writes first of the character of the speaker, then of the emotions, and after that of the character of the audience, because emotions are also considered as moral matters to the extent that speech is addressed to them, since emotions are properly discussed in rhetoric insofar as they are aroused or quieted in the souls of the auditors. On this account they can serve for both character and the emotions, and so they have been inserted between the first and the second part of the moral oration [*sic*]. Thus Aristotle first teaches that three virtues (*mores*) are to be evident in the orator, prudence, probity, and benevolence; then he treats extensively of the emotions, and indeed in a remarkable ordering, so that each emotion is easily understood following its definition, whom it affects, toward whom, and in what matters, and how each emotion is aroused. Beyond this he teaches how, for the four kinds of character that are usually found among the auditors, the oration is suited to their emotions, habits, ages, and fortunes; and this is the second part of the moral oration. The third part pertains to style, which Aristotle treats in the third book, and which we treat in conjunction with the other parts, so that we may retain our projected plan for ease of treatment. Aristotle adds the common propositions (*propositiones communes*) for the kinds of causes, and, in the last part of the second book, the topics of examples and enthymemes. And this is the first part of rhetoric from the viewpoints of order and dignity, namely, that concerned with things (*de rebus*).

The second part is concerned with words (*de verbis*), and it contains all the elements of style, in which both simple (*simplicia*) and compound words (*coniuncta*) are considered. Among simple words: proper (*propria*), foreign (*immutata*), and domestic (*domestica*), also metaphor (*translata*), epithet (*epitheta*), diminutive (*diminutiva*), frigidity (*frigida*), and simile (*imagines*). Among compound words: style that is pure (*emendata*), pompous (*tumida*), and appropriate (*decora*), as well as metrical (*numerosa*), continuous (*fusa*), and periodic (*versa*), both urbane (*urbana*) and agreeable (*conveniens*).

And just as the first part of rhetoric is concerned with things, and the second with words, so the third part is concerned with the parts of a speech and their arrangement (*dispositio*). Concerning this Aristotle treats how the sources of demonstrative exordia (*procemia*) are taken from praising and blaming, from persuading and dissuading, and from appeals to the audience; how the proper function of the judicial exordium is to indicate the purpose of the speech, among which are things common to other kinds of rhetoric (*communia*) and remedies (*medicamenta*) derived from the speaker, from the adversary, from the hearer, and from the subject itself (*a re ipsa*); how the deliberative exordium is taken from mere suspicion of a crime (*ab obiectione criminis*), from denying the fact (*a depulsione*), from exaggeration (*ab amplificatione*), from understatement (*a diminutione*), and from embellishment (*ab ornatu*). Thus narrations are appropriate for the demonstrative genus, not completely but in parts; for the judicial, completely; for the deliberative, in no way at all, unless they be assumed. And so amplification is appropriate for demonstrative proof (*fides*), the example, for deliberative, the enthymeme, for judicial. Then the function of the peroration is to dispose the audience properly, to amplify, to arouse, to refresh the memory. And all of these matters are treated in the third book, whose first part is concerned with style, whose second, with arrangement.

To Readers

Since our translation (*conversio*) differs in many respects from other translations, and to point out all of these would be too lengthy a task, we thought it worth the effort to note some few of these, from which the pattern (*argumentum*) can be transferred to all the others, and to leave the rest to your diligence, to let you decide what you can do easily should you wish to compare it with others. We have spared no labor to make it useful for you, and try without ceasing to help your studies as best we can. Meanwhile accept this explanation for the other places.

[After this, Riccobono references thirty-three pages in his translation, mostly concerned with particular Greek words and how he has rendered them into Latin. In ten of these he compares or contrasts his translation with those of other translators. Those most frequently mentioned are Petrus Victorius (1499–1585) and Marc Antonio Muretus (1526–1584). Two references are made to the work of Christophorus Rufus, a little known sixteenth-century author whose commentary on the *Poetics* is preserved in a manuscript at Ferrara. One reference each is made to the translations of the well known Marc Antonio Maioragius (1514–1555) and Vincentius Madius (1498–1564), and mention is made of a certain Mattheus Macinus, whose scholarship Riccobono admired but about whom nothing is otherwise known. Riccobono's own translation was much influenced by that of the Flemish Dominican William of Moerbeke (c. 1215–1286), composed around 1278, as explained above.]

ON THE NATURE OF RHETORIC

[201] Wishing to explain Aristotle's teaching on the nature of rhetoric, we must investigate its definition, since a definition is what explains the nature of a thing. So, since definition is composed of a genus and a difference, we first inquire into the proximate genus of rhetoric; then we turn to investigating its difference. In this enterprise we make special use of Aristotle himself, who defined it in optimal fashion, fashioning it from the art of reasoning and from tradition concerning morals and emotions, and from this made a unity that is perfect and complete. We proceed to our task.

The Genus of Rhetoric

Some wish to make the genus of rhetoric art (*ars*), others science (*scientia*), others faculty (*facultas*) or force (*vis*), or power (*potentia*). Which of these was Aristotle's opinion we explain briefly. But there is no doubt that rhetoric, from his teaching, is an art. This follows from the definition of an art he gives in Bk. 6 of the *Ethics*, [202] that it is a habit of making (*efficiendi*) with right reason, in which genus are found all operative arts. It follows more certainly from the argument he uses at the beginning of the *Rhetoric*, because all regard the function of an art to be to look into the cause on whose account men seek an end, and rhetoric clearly fills that function. There art is taken in a general way, so as to include all sciences and faculties and arts, both liberal and operative, all of which contemplate a cause so as to obtain an end. So art is indeed the genus of rhetoric, but not the proximate genus.

Moreover, it seems that Aristotle indicates that rhetoric is a science, since he wrote that rhetoric is to be estimated as from science and choice. But undoubtedly he named it a science from its being a faculty, since the nature of science is alien to rhetoric, for science is concerned with necessary things, rhetoric with contingents. For the same reason he also wrote as follows: "Should anyone try to construe dialectic or this discipline not as faculties but as sciences, he would implicitly destroy the nature of both, from the fact that the one joining them would pass into the sciences of certain subject matters, and not only in the manner of reasoning." He therefore used the word faculty as the proximate genus of rhetoric, not in the sense in which faculty is taken most broadly to denote all disciplines concerned with contemplating or with acting or with effecting, or including all powers that are principles of change in another, but strictly, namely, insofar as they include only arts that equally demonstrate contraries, and of these there are only two, rhetoric and dialectic, as Aristotle himself testifies.

First, therefore, it should be noted, as [203] Alexander teaches in the first book of the *Topics,* that faculties or powers are properly called such if they demonstrate contraries in similar ways, since that over which one has power one can do in contrary ways. He rejects the opinions of those who think that these arts are called powers because they instruct others who use them with power and excellence. That certainly would apply to the military art and the discipline of law, and then these also would be faculties, not our two alone, as Alexander writes. He also rejects that they can be put to good or bad use, for in this way they would be sciences as well as faculties. Thus the words of Aristotle are to be understood in the sense that rhetoric and dialectic alone equally demonstrate contraries, for he knew that they alone are properly faculties. So we read in the text: "But from the other arts, no syllogism concludes contraries; dialectic and rhetoric alone do this, for they similarly are both of contraries." Alexander puts it this way: "Those who are versed in the sciences, while having knowledge of contraries, nonetheless aim in their science definitely to establish the one side of the contrary that is the better: the doctor to cure, the wrestling master to safeguard a strong bodily constitution, and others to have the better outcome. For the knowledge of the contraries they pursue is not their principal object, for from the knowledge of one contrary that of the other follows, just as from the knowledge of things that produce health there follows the knowledge of others that give rise to illness. The dialectician and the rhetor, therefore, have as their object and in a similar way the demonstration of contraries." Thus [204] far Alexander.

Whence it is apparent that rhetoric and dialectic can argue equally to contrary parts; and whereas the other arts tend to one part, these do not incline more to one side than to the other. This despite the fact that Aristotle counsels that we should use rhetoric to demonstrate the true and the just, which are better by nature than their contraries. He also writes that one must be able to persuade contraries, just as we do in syllogisms, not that we should do both, because it is not proper to persuade to evil, but so that one not be unaware of how things are and be able to answer those who are proposing reasons that are unjust. This indeed is Aristotle's advice, and it is not the nature of the other arts to demonstrate contraries equally, we have just noted, and so ours should properly be called faculties.

With the proximate genus of rhetoric known, its differences are to be investigated, and these will be delimited through their end, their function, the matter they consider, and their mode of considering it.

The End of Rhetoric

The end of rhetoric is to persuade, despite what Quintilian may say, for he reproves Aristotle for not giving rhetoric its true end, which in his view is not to persuade but to speak well. But whatever is ordered to another is not an end, for an end is that to which all others are ordered and itself to no other. To speak well in the oratorical art is ordered to something else, namely, to persuasion. Therefore it is not an end, unless we understand end as something that is not the last but is ordered to it. But the end, Quintilian says, is not to be located in the event; it should always lie beyond it. We reply that end can be understood in two ways, either as the thing proposed, which is called the *skopon,* or as the attainment of the thing proposed, which is called the *telos.* Whence Galen wrote [205] that the *skopon* of the medical art is health, the *telos,* the attainment of health. We have already stated that in arts that are not sciences, the first is always the end whereas the second is not. Since they depend on other things and do not contain in themselves the way to achieve the object proposed, as do the mathematical sciences, wherein the attainment of the proposed end is assured, they do not always attain what they seek. Thus it is sufficient that they provide whatever one can toward attaining it. So, since the *skopos* of rhetoric is to persuade, the *telos* that the soul of the hearer be moved, it suffices for rhetoric to omit nothing that might conduce toward persuasion, even if it does not always actually persuade.

But there is a difficulty here: other arts persuade also, therefore to persuade is not the proper end of rhetoric. Proof of the assumption: one reads in Bk. 1 the following. "For from other arts one exercises the faculty of teaching and persuading in every matter subject to it; moreover, there is a third utility in rhetoric, for the other arts do not persuade all persons but only those who know their principles, whereas rhetoric persuades everyone." The doubt is thus removed by saying that persuade can be taken in two ways, one way in general, to include even that from the proper principles of the art, among those who hold them, and this is not the persuasion of rhetoric; the other in particular, when one is persuaded from probabilities and commonly conceded opinions, and this is proper to rhetoric. So also *to pithanon,* that is, what is able to persuade (the persuasible), can be understood in two ways: either commonly with the other arts, which comes from their particular propositions, or properly, which is found only in rhetoric and is accommodated to common understanding, about which much below. For which reason, when to persuade is said to be the end of rhetoric, this means in particular, not in general, and properly, not commonly.

The Office or Work of Rhetoric

[206] Having established the end, the office or work *(munus)* must be stated. As has been noted above, the function of an art is to look into the cause that explains why men attain an end; the function of rhetoric is to contemplate the cause that explains why those who speak persuade. It has been sufficiently established that the end of rhetoric is to persuade; thus rhetoric should contemplate things that are suitable for persuading, and all its contemplation should be directed to persuasion as to an end. Clearly therefore did Aristotle write: "Not that persuasion is its function, but to see what is able to persuade in any matter." Just as in the definition he uses the word *theoresai,* in explaining the function he uses the term *idein.* Quintilian takes this to mean discover, and reproves Aristotle because he includes only invention, whereas without style there cannot be a speech. Some reply that he has included style, against what Quintilian thinks; others that it has not been included, but this is not of interest. We follow the first opinion, that of Petrus Victorius and of M. Antonius Maioragius, outstanding men of our profession. For Victorius thinks that Aristotle takes style to be contained in the words *pithana* and *pithanon,* which include the power and use of words. Maioragius, on the other hand, takes him to apply invention not only to things but also to words. We would add that the argument for style being included would seem able to include the other parts of rhetoric also. For *theorein* and *idein* mean to intuit and to see, and these are apposite for persuading. So rhetoric is the faculty of seeing whatever is conducive to persuasion, that is, what invention, what arrangement, what style, and even what memory and delivery [207] are suited to persuasion. This is what a most noble and learned man, Augustinus Valerius—patrician of Venice, whom I think worthy of being honored above all, not only because he is bishop of Verona but because he is worthy of even greater honor than the episcopate—seems to hold, along with me. For passing over the less artificial parts he defines rhetoric as the faculty of discovering, arranging, and styling.

As to those who think that style is not included, they say that style is accidental to rhetoric and that what is accidental is generally not put in a definition. They adduce the authority of Aristotle, maintaining in Bk. 3 that style is a light matter, that it is necessary to address things themselves, and that everything apart from demonstration is more or less frivolous. This response does not appear very solid to us, since we think that style is accidental to the matter with which the orator is concerned, but not to the rhetoric. At the beginning of Bk. 3 Aristotle locates style among the three principal parts of rhetoric, and Cicero looks for it especially in the orator, since it is not from invention, nor from arrangement, or memory, or even from delivery that the orator gets his name, but rather from style, in Greek *rhetor* and in Latin *eloquens*. Also, because men can indeed be praised for their acumen of discovery and from their beauty of arrangement and of prudence, but it is only from eloquence that they are seen to be eloquent. With regard to the text of Aristotle we say: the expression *kai dokei phortikon* should be understood, not of eloquence, as Victorius, along with many others, thought it should be, but of delivery, as Robortellus, a man both most learned and most eloquent, has observed in his handwritten annotations to Aristotle's *Art of Rhetoric*. These were [208] shown to me by Salvator Bartolutius, a great friend of his and also of mine, respected for his great learning and outstanding character.

But, that we might give additional treatment to style, we say that something can be considered to pertain to rhetoric in two ways, as is gathered from Aristotle's own words: either as that which is correct or as that which, while not correct, is necessary for the orator. In the first way style is a light matter, for if we look to what is correct, everything apart from demonstration is frivolous; in the second way, much comes to be of value because of the depravity of the audience. We add that style is always considered to be in rhetoric in this second way as necessary, since there we read that the entire treatise of rhetoric is ordered to opinion and to the depravity of the audience. Therefore this distinction we have noted has validity. Many things should be retained in the nature of rhetoric apart from demonstration, such as emotion, character, style, and arrangement of the parts of a speech, about which more below.

The Matter of Rhetoric

After the function (*munus*) of rhetoric the next thing to be looked at is its matter or the things it considers. In so speaking we follow the custom of philosophers and bring out the cause of its proper matter. Elsewhere we will be partisan to the flowers, the charms, the festivities, the pretty arrangements, and the modulations of sounds of speech. Now, to begin with, we observe its matter. Aristotle's opinion here is not completely clear, for, in explaining the function of rhetoric he says that it is to see what happens to be persuasible *peri ekason,* and describing it he calls it a faculty of seeing what may be persuasible *peri ekason,* and elsewhere he tells us that rhetoric is concerned with those things about which we take consultation and for which there is no art, of which kind [209] are civil questions. And so he gives as the mode of rhetoric all matters that are addressed in the manner of civil questions. Because of this his view has received one or other interpretation from rhetoricians. Quintilian writes that Aristotle assigned all matters to rhetoric, and his words in Bk. 2, chap. 16 are the following: "It seems that Aristotle subjected all things to the orator when he said that his is the power of saying what can be persuasible in any matter whatever." But Cicero testifies that the opinion of Gorgias was one thing, that of Aristotle another, for the former said that the orator's subject was everything, the latter that it was only civil questions. So we read in the first book *On Invention:*

Gorgias of Leontini, almost the earliest teacher of oratory, held that the orator could speak better than anyone else on all subjects. Apparently he assigned to the profession a vast—and in fact infinite—material. Aristotle, on the other hand, who did much to improve and adorn this art, thought that the function of the orator was concerned with three classes of subjects, the epideictic, the deliberative, and the judicial (v, 7).

These two opinions are further explained by Cicero in Bk. 1 of *De oratore,* one in the person of Crassus, the other in the person of Antonius. Some most literate men remove the difficulty by restricting the expression *peri ekason* to mean not simply every matter proposed but only what pertains to human actions, and this can be contained within the three types of causes. So is it explained by the illustrious Count Jacobus Zabarella, chap. 18, Bk. 2, where he writes: "Rhetoric looks to action, not to knowledge, and it takes its end from this, that the term 'persuasion' is ordered to action, if its sense is properly considered, and then a person is said to be persuaded when he is convinced by it and wishes to act accordingly." Again in chap. 15 he offers examples, but only of the deliberative, judicial, and demonstrative types, [210] as when one persuades the citizen about things that are suitable and right for the republic, or persuades judges to make judgments justly, or so to act that, by praising the good, they induce others to imitate them or, by blaming the wicked, they draw hearers away from imitating them.

This is the opinion of trustworthy and learned men, but there can be enough doubt on the matter that I propose to mediate between them, not for the sake of refuting them but rather, by juxtaposing contraries, I may make the truth more apparent for those studying eloquence. And first it is true, and indeed very true, that the principal matter of rhetoric is things about which we consult, and things that we do, and these things we do are included among the types of causes just defined. But Aristotle, speaking generally, does not seem to exclude other matters from the function of the orator, not even those that pertain to knowledge, provided the orator treat them in a way that is appropriate for common understanding. For, when he argues that the function of rhetoric is not proper to other arts, he says that medicine is concerned with health and sickness, geometry with the properties of extension, arithmetic with numbers, and likewise the other arts and sciences in their proper subject matters, but the rhetorician with any matter whatever, in a way that is appropriate for persuading. He does not exclude what is treated in other arts, but makes all of them the province of rhetoric if their matters are treated in rhetorical fashion.

Nonetheless Aristotle says at the beginning of the *Rhetoric* that rhetoric, together with dialectic, is concerned with matters of the type that belong to no definite science, and, when he treats of the persuasible, that the function of rhetoric is to deal with matters for which we have no art, and in this way he seems to exclude matters that pertain to other arts. Yet, from the same [211] text, one can respond that, while it is not licit for rhetoric to treat matters pertaining to other arts by using enthymemes proper to those arts, it is licit to use enthymemes taken from common topics and accommodated to common opinion. For concerning proper topics we read as follows: "The more they attain them in this second way, the more they improperly recede from their own way." And, a little later, "The better one selects these types of propositions, the more he is in a science different from dialectic and rhetoric. For if he comes to the principles of some particular art, he will no longer be dialectical or rhetorical, but in the art whose principles he has gotten. Arguments that are common in this way I now call dialectical and oratorical syllogisms, and for these we say there are topics. But these deal commonly with matters of justice, with natural and civil questions, and with many other things that are different in kind, as is seen in the topic of more and less. Nothing is gathered from this type of syllogism, or is offered by an enthymeme, that pertains more to matters of justice than it does to those of nature or of any other subject, and all of these are different in kind."

From these words it is apparent that it is licit for rhetoric to use arguments drawn from common topics not only when dealing with civil matters, which deal with some proposed action, but also with natural things and indeed with any matter whatever. And this great utility of rhetoric was recognized by Aristotle, namely, that the other arts do not persuade everyone, since they use the formality of speaking that arises from the particular science; rhetoric on the other hand persuades all people, since it induces conviction and assent from common notions. Nor is it mindful only of the three types of causes, that is, those of the finite question, but also those of the infinite question, since in Bk. 2, after having taught the things to be investigated in any [212] genus, he says: "Likewise of these matters and of any matter whatever, as concerning justice whether it is good or not from those things that are present in the just and the good." Therefore Aristotle's *Rhetoric*, though it treats especially the three kinds of causes as its principal matter, does not reject other matters.

So we can say, from this teaching, that the matter of rhetoric is twofold: one infinite, the other finite, one more common, which Quintilian noted, the other more proper, which Cicero noted. This also seems to be the opinion of Alexander, when he writes as follows in the first book of the *Topics*: "The orator, therefore, treats of all things though not in the same way as the dialectician, and he is not concerned with any one definite species; so the orator also discusses medical matters, and likewise philosophical and musical matters, but particularly civil matters. And indeed we do not see why the term persuasion should not apply to knowledge, and particularly to popular knowledge, since it is more a kind of assent than is knowledge itself, in the sense that assent is given to those things that pertain to knowledge, and men are led to it by persuasion, that is, by the kind of conviction that is appropriate to common understanding." Here therefore it is proposed to us that most broadly conceived the matter of rhetoric is all things, most narrowly, civil questions alone.

Rhetoric's Mode of Consideration

The matters already considered can pertain to different arts, as the human body pertains not only to medicine but also to gymnastics, to the culinary art, and to others; but the mode of considering makes for one art, as the consideration of the human body precisely as it is healable makes for the art of healing. So the matter considered is common; the way of considering it gives a proper nature. Since rhetoric has the matter it considers in common with dialectic [213] and with politics, that is, the indefinite matter of all things with dialectic and the definite matter of civil questions with politics, it is differentiated from dialectic and from politics by its mode of consideration. For just as dialectic considers all things insofar as they are probable, and politics civil matters insofar as they can be directed to happiness, so rhetoric considers the same things insofar as they are persuasible. For we distinguish what is properly persuasible from the probable, as we explain below.

On this account we have another opinion, that of the illustrious Count

Iacobus Zabarella, who writes in Bk. 2, chap. 18 that, since on Aristotle's authority rhetoric is made up of logic and the civil faculty, it takes its form from logic, whence it gets its form of argumentation, and its matter from political science. But we think that its matter and the things it considers are common not to civil science alone but to logic also, that is, civil questions and all other things besides; and that its form, either, as modern philosophers say, its formal subject, or alternatively, its mode of consideration, are taken from its end. Moreover, since the end of rhetoric is to persuade, it should have its own proper mode of consideration, insofar as either all things or civil questions alone are persuasible. But the persuasible is indeed said to be proper to rhetoric not only in argumentation, or in oratorical demonstration, which it takes from logic, but also in its use of character and the emotions, which it takes from civil science. And this is what Aristotle teaches when he writes: "Artificial proof is threefold: ethics, the emotions, and demonstration." Even Zabarella agrees with this, in the same chapter, when he explains Aristotle's opinion in these words: "He says that persuasion can be effected in three ways, by arguments, by ethical oratory, and by arousing the emotions."

Definition of Rhetoric

[214] To this point the proximate genus of rhetoric and its differences have been explained, and from these Aristotle composed this definition of rhetoric, namely, that it is the faculty of seeing in any matter whatever what happens to be persuasible. Antonius Bernardus Mirandulanus holds, in the second section of Bk. 8, that this definition also applies to dialectic. We think that the probable and the persuasible are what differentiate dialectic and rhetoric, in such a way that dialectic is the faculty of seeing what happens to be probable in any subject matter, rhetoric, what happens to be persuasible in any subject matter. The whole difficulty here lies in the fact that some think that the probable and the persuasible are the same thing (as does Mirandulanus, Bk. 8, sec. ii), whereas others that they are not, and we follow the latter view. Therefore we first consider how the probable and the persuasible can be distinguished on the basis of Aristotle's teaching, and then reply to arguments to the contrary.

What Things Are Probable

Aristotle explains in the first book of the *Topics* that probables are, first, what is approved by all, that good is to be sought, and also health, wealth, and life, and that parents should have honor and other goods; second, what is approved by many, namely, that wisdom is preferable to riches, that the soul is more important than the body, and that the gods exist; third, what is approved by all the wise, namely, that the goods of the soul are greater than the goods of the body, that from nothing nothing comes, and that the virtues are good; fourth, what is approved by most of the wise, that virtue is to be sought for its own sake, that no body is without parts, that there are not infinite worlds; fifth, what is approved by the most outstanding among the wise, namely, that the soul is eternal, that there is a fifth essence; and finally, things that are repugnant to the opinions of the many, even though they are approved by some who are very wise, [215] namely, that whatever exists is unchanging and one, which was the opinion of Parmenides, and that contraries are the same, as Heraclitus thought, and that they cannot be contradicted, as did Antisthenus.

Again, in the first book of the *Art of Rhetoric* Aristotle teaches that rhetoric concludes and deduces not from things previously concluded from a syllogism, for these on account of their length are not suited to an orator, or for speaking to the arbitrator, who is supposed to be unlearned, nor even from things that have not been concluded from a syllogism, for they regard a true syllogism as not being concerned with persuasibles, since persuasibles are not from things admitted or even from probables.

What Is Persuasible

I gather that the persuasible is the acknowledged probable, that is, not the probable in an absolute sense, which can even be approved by some who are very wise, as that contraries are the same, but the probable of this type, that either all or many assent to it. In this sense Aristotle mentions also the acknowledged good and what is agreeable to the ordinary multitude of men, and this consists in a certain common sense or intelligence, and it is not examined, as Cicero says, with the steelyard of the artisan but with the scales of ordinary people. For he writes in Bk. 2 as follows: "For which reason it is fitting to speak not from all things that are probable but from specific things, namely, from what appeals either to those judging or to those who give approval, and which appear so to all or to many." Therefore the persuasible is not everything that is probable but definite things that appear that way to all or to many. Again, dialectic disputes on both sides [*aeque*] of all matters, whereas rhetoric is concerned more with civil matters. The former uses question and answer in the circles, disputations, and congresses of philosophers, the latter, continuous oration directed to the popular intelligence. The former treats more of universal matters, the latter more of singulars. [216] Whence it happens that the former takes for itself the probable as common and as more apt for philosophical discourse, the latter, the persuasible as less common but as more suited to the common intelligence. But the former, since it is concerned with the probable, embraces even the persuasible, insofar as a thing is probable to the extent that it will be approved by all or many; the latter, since its object is the persuasible, looks also to the probable, not in an absolute way as does dialectic, but to the probable that is persuasible. For everything that is persuasible is probable, but not the other way round. Therefore no clearer differentiation can be made between dialectic and rhetoric, in our judgment, than that, since each of them argues from probables, the former seeks the probable in an absolute sense, the latter, the probable that may also be called the persuasible. Things being put this way, certain contrary arguments now have to be examined.

Arguments on the Probable and the Persuasible

First. Mirandulanus has tried to prove that the persuasible and the probable are the same because the probable is also attributed to rhetoric, in these words: "Nor does rhetoric look to the probable that is singular, such as Socrates and Hippias, but to men so affected, just as does dialectic." The followers of Mirandulanus add that the persuasible is also attributed to dialectic, as in book one of the *Topics,* which reads: "There are problems and there are syllogisms concerned with contraries; for they contain a doubt whether things are this way or not, in support of which there are persuasible arguments."

Second. The same text shows that any syllogism that is dialectical is also properly rhetorical, so that the probable and the persuasible are the same, because if the probable and the persuasible were different the dialectical syllogism would be different from the rhetorical; for the one would be from probables, the other from premises that were not probable. The antecedent is proved [217] from the fact that Aristotle wrote that dialectical and rhetorical syllogisms are based on the topics of which he spoke, which are commonly concerned with matters of justice, and natural and civil matters, and matters very different in kind.

Third. Aristotle adds that common topics that do not pertain to any particular science are probables. But persuasibles are also common topics that do not pertain to any particular science, as is apparent from the definition of rhetoric and from the proof of the definition. Therefore persuasibles are probables.

Fourth. The last argument: the verisimilar is probable and the persuasible is verisimilar; therefore, the persuasible is probable. Thus far this learned man on the probable and the persuasible.

With regard to the first argument, we do not deny that sometimes the persuasible is attributed to dialectic, but we do not concede on this account that the persuasible is the same as the probable, since the probable is the genus and the persuasible a species under it. On this account it is not odd to attribute to dialectic the persuasible that is contained under the probable. Nor is the probable attributed to rhetoric absolutely, but only the probable that is persuasible. And since Aristotle frequently names the genus instead of the species, it does not seem remarkable that when treating of the persuasible as the proper matter of the enthymeme he should have called it the probable.

To the second argument we reply that the dialectical syllogism taken from common topics is also rhetorical, not unconditionally, but only when it is concerned with matters that are persuasible; and the rhetorical syllogism taken from common topics is also dialectical, not unconditionally, but insofar as it is contained under the part of logic that considers probables. For the one differs from the other in that the one has the wider extension, [218] the other the narrower, and the one is drawn from all probables, the other from those that are also persuasible. And so it does not follow that the probable is the same as the persuasible.

The third argument we concede, but since the persuasible is probable, we do not think that the one is so identical with the other that the two can be converted.

We can reply in the same way to the fourth argument, where the assumption is even weaker, for not every persuasible is verisimilar, for example the tecmerium and the unnamed sign, the one more perfect than the verisimilar and the other less perfect, and yet both are persuasibles. But more of this below.

Differences Between the Probable and the Persuasible

From our disputation it is established that the persuasible differs from the probable in the same way as a species differs from a genus.

To this may be added a second difference, that the probable is found only in argumentations, whereas the persuasible is found also in ethics and the emotions.

Also a third, that the probable pertains to opinion, the persuasible to belief and persuasion, since opinion is more universal than belief and persuasion, so that the former seems to pertain to dialectic, the latter to rhetoric.

Again a fourth, that the probable is more argued than stated, the persuasible more stated than argued. The former is treated by question and answer, the latter by continuous speech. For to argue is proper to dialectic, to speak, and even to speak clearly and eloquently, to rhetoric; this is apparent from the etymology of the two. For Alexander wrote of dialectic in

the following fashion: "Appropriately has this method been named dialectic. For *apo tou dialegesthai* means what is said by way of argument, and this
indeed consists in question and [219] answer. For the one who questions
about all matters and the one who answers alternate with each other, so
that the one answering takes from the questioner whatever it is they are
arguing about. It is well enough known that rhetoric and rhetor are called
such *apo tes rheseos*, that is, from speech and style, and this is found in continuous speaking.

Thus the difference between rhetoric and dialectic is sufficient from its
definition; the explanation of this advanced by Aristotle does not apply to
dialectic, as Mirandulanus thinks. Aristotle recognizes what is proper to
rhetoric in these words: "For the rhetoric on any matter, as I say, seems to
look into what is persausive."

Since, moreover, the persuasible includes a threefold belief, demonstrations, emotions, and characters; and demonstrations are taken from the
art of arguing, emotions and characters from civil discipline, appropriately
did Aristotle, so as the better to express the nature of rhetoric, write: "It is
sunkeisthai (composed) of analytical science and politics, and it is *paraphuesti*
(akin) to dialectic and politics, and *homoian* (similar) to dialectic and sophistic, and *antistrophon* (corresponds) to dialectic, and *morionti kai omoioma*
(a kind and similitude) of dialectic." What each of these expressions
means must briefly be considered.

Rhetoric Composed of Analytics and Politics

Rhetoric is said to be composed of analytical science and of politics,
which is concerned with morals. That is, from that universal and common
logic that makes use of the syllogism, and is said to be *Analytics* from analysis, that is, the dissolution of a thing into that of which it is composed, because the syllogism resolves to its principles; and also from civil science,
which studies morals and emotions. In this way rhetoric has a twofold nature, one from logic, whence it takes argumentation, the other from civil
science, whence emotions and ethics. For although in this [220] text only
ethics is named, yet emotions are related to ethics, since Bk. 2 divides
ethics into emotions, habits, characters of age, and characters of fortune.
Emotions are considered in rhetoric as a type of morals, to the extent that
speech can be applied to them; they are differentiated from morals by the
way in which they are aroused by the speaker in the souls of the hearers.
That is the reason Aristotle treated the emotions in the first and second
parts of moral speech.

Rhetoric Akin to Dialectic and Politics

Rhetoric is said to be somewhat akin to dialectic and to the discipline that treats of morals, which can with some reason be called politics. For dialectic and politics are like large trees from whose roots rhetoric rises like a branch. Dialectic is taken to mean the part of logic whose arguments treat probables and is called the *Topics,* as Alexander notes in his *Topics.* For, from the viewpoint of the matter, topics and dialectic are the same; but if invention is distinguished from judgment, then topics discovers probable arguments whereas dialectic judges from a collection of arguments which are necessary and which captious. According to Boethius, Aristotle gave no treatise on judgment, since, to use his words, his work "is full of and makes readily available ways of judging middle terms when one knows the extremes." Dialectic is taken in another way to mean the entire art of discourse, since it is written in the introduction to the *Rhetoric:* "to see those things that equally apply to all syllogisms, for dialectic is either a whole discipline itself or it is a part of another." Alexander adds that dialectic is taken by Plato to be a way or method of dividing, that is, of distributing one into many and of composing many into one. In the *Topics* Cicero takes [221] dialectic to mean the entire part of logic that judges all arguments, necessary, probable, and captious, and distinguishes it from the topics, which invents arguments. Politics, moreover, denotes in one sense the whole of philosophy concerned with action, and considers the ethics of individuals, of the family, and of the republic; in another sense it denotes only that part that treats of public administration. Since Aristotle already has said that rhetoric is akin to dialectic and to politics, we take him to mean the part of logic that treats probable arguments and the special part of philosophy concerned with ethics to which rhetoric is conjoined, what is treated in the *Republic.* And although rhetoric is akin to dialectic and to politics, it is akin to politics in a way different from dialectic. For it is not properly politics, as Aristotle indicates when he writes: "Rhetoric takes on the person of politics and appropriates it to itself, partly through ignorance, partly through arrogance, and partly for other human causes."

Rhetoric Similar to Dialectic and Sophistic

Rhetoric is said to be similar partly to dialectic and partly to sophistic, for it conforms its precepts, as Aristotle himself testifies, either to the truth, or to what appears true, and it demonstrates from things that are suitable in any subject matter to induce belief, and so, to the degree that it seeks truth it is similar to dialectic, to the degree that it seeks what appears to do so, to sophistic. For since in the form of argument, as he also says, the one who uses the syllogism is called a dialectician, the one who uses the apparent syllogism, a sophist; the former is thought to proceed from a faculty or a power, the latter from choice, since the former has the faculty of using false [222] and captious arguments but does not seek his advantage in doing so, whereas the latter deliberately chooses them. In the rhetorical art not only the one who uses the persuasive is called an orator, but also the one who uses the apparently persuasive, and he is said to do so either from a faculty, because he has the faculty of using either the true or the false, or from choice, because he sometimes seeks his own advantage from the falsely persuasive. Clearly therefore Aristotle does distinguish dialectic from sophistic, taking dialectic for the part that is concerned with probable arguments, and he puts the nature of rhetoric not only in the persuasive but also in the apparently persuasive.

Rhetoric *Antistrophos* to Dialectic

When rhetoric is said to be *antistrophos* to dialectic, the word *antistrophos* seems to be explained differently by Cicero, by Alexander, and by Aristotle himself. For Cicero to be *antistrophon* means "to respond on either side." This interpretation a certain Victorius, a famous expositor of Aristotle, reproves in these words: "He openly conflates their vicinity with their affinity; had he set aside the contrariety between them he would have mentioned only their similarity." But Maioragius, a most capable man, notes two defects in Victorius: one, that he uses the term contrariety, the other, that he wrote that Cicero introduced an opposition between rhetoric and dialectic. We think that in treating the arts one can make use of unusual words for the sake of preserving a property, especially if the novelties are from the precepts of the art of rhetoric, such as by similarity is meant the contrary of contrariety, just as by pious is meant piety. And "to respond on either side" means what are partly similar, partly dissimilar, so that the expression "to respond" means to be similar, and "on either side" [223] means the contrary. On this account if Cicero translates the *anti* as "on either side" then it does express some contrariety, since *anti* means "against" [*contra*] or "away from the region" [*e regione*]. But if he wishes to translate the whole expression *antistrophos esi* with one word, "it responds" [*respondet*], and adds "on either side" in view of Aristotle's words that follow, which show that rhetoric and dialectic are similar to each other in their matter, then he would not have pointed out any contrariety. Thus much of Cicero's meaning.

The following is the explanation of Alexander, who says in his writing on Aristotle's *Topics* that *antistrophon* means *isostrophon,* that is, what is concerned with the same things and treats the same matters. Rhetoric therefore is *isostrophos,* that is, equally corresponds with dialectic, since both concern all matters that are commonly understood.

It is not necessary, however, to seek other explanations, for Aristotle himself states this, as we read in his text: "For it is a kind of counterpart of, and similitude of, dialectic, just as we also said it takes its origin. For neither of them is a science of any definite subject matter, inquiring into its properties; rather both are kinds of faculties for preparing arguments." These words seem to state the principle of the art of rhetoric, in that Aristotle intended to indicate nothing more than a similarity between rhetoric and dialectic, and through the noun *antistrophon,* translated, he meant the proper noun *homoioma,* that is, similitude. Others have observed this before us. For we relate the passage, "Just as we were also saying 'coming forth from' [*exordientes*]" to the passage "It is a similitude." And so these arts are similar to each other, because both are about common matters for which there is no definite science. In our own translation we say that these arts [224] correspond to each other, that they agree in having the same matter and are concurrent. For the word *antistrophos* is said of things that have some agreement with each other, as happens in choral songs, in which there are some strophes that are sung previously and then antistrophes that correspond to the earlier strophes. The author Iulius Pollux, Bk. 4, chap. 16, speaks of sides [*de costis*] and says that the first two are called antistrophes; see also the same author in Bk. 2, chap. 57. In this way we express their similarity and quasi kinship.

Rhetoric a Counterpart of and Similar to Dialectic

Rhetoric is said to be a counterpart and similitude of dialectic because of oratorical demonstration. For with respect to its matter this type of demonstration is contained under dialectical demonstration, and the persuasible is a kind of probable. So also rhetoric is a kind of dialectic and a counterpart of dialectic, just as the rhetorical persuasive is a counterpart of the dialectical probable. And it is a similitude of dialectic, because both dispute on the same matters, both from probables, both on either side, even if there is a certain dissimilitude in that dialectic disputes on all issues, rhetoric more on civil matters; dialectic from all probabilities, rhetoric only from those that are persuasive; dialectic uses question and answer, whence it gets its special name, as Alexander notes, rhetoric, continuous speech.

Rhetoric a Part of Logic

Rhetoric therefore takes demonstration from universal and common logic and applies it to the matter of the persuasible, just as dialectic does for the probable, apodictic for the necessary, sophistic for the captious, and poetics for the imitable. For these are the parts of logic, which others state, both Ammonius on the *Categories* and Averroes on the first book of the *Posterior Analytics*. For rhetoric takes oratorical demonstration from logic, Aristotle begins, [245/225] naming dialectic for the whole of logic in this fashion: "Since therefore it appears that artificial method pertains to belief, and belief is a kind of demonstration (for we have the greatest belief when we think something has been demonstrated), and oratorical demonstration is the enthymeme; and the latter, as I shall say simply, is most efficacious for producing belief; and enthymeme is a type of syllogism; and to see those things that pertain to every syllogism is the work of dialectic, either in general or in its various parts; there is no doubt that dialectic can best see from what materials and how a syllogism is constructed, and that will also be enthymematic, since it takes up and is concerned with the type of things enthymemes deals with, and how it is different from logical syllogisms." Thus Aristotle. Whence it is easily seen that the rhetorician's knowledge of enthymemes depends on the logician's notion of the syllogism, with the result that rhetoric would be imperfect without logic.

Can Rhetoric Be Learned without Logic?

This was the reason why some thought that a person should first study logic rather than rhetoric, and that it would not be possible to know rhetoric unless one had first learned logic. Now we do not deny that for the perfection of the orator not only the knowledge of logic would be relevant but also that of other arts; but we do not think it so necessary that one should have completed all the books of the logic before being a rhetor, and that without them one could not understand rhetoric sufficiently to be able to persuade. For if rhetoric needs any matters from logic, it has those things translated for its needs, and it is sufficient to learn them from the *Rhetoric*. It is without doubt that Aristotle's intention was to consider the same matter in various arts, but to do so in different ways, and only as much as [246/226] seemed sufficient for the individual arts.

And so, to take an intermediate example, since the virtues arise from the powers of the soul, and for this reason one should treat of these powers in the books of the *Ethics,* it would be suitable for him to transfer this matter from the books *On the Soul,* which he calls exoteric (external), to the first book on morals and to consider it not in detailed fashion but only to the extent needed for ethical understanding. He shows that he did so in this fashion, and therefore that politics should also have some knowledge of the soul. But it should have this for the sake of, and only needs as much as can be applied to, the matters in question; for to inquire into more than is suitable would perhaps be more laborious than the project needs. Some matters that are more fully treated in the exoteric disputations are said about the soul, but they are to be used in this fashion, that the political theorist has merely a competent understanding, the psychologist, an expert knowledge of them and what follows from them. Therefore Aristotle did not wish to deter the student of ethics from learning about the powers of the soul, nor did he wish to restrict this study to the sciences of nature; rather he wanted to include it in the moral disciplines as well. But he said that the latter should have a theoretical knowledge of the soul for the sake of moral matters, and only what is sufficient for them, since a precise knowledge of the things he had already treated in *On the Soul* was not required.

So, to lessen work for students, he provides in the *Rhetoric* certain natural precepts that are deemed sufficient and that the student of the ethical faculty requires, lest he first have to study natural philosophy before doing work in ethics. Now, just as in ethics, where the detailed manner of learning everything in natural philosophy is not needed but only the things needed for an understanding of ethics, so in rhetoric, where one requires a less precise manner of knowing all matters contained in logic and only those that are worthwhile for the knowledge of rhetoric. [247/227] Concerning these matters there should be knowledge for the sake of, and only as much as can be applied to, the question proposed: for example, what is a syllogism, an enthymeme, induction, an example; in what way an enthymeme is an imperfect syllogism and what is lacking to it; that an example is an imperfect induction, as part to part; how an enthymeme is concerned with persuasibles and is made from verisimilars and signs; what the verisimilar is and also the sign; what the topical places are; and in what ways objections are raised. Although all these things are treated as if they were logic, they are always interpolated into rhetoric to the extent that they are needed there. Although nothing more may be required, if there are those who are not content with this knowledge that is sufficient for rhetorical purposes, they can always go to the primary sources themselves and fill up their souls with them.

We do not wish to argue this point further, nor do we wish to condemn those who, for the sake of greater erudition, wish to study logic before rhetoric (especially considering that among our students there are those who are studying both together), provided it be conceded to us that the knowledge of logic is not so necessary that it cannot be attained otherwise. For we do not require that the orator be *pantodan* (an all-knower), but only that he be suitably prepared to speak persuasively on civil questions. For rhetoric considers demonstration in much the same manner as does dialectic, although there is a difference in the force put into it, namely, that dialectic diffuses all probables through its demonstrations, whereas rhetoric contracts its probables to those things that are properly persuasive.

Rhetoric Requires Less Precise Knowledge Than Politics

Moreover, rhetoric considers morals and emotions just as does politics, but for a different reason. [248/228] For politics views them insofar as they lead man to happiness, rhetoric, insofar as they are instruments of persuasion. For that reason the former treat them in greater detail, the latter in lesser. That a less precise study is required for rhetoric than for politics Aristotle teaches in other places, for example when he writes in this fashion: "We need not inquire here so as to enumerate them completely and describe their precise forms, of which it is customary to treat, as of them themselves, by those seeking the truth; and so this is not for the art of rhetoric but for the art dealing more with prudence and truth." Therefore the matters that should be explained in rhetoric and those that are better left for consideration to the science of politics we will now explain.

Two Questions Concerning Emotions

While rhetoric along with ethics considers the emotions, one may doubt whether it considers them, as I may say, as domestic and its own, or as external and as foreign to its nature; moreover, is it proper for rhetoric to move the emotions? On these matters it is worthwhile to think about what Aristotle wrote, as follows: "And those who composed the arts of speech up to this time were very particular about what it contained. For belief contains only that which is artificial; other matters are extraneous additions. So they said nothing about enthymemes, which pertain to the body of belief, whereas they treated many other things that are external (*extra rem*). For incrimination, and mercy, and anger, and movements of the soul of this kind are not internal (*de re*), but are referred to a judge. And if they are found in all judgments, and even now in some cities, and particularly in those that are well constituted, they have nothing to say. [249/229] For all—some of whom think that it is proper for laws to be

cautious in such matters, some of whom retain this institution and pro-
hibit speaking *extra rem,* as they do in the Areopago—rightly indeed so
state: 'It is not fitting for the judge to turn the case about *(pervertere)* by
exciting to anger, or envy, or mercy, for that would be similar to one who,
making a rule out of usage, actually perverts it.'"

Are Emotions Foreign to the Nature of Rhetoric?

These words of Aristotle have led some to think that emotions should
be excluded from the nature of rhetoric. For they argue that belief, that is,
oratorical demonstration, contains only what is artificial; other things,
such as the emotions, are extraneous additions. Enthymeme, moreover, is
the body of opinion, whereas emotion is outside it, that is, external to
rhetoric. Emotion also can be absent from rhetoric if good judgments are
to be made, as are those of the Areopagites. Such arguments taken from
the above text seem to demonstrate that the emotions are foreign to the
nature of rhetoric. Add to this, from the authority of the third book, just
as with the emotions, so other matters apart from demonstration are vain
and superfluous. On this account the illustrious Count Iacobus Zabarella,
in Bk. 2, chap. 17, expressed Aristotle's view in these words: "He says that
the oratorical art consists in argumentations and asserts that these make
up the body of the oration. He reproves the rhetors of those times because, passing over the argumentative part, they were teaching only those
things that were extraneous and foreign to the nature of this art, such as
style and the arousing of the emotions, which were not permitted in a
well-governed city, just as in the Areopago; but they are allowed because
of the depraved customs of men. According to Aristotle, therefore, argumentation alone constitutes the nature of the rhetorical art; the arousing
of the emotions [250/230] is completely foreign to it, even though it is in
use because of the corrupt morals of the citizenry." Thus far this most noble and learned man, to whose authority I grant as much as I should.
Nonetheless, not so much to refute his opinion as to give more support to
the truth, I now offer some considerations that might induce one to hold
that the emotions in some way are not foreign to the nature of rhetoric.

First, Aristotle calls the treatise on the emotions a part of rhetoric, even
if only a small part. Then, when explaining what is apposite for inducing
belief in its proper signification he explains the rhetorical mode of consideration, which contains the emotions also, for persuasion is threefold,
demonstration, emotion, and character. Note that, as we have mentioned
above, rhetoric is said to be conflated of analytical science, that is, of those
things that pertain to demonstration, and of politics, that is, of those
things that pertain to emotions and characters. And so there are two prin-

cipal parts of rhetoric, one concerned with demonstration, the other with emotions and characters; and the latter part is such that it is even called necessary. For we read in Bk. 2 as follows: "It is necessary not only to look to the oration, how it will be demonstrative and worthy of belief, but also to the orator and to the judge, to see with what character they are endowed." On this account at the beginning of Bk. 3 it is taught that there are three things that should be treated in an oration: one, the matters from which belief is induced; second, style; third, how the parts of the oration should be ordered; and this first part of rhetoric that induces belief is divided into demonstration, emotions, and characters. That is the reason why Bk. 2 is written with such diligent attention to the emotions. The part of rhetoric, therefore, that treats of the emotions is indeed necessary, and is not [251/231] to be removed from the nature of rhetoric.

As to what has been said, that belief alone is artificial, and that other matters are extraneous, this can be explained, in our view, as follows. The artificial can be considered in two ways, either as to what is intrinsic (*de re*), and in this way of considering only belief is artificial, or as to what is extrinsic (*extra rem*), and in this way of considering the emotions are also artificial. That is the reason why Aristotle himself enumerated the emotions among the artificial parts of belief, even though he thought them to be extrinsic. Or, the matter of the art can be considered in two ways: either according to its right reason and the way in which things should be rightly understood, and so according to artificial demonstration alone; or according to necessity and how it is referred to the audience, who are presumed to be uneducated, and so according to artificial emotions. Rhetoric is always to be taken in the second way. For in Bk. 2 it is stated that rhetoric is for the sake of judication, and since counsels judicate and judgment is a judication, it is necessary to look not only to belief but also to emotions and characters; and the entire treatise of Bk. 3 is concerned with the opinion and depravity of the audience. Therefore the nature of rhetoric is made up of two things: both those things that are intrinsic, such as demonstrations, and those that are extrinsic, such as the emotions.

As to what pertains to the second argument, we do not deny that the enthymeme is the body of belief, but we hold that the nature of rhetoric is concerned not only with the body of belief but with certain additions also. Nor is the extrinsic (*extra rem*) to be taken to mean "outside rhetoric" (*extra rhetoricam*); rather it means the matter and the case with which the rhetor is concerned, not his rhetoric, as in the following words: "They are not intrinsic but are referred to the judge."

There follows the third argument, about which we have serious doubts, and which we may state as follows. Rhetoric is twofold, one kind that acts, another [252/232] that gives precepts. Emotions can sometimes be absent from the kind that acts, since an occasion may be given to the orator in which there is no opportunity to move the emotions, but not from the kind that gives precepts, for to it pertains that to which the orator should conform himself universally, such that, whatever the occasion that may be given, however he may wish to persuade, he may carry out his function in praiseworthy fashion. And if the movement of the emotions was prohibited in the Areopago, certainly this means that a large part of rhetoric was prohibited, which could be used to good effect and should not be completely rejected, as we shall prove a little below. And so, since orators could have used it—although they ought not to have done so if their audiences were endowed with wisdom and sanctity, virtues generally missing in audiences—they should seek by every means to gain victory, provided that they have a just cause. What is said in Bk. 3, that matters other than demonstration are vain and useless, this is valid, as we also have noted above, by reason of matter that is rightly ordered, but not considering the necessity of the case, according to which many other things are generally said in the same text to be valid. There is no reason, therefore, why the emotions should be ruled out from the nature of rhetoric.

Is It Licit to Move the Emotions?

And from the same text of Aristotle this argument is drawn: if it is not licit to pervert the judge, it is not licit to move the emotions. But it is not licit to pervert the judge, and it is no less perverse to provide him with a rule that he is to use; therefore it is not licit to move the emotions. We deny the consequent and say: through the emotions one draws the audience either to what is false, and then it is not licit, or to what is true, and then it is licit. Therefore if all audiences were of the type of the Areopagites, both holy and wise, there would be no need for the emotions; for it would be sufficient for them [253/233] to open up reasons and arguments showing the truth; but since those who hear are often reprobates and labor under great ignorance, for them demonstrations have greater force when they are conjoined with emotional appeals. This is what Quintilian says in these words: "What, therefore, is one to say? Is the truth to be obscured by moving the emotions? Not at all, for if the judge cannot be led to the truth otherwise, he should be led to it by moving them. Add to this that audiences are often led by the emotions on account of their own wickedness and ignorance, and this leads them into error, so that, if the same emotions were not removed from them, or if they were not impelled to contrary emotions, they would never be able to perceive the truth. It is necessary, therefore, to move the emotions so that the truth may better shine forth, and this should be undertaken for the sake of necessity, since the emotions gain great strength from the depravity of the audience, as Aristotle himself testifies."

Now it seems that the nature of rhetoric has been explained sufficiently, both from its definition, which is made up of its proximate genus and difference, circumscribed by its end, its office, the matter considered, and the mode of considering; also from its composition taken from analytics and politics; also from its affinity with dialectic and politics; also from its similarity not only with dialectic but also with sophistic; also from its agreement with dialectic, on which account it is said to be its counterpart and similitude. And since we have explained whether the study of rhetoric should be undertaken along with, or after, the study of logic; whether the emotions are foreign to the nature of rhetoric; and whether it is licit to move the emotions, it follows that, since rhetoric is directed toward belief, and artificial belief is threefold, [254/234] demonstration, character, and emotion, we now investigate the nature of this threefold belief.

ON THE NATURE
OF ORATORICAL
DEMONSTRATION

[254] Oratorical demonstration consists of the enthymeme and the example. The enthymeme argues from verisimilars and signs. Verisimilars and signs are gathered from forms, common propositions, and dialectical topics (*locis topicis*). Example argues from things either done or invented (*fictis*). On this account the first thing to be considered is what an enthymeme is and its matter and its form; then what an example is and its matter and its form; after that what verisimilars and signs are; then forms will be treated, then common propositions, after that dialectical topics, and last, things done or invented by way of examples, in all of which is comprised the nature of oratorical demonstration.

The Enthymeme

The first thing sought, therefore, is the nature of the enthymeme. Aristotle states this when he writes that the enthymeme is the oratorical syllogism. When certain things are posited, something different results along with them, and this occurs universally or for the most part. In dialectic, such a conclusion it is called a syllogism, in rhetoric an enthymeme (1356b15–18). Certain things are posited before the conclusion, namely, a proposition called the major and a premise, both of which are expressed in the syllogism, for example, "Virtue is desirable; justice is a virtue; therefore justice is desirable." One or other of these is unexpressed in the enthymeme, for example, "Justice is a virtue, therefore it is desirable." From these premises something different results either universally or [255] for the most part, because the conclusion is either universal or particular. The reason is that both the syllogism and the enthymeme are said to be *either* as a whole to a whole, when universal propositions prove a universal conclusion, for example, "Every vice is to be avoided; all injustice is a vice; therefore all injustice is to be avoided," and "All virtue is to be sought for its own sake, therefore all virtue is good," *or* as a whole to a part, when a universal proposition proves a particular conclusion, for example, "All philosophers are to be respected; Socrates is a philosopher; therefore he is to be respected," and "All wise men should be praised, therefore Socrates also." It is quite apparent that the enthymeme is an imperfect syllogism in which one proposition is lacking, and although it pertains to all arts and faculties, it is especially proper to rhetoric.

The Variety of Enthymemes

That the variety of enthymemes arises from the great variety of arts and faculties Aristotle states as follows: "Enthymemes differ greatly among themselves, and this is completely hidden from almost everyone. And this also happens in the dialectical method of syllogisms, and again in other arts and faculties some of which already exist and some of which have yet to be discovered" (1358a3–8). Thus far Aristotle.

The Matter of the Oratorical Enthymeme

The rhetorical enthymeme is understood to be what is concerned with matters that happen in such a way that they frequently happen otherwise, and that argue from verisimilars and signs, about which more below.

The Form of the Oratorical Enthymeme

The form of the enthymeme is seen in the fact that it is made from fewer propositions than the syllogism. About this Aristotle writes: "And from a few propositions, and often from fewer than those that compose the primary syllogism, for it is not appropriate to state which of these [256] propositions is known. For the hearer supplies this for himself, just as, when Dorieus won the contest at which a crown is the prize it suffices to say that he won the Olympics; it need not be added that the Olympics is the contest at which a crown is the prize, for everyone knows that" (357a17–22).[1]

Does the Enthymeme Sometimes Contain Everything That Is in the Syllogism?

The expressions "from a few and often from fewer" refer to the propositions of the enthymeme, and since Aristotle seems to say that the enthymeme is often made from fewer propositions than the syllogism, some gather that at times it is made from all the propositions and they ask how it can come about that it is an imperfect syllogism. On this matter there are various opinions that differ markedly from each other.

1. Certain people think that this is to be understood of potency and act, and this certainly is not free of difficulty, for when considered from the viewpoint of potency the enthymeme is always, and not sometimes, composed of all the propositions in the syllogism.

2. Some are of the opinion that the enthymeme is composed of as many propositions as the syllogism since it is the same as the syllogism with respect to form but that it is concerned with rhetorical matter; but this seems to go against the nature of the enthymeme, some premise of which is held in the mind, and on that account it is called an imperfect syllogism. Nor is it customary to confuse the enthymeme with the syllogism in this way, as though with respect to form a syllogism can be called an enthymeme on account of its matter and with respect to form an enthymeme can be called a syllogism on account of its matter. And apart from this the words of Aristotle seem to refer to the form and not to the matter of the enthymeme.

3. Maioragius explains this as follows. Sometimes the enthymeme is composed of all the propositions in the syllogism but in the reverse order, as when Cicero is used for Coelius: "There is no softness in Coelius, for he is given over to the study of the highest arts, and in such [257] a man no softness usually exists." If this is arranged in the reverse order a syllogism results in the following way: "Coelius is given over to the study of the highest arts; therefore there is no softness in Coelius." The same thing occurs in another way, for sometimes it happens that the major proposition is put in the last place when it is not as well known, and that is why Aristotle says that the enthymeme is made from fewer propositions than the syllogism, but not always. The major proposition is added in the last place in the following way: "Sensuality is to be sought for its own sake, since it is good; and every good is to be sought for its own sake." Therefore the enthymeme sometimes has all the propositions of the syllogism, but nonetheless it never has the same form of argument. And so Maioragius thinks that the form of the syllogism is violated if the order of the propositions is reversed. However, the common opinion of learned men is that changing the order of the propositions does not change the mode. So Philoponus writes that in the first figure, according to received usage, we can put the minor before the major as follows: "Every man is an animal; every animal is a substance; therefore every man is a substance." And, if the minor term is put at the beginning the conclusion also begins with it, in the following way: "Justice is a virtue; virtue is desirable; therefore justice is desirable." Aristotle himself affirms that the type of argument in which the conclusion is put first, the major second, and the minor third, is a syllogism, not an enthymeme: "Pittacus gives freely; those desirous of honor give freely; therefore Pittacus is desirous of honor." And so it is manifest that the form of a syllogism is not changed by reversing the order

of the propositions; nor is a syllogism reduced to an enthymeme simply from the fact that the propositions are not put in their proper place.

4. Not lacking are those who think that, since the syllogism is twofold, [258] the first without proofs, the second with proofs, if the enthymeme is compared in any manner of composition with the primary syllogism it will always be an imperfect syllogism because it lacks one of the propositions, either the major or the minor, and it often is composed from fewer propositions when it is without proofs; but rarely is it composed of all the propositions or even of most of them, since when one of the propositions is lacking, one proof or several is placed between the parts of the enthymeme. For proofs can be put between the parts of an argument, according to Cicero, Bk. 1 (58–77) of *De inventione,* where he proves that reasoning can sometimes have three parts, sometimes four parts, sometimes five parts. The three-part is composed of a proposition, a premise, and a conclusion; the four-part, of a major, a minor, the proof of either one, and a conclusion; the five-part, of a proposition, the proof of the proposition, a premise, the proof of the premise, and a conclusion.[2] And to those who deny that either a proposition or a premise can properly be separated from their respective proofs, or that an absolute proposition or a premise might seem perfect in itself when not confirmed by a proof, one may reply as follows: If in one argument it is sufficient to use a proposition and a premise and it is not necessary to add to them the proofs of the proposition and the premise, whereas in another argument the proposition and the premise are weak unless proofs are added to them, then proofs are something separate from the proposition and the premise. For anything that can be joined to or separated from another cannot be the same as that to which it is added or from which it is separated. Yet there is a certain type of argument in which the proposition and the premise do not require proof, and another type in which it has no validity without the proof. [259] Therefore proof is in fact separated from the proposition and the premise. And so it seems that the enthymeme has all the parts that the primary syllogism has even when it is lacking a proposition or a premise, provided the proof of one or the other is present. Then the conclusion is presented as follows: "Justice is a virtue, for it is a *habitus* consonant with a rational nature; therefore it is desirable; and virtue is desirable, for it is good; therefore justice is desirable." And if this be granted, nothing prevents an enthymeme from being also composed of many propositions and nonetheless being an imperfect syllogism, on the ground that it lacks a proposition, even though the proof of the proposition, the premise, the proof of the premise, and the conclusion are present. This type of enthymeme is found in the introduction to the *Rhetoric* (1354a12) and it reduces to the following five-part syllogism:

[1] Those writers said nothing about enthymemes, which are the sub-

stance of persuasion, but they say much about things that are extrinsic and they have constructed but a small portion of the art.

[2] The modes of persuasion alone are the true constructs of the art; everything else is merely accessory.

[3] These writers say nothing about enthymemes, but they say much about things that are extrinsic.

[4] The arousing of prejudice, pity, anger, and similar movements of the soul are not essential, but are directed to the judge.

[5] Therefore they have constructed but a small portion of the art.

The first thing posited is the conclusion;[3] the proposition is omitted;[4] second is asserted the proof of the proposition; third, the premise; and fourth, the proof of the premise. Thus an enthymeme of this kind is constructed of four parts. Indeed, in this explanation it is difficult to see how there can be [260] six hundred parts of an enthymeme but not three or four on the ground that proofs are multiplied in it; for proofs, seeing that they are separated from the proposition or the premise, are not to be regarded as parts of that argument, but of another in which its proposition or premise is made the conclusion. But, if they are parts, and this can be conceded in reasonings that are not simple but complex, a comparison in which the enthymeme containing proofs is compared with a syllogism without proofs does not seem to be a good comparison; for a part seems to be a condition in a comparison, as when a simple is compared with a simple and a complex with a complex, but not a simple with a complex, or vice versa.

5. When I proposed this difficulty to Reverend Father Thomas Peregrino, regarded in the opinion of all as most outstanding in the teachings of Aristotle, and also by those who teach *meta ta phusika* in our most celebrated university, I understood from this famous expositor that he thought without any doubt that in these words Aristotle was treating not the enthymeme alone but the syllogism in general, both perfect and imperfect, which is formed from few propositions when it is perfect and often from fewer propositions than the primary syllogism, that is, the perfect syllogism. In the case of the enthymeme this often happens, because frequently something is known that need not be expressed because the hearer himself supplies it, and the major proposition is known. In the following argument, "Dorieus won the contest for which a crown is the prize, for he won the Olympics," what is lacking is this: "Whoever wins the Olympics wins the contest for which a crown is the prize," and it is not necessary to add this, because everyone knows it. From this one can gather that, if the major proposition is not known, without doubt it should be provided. The type of argument that consists of a conclusion [261], a premise, and a major proposition will be, not an enthymeme, as

Maioragius thinks, but a syllogism, because it has everything that is required in a syllogism.

I have often had many and recurring doubts about how I could follow the opinion of this reputable man, which he proffers as true, since these words "from a few" seem to me to depend on the others, "and the enthymeme is" and what follows, so that they cannot be understood of the syllogism in general.[5] On the other hand, the authority of this man, whom I think should be as a divine light in interpreting the text of Aristotle, tormented me about Aristotle's other words, so that I did not know what position I should take. The truth finally illuminated me in this very obscure text, in which he, and I also on inspecting them, thought that this expression "and from a few" can depend on the words placed a little before. For it happens that to conclude from a syllogism, just as two things are said about the syllogism in general, first that something new is concluded from matters known prior to the syllogism and second, that the syllogism is needed to provide either proof or probability, so it is that one result is concluded "from a few" through the perfect syllogism, another result, and indeed more often, "from fewer" through the enthymeme. For there cannot be any doubt but that the orator also makes use of the perfect syllogism. So, just as it is customary to omit the major or the minor if these are known, if both are unknown, proofs of both should be forthcoming. And thus Cicero in *De arte oratoria* concedes perfect argument to the orator also, and admits that in orations integral syllogisms are sometimes found. And this being better known, it does not require lengthier discussion. So in this way that quite obscure text of Aristotle is illuminated in the foregoing fashion. Let these notations suffice for the enthymeme. The next matter we should now treat is that of the example.

The Example

[262] Aristotle writes that the example is oratorical induction, that is, imperfect, and since it can be demonstrated in many and similar instances that a thing is the way it is, in dialectic this is called induction, in rhetoric, example. But in induction these many's and similars are all the singulars that prove the universal, whereas in example it is not all instances that prove the singular. How this occurs will be made clear below.

The matter of the example is the same as that of the enthymeme.

The form is that it be as part to part, similar to similar, since induction is as part to whole. For induction proves the universal, example, the particular. Although induction also seems to prove the singular, as is found in Aristotle Bk. 2 (1398b): "If we do not give our horses to those who care poorly for the horses of others, nor our ships to those who overturn the ships of others, and a similar pattern in other matters of this type, neither should we commit our safety to those who have cared poorly for the safety of others." And this of Aspasia, from Cicero, Bk. I (51–52) of *De inventione:* "Tell me, I ask the wife of Xenophon, if your neighbor had better gold than you have, would you prefer hers or yours? Hers, she says. And if she had clothing and other womanly ornaments of greater value than those you have, which would you prefer, your own or hers? Hers, she responds. Tell me, he says, if she had a better man than you have, would you prefer your own to hers? Here the woman blushes. Again, this example: I ask Xenophon, if your neighbor had a better horse than you have, would you prefer your own horse to his? His, he says. And if he had a better country estate than you have, which country estate would you ultimately prefer? His, he says, the better one. [263] And if he had a better wife than you have, would you prefer your own or his? And here Xenophon likewise falls silent." On this account even Boethius, in his *De differentiis topicis,* wrote that not only the universal but also the singular can be proved through induction.

But one can reply that inductions of this type that prove the singular are imperfect and oratorical, and are properly examples, and on this account Aristotle makes no mention of them in his logic, but only in his *Rhetoric;* and Cicero considered them insofar as they serve the orator probably but not necessarily. But example is indeed different from induction not only by reason of the conclusion; it is true also of the similars that are gathered to prove the conclusion. On this matter Aristotle writes as follows in the *Prior Analytics:* "Example differs from induction in that induction, starting from all the singulars, shows that the extreme term belongs to the middle, but does not apply the syllogistic conclusion to both extremes; the example, on the other hand, makes the application, but it does not draw its proof from all the individual cases" (69a16–19). Here Aristotle brings out two differences: one, that induction, from all instances, shows the extreme to belong to the middle, whereas the example does not do so from all instances; the other, that the former does not tie the syllogism to the extreme, whereas the latter does. What these kinds of differences are we shall briefly consider.

Induction from the minor extreme that consists of all instances shows the major extreme to belong to the middle term. The minor extreme is man, horse, mule, and other animals of this type. The middle term is eliminating bile. The major extreme is long lived. So the argument goes: Man, eliminating bile, is long lived. The same for horse. The same for mule, and so for yet others. Therefore, all animals eliminating bile are long lived. The minor extremity is all animals. [264] And Aristotle teaches this in the following way: one must understand the minor extremity as a type of quiddity composed of all instances. For induction is effected from universals.

Moreover, induction does not join the syllogism to the extreme. For this reason he states the same result in the following way: "In a way induction is opposed to the syllogism, for the latter proves the middle term to belong to the third term by means of the middle, whereas the former proves the major to belong to the middle by means of the third" (68b32–35). Since therefore the syllogism ties one extreme to the other by means of the middle term, and induction, through one extreme, shows the other extreme to belong to the middle term, it appears that in some way induction is opposed to the syllogism.

An example shows the major extreme to belong to the middle term through something similar to the minor extreme. The minor extreme is the Athenians against the Thebans. The similarity is the Thebans against the Phocians. The middle term: to make war against a neighbor. The major extreme: evil. So the argument goes: To wage war against a neighbor is evil, as the Thebans did against the Phocians. Therefore, the same applies to the Athenians against the Thebans. This is a similarity to the minor extreme, and no "all" is involved.

Additionally, the example couples the syllogism with the extreme in this way. To wage war against a neighbor is evil, as the Thebans did against the Phocians; for the Athenians to wage war against the Thebans is to wage war against a neighbor; therefore it is evil.

Since Aristotle tells us that induction is made from all instances, whereas example is not, we seek an example of "not from all instances," whether this expression is understood of one instance alone or of several.

Boethius is thinking of one instance only, and his words are: [265] "Example is joined to induction and differs from it. An example argues to show some particular by means of a particular presented; for example, 'It is right for Tullius the consul to kill Catiline since Scipio slew Gracchus.' That both of these are particulars and not universals is shown by the inclusion of individual persons. So since a part is proved by a part, what we call an example has a kind of similarity to an induction. But because the parts it collects from which the result is produced are not more than one, it differs from induction" (De top. diff., II, 1184D1–5). Thus far Boethius. It may be added that Aristotle teaches that the example is like a part to a part, one similarity to another, and therefore one individual to another. And he teaches that both fall under the same genus, though one is more known than the other; therefore it is the one that proves the other. And when several instances are numbered together, there are several examples.

Nonetheless, Aristotle instanced in the *Prior Analytics* an example where the major term is proved to belong to the middle by means of a term that resembles the third, such as the following: "To wage war against a neighbor is evil, as the Thebans did against the Phocians, which is similar to this third, the Athenians against the Thebans," and he added that this comes about in the same way if the middle is proved to belong to the extreme through several similar instances (II.23, 68b37–69a12). And so it seems that an example can also be constituted of many instances, just as is found also in Bk. 1 of the *Rhetoric,* where that is discussed. The example: all instances are cited in reference to Dionysius, and they are not examples, although they all fall under the same universal proposition. The example is formed in Bk. 1 (1358a30–36), where Pisistratus, Theagenes, and as many others as we know are similars. The minor extreme is Dionysius. The middle term is to ask for a bodyguard. The major extreme: to aim at tyranny. And the argument runs in this way. One who asks for a bodyguard aims at tyranny, such as Pisistratus, Theagenes, [266] and others. Dionysius asks for a bodyguard; therefore he aims at tyranny. So in this example there are two similars, Pisistratus and Theagenes. In Bk. 2 another example is formulated in which the similars are Darius and Xerxes (1393b). The minor extreme is the king. The middle term is to take possession of Egypt. The major term is to cross over a frontier. And the argument runs this way. Those who take possession of Egypt cross over, as did Darius and Xerxes. The king will take possession of Egypt; therefore he will cross over. So in this there are two similars, Darius and Xerxes. What are we to make of this? What Aristotle himself stated openly in Bk. 2 near the end, that an example can be made from several instances? For having taught that enthymemes can be made from four sources, the verisimilar, the example, the tecmerium, and the sign, when explaining how enthymemes can be drawn from the example, he wrote as follows: "This occurs when they are the result of induction from one or more similar cases, and when one assumes the universal and concludes therefrom what is particular, from an example" (402b).

From the foregoing, responses can be given to the arguments to the contrary. The expression "not from all" can also be understood to mean "from some," contrary to the opinion of Boethius. And the example is indeed as part to part, but part may also be taken to mean many instances, as in the case of induction, which undoubtedly is constituted from many instances, if not from all. And nonetheless it is said to be as part to whole. And, when it is said that both fall under the same genus, and one is better known than the other, this should be taken to mean the example, from which the minimal argument is constituted. Nor should there be said to be many examples because there are many instances. For an example is not any particular similarity that is gathered up in an argument, but an entire argument whose proof comes from one, or [267] many, similars. Otherwise to follow that line of thought would lead to an absurdity, so that even the type of argument in which one instance proves another would not be called an example, but only the instance itself that is placed in the proof. And we think this to be foreign to Aristotle's teaching, that the example be one term, or one proposition, and not a complete argument.

Having explained oratorical demonstration in general, and what the enthymeme and the example are, since the enthymeme itself is composed of verisimilars and signs, we must now consider what a verisimilar is, and what a sign.

The Verisimilar

Aristotle teaches in the *Rhetoric* that the verisimilar is what happens for the most part, not always; others define it as what can happen to be otherwise, and it is related to that to which it is verisimilar as the universal to the singular. Thus two things are to be considered in the verisimilar, namely, that it is for the most part and that it presents itself as a universal. In the *Analytics* the verisimilar is a type of probable proposition. Many do not know that it is for the most part and they call the verisimilar what happens or does not happen, what is or is not the case, as to hate the envier, to love the beloved. Philoponus explains this to mean that it frequently happens that those who are envied hate those who envy them and that those who love love those whom they love. Victorius says that it generally happens that those who envy hate those they envy and that those who are loved love those who love them. We follow Victorius's explanation, especially since according to Philoponus's reading there seems to be more necessity than verisimilitude in the example, as if to say that no one is a lover if he does not love without limit.

The Sign

Aristotle treats this also in the *Rhetoric* (357b1) Among signs one type is the necessary sign, named the tecmerium; the other [268] is the non-necessary, which is unnamed. The latter is twofold: one type is the singular to the universal, which can be refuted even though what is said is true, because it is not concluded by syllogism; the other is the universal to the singular, which again can be refuted even though it is true. In the *Prior Analytics* (70a7) the sign is threefold, for either it is taken as in the first figure and cannot be refuted, or as in the middle figure and it can be refuted, or as in the third figure and again it can be refuted. Examples of all these will be given, as follows.

An example of the tecmerium in the *Rhetoric*: A man who has a fever is ill; he has a fever; therefore he is ill. A woman who has milk has given birth; she has milk; therefore she has given birth. In the *Analytics*: A woman who has milk is with child; she has milk; therefore she is with child.

An example of a singular non-necessary sign: In the *Rhetoric*, Bk. 1: Socrates is wise; Socrates is just; therefore all wise men are just. Bk. 2 (1401b): Harmodius and Aristogiton were lovers; Harmodius and Aristogiton were useful to the state; therefore all lovers are useful to the state. In the *Analytics*: Pittacus is wise; Pittacus is good; therefore all wise men are good.

An example of a universal non-necessary sign: In the *Rhetoric*, Bk. 1: A man who has a fever breathes hard; he breathes hard; therefore he has a fever. Bk. 2: All thieves are rascals; Dionysius is a rascal; therefore he is a thief. In the *Analytics*: Women who are with child are pale; she is pale; therefore she is with child.

Is the Verisimilar the Same as the Universal Non-Necessary Sign?

What the difference is between the verisimilar and the non-necessary universal sign has already been inquired into. Nothing seems to differentiate them, since neither is necessary and both are universal. But if no difference exists, Aristotle would seem to be less correctly understood in saying that the enthymeme is drawn from verisimilars and signs, since it would have been enough to have mentioned signs, which are [269] contained under verisimilars. For a division in which one part is contained under the other is a faulty division, as is the case with sources from which enthymemes are drawn being divided into verisimilars and signs; it would be vicious to divide in this way if verisimilars contain signs under them. In this question to be noted is what Cicero, Quintilian, Philoponus, and others thought about the problem, and to gather from them what seems the more probable.

1. Philoponus writes that the sign is divided into the tecmerium and the verisimilar.

2. Quintilian, that some signs, what the Greeks call *eikosa,* are not-necessary, that is, verisimilar. Thus both seem to think that the non-necessary sign and the verisimilar are the same. But in this they dissent from Aristotle in confusing the sign with the verisimilar and in attributing a name to the sign that is unnamed.

3. Cicero teaches in *De partitionibus* that the verisimilar is what happens for the most part, as, for example, that youth is more prone to self-indulgence, and that the essential characteristic gives a proof that is never oth-

erwise and supplies an indication that is certain, for example, where there is smoke there is fire. And, when he translates that verisimilars are found in persons, in places, in times, in facts, in events, in the natures and trans-actions of things themselves, he adds that "there is another genus of argu-ment that is taken from mere indications of fact, such as weapons, blood, a cry emitted, a stumble, a change of color, stammering, or anything else that can be perceived by the senses; also, some indication of preparation or of communication with someone, or something seen or heard or hinted at later on. Therefore, in place of the sign he names the individual character-istics of a thing and various traces of a fact" [Loeb ed., p. 341]. But what we are seeking he does not explain sufficiently. In Bk. 1 of *De inventione* he defines a sign as that which falls under any sense and which signifies [270] something that is gathered from it right away, which either existed previ-ously, or is in what is actually going on, or will exist subsequently; and nonetheless it is in need of testimony and more trustworthy confirmation, such as a cry, a running away, a pallor, dust, and things similar to these.

4. Maioragius and many others follow this definition, and they think that, since all of our knowledge has a twofold source, being either from sense or from intelligence, that it is necessary also that all arguments that cite any knowledge on our part should make some reference to sense or to intelligence. And, as to what pertains to sense, this should be called a sign, and it signifies something known through a sense, for example, sight, hearing, or the other senses; as to things that pertain to intelligence or opinion, on the other hand, these should be called verisimilars. Therefore, according to the view of these thinkers the difference between the verisimilar and the unnamed universal sign is that one pertains to the in-telligence, for example, that all mothers love their children, the other to sense, for example, that all who have a fever have difficulty breathing. These authors, however, do not see that for Aristotle a sign is also some-thing that pertains to intelligence, such as that all wise men are just since Socrates was wise and just. For the wisdom and justice of Socrates, which are habits of the soul comprehended by the soul, pertain as much to intel-ligence as do the love of all mothers toward their children. Cavalcantius, who treated the sermon before the *Rhetorician* of Hetruscus and who tried to give a simple explanation of Aristotle's view, replied that the wisdom and justice of Socrates pertain to sense, because men of the time in which Socrates lived comprehended these by sight and hearing. But the verisimi-lar is also comprehended in this way, since the effect of love in mothers is seen or heard. And therefore both the verisimilar and [271] the sign con-sidered in this way will pertain to sense. For it is one thing to comprehend a virtue, another, the effect of virtue; the former pertains to intelligence, the latter, to sense.

5. Maioragius adds: "There is that sufficiently obvious difference between the verisimilar and the sign that the verisimilar is reduced to causes and to common opinion, as that Malleolus should be sewn into a bag, an indication of patricide, and that Antonius should be judged an enemy, which implies a war against his native land. For this is known to all, namely, that those who kill their parents should be sewn into a bag and that those who wage war against their country are judged an enemy. Signs are taken from things effected, which fall under sense; for example, the Areopagites condemned the boy who tragically dug out eyes with buskins and then threw them away alive, for this they judged to be a sign of the greatest cruelty." But this distinction is facile and hasty. And you too, Maioragius, are facile and hasty. Indeed, it is not sufficiently clear to me, for I do not understand why the verisimilar could not also be seen from effects, as, for example: The man who got angry was slighted; one who is our benefactor is our friend. And a sign can be taken from causes, as, for example: The sun is over the earth, therefore it is day; there is fire, therefore there will be ashes. On that account neither does this explanation, which includes all signs, seem plainly to distinguish the verisimilar from the unnamed universal sign.

6. There are those who think that the verisimilar proposition is seen in itself as something that holds for the most part in the opinion of men, when no indication is given of any other thing. The sign, on the other hand, is a proposition that always gives indication of some other thing. This distinction, which is proposed by those most learned in the teaching of rhetoric and also by the most outstanding men in all of philosophy, is most [272] subtle. Nonetheless, to tell the truth, for me it requires a clearer explanation, for I do not see sufficiently how being a youth is less indicative of an inclination to self-indulgence than having difficulty breathing is indicative of a fever and a woman's being pallid is indicative of her being heavy with child, particularly since the verisimilar seems to be a more certain judgment than the sign, that is, the unnamed one. For it often happens that youths have more inclination to self-indulgence than those who have difficulty breathing are feverish or those who are pallid are heavy with child. Add to this that the sign, Socrates is just, is no more indicative that all wise men are just than is the verisimilar that a woman's being a mother is indicative that she loves her children.

7. Indeed for me in this pointed investigation there seems to be no other difference between the verisimilar and the non-necessary universal sign than that the former is a more probable proposition, the latter, a less probable proposition. For that the sign is not a term of a proposition but an integral proposition itself we shall prove below. On this account we think that they can be so differentiated if we say that there are two kinds

of signs, one that is more perfect than the verisimilar, which is called the tecmerium, the other less perfect which has no name and which is twofold: *either* it is as the singular to the universal, and it sins against the third figure of the syllogism, in which nothing can be proved from singulars alone, as, for example, Socrates is wise; Socrates is just; therefore all wise men are just; *or* it is as the universal to the singular, and it sins against the second figure, in which it is not licit to take a conclusion from particular affirmations alone, as, for example: One who has a fever has difficulty breathing; he has difficulty breathing; therefore he has a fever. Both of these are more imperfect than the verisimilar, because both sin against form, whereas the verisimilar does not sin against it. [273] And so Victorius, quite correctly, after many and various distinctions says, "Verisimilars have greater probative force than signs, and so they make for more certain arguments because they are true for the most part, whereas signs, unless they are proper and certain, are not so firm and often lead into deception. The verisimilar, therefore, is what happens frequently, as that the old are covetous, that mothers love their children; the unnamed universal sign, on the other hand, is what equally or rarely happens, as, for example: A man who has difficulty breathing has a fever; a woman who has a pallor is heavy with child. Thus it is that the *epitopolu,* that is, the *plerumque,* the 'for the most part,' which is said of the verisimilar, not of the sign, is what seems to distinguish the latter from the former."

Is the Sign a Term or a Proposition?

Up to now, as has been taught, among signs there is one type that goes from the singular to the universal, another that goes from the universal to the singular. A doubt has arisen for some whether this is to be understood of the terms of a proposition, one type of which goes from the singular term to the universal, the other from the universal term to the singular, or of the proposition itself, which is from a singular proposition to a universal conclusion, or from a universal proposition to a singular conclusion.

Alexander Piccolomini opts for the position that this is to be understood of terms, and he is followed by, among others, Raphael Cyllenius, in his *Tabulis Rhetoricis,* where the latter writes: "Of those signs that are related as singulars to universals, one type can be refuted, for example, 'Socrates was wise and just; therefore all wise men are just'; the other type is non-necessary, for example, 'The man who has a fever is ill' and 'The woman who has milk is child-bearing.'"

But Aristotle seems to hold the contrary, for we read in his *Prior Analytics* that a sign should be [274] a demonstrative proposition, either necessary or probable, etc. (70a7). Here only one proposition is mentioned, and it alone is the sign; if another proposition is added to it, then it is a syllogism. He adds that since the verisimilar is like the universal to the singular, if the terms of the proposition are considered and not the proposition, it will instead be like the singular to the universal. For example, in "Those who envy have hatred," "Those who are loved have love," envy is less universal than hatred and those who are loved are less universal than those who love. On this account, just as the verisimilar is said to be like the universal to the singular, not because of the terms but because it is a universal proposition leading to a singular conclusion, the same should be said of signs. What does this mean? That Aristotle treats sign in an unqualified way, that what is related as singular to universal can be refuted? This would be false of the tecmerium if for this reason it were understood to be like the singular to the universal, because in a proposition that is said to be a sign there is one term that is like the singular to the universal, as is the case of "having a fever" to "being ill" in the following proposition: "The man who has a fever is ill." For then Aristotle would in some way have to be corrected and it should be said, not that the type of sign that goes from the singular to the universal is *lutòn* (refuted), but rather that it is partly *alutòn* (unrefuted) and partly *lutòn,* just as Cyllenius was seen to correct it. Just how right he was is easily judged.

Since verisimilars and signs are taken partly from forms (*formae*), partly from common propositions, partly from common topics, the first things to be investigated are forms. I call forms, says Aristotle, propositions that are proper to any particular genus, and without doubt these cannot be known unless the genera of oratorical speeches are previously known. The genera [275] are three in number, deliberative, demonstrative, and judicial.

Two Questions About the Genera of Causes (*Caussae*)

Concerning these genera, before we come to the forms the first question we must consider is whether everything that pertains to the office of the orator is contained under these genera. And then, in what genus are the ecclesiastical orations preachers give in churches of our times to be located?

Is Everything Contained Under the Three Genera of Causes?

M. Antonius Muretus, a Frenchman, very learned and a skillful speaker, in his commentary on the second Catiline was intent on refuting teachings of ancient masters of speech, and he wrote that in no way would it be proper to say of the orator that his entire office is contained under the three genera of causes, the demonstrative, the deliberative, and the judicial. And a little later he adds: "You indeed, who would make Hippias the orator a kind of *pantodan* (all-knower), I ask of you, when he disputes about the motions of the heavenly bodies, of lightnings and earthquakes (when you wish these to pertain to his office), with which of these three genera would you say he is concerned? For he does not praise or blame, nor does he persuade or dissuade, nor does he accuse or defend." Thus far Muretus.

The response seems easy to us, that they are all matters of which the orator is to speak, but it is not true that all of them are within the three genera of causes, for there are infinite questions that at one time or another are treated by the orator and that are not causes. Aristotle himself attributed all things to the orator in his definition of rhetoric, and he recognized in the work of the orator not only the definite question, which includes the three genera of causes, but also the infinite question, as we have shown above. And so these questions are not to be confused. Nor is it to be doubted under which of the three genera are contained the questions about the motion of the heavenly bodies [276] and those relating to lightnings and earthquakes. For it is very well known that one can inquire about these either infinitely or definitely, and, first, the questions fall under none of these when they are infinite. Second, in some way they fall under the deliberative, when one wishes to use them to persuade or to hope for some good or to fear an evil, or to dispel a fear or anything else of this kind, for these are all natural things; or they even fall under the demonstrative, when they are brought in to praise or to blame a person. But matters treated by the orator definitely and singularly are contained under the finite question, and even though these matters are not clearly in these genera, their precepts are regarded as falling under them. This is what Cicero, Quintilian, and others have taught.

But Muretus thinks otherwise, for he professes that there are many things in the ancient teachers of rhetoric that he admires and yet does not approve of, although it seems without doubt to vindicate a major part of the glory that comes from the study of the art of rhetoric. Indeed, it was always the custom of great orators to hide their art lest it be too closely observed. And in this unfortunate situation seems to lie the condition of the art of rhetoric, that those who were most helped by it often withhold their gratitude, so that they seem to spurn it, reduce it to dregs, and rail out against it. Unless we should perhaps say, as the art itself teaches and considering the way in which a speech may be directed to contrary parts, that this function often works against itself, in order that what is being professed may appear to be more true. Muretus thus writes as follows: "For myself, if anyone asks me in what genus of cause or controversy an oration might be, say the kind it was customary to give many years ago in Athens for those who had died for their country, I shall reply in none; for there is no cause there, no controversy, or anything else about which one might argue, and nonetheless [277] it may be truly said of Plato's and Aristotle's doctrine that it is the *genos epideiktikon rhetorikou logou* (the epideictic genus of rhetorical argument)." And a little later, "Lest we prolong our examples, the one in the Catiline orations after the last considered, which often is said to be deliberative, cannot be included under any of the three kinds. Not under the judicial, for these are not matters that fall under judgment. Not under the demonstrative, for in the demonstrative it is only the pleasure of the audience that is considered, and that entire genus is given over to pomp and ostentation. Not under the deliberative, for in the prior example, as we have seen, no deliberation was involved, for Cicero was concerned only that Catiline should go away so that he himself might be able to deliberate with the senate about the republic; nor was he present to deliberate about anything or decide what was useful. This example, which we are now going to explain, and likewise the third, is one in which he did nothing more than explain to the people what his deeds were and to confirm him, and to counsel them to hope for the best." Thus far Muretus.

We reply that an oration about those who had died for their country was indeed demonstrative, and there was a cause and controversy, if not about the action itself at least about its quality and quantity; Aristotle recognized that controversies of this type are in the demonstrative genus in Bk. 3, where he treated of the demonstrative genus (1416b), and wrote that not only does it consist of matters that are inartificial, the speaker being in no way the author of the actions he relates, but also of those that depend upon art, and these consist in showing that the action did take place, if it be incredible, or that it is of a certain kind, or of a certain importance, or all three together. As to what pertains to the Catiline orations, we say from Aristotle's teaching that all of these pertain to the deliberative genus, and this is known from the audience, the parts, the time, and the end, for Aristotle teaches that consideration of these four locates a speech in a particular genus. For the hearer of the previous oration [278] is the senate, as also of the last; the end of the second and the third is to arouse, and its hearers are those of the deliberative genus. Since its two parts are exhortation and dissuasion, in the first Cicero urges and in a certain way impels Catiline to leave the city, and indeed his obvious advice is that he can do nothing more there. In the second and third he urges the people, through a narration of the things they have done, to defend their homes by guards and watchmen. In the fourth, about which not even Muretus was in doubt, he urged the fathers that they decide firmly and courageously.

Apart from this, undoubtedly in all of these cases he is treating of the future, and this time is most appropriate for the deliberative genus. And in all he is considering what is useful and what is not, and that is the end that is proper to the deliberative genus.

In What Genus Are Ecclesiastical Orations?

Some think that ecclesiastical orations are demonstrative in mode, others that they are judicial, and yet others deliberative, and they teach this in ecclesiastical rhetoric. It is not our intention to refute the opinion of these wisest of men who are most worthy of all reverence and respect, but we wish only to expose our view for what it is worth, and we say that they are always deliberative. For, since the genera of causes is differentiated by the genera of audiences, and the genus of the cause (*caussae*) is *sumbouleutikon*, since the hearer is *ecclesiases* (1354b33), one who would discern something about future things, the auditor for this type of speech is always being exhorted to be discerning about a future life. And so they are always in the deliberative genus, so that the oration, and ecclesiastical rhetoric, are nothing other than deliberative. Moreover, the parts of the deliberative genus are *protrope kai apotrope* (persuasion and dissuasion), and the total function of the preacher is located in exhortations, as St. Paul [279] wrote to the Corinthians, "We are ambassadors for Christ, such that God is exhorting you through us." So things of the future are always being considered, namely, a better life, the time that is most suited to the deliberative genus, and it is also truly *apo tou ekklesiasou*, or *apo tes ekklesias ekklesiasikon*, that is, preaching in an assembly, and this is the same as *demegorikon*, that is, for the people (1354b7). For this reason, in his introduction speaking of the deliberative genus Aristotle said *peri ta demegorika* and . . . *demegoriken pragmatoian*, that is, *ekklesiasika* and *ekklesiasiken* (1354b23–26). Nor can one object that praise and blame and accusation and defense are frequently used, for none of these are proper to it but are only taken up in it, and, when any genus is being identified, one should consider what its end is and not matters that are taken up in order to reach that end. For it often happens that to achieve the end of one genus the ends of others are taken up, as when Cicero wished to prove that it would be useful to have Pompeius in charge of the Mithridatic war he demonstrated that he was just and the right person to wage war against Mithridates. For the genera are intermingled, but there is always one genus that is principal. Aristotle taught in the following way how to take up matters that are proper to other genera to offer proof for a particular genus: "The end is different for each genus, and since there are three genera there are three different ends. For one deliberating, the useful and the harmful; for one persuading, that he persuade for what is better; dissuading, that he turn away from what is worse. And different matters may be taken up at the same time to achieve this, whether it be the just or the unjust, the honorable or the ugly. [280] For those in litigation the just and the unjust, although other concerns can be taken up with these at the same time. For those praising and blaming, the honorable and the ugly, although other interests also may be related to these" (R15; L35).[6] And since ecclesiastical rhetoric is the same as deliberative rhetoric, what Aristotle wrote about this genus can be applied to usage in our times, though with respect to its conforming with the rules of the art this is so perfectly written that it seems hardly possible now to add anything to it. For this reason preachers in our own day, and others too, should not contemn ecclesiastical rhetorics, especially those that do not depart from Aristotle's precepts. Of this type of rhetoric I hasten to recommend that of the most learned Augustinus Valerius, bishop of Verona, for preachers would be helped not a little in structuring their sermons according to this art if they would have recourse to Aristotle, the prince of philosophers and theologians,

Now we come to the forms of the individual genera.

The Forms of Individual Genera

We have noted above that the proper propositions of these genera, gathered from their ends, are called forms (*formae*). For Aristotle states that the orator, having proposed for himself the proper goal of the subject genus, whether this be the useful, the good, or the just, should consider what its end is and what its parts are, for example, what the useful is, what the good, and what the just, and how many kinds there are of the useful, the good, and the just. Also how, when taking counsel about the five most contingent matters in the deliberative genus, proper propositions for deliberating can be deduced from happiness and its parts, from goods acknowledged, controverted, and compared in relation to the good of each republic. And in praising and blaming, from virtue and vice, from agents that produce virtue and vice, and from what results from virtue and vice. And in accusing and defending, from the inspection of three factors: what causes injuries, by whom they are caused, and who are hurt by them. Since it would take too long to explain all the forms, we have proposed only [281] those that seem reasonable to us; not all are pointed out, but only those that need to be highlighted. Of these, some do not require very diligent examination, either because the matter itself does not require explanation or because it has been explained by others, some because to add anything would be superfluous. It will be sufficient, therefore, to note the principal headings of these forms and in explaining them to dwell only on those that seem to us to be more obscure, especially since in our translation the books themselves are so clear as to be easily understood by almost all. We have noted the numbers of our pagination for the greater convenience of the reader.

Deliberative Forms

Concerning the deliberative genus, which we have referred to as the more beautiful and the more civil because it concerns the more common good, we shall treat first of the matters with which deliberative forms are primarily concerned. They are not concerned with things that are necessary or with those that cannot be done or with those that occur naturally or that happen by chance, but with what comes from the human will, and first of all with taxes, with war and peace, with defense, with imports and exports, and with the handing down of laws. Next to be indicated are the matters from which deliberative forms are gathered, for they are collected both from what pertains to happiness and to the constituent elements of happiness and from things inside a person, as in the soul and in the body, or from things outside a person. Third to be enumerated are the forms of acknowledged goods. Fourth, of controverted goods. Fifth, of compared goods. Sixth, we shall consider the various forms of government to whose ends the deliberative genus must be accommodated.

The five genera of things that are brought to mind at the outset (R16; L39) can be referred to the causes that are listed in the third book of the *Ethics*, that is, to necessity, nature, and chance, [282] and beyond these to the human mind and to anything that is done by human beings. For under necessities are also included things that cannot come to be, for if it is necessary that something occur it cannot happen that it would not be, and if a thing cannot come to be it is necessary that it not exist. Therefore it is stated in the *Ethics* that there cannot be deliberation over necessary things which always occur in the same way, as the rising and setting of the sun. Nor can there be deliberation over things that happen in various ways but naturally, of which kind are droughts and rainfalls. Nor of things that are subject to cases (*casus*) of fortune, such as the finding of a treasure, but only to those that pertain to human nature. And not even to all of these, since the Lacedaemonians do not deliberate over how the Scythians should administer their government. We only deliberate over matters whose coming to be falls within our power.

Concerning the component parts of happiness (R23–24; L47–49), when the virtues of the body are treated these are called in Greek the *pentathli*, in Latin, the *quinquertiones*. Maioragius, when treating of beauty, explains the *quinquertiones* as recording the victory or reward gained from five contests, that is, the wrestling match, the run, the broad jump, the discus, and the weight or javelin throw. A little bit later, where the text is concerned with the faculty of competing, he does not seem to be consistent, since he writes, "The *pentathli,* which are called the *quinquertiones* in Latin, are those who came out victors in wrestling, boxing, and track, which can have five names, and are called wrestlers, boxers, runners, pancratiasts, and *pentathli.*" However, the common opinion is that *quinquertiones* refers to the five kinds of contests, namely, those Simonides refers to in his verse,

> Pythias devicit Diophon atque Isthmia, saltu,
> Et disco, et lucta, et iaculo, et pedibus.

Yet Aristotle makes mention of only three contests, [283] that of the track, wrestling, and boxing, so that in his opinion the *quinquertiones* are not those who take part in five contests but those who are in the five classes of those who do so. Thus those are called *pentathli* and *quinquertiones* who prevail not in five but in three contests, just as the *pancrasiastae* do in two (wrestling and boxing). Here we wish to give our support to the second position of Maioragius, which squares with Aristotle's words and mind. Here also should be observed that what others name an *akonta,* that is, a thrower, Aristotle calls a *plektikon,* that is, a boxer (*pugilor*), a fighter (*pungens*), and a striker (*percutiens*).

In acknowledged goods (R26; L61) two modes of following are enumerated, either simultaneously, the way health follows simultaneously with life, or subsequently, the way science follows after discipline. In compared goods there are three, with the following mode, called a faculty (*facultas,* potentiality) being added; for example, if one is sacrilegious a faculty follows, say, simple theft. Therefore first enumerated are the modes of following that actually exist, then all modes whatever. But since Aristotle teaches that the good that does not follow is greater, Victorius raises a doubt as to how learning is greater than science. For, according to Aristotle's rule, science follows after learning, and learning does not follow after science, therefore learning is greater than science. We approve Maioragius's explanation, that science is greater in quantity but not in quality. For knowing more can be understood in many ways, and that which does not follow is said to be greater in some way. For example, if a person is healthy it follows simultaneously that the person is alive. If a person is alive, it does not follow simultaneously that the person is healthy. Therefore to be healthy is greater than to be alive, that is, a greater good. If a person learns, it follows consequently that [284] that the person knows scientifically, but if he knows scientifically it does not follow consequently that he learns. Therefore to learn is said to be greater than to know scientifically, that is, it is more ample, of greater scope, and more general. If one is sacrilegious, a faculty follows when one also steals. If one steals, the faculty does not follow that one is sacrilegious. Therefore a sacrilege is more than a simple theft, that is, it is more of a vice (R30; L71–73).

Demonstrative Forms

Since, however, the demonstrative genus was discovered to praise, God first of all, then man, then animals lacking reason, and finally even inanimate things, and since whatever is praised is praised as being good, three principal forms of goods are enumerated by Aristotle. Thus goods include (a) virtues such as justice, fortitude, temperance, magnificence, liberality, meekness, and prudence, and especially those virtues that are most useful and in this sense are greatest, namely, justice, fortitude, and liberality; (b) those things that produce virtue, such as natural talent, memory, docility, education, and discipline; (c) plus those things that are the effects of virtue, such as the signs of various virtues, of which kind is the scar that covers a wound, and the insignia of a judge, and other things of this type that signify a virtue; and (d) finally works that proceed from justice, magnanimity, and other virtues (R43; L101). But since under these general forms many others are contained, this is especially worthy of observation: there is the praise of virtue and the encomium of works; then, in an unqualified way, the demonstrative proof of circumstances, such as nobility and discipline. On the matter of praise and encomium, read Bk. 1 of the *Ethics* at this place, "Praise is of virtue" (1101b32). For from it men are made apt to perform famous deeds. Encomia are of works, both those that proceed from the body and those that proceed from the soul (R44; L103); it should also be observed that, since there are three oratorical instruments, amplification is proper to this genus, and especially the kind made from comparisons, [285] just as the enthymeme is proper to the judicial and the example to the deliberative. And these are in Book 1. For it is taught in Book 3 that the oration is to be interwoven with demonstrative praises, as does Isocrates, who always inserted something, and this is what Gorgias said, for the oration is hardly ever lacking with him, because if he were to speak of Achilles he would praise Peleus, then Acacus, and then God, and similarly even fortitude, that he had done either this or that, or something similar. And even in Bk. 2 it is stated (R129; L295) that the more proper should be brought forth before the common. For some things are common, as when someone praises Achilles because he is a man, and that he came from semi-gods, and that soldiers came under him; these things, however, are found in many others and pertain to the praise of Achilles no more than they do to Diamedes. Other things are proper, as that he killed Hector, the bravest of the Trojans; that he slayed Cycnum, son of Neptune, who prevented all of the Greeks from disembarking, since he was invulnerable; that he was the youngest of all the heroes in the Trojan war; that he set out for that expedition without having taken an oath—for all these things happened to Achilles and to no one else (1396b). From this it is easily seen that Aristotle gives less approval to common praises, on which orators of our times usually dwell at length when they celebrate native land and family, rather than less common and more proper praises, of which kind are the sayings and deeds of the one who is being praised, which in Aristotle's view are the first things to be attended to.

Judicial Forms

Judicial forms are gathered from the inspection of three things: for what causes injury is done; who does it; and with what. So that the causes of injury may be known, seven causes of human actions are enumerated (R46; L109): chance, force, nature, custom, reasoning, anger, and cupidity; but these are not differentiated from others that effect injury. However, that the causes are three is indicated in Book 2 of the dialectical topics (*locis Topicis*) (R134; L305), [286] where it is stated that a topic is taken from division in the following way, "If there are always three causes of injurious action" and what follows. Victorius explains these as from utility, from pleasure, and from anger, and Maioragius in the same way. We think that the causes of injuries may be collected from the seven causes of human action we have just noted. When men act from the first three of these they are not said to act of themselves (*per se*). Thus injury is not that which is done by fortune, or by force, or by nature (R45; L107), because to cause injury is to act spontaneously and of oneself (*per se*), but such actions are not spontaneous. It follows that the causes whereby men are said to act of themselves, since these are four in number, can be accommodated only with great difficulty to Aristotle's words cited above. What to do? If mention had been made of more than three causes, as Victorius also indicates with a kind of supposition and by way of example, what if there are only three? A plausible explanation can be offered here, namely, that although four causes through which men act of themselves are named—custom, reasoning, anger, and cupidity—nonetheless these are reduced to three in the following text: "As for things they do of themselves and of which they are the cause, some are the result of habit, others of appetite, and of the latter some that participates in reason, some that is apart from reason" (R46; L109). And so three causes of injury do exist: habit, when this is bad, of which kind are the iniquities done by Clodius and Cataline; the appetite that participates in reason, also called the will; and the appetite that is apart from reason, that is, an emotion (*affectio*), such as anger and cupidity. And that topic can be explained by division, in such a way that the causes of injury are three, namely, [287] either habit, or will and reasoning, or emotion.

Common Propositions

Apart from forms (*formae*) attention should be paid to common propositions (*propositiones communes*), which Aristotle treats in Bk. 1. It is necessary for those who deliberate, litigate, or demonstrate to have propositions concerning what can or cannot come to be, whether something is a fact or not, and whether something will exist or not (R16; L39). Moreover, since all those who praise and blame, as well as those who persuade or dissuade, along with those who accuse and defend, attempt not only to defend what has been said, but also whether the matter is large or small, good or bad, honest or corrupt, or just or unjust—whether they speak absolutely or comparatively, comparing one thing to another—it is obvious that it is fitting that they have propositions concerning large and small and more and less, both generally and of each matter in particular, whether it be more or less good, or an injury, or a right, and similarly of other things. From this it is gathered that there are four kinds (*genera*) of common propositions: of what can or cannot be done (the possible or impossible); of fact or non-fact (present or past fact); of future or non-future (future fact); and of great and small. And although these propositions are said to be common because they can be accommodated to all kinds, nonetheless it should be understood that some are more accommodable than others. For Aristotle writes in Bk. 2: "Of the commonplaces, amplification is most appropriate for epideictic rhetoric, as has been stated; the past to forensic, since things past are the subject of judgment; and the possible and future to deliberative" (R117; L265).

The Topical Faculty: Source of Forms and Common Propositions

So that we may understand that the entire supply of arguments is obtained from the topical faculty (*topica facultas*), which we shall treat a little further below, it should be observed that both the kinds of forms and common propositions pertain [288] to the dialectical topics (*topicis dialecticis*). For although forms are deduced from the end of each genus contained under the topic of causes, as the deliberative from the useful, the demonstrative from the noble, the judicial from the just, so common propositions can also be deduced from the same dialectical topics.

Common Propositions Reduced to Dialectical Topics

As the first proposition of what is possible, from contraries: if one of contraries can come to be, also the other. The second, from similars: if a similar, also a similar. The third, from the lesser: if the more difficult, also the easier. The fourth, from a cause: if a beginning, also an end. The fifth, from an effect: if an end, also a beginning. The sixth, seventh, eighth, and ninth, from things that naturally follow or precede: if the later, also the earlier, and if the earlier, also the later; of matters that involve love and desire, these can come to be; of matters for which there are sciences and arts, if there are principles from which they arise, we can use them to urge and persuade. The tenth, from parts: if the parts can come to be, so can the whole. The eleventh, from a whole: if there are things that are wholes, so also parts. The twelfth, from a genus: if there is a genus, so also a form. The thirteenth, from a form: if there is a form, so also a genus. The fourteenth, from relatives that are contained among contraries: if one of the relatives, so also an other. The fifteenth, from a lesser: if something can be done without art or instrument, then it can be done better with art and diligence. The sixteenth, also from a lesser: if something from a weaker, inferior, more imprudent, then something better from their contraries.

Again, the first proposition of present fact is from [289] the lesser: if the lesser, also the greater. The second, from things that follow naturally: if the later, also the earlier. The third to the eighth are from causes and things that precede: if he could and would, he did; if he would, and nothing extrinsic impeded; if he could, and was angry; if he could, and was desirous; if it was future, that it would happen or he would do it; if it was past, whatever preceded it or was the reason for doing it. The ninth also is from things that follow naturally: if that whose cause it was was done, then also the thing caused was done.

In the same way the first and second proposition of future fact is from a cause: what is in one's power and volition will come to be; what is in one's desires, or wrath, or deliberative reason will come to be. The third is from things that precede: if nature requires that certain things come before, then they preceded. The fourth is from effects: if the cause of some deed has been placed, then it is likely that it will come to be.

And so likewise propositions relating to the great and the small, and from the comparison of greaters, lessers, and equals.

The Topic as Including All Forms and Common Propositions, and Those of Use in Conciliating and Arousing

Those forms themselves, and common propositions, and also those propositions which are useful for conciliating and arousing the souls of hearers, Aristotle calls topics *(loci)*, when he is writing Bk. 2. But for us there are also topics that are had for almost all individual forms that are useful and necessary, for propositions have been selected for each of them. On this account one should take from these topics enthymemes of the good or bad, of the fair or foul, of the just or unjust, and of characters and emotions and habits, in the same way as we have prepared the previous topics. These indeed are said to be the most powerful cause of the distinction of topics (R130; L295), for they do not [290] pertain more to one genus than to another and are suitable for proving any matter whatever and for demonstrating any question. Aristotle indicates as much when he adds: "Let us now endeavor to find topics about enthymemes in general in another way, assuming and saying . . ." and what follows (1396b/1397a).

The Topic of Selection *(Locus selectionis)*

In preparing arguments recourse should first be had to the topic that Aristotle calls the topic (or method) of selection and this is the first of the *Topics,* namely, that of selecting those factors that are in the thing itself *(in re ipsa).* For Aristotle teaches that in any question the orator treats, whether infinite or finite, he should hold to what is inherent in the subject. For example, should he inquire whether justice is or is not a good, he should argue from considerations that are intrinsic to justice and to the good (R129; L295). Should he be persuading the Athenians to take up or not take up a war (R128; L291), he should consider what their supplies are, whether their strengths are naval or military or both, and how strong these are, their sources of revenue, who their friends or enemies are, what wars they have already waged, with what success, and similar matters. Should he be praising the Athenians, he should know about the naval engagement at Salamis against Xerxes the king of the Persians under Themistocles' leadership, or the battle of Marathon against Darius the king of the Persians under Miltiades' leadership, or the war they waged for Heraclides, or something of that kind. Should he be censuring them, he should know how they subjugated the Greeks into slavery, and how they expelled the Aeginetans from their own cities, or slaughtered their youths, or left the Potideans with only a single garment, or any other wrongful act they committed.

Should he be preparing an accusation or a defense, he should consider matters that are proper and essential to the case. For the same reason should he wish to treat of liberality, magnificence, or other [291] virtues, he had better know the nature of each. If he should wish to urge the Venetian senate to undertake a war against the Turks, he should know both their supplies and revenues, their friends and enemies, and indeed other wars that have been waged by the Republic of Venice, and then argue from these. Should he wish to praise Emperor Charles V, he should take account of the latter's victories and his outstanding deeds. Should he wish to call someone to justice and make an accusation, he should know what he did that was wrong and dishonest. The same would apply to cases of opposition, vituperation, and defense. For any deeds that apply or any questions that are to be treated must be diligently and thoroughly known and understood.

This same message is given by Cicero in Bk. 2 of his *De oratore,* calling this precept not merely important but necessary. For, just as those who do not know what the crime is cannot say anything about it by way of reproach, so those who are ignorant can only puff up their cheeks and let empty words flow out in an effort to appear truly eloquent. Socrates meant this when he said that all are eloquent enough in matters they know, perhaps wishing by this to turn orators toward obtaining knowledge of their subject matter rather than turn them away from eloquence. For anyone who pays no attention to this precept will gain nothing from perusing books on rhetoric and from practicing speeches, for without doubt he will be thought incapable of speech or poorly prepared for it. Nor will he have the power of Demosthenes or of Cicero, for the only one who can excel in the praise of eloquence is one who knows his subject matter and the details that are proper to it.

Similarly matters that are prior to the subject should also be investigated. For Cicero saw how errors were made in matters that entered into the defense of Archias . . . [292–273² note change of pagination; 274²] . . . But we would be much too long were we to gather together all the errors that were made in that case. Thus much for the topic of selection.

The Definition of a Topic

The topic of an enthymeme *(locus enthymematis)* is the same as what is called an element *(stoícheion, elementum)* by Aristotle (R130; L295), just as it is said by Cicero to be the seat and quasi residence of an argument, the place in which an argument is located.

Two Meanings of Topic

Topics (*loci*) are said to be first axioms (*axiomata*) that are self-evident and illuminating (*illustria*), what Boethius in Bk. 2 of his *De topicis differentiis* calls first and maximal propositions, on the ground that they offer proof (*fides*) for all other propositions but do not themselves require proof from another source. Then there are rules (*paraggelmata*). These, as Alexander tells us in his commentary on the first book of the *Topics,* are like admonitions that have a certain wider application than axioms and are simpler, and from them others are discovered. Boethius calls them differences of primary and maximal propositions, such that axioms almost without number are differentiated under these headings. Therefore, as can be learned from Alexander, Theophrastus and many other peripatetics, when considering axioms simply and absolutely, called them topics; the others whence they arise, they called either rules and admonitions, or with the addition that they are *paraggelmatikous,* that is, preceptive and advising topics, and this [275²] they think was Aristotle's teaching about the topics of arguments. Others would call topics the universal genera and supreme headings under which axioms are contained, and this they have said was Cicero's teaching.

Two Kinds of Topics

Aristotle taught that there are two kinds of topics. The first is that of true enthymemes which are either apposite for demonstrating that something is the case (R130; L295), for example, that the glory of the Roman people was the result of the Mithridatic war, or not the case, for example, that an army cannot be controlled by an emperor who cannot control himself, or apposite for disproving, for example, that is licet to kill a man for some cause, against what Milo's adversaries were saying. Another kind is that of apparent or adumbrating enthymemes (*enthymematum adumbratorum*), which are found either in speech, for example, when a term is offered after the fashion of a conclusion with no syllogism given, or in reality, for example, if an argument were based on a sign, that all wise men are just because Socrates was wise and just.

How Many Topics Are There?
Cicero's Eighteen Topics

Aristotle enumerates twenty-three true enthymemes for demonstrating (R130; L295) and seven for refuting (R138; L317). Since for ease of treatment these are reducible to the topics enumerated by Cicero in his *Topics* (II,23–26), it is best first to consider Cicero's topics, which are eighteen in number. On this account, as is apparent from the *Prior Analytics,* since the matter being treated, that is, the terms of a question, is either a subject or a predicate, five things may be inquired into, namely, what precedes, what follows, what is convertible, what is incompatible, and what is conjoined, there are three topics (*loci*) that precede—genus, cause, and antecedents; four that follow—species, effect, conjugates, and consequences; three that convert—definition, enumeration of parts, and etymology (*notatio*); three that are incompatible—difference, contraries, and incompatibles; and five that are conjoined—similars, adjuncts, [276²] greaters, lessers, and equals. These are enumerated by Cicero as follows: the first locus is for him from a definition; the second, from an enumeration of parts; the third, from etymology; the fourth, from conjugates; the fifth, from genus; the sixth, from form or species; the seventh from similarity; the eighth, from difference; the ninth, from contraries;[7] the tenth, from adjuncts; the eleventh, from antecedents; the twelfth, from consequents; the thirteenth, from incompatibles (*a repugnantibus*); the fourteenth, from causes (*caussis*); the fifteenth, from things effected; the sixteenth, from greaters; the seventeenth, from equals; and the eighteenth, from lessers. For the sake of brevity Aristotle's topics may be reduced to these eighteen, so that one listing may readily be compared to the other.

The Reduction of Aristotle's Topics to Cicero's

"One topic of demonstrative enthymemes is derived from contraries" (R130; L297). This is Cicero's ninth, although for him it has a wider extension, since "contraries" (*contraria*) means not only what Aristotle calls *enantia*, which he names *adversa*, but also *serētika, ta pros ti, apophatika, privantia, relata,* and *negantia,* that is, all kinds of *anti-keimena* or opposites. For a contrary differs from a difference, for things that are contrary differ not only from each other but also from other things the contrary excludes, as virtue and vice. Things that merely differ, as man and plane tree, do not do this. Moreover, one thing is said to be contrary to one other, but the one is different from the many. A contrary also differs from an incompatible, for incompatibles are not contraries but rather one contrary that is opposed to what follows from another contrary, the way in which love is contrary to hatred and is incompatible with the evil deed that results from hatred.

"Another topic is from similar inflections (*ex similibus casibus*)" (R131; L297). This is Cicero's fourth [277²], which is said to be from conjugates. For with Cicero in the second part of the *Topics* conjugation is said to be a neighbor of etymology (*Topica* III.12), because etymology is taken from the force of the name, and again, conjugation is contained within a similarity of designation and is perceptible from derivation, as Boethius has noted. With Aristotle in the second book of the *Topics* (II,9) conjugates differ from inflections, for all inflections are indeed conjugates, but not all conjugates are inflections. For inflections are modes of action, as justly, strongly, healthfully, suited for a strong bodily constitution, and these are to be distinguished from conjugates that are things themselves, such as the just woman, the just man, and justice itself.

"Another topic is from things that relate to each other (*quae conferuntur ad se invicem*)" (R131; L297). This is reducible to Cicero's ninth topic, from contraries.

"Another topic is derived from the greater and the lesser" (R132; L301). The topic from the greater is Cicero's sixteenth, that from the lesser his eighteenth. In these topics it seems to many that he has departed considerably from Aristotle's teaching, for they think that the argument he calls from the lesser is really that from the greater. For, if that which seems less and is less verisimilar is present, much more will that which seems more and is more verisimilar be present. For example, on behalf of Sextius: If you wish to save the reign of Tigranus, who was an enemy of the Roman people, how much more ought you wish to conserve that of Ptolemaeus, who was always an associate, always a friend. On behalf of Caecinna: The army that moves those who are armed, would it not seem to have moved those called to the toga? And in ecclesiastical rhetoric: Our Lord Jesus Christ forgives the gravest and most serious sins we daily commit; and we are not able to bear the slightest injuries of our brothers? [278²] Some say that these arguments are from the greater; we say from the lesser, that is, from the less verisimilar, following the teaching of Aristotle, which looks to the verisimilitude in the comparison, not to the magnitude of the deed.

"Further, if there is no question of greater or less" (R132; L301). This is Cicero's seventeenth topic, which is different from the topic of similarity, since whereas quantity respects equality, quality respects similarity.

"Another topic is found in time" (R132; L301); this reduces to the topic from an equal.

"Another consists in turning upon the opponent what has been said against ourselves" (R133; L303). From the greater.

"Another from definition" (R133; L305). This is Cicero's first.

"Another topic is derived from different significations of a term, as is correctly said of it in the *Topics*" (R134; L305). Concerning the "correctly" (*recte*), this is commonly taken to mean the different ways terms are understood when taken correctly. We think, without any doubt, that Aristotle is looking here to the third (read: thirteenth) chapter of the first book of the *Topics* (I,13), which is concerned with multiple meanings, and by the words "of it," the "it" refers to multiple significations, so that the expression means that the matter of multiple significations has been treated correctly in the *Topics*. That the most learned Robortellus thought the same we have seen in the annotations to his manuscripts, and also Salvatore Bartolucius, with whom he had the closest friendship, and indeed that most noble and learned man Ioannes Vincentius Pinellus, whose explanation seems to postulate that the text be read to include the terms *peri tou orthōs* [see Loeb ed., p. 305, note d]. This topic can be reduced to Cicero's fifth, that from a genus. For a homonym, which has multiple meanings, is like a genus to different significations.

"Another, from division" (R134; L305). When a genus is divided, either it is eliminated, or it is put in a more universally posited genus, or it is made a species, and this is Cicero's fifth topic, [279^2] from a genus. For example, animal is divided into man, lion, donkey, and species of this kind. Animal is not; therefore, man is not. Every animal is eliminated; therefore, so is man. Wrong-doing occurs from either habit, or reasoning, or passion; for these are the species of wrong-doing we have enumerated above. There has been no wrong-doing; therefore, neither has there been wrong-doing from habit. All kinds of wrong-doing have occurred; therefore, there has been wrong-doing from habit. Or, if all species are eliminated the genus is removed; again, if there is one species, the genus is also posited. This is Cicero's sixth topic, from a species. For example: There is no man, no lion, no donkey, nothing of this kind; therefore, no animal. Or, there is a man, therefore, an animal. No wrong-doing was done by habit, or reasoning, or passion; therefore, no wrong-doing. Or, he broke the law by habit; therefore he did a wrong.

"Another topic is from induction" (R135; L307). This reduces to Cicero's seventh, from similarity.

"Another is from a previous judgment in regard to the same or a similar or a contrary matter" (R135; L309). This seems to pertain to Cicero's tenth topic, from adjuncts.

"Another, from parts" (R136; L311). This is a common topic from the parts of a genus, of wholes, or of homonyms, and it is reducible to Cicero's second topic, from an enumeration of parts, since when all the parts are removed so is the homonym, the genus, or the whole. And, to the degree that the homonym is said in many ways, so the topic is taken in many ways; to the extent that a genus is divided, so is the topic from division; in whatever way parts are enumerated, if these parts are taken away, so is the homonym or the genus or the whole. This is the topic from parts, which is to be distinguished from the topic from species because the former is more universal; moreover, the topic from parts always contains several parts, whereas the topic from species can be from a single species.

"Another, since in most human affairs something good or bad can eventuate [280²], there is a topic to employ consequences either to persuade or dissuade, to accuse or defend, or to praise or blame" (R136; L311). This is Cicero's twelfth topic, which can also be connected with his eleventh, from antecedents, and his tenth, from adjuncts. Although for Cicero there is a distinction here on the ground that antecedents and consequents are necessary and adjuncts are not, Aristotle seems to take consequents generally to include things that do not follow necessarily. Apart from these there are consequents of nature and consequents of arguments, and the same holds for antecedents. For the sun rising is an antecedent of nature; day is a consequent. The antecedent of argument is of many types: either something less universal than the consequent, as, if man is, animal is; or something more universal, as, if all animals sense, so does man; or later than the consequent, as, if she gave birth, she slept with a man; or earlier than the consequent, as, if he is arrogant, he is offensive; or equal to the consequent, as, if he is man, he is by nature risible; or contemporaneous with the consequent, as, if the moon is eclipsed, the earth has blocked the sun. In this way there are also many types of consequent. Here in this text Aristotle takes account of consequents of nature that are antecedents of arguments. For example, if one does not wish to be envied, one should avoid being educated. Here also can be seen an argument from adjuncts, in the following way: if he is educated, tied to this is that he be envied; if he is educated, tied to this is that he be wise.

"Another topic arises when one must persuade or dissuade in regard to two opposites, and one must use the method just considered for the one or the other" (R136; L311). This reduces to the topic from contraries.

"Again, since one does not praise the same thing in public and in secret, but in public chiefly what is just and beautiful, [281²] in private what is more pragmatic, another topic consists in interchanging these respective objects" (R136; L313). This reduces to Cicero's eighth topic, from difference.

"Another topic arises from analogy" (R137; L313). This is equivalent to the seventeenth topic, from equals.

"Another consists in concluding from the identity of what happened to the identity of its antecedents" (R137; L313). This reduces to the twelfth, from consequents.

"Another topic comes from the fact that the same person does not always choose the same thing before and after, but the contrary" (R137; L315); to the eighth topic, from difference.

"Another topic, if a result intended is not achieved, to affirm that it is or was the cause of the action" (R137; L315); to the fourteenth, from causes.

"Another, common to forensic and deliberative rhetoric, considers what is persuasive and dissuasive, and what causes men to act or not" (R138; L317); again, from causes.

"Another, from things that seem to happen and yet are incredible" (R138; L317); to the fifteenth, from effects.

"Another, appropriate for refutation, to examine incompatible elements (*repugnantia*)" (R138; L319). This is Cicero's thirteenth topic.

"Another, when actions or individuals are attacked by slander in a way thought to be unjust, to explain the cause of the paradox" (R139; L319); to the topic from causes.

"Another, from the cause, and if this exists, so does that, and if it does not exist, neither does that" (R139; L319); to the topic just noted, from causes.

"Another topic, to consider whether there was or is a better course than that advised or is being, or has been, carried out" (R139; L321); to the topic from the greater.

"Another, when something is to be done that is contrary to what has been done, to consider both together" (R139; L321); to the topic from incompatibles.

"Another topic consists in making use of past wrong-doing for purposes of accusation or defense" (R140; L321); this can be reduced to the topic from causes.

"Another, from the name" (R140; L323). This is Cicero's third topic, from etymology.

[282²] Apart from the topics of true enthymemes Aristotle enumerates topics of apparent or adumbrating enthymemes, four in speech (R141; L325) and six in reality (R142; L329). He also adds two ways in which enthymemes may be refuted, and since enthymemes are drawn from four sources, the verisimilar, the example, the tecmerium, and the sign, he teaches how each of these may be refuted. All of these matters are taught in Aristotle's own words (R145; L33).

The maxim (*sententia*) also pertains to the enthymeme. For, there are two kinds of maxim, one without an epilogue, and this is *per se* evident, the other when an epilogue is added, and this is either part of the enthymeme or it is enthymematic (R123–124; L279–283).

But all of this is about the enthymeme, which is the first oratorical demonstration; for the second is the example, which also reduces to the enthymeme, as when Aristotle explains how certain enthymemes can be drawn out of examples. For the enthymeme, taken in a broad sense, also includes the example, although taken strictly it is distinguished from the example. It seems to have been broadly taken in the following words from the introduction: "And yet they say nothing about enthymemes which are the body of proof" (R2; L5); and taken strictly when describing the general characteristics of rhetoric, where the words read as follows: "The proof that it demonstrates, or appears to demonstrate, as in the case of dialectics, is either induction or the syllogism, or what appears to be a syllogism, and so it is in rhetoric. For the example is an induction and the enthymeme a syllogism" (R8; L19).

Examples of Two Kinds: Facts Real or Invented

Examples are taken from facts that are either real (*facta*) or invented (*ficta*). An example of real fact would concern an event that actually occurred. An instance is the following: Darius did not cross over to Greece until he took Egypt, but when he had taken Egypt he crossed over. [283²] Again, Xerxes did not attack until he occupied; but when he had occupied he attacked. So this king, if he shall have taken Egypt, will cross over. On this account we must make preparations against him and not permit Egypt to fall under his power (R120; L275).

An invented example is either a comparison (*parabola*) or a fable (*logus*). A comparison is based on invented events that manifest similarity, as to say that magistrates should be chosen by lot is similar to saying that atheletes should be chosen by lot, not on the ground that they could compete but on the ground of their being lucky; or choosing any particular sailor to be helmsman by lot, on the ground that the choice should be decided by one's fortune and not by one's knowledge (R121; L275). A fable is concerned with events that show little similarity. An example is that of Stesichorus, among the people of Himera, against Phalaris, who used the fable of the horse that, wishing to punish the stag, ended in servitude to man. Or of Aesop, among the people of Samos, against a popular demagogue, who used the fable of the fox that, being afflicted by dog-fleas, would not permit the hedgehog to remove them (R121; L275–277). This is concerned with the first artificial proof, which occurs in a proof; the second is found in moral matters. Aristotle calls this the "second" at the beginning of his treatment of the demonstrative genus, when he writes: "When speaking of these, we shall at the same time bring to light the means of making us appear to be endowed with character, which is a second type of proof (*fides*)" (R38; L91).

ENDNOTES

1. This passage reads as follows in Riccobono's Latin translation: "Quare necessarium est, enthymema esse, ut etiam exemplum, de iis, quae ita contingunt, ut saepe se habeant aliter, exemplum quidem inductionem, enthymema vero syllogismum. Et ex paucis, ac saepe paucioribus, quam ex quibus primus syllogismus existit. Si quid enim horum notum sit, non oportet dicere. Nam id ipse supplet auditor, quemadmodum cum Dorieus vicerit coronarium certamen, satis est

dicere eum vicisse olympia, esse autem olympia coronarium certamen, non oportet adiungere, nam id omnes cognoscunt."—*Aristotelis ars rhetorica,* (Venice, 1579), p. 10. Hippocrates Apostle's translation of this, made rather literally from the Greek, reads: "Enthymemes and examples, then, must deal with things which are possible for the most part but can be otherwise, in which case an example will be an induction and an enthymeme will be a syllogism; and enthymemes should use few premises, and often fewer than [what] are required by a primary syllogism, for what is familiar need not be mentioned; the listener supplies it for himself. For instance, in showing that Dorieus was crowned by being a victor in the Olympics, it is enough to say that Dorieus was a victor in the Olympics, without adding that victors in the Olympics are crowned, a fact which everybody knows."—*Aristotle: Selected Works,* (Grinnell, Iowa, 1982), p. 611.

2. The example Cicero gives in *De inventione* II.58 runs as follows. The first part should state the basis of the argument, such as "Things done by design are managed better than those without design." This should be supported by a variety of reasons, e.g., "The house managed with a reasoned plan is better than one without," "An army commanded by a wise general is guided better than one managed by a fool," "A ship navigated by an expert pilot has the most successful voyage." These make up the second part, the proof of the major premise. The third part then states the minor premise, such as "Of all things nothing is better managed than the universe." The fourth part will provide the proof of the minor premise, citing the orderly risings and settings of the constellations, the changes of the seasons, the alternation of night and day. In the fifth part comes the conclusion, which either states merely that "Therefore, the universe is administered by design," or which sums up the entire argument as follows: "Therefore, if those things are administered better which are governed by design than those which are administered without design, and nothing is governed better than the universe, then the universe is governed by design." (Loeb ed., pp. 101–3)

3. That is, that writers have constructed but a small portion of the art, which Riccobono gives as [5] in his enumeration.

4. The proposition that is omitted is that enthymemes are the substance of persuasion.

5. See the text cited in note 1 above.

6. In what follows, the pagination of Riccobono's Latin translation is indicated by a page number preceded by an R, e.g., [R16]. The corresponding pagination of J. H. Freese's English translation in the Loeb edition is indicated by a page number preceded by an L, e.g., [L39].

7. In listing these contrarieties Boethius expands *ex contrariis* into four subdivisions, thus giving his ninth, from contraries *(ex adversis),* his tenth, from privatives *(ex privantibus),* his eleventh, from relatives *(ex relativis),* and his twelfth, from contradictories *(ex negantibus).* Thus Boethius's listing of intrinsic topics comes to a total of twenty-one, as opposed to Cicero's eighteen. See Niels J. Green-Pedersen, *The Tradition of the Topics in the Middle Ages* (Munich-Vienna: Philosophia Verlag, 1984), p. 56.

THE NATURE OF THE
ORATION OF CHARACTER

[283²] Character is what makes people appear to be of a certain type, and it is considered by psychologists, ethicists, poets, and orators, each for a different reason. By psychologists, insofar as it affects the powers of the soul. By ethicists, insofar as, if [284²] good, it conduces to happiness, if bad, it destroys happiness. By poets, as it pertains to imitation, which Aristotle treats when he writes about tragedy, explaining that characters are good, appropriate, genuine, and consistent (1454a15–b18). By orators, insofar as they are an instrument of proof, and indeed the most powerful instrument, practically containing proof within themselves. Let us set aside other considerations and investigate those that pertain to the orator, to which we are led to observe first of all that we should look at character under three aspects, as it is in the speaker, in the audience, and in the speech itself. We now treat each of these in order.

The Character of the Speaker

The character of the speaker is constituted by the qualities he presents himself as having, that is, as possessing trustworthiness, prudence, and benevolence, and so appearing as worthy of confidence, prudent, and benevolent. In the first book, in enumerating artificial proofs Aristotle mentions only the speaker's being worthy of confidence (R7; L17), but this can be understood in two ways, either from the opinion of the audience in anticipation of good deeds on his part or from what he actually expresses in the speech. Here Aristotle takes it in the second way, that it suffices for the speaker to present a good character in his speech even though he does not possess it himself. For an orator may be good or bad, he also explains (R6; L15), when he presents the speaker from the viewpoint of his ability, that is, his faculty or power of using a false persuasible, or from the viewpoint of deliberate choice, as when he seeks glory for himself through the use of false arguments.

On this account Quintilian, whatever he intends, speaks of a good man speaking well. For that can mean that the man is good, but not necessarily, for a bad speaker who appears from his speech to be worthy of confidence will be more persuasive than a good man who is unable to express his trustworthiness in words. Indeed, the person who, even before speaking, is thought to be good because he is actually so, [285²] and then in his speech shows himself worthy of confidence, will without doubt be the better persuader. The first quality is of course useful, but the second is necessary besides.

When Aristotle treats of the Republic in the same first book (R37; L89) he adds good will to probity in the following way: "For proofs are established by ethical argument, since we have confidence in an orator who exhibits certain qualities, such as goodness, good will, or both." But in the second book (R74; L171) he makes mention of three character traits, prudence, virtue, and good will, meaning by virtue genuineness, goodness, and probity. For, treating of the same matter, he sometimes calls it *tous epieikeis*, sometimes *tous hagathous*, and sometimes he opposes it as a virtue to *machthērian*.

The Character of the Audience

The character of the audience is that according to which auditors appear to be of a certain type, and this on four counts, by reason of their emotions, their habits, their age, or their fortune (R107; L247). The emotions are, for example, pleasure, desire, fear, and sorrow. Character traits associated with pleasure can be seen from the matters treated in the first book on pleasurable things (R49; L115). Those associated with desire are known from the treatise on the emotions, for example, wrath, whose contrary is gentleness, love and hate, friendship and enmity (R75; L173). So we have character traits arising from fear, whose contrary is confidence, whose parts extend all the way to modesty, and character traits associated with sorrow, whose parts are mercy, indignation, envy, and jealousy. Character traits associated with habits are those of justice, courage, self-control, magnificence, magnanimity, liberality, gentleness, prudence, wisdom, and the habits of their contraries, which are treated in the first book under the demonstrative genus (R39; L91). Character traits associated with age (R107; L247) are those of the young up to their thirtieth year and of the old beyond the age of forty-nine; of men, with respect to their bodies, from thirty to thirty-five, with respect to their souls, up to forty-nine. The characters of the young and the old are almost [286²] the opposite of each other, and those of men fall between the two. These are treated in the second book (R108–112; L249–257). Character traits associated with fortune are those of noble birth, wealth, power, good fortune, which are also treated in the second book (R113; L261).

The Character of an Oration

Character traits associated with an oration are those according to which the speech appears to be of a certain type, in such a way that it corresponds to the kinds and habituation of those to whom it is addressed (R163; L379). The kinds are said to be age, as boy, man, aged; sex, as woman, man; nationality, as Laconian, Thessalonian. Habituation is said, for example, of being an uneducated or an educated person.

The Employment of the Oration of Character

With respect to the character of the speaker, the character traits include prudence, virtue, and benevolence. Of the first two Cicero writes in the second book of *De officiis* as follows: "Faith that these are possessed can be effective of two things, if we think that the speaker has prudence added to justice. For, from these, we obtain trust in those who know more than we think we do, and we believe that they can see the future, and when it comes to acting, they are able to make proper judgments, expedite matters, and take counsel at the right time. For all regard such persons as true and prudent citizens. Such good and faithful men are held in such good faith that there is no suspicion of fraud or injustice in them. And so we feel that we can most rightly entrust to them our safety, our fortune, and our children." The third character trait is added to signify that they should be disposed in mind to be of good will. Cicero writes especially well of this: "We are forced, as it were, to love those in whom the following virtues are found: love for the multitude, ability to do good for them and gain their trust, ability to move them by the good opinion they induce of their liberal beneficence, justice, trust, and all the other virtues that pertain to gentleness and ease of character." And Aristotle teaches in the second [287²] book that we should love those who have done good either to us or to those whom we hold dear (R84; L193). On this account the orator will be especially loved for his disposition of soul to do good, for thus he will also be thought to be benevolent and a friend. For a friend is defined as one who wishes for another the goods he believes to be good, for the other's sake but not for his own, as far as lies in his power (R83; L193). For not a little sign of a well-wishing soul is the praise that seems to come not from adulation but from the truth. And so among the many reasons men are thought to be benevolent that we can take from Aristotle when he is treating of love, two especially stand out as making the orator appear good-willing, namely, memory of his deeds and the offices he has performed without arrogance, and the true praise he receives from his hearers without adulation (R83; L193). . . .

[Riccobono then goes on to cite particular examples of persuasion through character traits in the following works:

Cicero
>
> *Oratio pro Sexto Roscio Amerino*
> *Actio in Verrem*
> *Oratio pro Lege Manilia*
> *Oratio pro L. Flacco*
> *Academicae Quaestiones*, Lib.2
> *Oratio pro Marcello*
> *De Partitione Oratoria*
> *Oratio pro Milone*

Demosthenes
>
> *In prima Olynthiaca*
> *Adversus Midam*
> *Oratio de Corona*

Aulus Gellius
Q. Metellus Numidicus
Scipio Africanus
Sophocles de Neoptolemo
Homer
Xenophon
Horace]

Ludovico Carbone's
On Invention

DE ORATORIA
ET DIALECTICA
INVENTIONE

Vel

DE LOCIS COMMUNIBUS
LIBRI QUINQUE

*In quibus plana, qua de omni re proposita, expedite disserere,
copioseque dicere, et aliorum scripta recte exponere liceat,
demonstratur ratio: Dum omnium, qui in
Rhetorica et Dialectica traduntur, locorum communium
natura, vis, et usus plene, facileque explicantur*

Auctore

Ludovico Carbone, a Costaciaro

*Academico Parthenio et Sacrae Theologiae in almo Gymnasio
Perusino olim publico Professore*

Cum triplici Indice

Cum Privilegio

VENETIIS, M.D. LXXXIX.

Apud Damianum Zenarum

FIVE BOOKS ON ORATORICAL AND DIALECTICAL INVENTION

or

ON COMMON TOPICS

*In which everything proposed is discussed fully and expeditiously
and the writings of others correctly explained, while the contents of
Rhetoric and Dialectic are being covered and the nature,
power, and use of common topics are explained
in full and simple fashion*

by

Ludovico Carbone of Costaciaro

*of the Parthenian Academy
Former Public Professor of Sacred Theology
in our University of Perugia*

With three indexes

With Privilege

VENICE, 1589

From the Press of Damian Zenaro

Ludovico Carbone on Invention

Carbone's book on invention ranks just below his treatise on sacred rhetoric as a window opening into his classroom, where interdisciplinary teaching created a remarkable opportunity for gaining erudition, critical acumen, and practical advice. The book contains the fruits of his vast knowledge of philosophical and rhetorical thought and it shows his enthusiasm to impart as much of it as seemed appropriate to the subject. At 647 pages, that may be more than students could absorb. Nevertheless Carbone apparently did attempt to teach the content of the work, if we can take him at his word. He relates that he took pity on his students, who were struggling to get down on paper, "not without great labor and loss of time," what he recorded here and so he hastened to publish "this rough work" at the behest of many friends. (See the advice to the reader that follows for his apology, typical of Renaissance literature, but in his case also credible.)

Carbone's book was meant to supply what he found to be lacking in current textbooks. No one, he says, has adequately treated the foundation of topical argument in the *Categories,* the first treatise in Aristotle's *Organon,* nor has anyone fully explained the dialectical topics and made them clear with enough examples. Another shortcoming: examples given for topics were not related to specific kinds of rhetoric.[1]

To remedy these defects, in book one Carbone first establishes the nature, use, and necessity of rhetoric, then treats the question and the foundations on which questions are based. This leads to a detailed explanation of Aristotle's ten categories, then to argumentation and the ways in which middle terms can be used to answer questions. The concluding part of the book explains what topics are, their various kinds, and their uses in probable argument. This book is here translated in its entirety.

The second book provides extensive exemplification of rhetorical topics, but in view of the detailed treatment of this subject matter in preceding sections, this book is not translated here. The third and fourth books then give similar treatment to dialectical topics, the third being devoted to intrinsic topics and the fourth to extrinsic topics. Forced by the detail of Carbone's exposition to be selective, we have decided to give here only our

---

1. For a full discussion of the intellectual context of this volume, see Jean D. Moss, "Antistrophic Rhetoric: Aristotelian Rhetoric in Renaissance Rome and Padua," *Philosophy in the Sixteenth and Seventeenth Centuries: Conversations with Aristotle,* edited by Constance Blackwell and Sachiko Kusukawa (Aldershot, Hampshire: Ashgate, 1999), chapter 5.

translation of chapters twelve through eighteen of book three—a portion that explains Aristotle's teaching on the four causes and how these may be used in dialectical argument. This is of particular interest for two reasons. The first because it is the most innovative element in Carbone's view of dialectic, considering that causes are the preserve of the *Posterior Analytics* and their most important use is thought to be in demonstrative argument. The second is that it provides an illustration of the different levels of instruction in rhetoric and dialectic within the Jesuit system of education. Carbone's treatment of the four causes as topics for probable reasoning at the elementary level has already been given in section one, in the overview of dialectical reasoning provided in his *Introduction to Logic.* Here we offer essentially the same material, but now at an advanced level and with extensive exemplification from classical philosophy, literature, and contemporary works, including frequent references to Agricola. In his exposition Carbone clarifies difficult points and his illustrations are copious, shedding great light on the range of literature his students were expected to know. His citations are actually included in the text of the original, but for editorial reasons we have removed them from the text and provide their essential content in endnotes as "Glosses and Notes."

The fifth book gives special attention to topics employed by both orators and dialecticians. A brief excerpt from chapter eleven of this book is included in our translations because it describes in some detail the differences between the ways in which orators and dialecticians make use of the topics.

The five books reveal the metamorphosis in the teaching of invention that was taking place in the early modern period. Dialectical invention, sequestered during the Middle Ages in theoretical philosophical and theological debate, has now been appropriated by rhetoricians. The Jesuit Fathers in particular seem to have taken to heart Aristotle's advice in the *Rhetoric,* that he who would become a master of rhetorical argument should study logic and the *Topics* in order to understand the similarities and differences in the two kinds of arguments (l.1, 1355a11). The blend of the two kinds of invention was reflected even in the *Ratio studiorum* of 1599. It suggests that students in the academies be expected to engage in disputations in an oratorical rather than in a dialectical style and that the best of these exercises should be offered in public exhibitions.[2]

2. Flynn, *The "De Arte Rhetorica,"* Part I, 18–19.

TABLE OF CONTENTS

❧❧

BOOK ONE

BOOK TWO

TO THE READER

If ever a writer or painter were permitted to use an imperfect word or picture, my reader, in your humanity allow me the same indulgence in the composition of this book, since in putting it together I could not apply all the care that a work of great labor and judgment requires. So I wish you to know—for what I here propose you are capable of noting by yourself— that our treatise on invention is not as polished and complete in its details as it would have been were it not necessary to publish it before its time.

But here a prudent and experienced reader would say, why not adopt that best and solid counsel of Horace, who, speaking of the editing of books, said "let it be printed in the ninth year." And this I would have done, if a certain necessity and usefulness for others, which is my principal motivation for writing and editing, had not impelled me to a premature edition. For, while explaining to certain of my students the art of invention, the work then not yet finished—when I saw how they were grasping what I was teaching by pen, as is the custom, not without great labor and loss of time—so as to lift from them such a heavy task and to satisfy the wishes of many friends requesting it of me, I allowed this still rude and rough work (later, with God's help, to be more properly polished) to be taken from my hands.

Indeed, lest while reading this you incline to the opinion that you will receive little or nothing from reading our treatise, we make mention of what others have written on this subject. Then, by comparing their work with what we have written you will see right away what profit can be gained from our labors. Moreover, although many learned and excellent men have treated of invention, if you consider diligently the printed books that are now extant, and what must be known for a perfect understanding of invention, you will not find a single work among those that have been produced that is adequate to the task. For some have said practically nothing about the categories, which are the basic sources of good speaking and writing and the necessary elements and foundations of all the topics. Others explain some few topics in juvenile fashion and meagerly, providing only one example and mode of arguing; others make no mention of the oratorical topics accommodated to the three genera of causes; others pass over in silence the axioms of the compared question, of which there is maximum utility in every art; others think it is licit for them to leave untouched topics they call inartificial; others say nothing of the use of topics, which certainly is a principal concern in this treatise; and finally, lest I note too much omitted by others, others teach nothing concerning the judicative part, a knowledge of which is completely necessary for the use of the topics.

And these things I have said not to make you think I am criticizing other writers, who perhaps in writing have proposed for themselves a goal different from my own, but that I may lay out what should be explained concerning invention. All of these matters, and others besides, we touch on quickly when sketching the scope of this work and explaining how we have covered the matter in the individual books.

Our intention in this work has been to explain the universal art of invention and all the common topics that are necessary both for writing and for speaking. To achieve this end, when explaining the subject matter of the first book we have treated the question and the foundations of all questions and topics, while briefly explaining the ten categories, and also the argument, to whose discovery this entire art is ordered, and the nature and kinds of topics. In the second book, beginning the explanation of the topics, we have written first of the topics of persons, which serve the demonstrative genus, and here we have enumerated and defined several individual virtues. Then come the topics of the deliberative genus, where we consider the true and the good and their parts, the causes of human actions, and the passions and characters of individual age groups. To these we have added the topics of the judicial genus and also those of circumstances. In the third book we go on to the explanation of the topics that dialecticians customarily explain; and first of all the intrinsic topics, using the following method. First we set out the nature of the topic, then all its modes of arguing, illustrated with various examples, and finally, the use of the topic. In the fourth book we discourse of external, intermediate, inartificial, and comparative topics. Finally, in the last book we treat many matters relating to the use of the topics, and here we explain the judicative part, that is, the method of arguing used by both dialecticians and orators. And from this overview you can judge for yourself whether you cannot gather some fruit from this work, which is not yet, as I said, sufficiently finished and polished. Therefore, should you find anything that is less than pleasing, you have good reason for excusing me, while taking from it all that is good and just. Farewell.

BOOK ONE

Chap. I. The usefulness and necessity of the art of invention

[1]¹ Among the principal gifts given to the human race by the Supreme and Immortal God, men of learning have with reason listed the faculty of speech, for with it not only are the feelings of the body expressed by the imperfect sounds animals make, but it is given to us also to explain all the sensations and thoughts of the soul and communicate them fully to the ears of others.² For by speech, and especially serious and embellished speech, our discourse is brought by a kind of vehicle into the ears of others, [2] and when it has entered there it so affects and arouses the souls of hearers that it draws and impels them wherever it wishes. Nothing, as experience itself teaches, is more apt to attract human minds in a variety of ways, is more efficacious, than a thought expressed in suitable and embellished words. Thus it happens that those who have perfected this power of speech with practice and care and have equipped themselves with a supply of things to say always seem to stand out above other men, just as man himself by simple speech shows his superiority over dumb animals.³ So with reason eloquent speakers are heard with admiration and are adorned among all peoples with highest praise and the most ample rewards. From this you can easily gather how much work and how much struggle those ought to take on, who, inflamed with an honest love of glory and aspiring to stand out above others, seek to enter into this part of rhetoric, which is indeed the most abundant source of all human eloquence.⁴ And this part, namely, the part called invention, as all learned and experienced men teach, with merit takes highest place over all others. Through the power of invention you are prepared to think about all topics that enable a person to explain fully and ornately any matter proposed. [3] Finally, those who have fully understood and treated these topics will finally have found the sources of perfect eloquence. Thus I explain in the beginning how great an advantage this treatise offers, so that having perceived its utility, those desirous of speaking and discoursing well may be more disposed to attain knowledge of the topics to be discoursed about. And granted that one might have a lengthy discourse on the matter proposed, for us who are lovers of brevity, to have attained it to some slight degree will be sufficient.

So first, the faculty of invention brings much to the common and familiar speech we daily are accustomed to have with our friends.⁵ Indeed, one who possesses these topics always has at hand what to say, what to object, how to reply, and understand what others are saying, what they mean, and how to evaluate it, and from this arises much delight. Then it makes one prepared and ready for undertaking domestic affairs, for entering into commerce, for settling disputes, for entering into and dissolving contracts, and finally for any struggle whatever; since through it anyone is enabled to defend his own rights and contest those of others; and from all this arises not a little advantage.

[4] Toward these, through this power of discovering, the person who would sustain a public persona will see immediately if advice needs to be taken, if an opinion is to be sought about some doubtful matter or about any matter whatever that is perplexing and obscure, what stands in the way, what hastens along, what helps, what hinders, what is to be cautious about or let go, lest he have to spend a lengthy period of time deliberating. In this way he will state his position expeditiously, not without the admiration of others, whence he will receive maximum praise from all. Whoever lacks this faculty spends his time reading the writings of others without pleasure or fruit, because he perceives neither the ability, nor the art, nor the industry of the author, and, as necessarily follows, cannot in any way imitate or put to use the things he has read. Whoever lacks this faculty will seem to be dull, slow, dumb, and in some way lame, since he will be able to understand nothing, to grasp nothing, to state nothing. Whoever is not endowed with this faculty always falls unarmed and defenseless on the battleground of letters.

Just how great and how powerful this force and power of inventing is, I do not say useful but necessary, for those who wish to commit anything to writing, I think can hardly be expressed in words. For whoever knows the topics [5] finds the most fruitful sources, whence he draws the most plentiful rivulets to all parts;[6] whoever knows the topics has the greatest treasure, from which he can easily draw what he wishes, how much he wishes, and whenever he wishes; whoever knows the topics raises up the lowly, illumines the obscure, clothes the naked, and frees himself from whatever difficulties he encounters; whoever knows the topics easily enlarges, destroys, fights against, fights for, overcomes, and presses his adversary and drives him into a corner; whoever knows the topics . . .[7] And finally, whoever possesses the topics shows himself to be truly rich in every place and in every way.

On the other hand, whoever does not know the topics is in need of a large supply, is in great difficulty with the most ample matter, is blind in the light, is fearful at the appearance of an adversary, falls, and offers his hands to be bound with no honor. Without the topics the orator is dumb, the poet languishes, the lawyer loses his case, the philosopher admits defeat, the grammarian explains nothing correctly, the historian is dried up and without food, and lastly, every artisan appears completely lifeless.

We conclude therefore that he alone is truly rich who is filled with knowledge of the topics, for he can discourse on either side of any question that is proposed, than which nothing can be more delightful, [6] as has always been thought by educated men, nothing more laudable and worthy. No one can express even with the lengthiest of speeches just how great is the usefulness and the necessity of the common topics. No one, I say, of those who seek to attain for themselves some measure of erudition and to exceed others in excellence, who desire to obtain the greatest advantage from these studies, an advantage joined to the greatest of pleasures, who do not embrace with all their heart this one faculty of discoursing rightly and of speaking with eloquence.

Chap. 2. The matter, division, and title of this work

The usefulness and necessity of invention being demonstrated, its nature should now be explained, and this we would indeed do if we had not already done so in our other book *De arte dicendi,* which came out some time before these five books *De inventione.* These matters having already appeared, since I have covered in the place cited what should be said about the name, division, definition, and parts of invention, I will discourse more fully on questions and the nature of topics, which are the proper subject matter of this treatise. But before I proceed to this task, [7] I propose in this chapter to say a few things about the definition of invention previously given and the matter, order, and scope of this work. Thus invention, as Cicero conceives it, is nothing other than the thinking out of an argument, that is, of some kind of probable reason.[8] Or, invention is a faculty, or an art, whereby one can excogitate arguments that are suitable for proving any question.[9] In this work therefore, we with the help of God explain this method of finding arguments. The work itself is divided into five books.

The first book treats the matter of invention, that is, the question, the speech, the argument, and the argumentation, which we use as instruments for proving questions, and then the nature of topics and their division. The explanation of these things is very useful and necessary for all that we are to say about the art of invention. In the second book, proceeding to the treatment of topics, first we explain those that are special, the ones that orators customarily use. Then we move on to the exposition of the topics that are the province of dialecticians, and so in the third book we treat these, what the latter call intrinsic topics. [8] In the fourth book we discuss extrinsic topics, mediums, non-artificials, and other matters that bring much to treating questions comparatively. And finally, in the last book, beyond those matters that we have offered for individual topics, we give precepts designed for the use of the topics; also we write more fully about judgment, that is, the method of argumentation. And although I could put together many books on this material, and even treat more fully what I have already written, nonetheless, since I wish only to teach and to offer only matter that is proximate to the subject, I have restricted the vast material to what I can cover in these five books, and I have reduced it in a way as to omit nothing necessary and still make it easy to remember.

Granted that there were many ancient authors, and in our own times not a few learned and experienced men who are well versed in this subject matter, still, should anyone read our work he will not be sorry for having done so. For this I could give many reasons, listing more fully the advantages and utilities of our work; but, to avoid the vice of envy, I leave to the judgment of others just what and how much I have accomplished in this task, on which so many famous and distinguished men have also labored. This one thing I do say, and this [9] something most needed in writing on the topics, I have treated more fully than any other author I know how to use the topics, especially with regard to oratory.

But now one might ask why I have entitled these books *De inventione oratoria et dialectica,* since there is only one invention, and this, as some say, is proper to dialectic. To this inquiry you may be satisfied with what I have written in the third disputation of the book cited above,[10] where I have demonstrated that the invention of topics pertains not only to dialectic but also to oratory or rhetoric. Add also that there are certain topics that are completely proper to oratory and there are others that are the concern of the dialecticians. And finally, since we have treated of the topics in this way, our method of explanation is best suited to all uses, to those of both orators and dialecticians, not to say of all craftsmen. Thus, having explained the subject matter of this work, its scope, order, and the reason for its title, we now proceed to the task itself.

Chap. 3. What a question is and its kinds

[10] Since the entire power or faculty of invention is concerned with investigating topics that are used in answering all questions, we begin with the question as the proper subject matter of this treatise. Concerning this we explain what it is, what its kinds and divisions are, and by what method it is to be found and understood.

As to what pertains to its definition, therefore, Rudolf Agricola, whose *Dialectica* has elicited great praise ever since it appeared, defined the question, so named from the Latin *quaerendo,* as follows. A question is a speech (*oratio*) raised with an interrogation.[11] Examples would be if one were to ask "Is the world to come to an end?" "Are riches to be sought or not?" This description causes some serious authors to be amused,[12] but there is no reason why we should dwell on this confrontation, since in this work we wish to avoid disputations. Boethius describes it in this way: a question is a doubtful proposition. This description pleases neither Agricola nor others. However, if one compares this definition [11] with the previous description of the question, one will see, as Phrissemius has rightly warned, that there is no reason to condemn this teaching.[13] Others, finally, have thought up this definition: A question is a sound (*vox*) raised with an interrogation, whether this be an utterance (*dictio*) or a speech (*oratio*). Examples: "What is man?" "Are the heavens round?" "Does virtue make a happy life or not?" Otherwise, no matter how one defines it, it suffices for us that we understand what the question signifies, and for what reason. The question or the query, in Greek *problema*, is usually called in Latin *percunctatio*;[14] although the only type of question that is properly called a *problema* is one that can be argued on either side; that which inquires about one part alone is simply called by Aristotle a proposition. So much for the definition.

Concerning its division, first, the question can be divided into the simple and the enunciative. The simple question is that in which we inquire about any thing straight out, for example, "Are there demons?" "What is a contract?" "What are the parts of eloquence?" The enunciative is one in which we inquire about an enunciation or in which we ask whether the thing signified in it is true or false, as, "Are brute animals endowed with reason?" "Is sound a body?" [12] "Are riches to be sought?" The simple question, as some teach,[15] is distributed into eight parts: the first of these is the meaning of the term or its signification; the second inquires about the existence of a thing; the third, the nature or definition of a thing; the fourth, its quality, as when the accidents of a thing are inquired into; the fifth, the cause on account of which a thing is, and especially the efficient cause, as "What makes the moon wane?"; the sixth, the effect and function of a thing, as when one inquires into its purpose; the seventh, its parts, what they are and how many, as when one inquires how many meanings a term has, or the members of a body, or the species of a genus; and the eighth, when one asks about anything that pertains to a thing in any way, as things that have an affinity or a similarity, or contraries and repugnants. And since on any matter proposed we can dispute in two ways, either absolutely or comparatively,[16] hence two kinds of questions arise, the one absolute, as, were one to inquire, "Is the good to be sought?" the other compared, as, "Is the good to be [13] preferred to the useful?"

The enunciative question is twofold, the one categorical or absolute, or, as they say, predicative, in which one attribute is inquired of one subject;

the other composite, commonly called hypothetical, in which many attributes are inquired of many subjects through some type of conjunction. The categorical or simple question is divided by orators into three types: of these the first inquires whether a thing is, that is, is it true, does it really exist? For example, "Is it true that there are antipodes on the earth's surface?" This type of question can also be raised about something past or something future. Another type inquires into what a thing is, or whether this is that, for example, "Is an utterance a sound?" The third type inquires what kind it is, or, as Agricola puts it, how this is said of that, that is, for what reason is this said of that; for example, "Is the war just or not?"[17] To these philosophers add a fourth question, why is it, that is, what is the cause of the thing, as "What causes the moon to wane?" "Does virtue produce a happy life?"[18] Orators call this "why it becomes so," and some reduce this to the first type, others to the third.[19]

The composite question is divided into the copulative, the disjunctive, and the conditional. A copulative question occurs when two or more simple enunciations are joined [14] with a copulative particle, for example, "Is God truthful and man a liar?" A disjunctive question uses a disjunctive particle, as "Is the man at rest or in motion?"; and a conditional question, a conditional particle, as "Is it the case that, if it is day, the sun has risen?" Again, an enunciative question is twofold: one type is simply posed, as is seen in the examples given; the other type adds to it some kind of modality, such as necessary, probable, contingent, and impossible.

Furthermore it is customary to divide questions on the basis of the things they seek to explain, or according to the arts that treat questions of this type,[20] and on this basis the genera of questions are usually numbered as three. Some are called moral questions,[21] as, for example, "Are laws to be obeyed?" "Is a good man also a good citizen?" Others are natural questions, those that inquire about the hidden aspects of nature, as "Is the soul immortal?" "Is there such a thing as divine providence?" "Will the world cease to be?" Yet others are called dialectical or logical questions, as "Are contraries dealt with by the same science?" From this arises another division of questions, according to which some are said to be problematical, either side of which can be disputed with probability, and these are treated by the dialectician; others are said to be demonstrative, only one side of which is necessarily demonstrated by the philosopher, who either proves it or disproves it. For example, "Is the soul [15] immortal or not?" "Is honesty praiseworthy or not?"; only one side of these questions can be proved rightly and truly.

There is also that common division of the question, accepted by all, into the infinite question,[22] which inquires generally about something, as, "Is not philosophy something to be learned?" "Is it licit to repel force with force?" and the finite question, which is contracted to certain persons, times, and places, as, "Are priests to be burdened with physiology?" "Was it licit for Milon to kill Clodius?" This genus the Greeks call a *thesis,* the Latins a *propositum* or *consultatio* (the latter the Greeks call a *hypothesis),* and we ourselves a *causa.*

Frequently there is invoked that other distinction of the question[23] wherein some are directed toward knowledge, when we inquire only because we wish to know something, as are questions about things we cannot influence ourselves, for example, "Is the sun larger than the earth?" "Are the heavens completely free from corruption?" and others toward action, when we inquire about something we can do ourselves, as, "How does one cultivate friendship?" "Should a wise man marry a wife?" But enough of these divisions. In the following chapter we explain a division proposed by Aristotle that is somewhat obscure.

Chap. 4. The four kinds of questions assigned by Aristotle, and the five common attributes of all things

[16] Not everyone approves of what Aristotle says in one place,[24] that every question concerns either a genus, or a definition, or a property, or an accident, for there can be many questions in which none of these is inquired into, as, were one to ask, "Are riches to be spurned?" or "Is God everywhere?" etc. But to open up this division of questions and explain Aristotle's meaning, we explain briefly what a genus is, and also a species, a difference, a property, an accident, and a definition, since reference is made frequently to these terms throughout the entire treatise.

A genus, omitting other meanings of this term, is what is said of many that are different in species when asking the question "What is it?"[25] That is, it is the way one responds to the question when one is asked what a thing is; for example, animal is the genus of man, and virtue the genus of justice, for if one were asked what man is, one will say an animal, and [17] if asked what justice is, one will say a virtue. Or, a genus is that which contains different species, as virtue, virtue of knowledge and virtue of action, and the good, honorable good, useful good, and pleasurable good. Genus is threefold, for one type is said to be supreme, that which has nothing over it, such as substance and quality; another is lowest, that which has no genus under it, such as animal; and a third intermediate, because it has another genus under it. This division will be made quite clear in what is said below. Note there that the Latins frequently use the term genus to designate a species. Also, genus at the moment is not being considered as it is a topic, or as it indicates an argument, but only in the way it is used in a question. And thus briefly of genus.

A species is that of which a genus is said in answering the question "What is it?"[26] Or, it is that which is proximately placed under a genus. Or finally, it is the common formality that is said of many individuals when one inquires about them with the question "What is it?" A species differs from a genus in that a genus is said proximately of species and a species is said proximately of individuals. Species is divided into two kinds: one is called an intermediate species, for it is a nature that is [18] contained in a genus in such a way that it can itself be a genus, since it contains other species under it; another is the lowest species, which is said proximately of things that differ only in number. Examples are man and horse, and these are species in the proper sense.

A difference is a form or a formality by which one thing differs from another or from itself at one or other time.[27] It is threefold: one kind is most common, and it is any accident or formality by which things differ among themselves, as a learned man from an unlearned, or a thing from itself, as boy from adult, standing from sitting. Another kind is a proper difference, whereby one differs from another by some property or non-separable accident, as being able to laugh in man, neighing in a horse. The third kind is maximally proper and is also called a specific difference, which is non-separable and pertains to the nature of a thing as its intimate part, as to sense in animals and to be capable of reason in man. From this one can gather that differences are of two types, one general and the other specific; the former constitutes the type of species that can also be a genus, the latter gives rise to a lowest species. The former may be described as follows: a difference is a formality that is said of many that differ essentially in species, in the question [19] of what kind of essence they are. For example, if asked concerning a lion what kind of living thing it is, one would respond, sentient; and of a stone, what kind of substance it is, corporeal. If one removes from this definition the expression "that differ in species," the definition would also apply to a specific difference, which is said to be a difference in the most proper sense. Yet another kind of difference may be signalled, that whereby one individual differs from another; Cicero would call this a note (nota). A difference has two functions: one is to divide a genus, the other, along with a genus to constitute or give rise to a species. Thus sentient along with animated makes an animal, and animal along with reason makes a human being. And hence it is that a difference is said to be that by which a species exceeds its genus, since it includes something more than the genus, namely, the difference.

Property is not said in any single way,[28] for sometimes it is used when it applies to an individual alone and not to all of the species, as "theologian" applied to a particular person; sometimes it applies to all of the species but not to these alone, as "two-footed" said of the same person; sometimes to the individual and to all of the species, but not always, as "becoming bald" said of men; and finally, when applied to all of the species, to these alone, and always, as for a crow to "caw" and a horse to "whinny." And the latter is truly a property, which will be described in the following manner. [20] A property is that which is said of many, both accidentally and necessarily, in answer to the question "What kind is it?" or it is that which belongs to a thing universally, uniquely, and always; this applies to all properties that flow from the nature of the thing, for example, to be risible and to be teachable in the case of man. It applies also to the functions of all arts and services. There are two kinds of property: one is general, which belongs to a genus and always accompanies it, as to be sentient, for animals; the other goes with the species only, as to be risible, for man.

Accident sometimes designates anything that is other than the nature of a thing, and in this sense even a property is said to be an accident; sometimes it means anything that belongs to a thing in such a way that it does not necessarily follow from its nature, and it is of this we here speak, which is usually described in this way. An accident is that which is either present in a thing or absent from it, without its ceasing to exist;[29] in this way "black" is in a crow and "white" in a man. In this understanding an accident is that which is said of many, both accidentally and contingently, in answer to the question "What kind is it?" as, for a man to be black or white. Among accidents some are separable from a thing, such as anything that can be easily removed, as "sitting" from a particular man; others [21] are not separable, as "white" from snow, "black" from a crow. Although such accidents are not separated in the thing, they can nonetheless be separated in thought. Again, some accidents are or can be in an entire thing, as white in a man, whereas others are only in a part, as hazel-eyed or curly-headed.

As to what pertains to definition,[30] we here speak of this only briefly, since much is said about it in its proper place.[31] A definition is an expression that explains what anything is; or, to get closer to the thing, it is an expression made up of a genus and a difference that explains the nature of a thing, which is conflated from these two parts. For example, this expression, "the art of speaking well," which makes clear the nature of rhetoric, and "an animal endowed with reason," which explains the nature of man.

These things understood, we respond to the proposed difficulty in this way. When Aristotle says that all questions are either about genus, or definition, or property, or accident,[32] this is not to be taken as if he means to state that in every question we expressly inquire about one of these, as if we were to ask a person where he is coming from or where he is going to or what he wants. Rather, this learned man simply means that every question can be [22] reduced to one of the four kinds, as it truly can.

But here one might wonder, since there should be as many questions as there are things about which they can inquire, which, as is plain, are five in number, namely, genus, species, difference, property, and accident, and there are neither more nor less than these that can be attributed to a thing, why did Aristotle not list five kinds of questions, and why did he omit species and difference and list only definition? To this difficulty one might respond in this way:[33] Aristotle means by the term genus any common attribute that belongs to a thing intrinsically, and so this also contains within it a question about species and difference, unless one wishes to reduce this to a question of definition. Proceeding in this way one can formulate each of the five questions individually, although it is legitimate to reduce all of them to four, in the following way. In every question an attribute either belongs to or does not belong to a subject; if it belongs, either in such a way that it cannot be transferred to another thing, and of this kind are definition and property; or it can be transferred, as can genus and accident; and just as definition and genus belong essentially, so property and accident belong accidentally; if it does not belong, [23] then a legitimate question does not arise. Or, in this way every question inquires either what, or what kind, or what kind of essence: the first asks for genus and species; the second, for accident, either proper or common; the third, the thing's definition.

Finally, there remains a problem about the question whether a thing exists, which does not seem to be reducible to any of the four kinds. One can remove this doubt by saying that it is reducible to the question of genus, because when one inquires whether a thing exists one is asking whether it is contained in any genus. The question of why a thing exists may be reduced to a question of accident or of property, as, for example, if it be asked whether things outside ourselves make for a happy life.

Here it should be noted that the question of genus, and what I have said about genus, is basically the same for the other three questions and can be handled in two ways: in one way, expressly, if one were to ask, "Is virtue the genus of justice?" or tacitly, as in "Is justice a virtue?" Other examples: "Is sound a body?"—here genus is sought tacitly; "Is time a motion of the heavens?"—here, definition; "Is man alone risible?"—here, property. Thus it is possible to reduce all questions to one of the four kinds pointed out by Aristotle, whose mind some [24] have tried to read[34] but whose teaching in this matter they have wrongly condemned. It is of course true that one can separately pose questions relating to both species and difference, as, for example, by asking, "What is Socrates?" and "In what way does man differ from a brute animal?" and relating to definition, by asking

"What is man?" Since therefore what we have already said makes clear the various kinds of question, we now turn to other matters.

Chap. 5. The two supreme genera, substance and quantity, and questions concerning them

Just as every question can be reduced to the four discussed, or, if you wish, to the five, so also their entire variety can be reduced to the ten supreme genera of things,[35] that is, to substance, quantity, quality, relation, action, reception, where, when, location, and possession. These are the common fonts of all questions, in the sense that some questions concern substance, others quantity, others relation. For this reason, both that the great variety of questions be known and that what we shall say later about the topics may be more easily understood, we now explain briefly these ten attributes of things and their heads and [25] common topics, to which everything in this universe of things can be reduced.

Substance, what Cicero calls nature, is that which exists in itself, and subsists, and is not in any other thing, but rather all other things are in it, as clothing on a body, and thus it is said to be a quasi basis and foundation of accidents, which are in some way the clothing of substance. Substance does not fall under the senses except through its accidents, and in its nature it is devoid of mass and extension. Substance is also twofold:[36] one is called first substance, which is neither in a subject nor said of a subject, and of this kind are single individuals of all kinds, as this man, that tree, this stone; the other is called second substance, as are the genera and species that are separated by thought from first substance, as man and animal.

If substance is considered universally, first substance is divided into non-created and infinite, as is God, and created and finite, as are all things other than God. Created substance, which properly makes up this genus, [26] is divided into incorporeal substance, as are intelligences and the human soul, and corporeal or bodily substance, in which all others are contained. The latter is either simple or composite, that is, made from other substances. Simple substances are either free from all corruption, as are the celestial orbs, or subject to change, as are the four elements: fire, air, water, and earth. Composite substances either lack a soul or make use of a soul: the former are either perfect, as are all metals and stones, or they are imperfect, as are those that are generated in the atmosphere, as are hail, snow, lightning, and other things of that kind. The latter are either devoid of sense, as are herbs, fruits, and trees, or they are endowed with sense, as are all things that have the power of sensation. The latter again are either devoid of reason, as are brute animals, terrestrial, aquatic, or aerobic, or they are endowed with reason, as is man. In sum, substance, either incorporeal or corporeal; corporeal, either inanimate or animate; animate, either non-sentient or sentient, as is animal, which is divided into brute and rational.

Composite substance has parts of which it is formed, matter and form:[37] the former is a somewhat imperfect substance that is perfected by the other, that is, by form as by [27] perfect act. This nature is known through these properties: that it is not in another, that it has no contrary, that it is not susceptible of being greater or less, and that it is the subject of contraries. From this category only two kinds of questions of the four listed above can be taken, those of genus and definition, or, as some prefer, also of property, since this type of question can be reduced to the category of property. For example, "Is a sponge an animal?" "Is any brute animal capable of reason?" "Is man alone endowed with speech?" Of these the first is a question of genus, the second, of definition, the third, of property. In this category there can also be a question of accident, as when one inquires "Is a swan white?" This is rejected by some as not being a natural question, as is explained more fully below.

Quantity is a nature or thing that has bulk and parts, such as a line, the number five, etc., or it is that by which a substance has parts, so that it can be divided. Of this nature there are two kinds:[38] one is continuous quantity, as is that whose parts are joined by a common term, for example, a line, whose parts are united by a single point; another is disjoined or discrete, [28] whose parts have no term in common, as the parts of five or of any other number. Continuous quantity is subdivided into the line, which consists of length alone, and this is either straight or bent; the surface, which also has depth and is either even or uneven; the body, in which there is length, depth, and thickness, and it is either spherical or angular; time, whose parts are the present, past, and future; and place, which is space or the extremity of a body surrounding another. Discrete quantity is divided into number and voice. Number is either simple, as even and odd; or brought together, as double, triple; or figured, as triangular, rectangular. In voice one looks to harmony and rhythm. In the first kind there is magnitude, in the second, multitude; the first looks to all magnitudes, the second, to all numbers and sounds. The first kind are considered in geometry and astronomy, the second in arithmetic and music. The properties of this category are: it has no contrary, it is not susceptible of being more or less; and by it things are said to be equal and unequal. As to the matter of questions, the question of genus: "Is time a continuum?"; [29] of definition, "Is time a measure of motion?"; of property, "Is quantity alone capable of division?"; of accident, "Is the moon larger than the earth?" In sum, to this category pertain all questions that inquire into the size, measure, and number of a thing.

Chap. 6. Quality and relation, and their questions

Quality is the thing or form by which things are named to be of a certain kind, as white, holy, learned, or an affection of any kind.[39] Its species are: habit and disposition, or affection; natural power or incapability; sensible quality or passion; and figure or form. A habit is a firm quality acquired through long use and strengthened by exercise so that it can hardly be eradicated. A disposition or affection is a weak quality that is easily removed. Some habits are of the soul, as are the virtues and sciences; others of the body, as are the gladiatorial art and the ability to swim, and so they designate a certain state of the body acquired through use. How many habits there are in the soul, either of thought or action, is discussed later.[40] A power, or natural faculty, is that by which any nature is said to be perspicacious, alert, [30] skilled, docile, or suitable and in a good state to perform another action; to it is opposed a natural reluctance or incapability whereby one is said to be obtuse, oblivious, sickly, and unable to resist. This kind is different from the previous kind in that the latter is adventitious whereas the former is inborn or innate. Thus by this kind one is said to be able or not able to do, or undergo, or to suffer anything whatever.

Natural power is found partly in things lacking a soul, such as stones, heavenly bodies, and the elements; partly in those that use the soul, and then it is either in the body, as strength and swiftness, or in the soul, as the generative, nutritive, augmentative, and other powers; or in sentient things, as are the five external senses, sight, taste, and the others, and the three internal senses, central sense, imagination, and memory; the power of self-movement or of appetition, by which an animal seeks after something or flees from it; or, in an intelligent soul, intellect and will. A sensible quality is that which either moves the senses, as do colors, tastes, odors, and qualities that are perceived by touch, or which takes its origin from some motion or affection, as lasting color in a body, insanity in [31] the soul. An emotion, or passion, is a certain flowing and brief transient quality that either moves a sense or arises from a motion, such as the blush arising from shame, the pallor from fear; again, joy and the other kinds of emotion with which the orator is accustomed to deal, as we shall describe fully in another book.

Figure is a mode of quantity simply considered, or it is a kind of quality that is composed of one or many lines, as the shape of a circle, triangle, square, and the like. Form, as understood in this context, is a kind of composition or skillful connection that arises from an apt constitution of members in animals, and in other things from a proper arrangement of their parts whereby they are said to be beautiful and handsome. Here rectitude refers to smooth, rough, thin, thick, and oblique.

Properties of the category of quality are: to have a contrary, to be increased and decreased, and to be that by which things are named to be of some kind. Examples of questions taken from this category are these. Of genus: "Is eloquence a virtue?" "Are virtues sciences, as the Stoics maintained?" Of definition: "Is virtue a good quality of the soul?" "Is emotion a voluntary act opposed to reason?" Of property: "Is it especially proper to quality that from it we are said [32] to be of a certain kind?" Of accident: "Is glory to be avoided?"

Relation, or collation, is that by which anything, by what it itself is, is referred to another; for example, equality, by which things are said to be equal, or similarity, by which they are said to be similar, such as slavery, mastery, etc. Things related, or collated, affected, and connected, as Cicero says, or compared with another, are those things whose power and entire nature consist in this, that they are in some way brought to another;[41] examples are father and son, master and slave, creator and creature, man and wife. Thus collation is nothing other than the mutual affectation of two things by themselves. Of things related some are of equal comparison, as are things of the same nature and name; for example, two similars, two equals; others are of unequal or diverse comparison or of different name, as father and son, master and slave.

Again, of things related some are simply collated, as are those things that of themselves alone form the relationship and imply nothing absolute; for example, teacher and disciple, buyer and seller, which are said to be related *secundum esse* (according to being); others designate something absolute along with the affecting, as scientific knowledge and its object, what is known, since science primarily designates a habit [33] and afterwards a type of relationship to the thing known, and such things are said to be related *secundum dici* (according to speech). The properties of this category are that they are by nature simultaneous, that they are reciprocal, that they have a contrary, and that they can be intensified and diminished, although the last two are not found in all relationships. By this category not only are substances related to each other but also accidents. One substance is related to another by all of its accidents: by quantity it is said to be equal and unequal, even and uneven, first and second; by quality, similar and dissimilar; by action and reception, father and son, uncle and nephew, prosecutor and defendant, buyer and seller; by location or where (*ubi?*), upper and lower, nearer and farther; by time or when (*quando?*), of the same or equal age; of situation, prone or bent over, standing or sitting; by having, rich and poor, containing and the contained. Similarly, individual categories can be compared among themselves: quantities, as a line with a line, a flask with a pitcher; qualities, one whiteness with another, virtue with vice; actions, teaching with learning, buying with selling, leasing with renting; receptions, being intensified with being diminished, and so in other categories. Subjects of these categories are all things that have mutual reference, as the names of relationships, [34] affinities, contracts, and numbers. Examples of questions taken from this category are these: of genus, "Is triple multiple?"; of definition, "Are species things that come under genera?"; of property, "Are related things such that one cannot be known without the other?"; of accident, "Is the man a disciple?" "Is four a double or square?"

Chap. 7. Three other supreme genera: action, reception, and location, and questions relating to them

Action is the act of an agent, or an operation or motion as it comes from the agent,[42] or concretely, to act is to apply one's force on another, or simply, to exert one's force, as, to whip, to walk, to think. There are two kinds of action:[43] one type are in the thing affected, as those things by which something is effected and after which something remains in the effect, for example, building, generating, and like things; the other type are those that remain in the agent, as are those through which nothing is produced, such as jumping, thinking, and seeing. Again, some actions are from nature and are necessary; others are from the human will and are not [35] produced necessarily. Of the former, some are concerned with substance, as generation and corruption: a thing is generated either according to nature or contrary to nature, as from seed, or from transplantation, or from putrefaction, and for the same reason there are many ways in which a thing can cease to be, and these need not be listed here. Others are concerned with quantity, as augmentation and diminution, which also can be brought about in various ways. Some are concerned with quality, as to heat, to make joyful, to bring sorrow upon, and so on. Others are concerned with place, as to go upward or downward, to swim, and to fly. Thus universally there are six parts of action or motion,[44] generation, destruction, increase, diminution, alteration, and migration. Of human actions some proceed from deliberate reason, others do not:[45] those that do are called human actions, those that do not are called acts of man, since they are done by a human being but not with deliberate reason. To this category belong all verbs that signify doing or quasi-doing something, and nouns derived from them that designate an action, such as birth, death, coming close to, getting warmer, reading, etc.

Reception or enduring is the act of the patient or the receiving of an action; or, to undergo is to receive the power of the agent, as, to be generated, to be destroyed, to be augmented, [36] to be set afire, and to be changed. This category is divided in the same way as the category of action. What we have said of that regarding its division, therefore, should be regarded as applying to reception. The common properties of these two categories are to have a contrary and to undergo more or less. With respect to questions, these are some examples: of genus, "Is sensing the same as understanding, or sensation as intellection?" "Is creation an action?" "Is seeing an action or a reception?"; of definition: "Is motion an act or perfection of that which is in potency, precisely as it is in potency?"[46] "Is motion a change from one contrary to another?"; of property, "Is it proper for motion to flow gradually?"; of accident, "Is an action performed out of fear a human act?" "Is throwing cargo overboard in a storm a voluntary act or not?"[47] These examples also serve for instances of reception.

Location, or being in place, is defined as circumscription by place in such a way that the thing exists, acts, and receives action in that place and not elsewhere.[48] In the category of quantity place is said to be an interval; here it designates where a thing is. To this category also pertain other modes whereby things stand in some relation to place, as whence, wherefrom, and whereto. The divisions of this genus are above, below, before, behind, to the right of, and to the left of. Again, one kind of place [37] is common, as that in which many things are located, for example, a city, a plaza, and a house; another is proper place, which is that of each thing, in such a way that the highest specification would be "in Venice," the lowest, "in one's room." The properties of this category are: not to have a contrary and neither to be increased nor to be decreased. This category supplies a great number of questions for one who would know the varieties of places in the entire world. This category easily lends itself to conjectures, praise, and disparagement. Examples of questions from this category are the following: of genus, "Is God everywhere?" "Is Venice on land or in the water?"; of definition, "Is the higher place where light things tend?"; of property, "Is it a property of place to conserve things contained in place?"; of accident, "Are stars in the eighth orb?" And compared questions: "Do vines grow better in one place than in another?" "Is it better to live in the shadow than in the public light?"—a controversy often disputed by learned men.[49]

Chap. 8. The last three supreme genera: when, how situated, possession, and questions relating to them

[38] When, or being in time, is to be contained in time and affected by time in the sense that a thing exists or comes to be in time.[50] To this cate-

gory pertains any expression that is a legitimate response to the question "When?" as, for example, yesterday, today, last year, etc. Time as it designates an interval indicated by the expression "How long?" or any other numbering of the parts of time pertains to the category of quantity. There are three kinds of time, the instant, the past, and the future. The principal parts are a generation or *saeculum,* a year, a month, a week, a day, and an hour; these can also be further divided, as the year into spring, summer, autumn, and winter, the day into the natural, the civil, the feast day, the working day, and so on. Properties of time are to flow, to lack a contrary, and intensification and remission. Questions from this category are: of genus, "Does generation take place in time?"; of definition, "Is time the numbering of motion according to before and after?"[51]; of property, "Is it proper to time to flow perpetually?"; of accident, "Should [39] classes be cancelled on feast days?" And of the compared question: "Is it more comfortable to live in summer than in winter?"

To be situated is to have the parts of a body disposed or arranged in a certain manner, or, as Quintilian says, to be composed in such a way as to be neither acting nor receiving action,[52] as to sit, to stand, to recline, to be prone or bent over, standing, seated, or lying down, looking to the east or to the setting sun. Thus situation or position designates an arrangement of parts with a fixed relationship to each other and to place. From this it follows that situation applies not only to animals but to things that lack sensation, such as trees, cities, mountains, and like things. Yet the situation of animals is variable, that of inanimate objects fixed. Situation is twofold: one is natural, conferred by nature, the other voluntary, which depends on art or the human will. Also pertaining to this category are neutral verbs that designate a position without any operation, and nouns derived from these, such as a recliner, a sitting, a proneness, and others of this kind. From this category one obtains descriptions of places. The properties of situation are not to have a contrary and to undergo neither increase nor decrease. [40] Four examples of questions are: of genus: "Is turning a situation?" "Is a person who is getting up standing?" or "Is raising up a status?"; of definition, "Is standing the same as having the entire mass of the body directed toward the heavens?"; of property, "Is man the only erect animal?" in such a way that one might ask whether it is true, as did Ovid;[53] and of accident: "Should a house face to the western sun, or to the meridian?"

Possession is being dressed or covered or adorned with something, such as a toga, a legging, a helmut, a ring, a fasces, hair, scales, claws, horns, saddles, etc. From this it follows that nouns of clothing do not pertain to this category but rather adjectives derived from them, such as helmeted, mantled, armed with a spear, clothed in silks, and other terms derived from nouns designating clothing and armor. From this one should understand that this category does not designate the type of habit that the name clothing generally indicates; rather it should be called covering. By the term covering is then understood things that cover not only men but also brute animals and other things that lack sense, [41] as to be bristled, leafy, mossy, and so on. One can also use the expression "to have" in place of "to possess," as to have gold, a manor house, a wife, and even the verbs "to take" or "to contain," as to be full of liquor, or of corn, and similar things. The properties of this category are: to be capable of increase and decrease, and to have a contrary, as to be armed or unarmed, naked or clothed. Examples of questions are: of genus, "Are some men adorned with shaggy hair, like beasts?"; of definition, "Should a dress toga be oblong and reaching to the ankles, to which purple would be attached?"; of property, "Is it proper for birds to have wings?"; of accident, "Is the Greek pallium more illustrious than the Roman toga?" "Is white the preferred color, or purple?"

To this point we have treated the ten categories and their questions. To these it is customary to add what are called the postpredicaments, such as opposites, agreements, the ways in which things are said to come before or be simultaneous, motion, and having. We say more about opposites when we treat of them in their place; the kinds of motion we have enumerated in the category of action, and in the last category, possession, what we have said there suffices for having.

It remains to discourse briefly [42] about the rest. With regard to agreement, one kind of agreement is that by which brutes and man agree in their animal nature; another in species, as two men in their human nature; yet another in number, as Cicero and M. Tullius, where the two names designate the same man. In the same manner things are said to differ, namely, in genus, as a man and a tree; in species, as an ox and a lion; in number, as Socrates and Plato. A thing is said to be "before": either in time, as yesterday was before today; or in the order of nature, when two things occur at the same time but one supposes the other and they do not reciprocate, such as man and animal, accident and subject; or in situation, as the head is before the neck, letters before the syllable; or in dignity, as the consul before the praetor, the soul before the body; or in the order of causes, the way the rising of the sun is before the day. Things are said to be "together": either in time, as the sun and its sunlight; or in nature, as things that reciprocate but one is not necessarily the cause of the other, as father and son, double and half; here are pertinent also the species of any subject genus.

From what we have said concerning the ten categories [43] one may understand just how many questions can be reduced to these supreme genera, which are like ten common topics from which all arguments are brought forth, as is discussed elsewhere. This much explained, we cover in the following chapter how questions are differentiated.

Chap. 9. How the four kinds of questions are discerned

If some knowledge of the categories is necessary for all the arts, it is especially beneficial for those who wish to teach the art of invention and how to uncover the fonts of arguments, since from these ten categories and their parts all questions are constructed and anything that facilitates praising, advising, and especially proving is obtained. Meanwhile I omit many other advantages that the faculty of invention takes from the knowledge of all things here adumbrated. Thus, having explicated the matter and variety of all questions, we now disclose the way in which the four kinds of questions are discerned and how a [44] question can be discovered.

To expose what is required to discern questions, it should be noted that some questions are said to be right or natural,[54] as are all those in which an attribute or predicate is attributed to its natural and proper subject, one in which it is naturally present; others are non-natural, as are those in which the attribute does not belong to the subject, such as these: "Are virtues sciences?" "Does an animal lack sensation?" "Are men incapable of grasping disciplines?" To recognize the kind of question, whether it is a question of accident, of property, of genus, or of definition, it is first necessary to examine whether the question is natural. Then it should be noted, that although there are only two terms in a question, as dialecticians say, the subject and the attribute, it is only from the attribute that the question takes its kind. We can, of course, discern from the subject to which the attribute is applied whether the question is natural or not; if the question is not natural, it will not indicate the true kind of question. Note also that, since all things that exist are either a substance or an accident, all [45] questions can be reduced to these two heads, since every question is either of a substance or of an accident. On this account a rule will be given for recognizing these two questions. This much noted, we posit the following rules for discerning questions.

First, a question will pertain to the category of substance, provided it is correct, if its attribute is a substance; that is, if it is a genus, or a definition of the subject, or a difference, or even a property, as some claim (while others reduce this to a question of accident, as we have also written above). The question will be of an accident if the attribute is an accident. Otherwise, all questions of genus and of definition, even if the subject be an accident, can in some way be said to be questions of substance, or of nature, when they go with their subjects necessarily.

Second, a question of genus, of definition, and of property can be in all categories, and a question of accident also, provided it is not in the category of substance, for nothing goes with a substance fortuitously—we are speaking of a natural question.

Third, when an attribute cannot not go with the subject, the question will either be of genus, or of definition, or of property; when it goes in such a way that it can [46] also not go, it will be a question of an accident, whether the subject be a substance or an accident.

Fourth, there will be a question of genus, of definition, and of property whenever the attribute is either a genus or a definition or a property of the subject.

Fifth, not every question in which the attribute is an accident is a question of accident—I speak now of accident that makes the fourth kind of question; on this account many questions seem to be questions of accident when they actually are not. For example, "Is white a color?" "Is justice a virtue?" "Is a virtue a good habit?" "Is quantity alone essentially divisible?": in all of these the attribute is an accident, but the first is a question of genus, the next two, of definition, the last of property. It remains therefore that a question of accident is one in which an attribute is predicated of a subject in such a way that it need not be predicated. And from this it follows that all questions concerning accident are compared questions.

Sixth and last, when a question is proposed, first it should be seen whether it is of a genus, or of a definition, or of a property, or of an accident, then in what category and in what seat it should be located. We could illustrate all of these rules with examples, but because they are easy to understand from what has been said and the examples already given, we do not wish to dwell on this any longer. From [47] this you thus have the method by which the four genera of questions can be discerned. Let us now speak of the invention of the question.

Chap. 10. The method of inventing a question

Since there cannot be a disputation unless a definite question has been proposed, for whose proof definite topics must be excogitated, it is necessary at the start, before the invention of topics, to ascertain the question, as we demonstrate more fully in another book we are writing on status. If therefore the person who speaks has an adversary, such that there are two persons arguing between themselves, it is easy to discover the question from their mutual conflict. This usually happens in courts, in civil cases, and also in schools of philosophers. In these, when one comes to something on which the parties take stands and differ between themselves, the question to be disputed and for whose treatment discourse ought to be directed arises immediately.[55] But when no adversary obviously appears, as happens particularly in the demonstrative genus and in its parts, such as reconciliations, laudatory [48] and gratulatory actions, it is not so easy to investigate the question and the heading to be treated.

In this kind of matter, as Agricola has noted,[56] we can investigate the question or the status if we shall have considered whether we are contending about persons, or causes, or a goal, or what to do—which he calls a *conatum* or undertaking, others a status. Persons are those who act or speak, and those with whom they act or among whom they speak; those through whom they act are called agents. With persons one ought to consider their conditions, status, and affections, and these should be compared among themselves as to whether they are equal, related, agreeable, and inimical. The cause is the matter being treated, which may be something past or future, such as the dignity to be obtained in gratulation, the property lost in consolation, or the benefice accepted in the giving of thanks. The undertaking is that which we wish to accomplish in speaking and to attain which we are working.

If the undertaking coincides with the cause, this gives rise to a certain type of question. For example, in consolation the cause will be that which is lost or that which offers a friend cause for sorrow; the undertaking or goal is for us to establish by speech that the friend ought not be sorrowing. If we join these two the following question arises: [49] should this matter, for him, be cause for sorrowing? For treating this question suitable topics should be found with which you may prove that he ought not be sorrowing, if you wish to argue this side. In rendering thanks, the persons are friendly with each other; the cause is how to access some benefit or utility for another; the undertaking, that we may show for the sake of benevolence that the thing given will produce joy. Hence the question arises: will we be happy for having received this gift? And if we diligently have considered the persons, and if we have seen correctly how that cause affects the person, the undertaking is readily apparent; when this is connected with the person, the question is raised.

From this it happens that the same cause, compared to different persons to whom it may apply, gives birth to different questions. For example, if someone is to make a speech at a wedding, if he looks to the persons to be united in matrimony and considers what should be the goal, he will elicit the question: Are these nuptials desired by those contracting them? Then if he considers the persons who are attending the wedding he will draw the following question: Is there cause for their rejoicing in this particular marriage? Similarly, in a funeral oration, if he looks to the immediate family and the relations, [50] the speech will be directed at their consolation; if to a stranger, he will have praise for his goal. In this kind of speech, as Agricola advises, we should first pursue the praise aspect and then offer the consolation. With persons, however, one ought to note whether the persons are private and individual, or universal and public. And this much for the question of invention. We say more in our book on status, where we explain clearly the individual methods of finding the status in any proposed speech whatever. The way in which the question can be expanded and amplified we cover below in the fifth book.

Chap. 11. Definitions of sentence, argument, and argumentation

Just as when an artist has material at hand to work on he must have knowledge of the instruments required for that work, so when a person with a faculty for dealing with topics has found a question, which is his material, he requires an explanation of the instrument required to work on the question. That instrument is nothing more than the sentence and the argumentation, of which [51] we discourse briefly, as required for our purposes. And although many authors have written much on the matter proposed, since we do not wish to digress from our main intention, we touch only on matters that bear directly on our project and treat first of the sentence, what it is, and its various kinds.

As to the sentence's definition, as Aristotle holds, a sentence is a sound that signifies and some part of which has meaning,[57] but like a noun, as a simple utterance and not as an affirmation. This part of the definition excludes connected or composite sentences whose parts, as affirmations, can signify. If we wish to include all kinds of sentences in the definition, we should describe it in this way: a sentence is a sound a part of which has some meaning, to distinguish it from simple utterances whose parts do not signify; in this way a simple sound cannot be a sentence. Or in this way: a sentence is a group of words that signify by convention.[58] It is said to signify by convention so as to exclude sounds that signify naturally, for sentences are not made from these. Or finally: a sentence is a thought expressed in words.[59]

[52] There are two kinds of sentences: one is an imperfect sentence, which does not generate a complete thought in the mind of the audience but leaves its hearers in suspense; for example, if you say, "If they had done what I . . .", the other is a perfect sentence, which conveys a complete thought, as this: "Man is an animal," and the expressions in Horace and Juvenal.[60]

Perfect sentences are again two in kind, one of which expresses something true or false, which orators call a pronouncement, dialecticians an enunciation, as, for example, "God is truthful," "Man is not endowed with reason"; the other kind expresses nothing that is true or false, as are commands, wishes, questions, and exclamations, with which some thought is expressed, but not one signifying truth or falsity, such as these: "I wish you liked me," "Love me." Here we omit other divisions of the sentence offered by dialecticians and grammarians, since we have no future use for them; we add, however, two other divisions from Agricola that are useful for our purposes.[61] There are two kinds of sentences, one is full (*continens*), that is, [53] expanded and amplified, of which type is the orators' sentence, especially when they praise and exhort; the other is concise (*concisa*), which we customarily use in dialectical disputation. One may compare the former to the open palm, the latter to the clenched fist. Agricola then divides the sentence into one by which we expose something and another by which we prove something, such that one is an exposition, the other an argument. We use the former when we teach someone who is disposed to give assent, the latter, when someone has to be urged to believe something by the force of the speech; the former simply narrates the matter, the latter makes use of reason to evince assent; the former is best used in narration, the latter in confirmation. Thus exposition is a speech that makes apparent the mind of the speaker without bringing in any matter that serves immediately to produce belief; argumentation, on the other hand, is a speech wherein we try to induce belief in the matter on which we are speaking. An example of exposition taken from Virgil is from the first book of the Aeneid.[62] [54] An example of argumentation from the same poet is also found in the first book.[63]

These two forms of speech are so related that one can sometimes be changed into the other, as when someone in exposing some matter first explains its cause and then, afterwards, takes up that very cause as the reason with which he proves what he has exposed. Sometimes also, an argumentation is inserted into an exposition, and an exposition into an argument; this type of speech, which seems to be mixed, takes its name from the form that is principal in it, since, as Anaxagoras taught, a thing should be named not from what it is but from what it maximally is. The faculty involved in treating and using topics makes special use of argumentative speech, and thus we discuss it in this place; elsewhere, when we treat of narration, we treat expository speech more fully.

[55] An argument is described as follows by Cicero:[64] An argument is a probability invented to produce belief. The entire faculty of invention is involved in finding such an argument, in such a way that it might be called the matter of invention. What Cicero calls an argument the dialecticians call a middle; when this is taken and proposed through an argumentation, that is, through an explication of the argument, the question is proved. Whence an argumentation is an explication and treatment and artificial

polishing of an argument whereby some definite form of reasoning is constructed. The middle that is used to prove a question is called an argument because it argues a dubious matter, makes it verisimilar and manifests it, for sometimes the term in Latin means "to argue." This meaning is also found in Virgil, when he says *Degeneres animos timor*[65] [Fear departs from souls]. For then, as we said earlier, what is invented argues and produces belief, when a good reason is contained in the speech; in other words, when an argumentation is used in it. But when outside a proof, an argumentation that has the force of proof can be called a cause, that by which a thing is, but not a reason [56] or argument, since we use reason or argument to indicate something through which a doubtful matter is resolved. Here argument is taken not only for an invention or probable argument but generally for any reason by which something is concluded either probably or necessarily. Whence it should be understood that Cicero and logicians use the term argument differently.[66] By an argument the former means what is invented, the middle; the latter, the argumentation itself, the exposition of the argument.

In an argumentation that we use as a kind of instrument to produce belief we must attend to two things: the propositions and statements from which it is constructed as from matter; and the form, that is, the definite manner of arranging and concluding that logicians treat when they teach how to construct a syllogism. Rhetors also use a special form or deduction in constructing their argumentations, and this is somewhat different from that used by dialecticians. All of this we treat in the fifth book when treating of the judicative part of rhetoric. For the present we are concerned only with the argument or the middle used in proving a question, for finding what topics must be thought out, or certain notes [57] that indicate where arguments lie hidden, as we explain more fully later on.

Chap. 12. The argument, or middle, used for resolving a question

Therefore, having invented or being proposed a question on which one must dispute and speak, since no question resolves itself, because a proof is always taken from something more known than the matter under doubt, it is first fitting to turn the mind to discovering what is suitable for answering the question. Indeed, not everything whatever, true though it may be, should be thought suitable for supporting any case, but only what has some affinity and relationship with the matter under dispute. For it does not follow from the fact that the heavens are free of corruption that man is rational, even though both statements are true. I shall explain this point with an ingenious and apt example used by Agricola.[67]

Before I explain this, note that in any question [58] two phrases are contained, either actually or virtually, or two things are designated by two phrases, one of which is called the subject and the other the predicate, or attribute, or apposite, which are connected by a word that logicians call a copula. For example, "Whether man is an animal?" This question being proposed, we wish to inquire whether these two are related so that they be joined to each other or disjoined, and to do this we need some kind of rule or measure. This is no different from someone wishing to know which of two bodies that cannot be joined together is the larger; to do this it would be necessary to find some measure or quantity that can be applied to the two bodies. And this measure should be such that it is at least equal to one of the bodies; if it is brought to the other body and is found to be equal to that, then one will conclude right away that the two bodies are equal to each other, since they are equal to the third body; if it is found to be smaller, we conclude that the two bodies are not equal. For the same reason, in nature and in matters on which there is a dispute, if that third thing with which we wish to see whether an attribute belongs with a subject agrees with each of them, that is, can be accommodated to both, we conclude that the thing is so, by [59] confirming; if it agrees with one but not with the other, that is, cannot be accommodated to it, we conclude that the thing is not so, by refuting. Therefore, in order to prove that one thing goes or does not go with another, it is necessary to take some third thing of which we can know for certain that it goes with or does not go with either of them.

For example, the question proposed is "Are riches to be sought?" For the affirmative part we must think up an argument that goes with, or certainly appears to go with the subject "riches" and with the attribute "to be sought," and this is "the good." Then we reason as follows: "Every good is to be sought; riches are a good; therefore they are to be sought." But to prove the negative part we must find something that seems not to go with the one but to go with the other, for example, "the harmful." Then we argue: "Nothing harmful is to be sought; but riches are harmful; therefore they are not to be sought." But were we to find a third term of the type that it does not go with either the subject or the attribute, this would be useless for inducing belief; an example would be: "An animal lacks sensation; therefore, man is rational." Thus, to conclude correctly, whether one is proving or disproving, it is always required that that third thing agree with both for this reason, [60] that otherwise the argumentation will not be a suitable instrument for inducing belief. On this account, if the two extremes seem to agree with this third, but in reality do not agree, the argumentation will be fallacious. For example, if we say, "Some animal laughs; a goat is an animal; therefore it laughs," here "laughs" seems to be joined to every animal, whereas it is not. Hence it is obvious why this third term is called a middle by logicians, because it joins together and sort of binds the two extremes, namely, the subject and attribute, for the one who reasons takes the three terms and with them ties a knot that restricts and binds his adversary. And the entire faculty of invention consists in this, that through it we are rendered adapted and skilled at finding arguments or middles by which we can resolve any question proposed. From this one can easily understand Aristotle's saying that every question is concerned with a middle, that is, when any question is proposed, we are inquiring into the middle with which the doubt is dissolved.

Since, as is apparent from what has been said—no medium is suitable for dissolving doubt in all matters, but sometimes one is deceived, [61] so that we can use a middle that is truly inadequate even though it appears to be apt and suitable—it is necessary that beyond invention we possess another faculty that makes us capable of judging whether a middle is proper or not. Nor can we use a measuring cup, or a vessel for measuring continuous quantities, or the Lesbian rule, which bends to the shape of the wall, without falling into error. So it is that beyond the teaching on invention there is need for a judicative faculty by which we can know what can be inferred or not inferred from any middle, either necessarily, or probably, or fallaciously. This is the teaching Aristotle treats in his *Analytics*, where he teaches the rules for reasoning correctly and for distinguishing necessary arguments from those that are probable or false—rules which are not our present concern. Otherwise we do say something in the following chapter about the threefold material of argumentations and syllogisms, for these are of considerable importance for our purposes.

Chap. 13. The threefold matter of argumentation

In argumentation, the instrument for producing belief, since it is quasi [62] composed, one must consider two things, the form, which consists in a certain arrangement of the three terms, and the matter, which are the elements or propositions from which the argumentation is composed as its parts. If one looks to the form, it is one and the same for all argumentations, since all discourse is finally reducible to reasoning or the syllogism, just as the form of a circle is the same regardless of the matter in which it is found, whether this be expressed in copper, stone, or wood. But the matter to which this form is applied is not the same but comes out to be three types, for some is necessary, some is probable, and some is sophistic.

Necessary matter is recognized by these four characteristics: first, when the attribute or the predicate is the definition of the subject, as when you say, "Man is an animal endowed with reason," "Rhetoric is the art of speaking well." Second, when the attribute is a part of the definition of the subject, whether this be an intrinsic difference or a genus or something higher and more common, as "Man is an animal, is living, is endowed with reason." Third, when the attribute is a property or a proper passion of the thing to which it is attributed, as "Man is risible; it is proper for a dog to bark, a crow to [63] caw." Fourth, when a proper effect is attributed to the cause from which it flows necessarily, as the day from the sun, birth to the newborn, death to the strangled, and so on. Therefore, if reasoning is based on propositions of this type, there arises a kind of proof that is called demonstration, whose proper effect is to generate science, that is, certain and indubitable knowledge, from which anyone who grasps its force cannot dissent, whether the effect is demonstrated from the cause or the cause from the effect. Thus in this context we understand by demonstration any reasoning that concludes necessarily. Nor are we to go into detail about this in our enterprise, for logicians do this.

Probable matter is that in which the propositions of an argumentation are of the type where the attribute is connected to the subject to which it is attributed not necessarily but contingently, or, should it be connected necessarily, this is not apparent and so the intellect can dissent from them; but, because either they can be true or they are received by common consent and taken to be true, they are said to be probable. From this type of reasoning is generated only a kind of opinion, that is, [64] knowledge that is not completely clear, certain, and indubitable, and so it is possible for it to be false. This type of reasoning is said to be a dialectical or topical syllogism, which is generally used to resolve questions or problems that are disputed with probability on either side of the issue.

There are various kinds of probable propositions: some are probable for everyone, such as that friends should be obliging, that mothers love their children; others for the majority, as that riches should be shared, honors should be sought; others for the very wise, as that virtue alone is desirable for its own sake, that the honorable should be preferred to the useful; and others finally to the moderately wise, as that not all emotions are bad, that virtues are not sciences. Argumentations taken from these types of propositions serve to generate opinion or belief, which is twofold: one type is popular, which is produced by propositions and causes that are easily perceived and resolved by the people; the other is the type that those who have some schooling try to attain, but since they are unable to demonstrate and achieve scientific knowledge they come as close to it as they can; we say that the former is proper to the orator, the latter to the dialectician.[68] Cicero seems to distinguish this [65] twofold belief or method of discoursing in the preface to his *Paradoxa* when he says that Cato was accustomed to treat certain serious topics that were taken from philosophy but were abhorrent to forensic and public use. He seems to imply that these should not be used and that Cato should have spoken in a popular way; thus there would be two types of speech, one for the learned, the other for the people.

Finally there are other propositions from which an argumentation is formed that are neither true nor probable but false, although they appear to be true or probable. From these are formed a kind of instrument of deception that is called a sophistic syllogism, the fallacy of which is recognized by the judicative faculty. Philosophers, therefore, use demonstration, dialecticians and orators the probable syllogism, but since their probable matter is not the same, as noted in the first book of *De arte dicendi*,[69] we have not taught about them in the same place. Sophists, that is, those who deceive by using false arguments and wish to appear wise, use the sophistic syllogism, about which we have written much elsewhere.[70]

Thus all artists who dispute necessarily or probably or insidiously have need of topics or middles or argumentations, [66] since nothing can be resolved or made to conclude without a middle. It is true that sophistic invention is vacuous since the middle does not go with the extremes, nor does it fit the parts of the question, nor do the parts agree with a third term, as it does in the demonstrative and the topical, in the first of which the agreement is recognized as evident, in the other as credible. From this one may infer that the inventive power is of service not only for disputing with probability but also for constructing demonstrations, since topics are well adapted to serving the needs of both.

Chap. 14. Why the invention of topics is necessary, and how they were found and defined

Thus far we have spoken of the question, which is the subject matter of invention; we have also spoken of the argument and argumentation, which is like an instrument we use to resolve a question and induce belief, and also of the threefold matter of argumentation. It now follows, according to our proposed ordering, that we say something about the nature of topics generally, so that [67] having said this, what we shall say about individual topics may be more easily understood. But before we expound on the nature of the topic, we explain briefly the necessity for inventing topics and how they were invented.

As to the necessity of finding topics, we can take this mainly from three headings. The first is from the nature of human acts, for, since they are ambiguous, perplexing, and open to various objections, argumentation was necessary for explaining, elucidating, and terminating them, and this could not be done without the discovery of topics. Then, from the variety and multitude of the things from which topics are taken, from which it results that it is not easy for anyone to be able to excogitate certain and suitable arguments. For which reason, just as philosophers, to achieve knowledge of all things, had to reduce everything that exists in the universe to certain supreme genera, so those wishing to find arguments with facility sought to reduce the method and variety of all arguments to certain topics. Finally, from the condition of human nature, for, since this is dull, slow, and with little skill, it was fitting that some brief and easy way be offered to it by which it might go to topics, [68] whence it might seek arguments, which, as we have said above,[71] have great use and utility in all walks of life. And this should be sufficient for the necessity of inventing topics; now we treat briefly of the method of invention.

Since therefore human matters, as we have said, are dubious, uncertain, and open to controversy, there is need of the question and reasoning to explain and confirm them, and since arguments for treating questions are not readily available to all, so that those who are slow and gross might use some ingenuity, there were certain people of acute mind, quick wit, and perspicacity who had acquired experience in discoursing. These individuals gradually noted certain seats of arguments and made certain headings for the great variety of matters and their great supply of arguments, and assembled them in common topics, which, because of the order and relationships found in things themselves, are suitable for making affirmations about them in the ways we have explained in the twelfth chapter above. And so even more ingenious individuals put together the common orders and indices of things [69] by which we are shown what may be valid for a proof and whatever can be found doubtful in any way whatever, considering the different relationships among things that are to be discovered in any matter that may be proposed. These are the causes of things, their parts, affections, adjuncts, contraries, comparatives, and others of this type. This was done with diligence so that one who is adept at this faculty, when hearing of any problem, understands immediately and, for any question proposed, sees the middles that are proper for explaining it. This is not otherwise than the way in which a philosopher, as soon as he sees a substance or hears its name, knows immediately in what category it should be put. And so much for invention; now we turn to the definition of a topic.

Agricola describes a topic in this way:[72] a topic is a certain shared characteristic of a thing by whose direction what is probable in each thing can be discovered. By characteristic he means a sign or an indication, such as the statue of Mercury that at one time was placed at crossroads, and now a wooden hand, that shows a traveller the direction in which he should go. Boethius defines it in this way: a topic is that from which one draws an argument appropriate to the question under consideration. From Cicero[73] and Quintilian [70] is gathered this description of a topic: a topic is the seat of an argument, for arguments are resident in certain places from which they can be drawn when we wish to prove anything. From these one can infer why the source from which arguments and middles are taken is called metaphorically a place, because arguments lie hidden there as in a type of place. And, as Agricola says, they are called places because all the instruments for engendering belief are deposited in them as in a receptacle or kind of treasury. With the result that, as Cicero states, when things hidden are pointed out and their places noted, finding them is easy;[74] and so, when we wish to investigate any argument, we must know the topics.[75] And so that they not be distributed all over the earth, but different things in different places, such that no argument comes from just anywhere, one must know whence they arise, so that when they have been found we may easily see what is in them. Aristotle called the source from which arguments are taken not only a place but an element,[76] possibly for the reason that it itself is simple and the origin and beginning of many arguments. What has now been said briefly of the necessity of finding topics, and the method and description of their invention, should be sufficient.

Chap. 15. Kinds of topics, maximal topics, and maximal differences

[71] Having explained the definition of a topic, we should say something about its division. Topics are commonly divided into the topic that is called maximal and that which is called the maximal difference. The former is described as follows:[77] a maximal topic is a universal proposition that is probable per se and on whose truth many argumentations depend. It is said to be a universal proposition because it is one and maximal and serves, not for one argumentation alone, but for many in different subject matters, as, for example: "What is said of the thing defined is said also of the definition," which is useful for all argumentations drawn from the thing defined. It is said to be probable because it is assumed as certain, so that it does not require proof, nor is it usually proved. It is said to be supportive of many argumentations because all the force of the argumentation depends on it. That it should be so called is proved by Boethius from the fact that such a proposition contains several argumentations in its embrace, and this is proper to a topic. [72] The fact that it contains several argumentations is apparent from its definition. Such propositions are said to be maximal either because they are not generally taken into an argumentation, whose parts are the minor and the major, and they stand outside the argumentation, and ascend over the other propositions as by a higher degree, or certainly because they have the oldest and fullest approval, since they induce so much belief for other propositions that they themselves do not require proof.

There are two kinds of maximal topics: some can be put in an argumentation in the first place, as are the major propositions of a syllogism;
others do not enter into the argumentation. For example, should one argue using an enthymeme as follows: "Virtue is longer lasting than riches,
therefore it should be more sought after," this argumentation is based on
the maximal approved proposition, "What is longer lasting is more to be
sought after." If this enthymeme be reduced to ratiocination, this maximal
topic will take the place of the major proposition. From this one may infer
that every major proposition, if it is known *per se,* can be called maximal
because it generally explains the relationship between the middle and the
major extreme, [73] and on this depends the deduction of multiple conclusions in view of the variety of minor extremes in the syllogism.[78] However, if one were to argue as follows: "Man is not liable to corruption
because he is an animal endowed with reason," the force of this argumentation depends on the maximal topic, "What is said of the thing defined is
said also of the definition," which does not enter into the argumentation.

Maximal topics of the first kind explain the relationship of the things
signified to the argument itself through the terms placed in the question,
and they are not explained by logical statements; of this kind are the following: "All mothers love their children," "The more lasting good is to be
more sought after," "Wise men are not envious," and others similar. Those
of the second kind expound the dialectical relationship of terms and are
explained by dialectical sayings, such as: "Contraries are attributes of contraries," "A cause being removed, the effect is removed also." These maxi-
mals and topics are properly those of dialecticians: they state the general
relationship between the argument and the question, and in them reside
many arguments or many propositions, each of which can be the antecedent of a dialectical syllogism. For example, "An animal endowed with
reason has the capability of talking, navigating, preaching, and therefore
he is human"; [74] all of these argumentations are based on one dialectical
maximal topic, which is, "What is attributed to the definition is also given
to the thing defined." Again, maximal topics of the first kind help in
knowing whether an enthymematic argumentation is good and probative
on the part of the matter, whereas maximal topics of the second kind,
which are especially useful for invention, are applied to the enthymeme to
show not only that the matter is good but also the consequence.

From this one may inquire whether the consequences of enthymemes
are justified through maximal topics when the arguments are taken from a
definite topic; Agricola denies this, whereas others affirm it. For they can be
proved very well through maximal topics of the first kind if they are not
placed in the argumentation, but not if the argumentation is reduced to a
syllogism whose antecedent refers not to the consequence but to the consequent. So a consequence is proved correct by maximal topics that are placed

outside—a material consequence by maximal topics, a formal one by syllogistic maxims. From this there arises another division of maximal topics: some are dialectical, or topical, by which the consequence of an argumentation is proved by reason of the matter, as are those we shall offer below; others [75] are syllogistic, that take the force of their proof from the form of the argumentation, as are those in the *Prior Analytics,* of which kind are the following: "From two negative premises nothing follows," "From two affirmative premises in the second figure nothing can be inferred by reason of form," and others similar to these. The former pertain to invention, the latter to judgment. This is enough for the topic referred to as maximal.

The topic of maximal difference is defined as follows by Boethius: the topic of maximal difference is a general heading of things wherein one maximal proposition differs from another, or, it is that by which several maximal topics are distinguished and separated from each other, or, it is a receptacle containing several maximal topics. Just as different maximal topics give rise to different arguments, so they are variously named, and such denominations are called topics of maximal difference, such as the locus from a definition, from parts, from contraries, and similars, as will become clearer below. Here it should be noted that topics of maximal difference do not differentiate individual maximal topics, since each of them contains several within its embrace, but they do supply different appellations for different orderings of maximal topics. A maximal difference [76] under this general heading is called a topic because, just as many argumentations are contained under one maximal topic, so many maximal topics are contained under one maximal difference or under one heading, as will be seen more clearly in our exposition of topics.

Before we divide the topic of maximal difference we explain briefly whence the division of topics is to be taken, whether from a maximal topic or from a maximal difference. That this may be explained more clearly, note that three terms or expressions are employed in a dialectical argumentation: one is that from which something is inferred, and this is placed in the antecedent; another is what is inferred, and this is placed in the consequent; and the third is common, and this is placed in each part of the argumentation. For example, "The wise man is not envious, therefore the philosopher is not envious." Here the subject is found in the conclusion, but if a syllogism were formed, the subject would be in the minor proposition; the common term is the predicate in the conclusion, but if a syllogism were formed, it would be the predicate of the major. That is to say, "No wise man is envious; the philosopher is a wise man; therefore the philosopher is not envious." What we have said applies to a correct and simple argumentation that can be [77] reduced directly to a syllogism.

These three terms are those of which we have written in the twelfth chapter above, two that are placed in the question and the third which is taken as a measure, so that from their agreement or disagreement one can discern whether the terms placed in the question agree or disagree. The third term in which the comparison is made in the enthymeme, where one of the propositions of the syllogism is suppressed, is the inference term that is placed in the antecedent and it is the term that is repeated twice in the syllogism. From this one can see that the inference term is the term that makes one maximal topic differ from another. For example, if one infers the definition from the thing defined, or the effect from the cause, here the topics would be said to be from the thing defined, from the cause, and so on. Thus it is appropriate that the topic be called the seat of the argument, since it is what contains the source through which belief is secured in a doubtful matter, or that from which an argument is drawn appropriate to the question proposed; so that a maximal topic is what induces belief *per se,* and a maximal difference is what, taken with another, constitutes a proposition that *per se* is conclusive of the question.

In light of this explanation, it should be easy to see whether the differentiation of topics should be taken from a maximal topic or from a maximal difference; and this done, [78] if we wish to see the common opinion, the reason for it should be taken from a difference of the maximal topic. So hold Cicero and also Quintilian, Themistius, Boethius, Agricola, and practically all other authors who have written on this matter. And since topics that are placed in differences are far fewer than the maximal topics of which they are differences, they will also be more universal and hence will contain more, and will have more the nature of a topic, and as a consequence will be better committed to memory and will be more easily found. Nor are these topics vague and uncertain, but they are contained in a definite ordering that shows how a maximal topic is used for demonstrating a particular matter, as we have explained above, and if this ordering and grouping is removed, there is no argument, and thus, no topic.

Since this relationship of the argument to the question to be resolved is various and diverse, different enumerations of topics have been offered by different writers. There is no need for us to explain whence springs this diversity in the numbering of topics, since some enumerate many, others few, some these, others those; those who are interested should consult Boethius and the Louvain Doctors. In this matter we ask only that the same faculty be conceded us [79] as has been conceded other writers, so that we be permitted to list topics in a way different from others so that they may be seen more readily and with greater perspicacity, and this we do after having exposed other enumerations of the topics. So, having posited the first division of topics, according to which one topic is called maximal, another maximal difference, those who treat of this matter usually subdivide the topic of maximal difference in various ways, as will be apparent from the tables that follow.

Chap. 16. Different enumerations of topics taken from various authors

Since different topics of invention have been enumerated by various authors, we offer here three of the more famous enumerations, and these, so as to make them more easily grasped, we put in the form of tables. The first is that of Cicero, the second that of Agricola, and the third that of Themistius; later dialecticians have adopted these more or less freely. [80]

Cicero's Enumeration of Topics

Topics are intrinsic or innate, and these are 16 in number, i.e., from:

definition
enumeration of parts
notation [description of significant features]
conjugates
genus
form
similarity
dissimilarity
contraries
adjuncts
antecedents
consequents
repugnants
causes
effects
comparison
     with greaters
     with lessers
     with equals,

or they are extrinsics or remotes and things assumed; these, according to Quintilian, are six:

prejudices
reputations
torments   Cicero includes all of
tables   these under testimonies
oaths
witnesses

Agricola's Enumeration of Topics

[81] Some topics are internal, and these are

partly in the substance of the thing, as

definition
genus
species
property
whole
parts
conjugates, or

partly surrounding the substance, as

adjacents
actions
subjects;

other topics are external, and these are either

cognates, some of which are

causes through which a thing comes to be
efficient
final, or
other events that come to be through causes
effects
things destined, or

applied things, as

place
time
connections
contingencies, or

accidents, of which there are five genera

pronouncements
the thing's name
comparisons
similars
dissimilars, or

repugnants, as

opposites
differences

Themistius's and Boethius's Enumeration of Topics

[82] Topics are twofold, either maximal, or
maximal differences, which are threefold:

internal, either

    from substance, as, from

        definition and the thing defined
        description and the thing described
        interpretation and the thing interpreted, or
    from concomitants of substance, that is, from

        whole or parts of the same

            integral whole
            universal whole
            quantitative whole
            modal whole
            temporal whole
            locational whole, or from
        cause and effect, i.e., from

            efficient cause
            material cause
            formal cause
            final cause, or from
        generation, or
        corruption, or
        accidents in general; or

external, either from

    opposites, which are

        relative
        privative
        contrary, or
        contradictory, or
    disparates
    greater or lesser
    similar or dissimilar
    proportion or disproportion or transmuted proportion
    transumption
    authority, or

intermediate, that is, from

    conjugates
    inflected cases
    division

[83] It is this last enumeration of topics that we regard as best when we come to explaining the dialectical topics, although for reasons of facility we have expanded one or other topic and changed others. Otherwise, since we have worked out an alternative way of discovering and explaining the topics, our own treatise on invention is divided following another method, which we set out in the next chapter.

Chap. 17. The division of topics proper to this work

Here our proposal is to make clear, to the extent of our ability, all the force and nature of invention simply and clearly, and also to explain the topics that dialecticians usually regard as their own as well as others that are adapted to rhetoricians and to common use, which many of those who treat of invention omit. For these reasons our treatise is divided differently from those of others. For we think that all the multiplicity and variety of topics can be reduced to two headings, in one of which the topics of persons, in the other the topics of things, are contained.

[84] In persons we can look at two things: their attributes and their actions; and in actions, both their causes, or those things whereby men are moved either to act or not to act, and the circumstances that surround such actions. And that you may understand how men are moved to act or to pursue one thing and avoid another, note that there are two powers of the soul, one by which we know and which has as its goal truth, the other by which we will or desire, which is moved by the good. For this reason, whoever wishes to find topics suitable for persuasion ought to know these and propose them to those whom he wishes to influece by the power of knowing or of seeking; and these are the true and the good, and their parts. And just as topics taken from persons individually serve the demonstrative genus, that is, those things that conduce to praising and to blaming, so the topics taken from things by which men are affected and excited to seek one thing and to flee another serve the deliberative genus. And indeed, all of these topics, which are reducible to these two headings, pertain properly to orators and to rhetors, just as those that look to things pertain to dialecticians.

We do not deny, however, that the prior topics [85] also pertain to dialecticians and that the posterior similarly pertain to rhetors, since the treatise on invention and on topics is common to both dialecticians and to rhetors, as we have demonstrated more fully in another place,[79] though they do not take on the same formality, nor do they have the same goal. Therefore the topics that pertain to persons are either their attributes or their actions, and of their actions either the causes or the circumstances.

The topics of things are discovered on the one hand by art and are in the thing itself, and these are named artificial; on the other hand, they are taken from without and supplied in abundance from the genus of cause, and these are called inartificial.[80] Matters that are sought in the thing itself can be divided, as by Themistius, into intrinsic, extrinsic, and intermediate; and we usually follow this division; those that are associated extrinsically, as Quintilian divided them.[81] Again, topics universally considered are divided into two parts: for some are said to be absolutes, which are used for resolving an absolute question; others comparatives, which we employ to treat a comparative question—and of these we treat at the end.

In sum, therefore, topics are either of persons or of things: those of persons pertain either to their attributes or to their actions and to the causes and circumstances of actions. Topics of things are either artificial, and these are either [86] intrinsic or extrinsic or intermediate; or they are inartificial, as are presumptions, tables, rumors, etc. And this should suffice to explain our general division of topics, which we further subdivide later at the proper place.

Now, since what are referred to as common topics have been explained in various ways, I treat a few matters in the following chapter concerning the way in which this expression is to be understood.

Chap. 18. Common topics and proper topics, and divisions of common topics

There are various appellations for common topics among both dialecticians and teachers of oratory. Sometimes the term "common topic" designates a famous sentence or proposition in common use and generally received, and this the dialecticians call a maximal topic, or, in Latin, *axioma*.[82] Sometimes common topics are said to be common attributes that are found with some genus or common nature and are attributed to individual forms or species. And things that are affirmed of virtue and of animal are also said of their species.

[87] Otherwise common topics are the general headings under which things are located that are treated in any art or science,[83] as, in theology, God, angels, man, virtues, vices, and other matters that are considered generally in this science. In civil law, persons, things, possessions, contracts, and actions.[84] In medical matters, naturals, nonnaturals, and preternaturals; and these are subdivided into other parts. And finally in philosophy, the ten supreme categories of things, under which all natures are contained. Again, common topics are sometimes said to be various sentences, collected from various writers in one place, which we use for treating and elaborating different matters; there are various extant works that contain such common topics.[85] And we, God willing, shall soon publish a

volume of this type in which the flowers of the ancient and best writers will be contained. Again, a common topic is said to be a question that is infinite and treated universally,[86] whether it is referred to a finite question or not; for example, one concerning the power and nature of God, providence, adultery, poetics, the office of judge.[87]

Finally, common topics are said to be certain headings that are proper to consider in each matter, from which many arguments can be quickly drawn in a disputation, [88] as the topics from definition, from causes, from effects, and other similar things, of which we have written elsewhere.

With respect to the division of topics, apart from those we have given above, some topics are called proper and others common. Proper topics are said to be those that belong in one cause, or thing, or art, or science; common topics are those that can be accommodated to several causes and things. Or again, common topics, whether they are maximal topics or maximal differences, are said to be those notes, universally considered, that alert us to where arguments lie hidden; and their explication pertains to the common arts, which are dialectic and rhetoric;[88] for example, the topic of definition, of cause, of effect, and others, since these are not restricted to any particular matter. Those that are contracted to a particular kind of thing come to be proper; for example, topics from the definition of virtue, of justice, of nature, of contracts, of fevers, and of other particular things, because under this formality they pertain to individual arts and sciences.

From this division yet others flow, for some topics are said to be dialectical, others rhetorical; the former are explained and used by dialecticians, the latter by orators, as explained above. Again, topics are divided by masters of speech[89] according to the three genera of causes or cases, [89] and so some topics are of the judicial kind, as the just and the wicked; others are of the deliberative kind, as the useful, the useless, the easy, the difficult; others are of the demonstrative kind, as the topics of persons. Again, they are divided according to the three statuses, since some serve conjecture, others definition, and yet others quality. Again, some topics are said to be major, for these can be regarded as the fountainheads of others, and these Cicero enumerated and explained in his *Topics;* others are minor, for these belong to individual cases and states.[90] Finally, some topics are suitable for blaming and accusing, as the topics against lying, against adultery, against patricide, and similar things; these are usually treated in digressions and amplifications. Others contain matters for pleading and excusing, and are used for arguing against the previous type. Yet others can go either way, as the topics from riches, from honors, from voluptuousness, and similar things.

Thus is apparent the way common topic is used in various ways by authors and for this reason has been used by us in this treatise. Therefore, what a question is, and the various kinds of question, and what a topic is and its various divisions, we think should be clear from the matters thus far considered. [90] And since in this first book we have explained the matter of the entire work and things that should make it easily understood, we move on to the second book where we take up specific details, following the order proposed.

END OF THE FIRST BOOK

BOOK THREE

Chap. 12. The nature and division of cause, and the way of arguing from material cause

[326] Of all topics the most ample and the most frequently used among all writers is this topic of causes, and therefore we explain it carefully with the following method. First, we teach the order of topics in which it should be placed; then, what a cause is, and [327] how many kinds of cause there are. After that we treat of single causes individually, and finally of the effects of causes.

Concerning the first, some[1] put this topic among the "extrinsics"; others partly in the "intrinsics," as the topic of matter and form, partly in "extrinsics," as the topic of end and efficient cause; others locate all among the "internals," as do Themistius, Boethius, and the Louvain School. It is the last opinion we follow. And what pertains to matter and form is most certain, since from these two causes each thing is proximately constituted. But the end and the efficient cause, even though said to be outside the thing, also have much to do with constituting and making known its nature. Again, by the fact that they are said to be causes of a thing they would seem to pertain to its essence. Indeed, to be properly called extrinsic a cause would not be included in the nature of the thing, nor would anything of it. But these two causes are not of this kind, as is apparent, especially since demonstrations are best made from the final cause, and every nature whatever depends on its final cause.

Concerning the second, a cause in general is described in various ways. Agricola describes it as follows: a cause is that with whose force or power something is done; others in this: it is that from whose force or power something follows; or, it is that [328] from which an effect follows in the order of nature. Yet others,[2] whose definition is more in use, define it in this way: a cause is that on whose existence another follows, that is, a cause is that from which, flowing out as it were, something else proceeds immediately that is posterior to it at least by nature even though they may be together in time—as from the existence of fire heat follows. We may say in passing that we do not agree with what Agricola attributes to Cicero, that he reduced all causes to the efficient cause, since in actual truth he made mention of all the kinds of causes, as may be clearly seen in his *Topics*.

Concerning the third, as all philosophers teach, there are four kinds of cause: matter, form, end, and agent, from the perfect knowledge of which one attains scientific knowledge of any object whatever. Virgil says the same,[3] and another poet encourages us to such knowledge.[4]

Concerning the importance, order, and power of these causes, this is not the place for treating this matter extensively. But, when treating the individual causes we do speak of the way in which each of these can be described and divided into types. [329] Turning now to each cause in particular, I first treat of matter, concerning which I cover the many ways a material cause is understood, what it is and how many kinds there are, the modes of arguing it offers, and its use.

As to the first, matter primarily and properly is said to be that from which anything is made, whether this is done by nature or by art. In this way the elements are the matter of compounds, stones and wood the matter of a house and brass of a statue, concerning which we may quote Virgil.[5] Then, by *catachresim,* matter is said to be what is treated in any science or art. In this way every expression is said to be the matter of grammar; persons, things, and actions the matter of civil law;[6] and harmonious sounds that of music. Horace spoke of matter in this sense in his *Ars poetica.*[7] Moreover, by the term matter is designated that around which any thing turns or rotates, or that on which art imprints a form. In this way the canvas is the matter of the picture and the marble the matter of the sculptor. Finally, matter is said to be any thing in which any form or actuality inheres, and this properly [330] is called the subject. In this way substance is the matter or the subject of all accidents, and the human soul of virtue. And we use these three notions of matter in this topic, and especially the first, in which meaning matter is usually described in this way: matter is that from which something is made and exists in it; or, it is that from which something is made and into which it is resolved.[8] Matter thus has two properties: one, that from it something is made; the other, that it remain in the thing effected, and if the thing is destroyed, it is resolved back to it, as the human body into the elements, words into letters, and a shepherd's pipe into stalks of hemlock.

Although matter can be divided in many ways, we attend only to divisions that are appropriate to our consideration. Matter taken in this way is twofold; one is natural, from which nature fashions its works, as clouds are the matter of rain, elements the matter of compounds, and the basic unformed substrate from which all things are made [i.e., prime matter] the matter of the elements. The other is artificial, which either nature supplies to art, or one art supplies to another, and in this way earth is the matter of walls and walls the matter of a house; food the matter of a banquet, gold of a crown. Again, matter is twofold: one is permanent, which remains in the thing effected [331] as part of its substance and can be resolved back to it; in this way stones are the matter of a house and silver of a vase. The other is changeable, and its nature does not remain in the thing effected and thus cannot be reduced back to it; in this way wheat is the matter of bread, honey and vinegar that of oxymel. Finally, matter is twofold: one proximate, from which the thing is made directly, as the hewn wood from which the bench is made and the expressions from which a speech is made; the other remote, which is presupposed by the artisan or by the efficient agent, as are the wood in the forest from which the bench can be made and the syllables of the spoken word. These matters thus explained, we begin to explain the modes of arguing from matter taken in this first meaning.

One may discern a threefold mode of arguing from the topic of cause: one from the cause to the effect, another from the effect to the cause, and a third from the attributes of the cause to the effect; in the present treatise we explain the first and the third when treating of causes, the second later when we treat of effects separately.

From the matter from which something is made arguments for affirming and denying may be taken in the following way. First by proving, from the positing of the matter, whether permanent or not, that the effect can occur, [332] but not absolutely, since other conditions apart from the matter are required for the thing to be effected. For example: clouds appear, therefore there can be rain; there is wool, thus a garment can be made. The eunuch of whom mention is made in Sacred Scripture,[9] took an argument from this topic, when, having come to water, he said to Philip, What prohibits me from being baptized? There is vacant property, therefore it can be put to use. The common topic: if the matter is found the effect can follow. Second, for refuting, from cause to effect: in a permanent cause using the present tense, as follows. There is no iron; therefore there are no iron weapons; there is no wood, therefore no ships. The common topic: if the permanent matter is lacking, so is the effect. In changeable matter, however, one would conclude wrongly using the present tense, saying, for example, there is no flour, therefore there is no bread; yet one may use the past tense as follows: there was no flour, therefore there is no bread; and one may also argue licitly, there is no flour, therefore bread is not being made. The common topic: if changeable matter has not preceded, the effect is not.

The third mode is from the attributes and the nature or the affections of the matter to the effect; this mode is easily seen. The house is made of stone; therefore it is not in danger [333] of being destroyed; it is made of reeds and straw, therefore it would take little to damage it; animals are composed of contrary elements, therefore they will ultimately die; stars

are removed from all material disturbances, therefore eternal; some thing
is stolen, or sacred, therefore it cannot be possessed by prescription;[10] and
a text from Horace.[11] From this place Martial has censured a certain person's avarice and untimeliness with a diptych.[12]

If the term matter is taken in the other three modes recounted above, it
may be described as follows. Matter is that in which, or around which, an
art revolves or in which something is present. Concerning the matter in
which something is found as in a subject, we speak separately a bit later.
Concerning the matter with which an art is concerned or on which it acts,
the following may be said: from it the dignity and the importance of all
arts are taken,[13] since the more worthy the subject matter [334] the more
worthy the art that considers it, as philosophers generally teach. In moral
philosophy, the formality of a virtue and a vice and greater or less praise or
blame is taken from this matter. Orators and poets present this matter
when something is to be said, as did Virgil in his *Georgica.*[14] On the basis of
this topic sacred theology is preferred to all other sciences and moral philosophy to mathematics; using it Cicero beautifully castigated the science
of civil law in his oration *Pro Murenam.*

Now let us discourse briefly on how the material cause is used by writers. Historians, orators, and poets use this topic when they describe any
object or offer praise on the basis of the matter from which something is
confected: in this mode Caesar at one time described ships he had built,[15]
and Ovid the reign of the Sun in his *Metamorphoses.*[16] Virgil used the same
topic for the gifts given to Dido by Aeneas and the banquet Dido prepared for Aeneas; [335] and Horace, the feast of Nasidienus.[17] From it jurisprudents separate out the following considerations: if anyone make a
vase from another's silver, or build on another's field, or paint on his canvas. On its basis orators differentiate various kinds of speaking: sublimely,
slightly, and temperately. From it philosophers and theologians distinguish
one vice or one virtue from another, and assess the gravity or importance
of various virtues and vices. There are also those who reduce to this topic
arguments taken from the attributes of places in which things are generated, as, for example, that fish are humid because they are generated in water; but we discuss these matters in another place.

Chap. 13. The topic of formal cause

The topic of form will be explained sufficiently if we speak of its name,
its definition, and its division, and open up the modes of arguing and uses
of this topic. Among philosophers, form is taken for the part of a composite object that liberates it from matter and constitutes it with a definite
nature; in this way the human soul is said to be the form of man. Philoso-

phers also take form to mean the figure by which things [336] confected by art are distinguished one from another. In this way objects made of wood are diversified by their different shapes; so we say that some have a round figure, others a triangular, others a square. Again, among philosophers any accident that inheres in a subject is called a form, and generally, whatever is attributed to a thing; in this way whiteness is the form of a white object, sweetness of a sweet object, and being grammatical of a grammarian. Finally, form sometimes has the same meaning as species, and also as beauty, which is called *venustas* or being Venus-like in women and is named dignity in men.[18] This form is what is meant in a work by Ovid.[19]

The formality of this form is noted and recognizable not only in humans but also in things lacking reason and sense, as in brutes, in trees, mountains, fountains, and other things of the same genera; whence it happens that something may be said to be formed or deformed. This is seen in what Seneca once wrote.[20] It is usually described as follows: form is what gives existence to a thing and conserves it in being; or it is what [337] gives a name and an essence to a thing. Or it is that through which each thing is distinguished intrinsically from other things and constituted in a certain species.[21] Or finally, form is the cause by which a thing is what it is. Thus the form is the ultimate perfection of a thing, by which (along with matter) the entire thing is completed and conserved in being.[22] If form is taken for figure, it is nothing more than a mode of quantity by which a thing is said to be round, square, oblong, or angular. If it is taken for any nature by which a thing is affected in any way whatever, form is said to be that by which the subject receives its name, as to be white from whiteness, to be lucid from light. The form that designates beauty is nothing more than a certain ordering of parts and a symmetry, or an apt arrangement of members, with a certain agreeableness in color.[23] Thus much concerning the definition of form.

As to what pertains to its kinds: some forms are essential, as are those that constitute a thing in a certain species, to which are referred all intrinsic attributes taken from genera, species, and proper differences that are said concretely of their subjects, as humanity in man. Others are accidental, those [338] that affect and name a thing extrinsically, as are all accidents (as opposed to substances). Of accidental forms some are natural, as those that arise from nature, and of this kind is whiteness in man and light in the sun; others are from art or the human will, as the square form of a house, this or that term in contracts. This suffices for the division of form, more divisions not being required here.

Before we explain the modes of arguing, note that philosophers reduce the cause they call an exemplar to the genus of formal cause. This is nothing more than the formality or the model in whose similarity or imitation something is made or done.[24] In this way the painter paints an image based on an exemplar; and from such a cause arguments may occasionally be taken. The exemplary cause differs from other formal causes in that it exists outside the thing whereas the others are in the thing itself.

This much explained, we now detail the various modes of arguing by running through the individual kinds of forms. To better understand these, again note that form not only constitutes and composes a thing in itself but also gives it a power and faculty of acting.[25] On this account we can prove from this cause not only that [339] a thing exists but also that it has a particular type of operation or ability to operate.

The following arguments are taken from the essential form. This is a soul endowed with the capacity for reason, therefore a human being, therefore one able to contemplate; reason is denied of beasts, therefore they do not think; these vessels were rightly consecrated to God by the bishop, therefore they are sacred.[26] The common topic is, in brief: the form being posited, that of which it is the form is posited, or its operation, or at least its power to act. Then arguments can be taken from the attributes of the form: it is licit to affirm them of things in which the form is found, and to deny it of those that lack such a form. For example, reason foresees the future, therefore it belongs to one endowed with reason to foresee the future; heat expands and cold contracts, therefore fire can separate the dross from gold and cold can solidify clay and straw; the soul of a brute animal is subject to corruption, therefore so is the brute animal; sickness is not compatible with hilarity, therefore neither is the sick person. "You, since either God or your mother or, so to speak, the nature of all things has given you a soul, than which nothing is more important or more divine, should you not reject from yourself and see to it that nothing be seen to be common to you and a four-footed creature?"[27] [340] Here is pertinent that saying of our Savior: "Do not fear those who kill the body and are unable to kill the soul; rather fear him who can cause soul and body to be lost in hell"[28]; there he is arguing from the nature of the soul.

Arguments from an artificial form or shape are the following. The heavens are round, therefore they rotate easily; a sharp object penetrates easily, therefore a sharp knife cuts easily; the broader a board is, the more adapted it is for floating. From this topic Menalcas elegantly praised his potions in the words of Virgil.[29] This topic offers ample material for praising artisans such as painters, sculptors, architects, writers, and others, on the basis of the forms they produce in things. From an accidental form endowed by nature are taken the praise and description of mountains, fountains, trees, and things of a similar kind. Thus is pertinent another text in Virgil.[30] [341] And this elegant description of a port by the same author.[31] From such a form is also taken the basis for proving that a field inundated by the force of a river does not cease to be owned by him who had it before, that inundation does not change the kind of what is underneath.[32] Also, the form that is beauty offers the occasion not only to prove and refute but also to praise. For example, one may argue from the structure or form of his body that man ought to look up into the heavens; it is this topic that Sillius the Italian, Manilius, and other writers have used; and Naso, when he sang in Ovid's *Metamorphoses*.[33] And Virgil gave wonderful praise to Aeneas from the topic of form.[34] From the same form, or beauty, are taken conjectures judging of spirit or of morals. This form also has the power to attract souls; Corydon used this topic to counsel benevolence of Alexis.[35] [342] Things that are attributed to the form are also easily attributed to those possessing it.

From the external form, or from the exemplary cause, Aristotle proved that it is most natural for plants and animals to procreate progeny similar to themselves; that all creatures, as much as they are able, seek unending conservation in imitation of the divine Godhead.[36] This was also used in the Holy Scriptures when it was written that the blood of man is not to be spilled since man is made to the image of God.[37] And this: "We ought to love our enemies and do good to them, that we might be sons (that is, that we might imitate our heavenly Father), who makes the sun rise on the good and the bad."[38] Hence also is it rightly sanctioned that a minor cannot adopt an adult, since adoption imitates nature, according to which a father is not minor to a son.[39] From this topic preachers take verisimilar arguments to prove that children and peoples cannot be good if they do not have good parents, good princes, and good pastors. Claudian wisely sang this.[40]

[343] And that we might put an end to this chapter, let us add something concerning the use of the formal cause, although its quantity and quality can easily be understood from the foregoing. The greatest use of form in every art and science is to define and to demonstrate the existence, attributes, and properties of an object. Through it moral philosophers discern the vices and the virtues; historians, orators, and poets graphically describe, put before the eyes, and wonderfully praise things with which they are concerned; through this physiologists make predictions concerning the customs of men. And finally, the science of mathematics, for the most part, is concerned with the explication of this cause when it considers the numbers and figures of quantified objects.

Chap. 14. The topics of subject, adjacents, and acts

In this description of the topics we have been persuaded that it is much easier and more expedient to work from a distinction of many topics than from an enumeration of a few, with the accompanying difficulty of recognizing them. [344] On this account no one will regard us as playing a game when we distinguish a multitude of topics. Although topics from a subject, adjacents, and acts may easily be perceived from what we have said about form and matter, since a subject is a type of matter and adjacents and acts quasi forms, nonetheless something needs be said about them separately, using the method already employed.

A subject is properly said to be that which is thrown under something, as pavement under the feet.[41] By translation, a people is said to be the subject of a prince; and, *per catachresim,* that which is treated in any art, and that on which something acts and in which it inheres. This can be described as follows. A subject is that in which something exists, the foundation of adjacents and acts, and everything that is the ground for action. Of this kind is substance that is such primarily and essentially, and secondarily quantity, through which sensible accidents inhere in a substance. For this reason we say that fire is the subject of heat, snow of whiteness, wood of heating, and the human mind of intellection. Thus people speak improperly [345] when they call things that fall under our senses and our intelligence subjects. Since knowing powers do not inhere in them and nothing acts on them, they should be called agents and movers rather than subjects. A subject therefore is twofold: one, in which accidents inhere, from which it gets its name, as the white from whiteness; the other, that on which an agent acts, which is simply the matter in which an agent exercises its operation.

Arguments are taken from a subject as follows: if they were not mortals, they could not be said to be sad; he lacks bile, he is not irritated;[42] if there are no pygmies, they cannot fight with cranes; if the land is taken away, so also are the profits accruing from it.[43] The common topic: if the subject is posited or taken away, so are the adjacents and acts. Arguments deduced from this topic can be refuted, since acts and adjacents are non-necessary beings.

Adjacents are things from which a subject takes something other than the name of substance; in this way it comes to a man to be grammatical, wise, and white. More explicitly, from Agricola: an adjacent [346] is a certain mode existing in a thing by which it is denominated something other than substance. Thus anything whose formality is other than substance may be an adjacent, provided it not be placed in agitation or in quasi motion, as are action and passion—even though these also, since they are accidents, are adjacents in the sense of being "thrown to" a subject. Adjacents, from the same author, are distributed in this way: some adjacents are perceived by the senses, as whiteness, taste; others are comprehended by intelligence alone, as wisdom, goodness. Again, some are native, which are inserted by nature, as heat in fire, wetness in water; others are adventitious, which come after birth, as virtues and vices in man, and heat in water. Of the latter some are not easily removed from a subject, of which kind are habits; others are easily removed, as the redness born of a blush and other affections of mind and body that the Greeks call dispositions. Finally, there are some that are present in inanimate objects, others that are found in things having a soul.

From this topic arguments are taken as follows: there is absolute lightness, therefore there is fire; people are either sad or happy, therefore they must be mortal; liberty is not found, therefore neither are free men.[44] Faith is not kept, [347] therefore there are no men of faith. The common topic: having posited or removed adjacents, their subjects are posited or removed. Similar to this topic is the topic from properties and from adjuncts; the former inhere perpetually, the latter only for the most part. But concerning adjuncts we will speak more fully below. From this topic are sought descriptions of oratory and poetry, of persons, places, and times, and of any matter whatever.

Concerning acts, an act is the same as a motion, whether this be action or passion. Whence an act is an accident posited in a certain activity, as to write, to talk, to move, and to fear. These acts take their origins from adjacents, or, to speak more forcefully, from certain consequences, as from heat, heating, and from the faculty of sight, viewing. Acts are usually divided by philosophers and dialecticians in different ways. To be brief, some acts arise from native adjacents, as to see, to taste, to radiate; others arise from adventitious adjacents, whether these are firm, as to write, to speak well, to cure, or changeable and temporary, to blush from shame, to dance from joy, to tremble from fear. Again some are perfected in the operation itself, as to jump and to sing; others in something that is done, as to paint, to build, to weave. Again others [348] have some end as their purpose, as to walk, to fight, to dispute; others have no end proposed, as to rejoice, to delight, and to be sad. Again, some acts are born of present things, others from future goods or evils. Finally, some acts are free, namely, human acts, which are bad or good, and consequently capable of punishment or reward, arising as they do from knowledge and deliberation. Others are not free and they are done either unwillingly or from ignorance, and so lack culpability.

From acts the following arguments are sought. The spirit leads, therefore he lives; he built the house, sold it, or gave it away, therefore he has property.[45] Bias always brought good things with him, therefore he was adorned with goods of the soul. Whoever safeguards the peace is of the people, and Cicero did this, therefore he is of the people.[46] From this topic Horace elegantly demonstrated the daring of men with the third ode of the first book.[47] And in Scripture: "He distributed his goods and gave to the poor, his justice remains forever";[48] [349] "Lord, if I did this, if there is evil in my hands . . . ,"[49] and what follows. The common topic: acts being posited, the subjects and powers or faculties from which they proceed are also posited; the former being taken away, the latter are also removed. We can also take arguments from the genus or the quality of the action and apply them to the agent acting, and then to other attributes of praise and of blame that follow from such an action. For if the actions are proper, we can reduce the argument taken therefrom to the topic 'from a property': as, he gives to each his due, therefore he is just; it barks, therefore it is a dog.

The topic from acts is of great use to physicists and physicians, who proceed from effects to knowledge of causes; to theologians, who recognize divine power from created things;[50] and to those who write about the properties of things, which they discern from their acts. Again, to moral philosophers, who treat human actions in particular, and to jurisprudents, whose science is drawn mainly from knowledge of actions. And, to conclude briefly, orators and poets praise, describe, and take their conjectures from this topic.

Some refer the mode of arguing called 'from existence and being denominated' to the topic of subject and of adjacents,[51] or to the topic of form, [350] whether the denominator is adjacent or the force is another attribute. Thus, whiteness is in the swan, therefore it is white; heat is in the fire, therefore the fire is hot. For a denomination to be perfect, however, the denominator should not be only in part, as the whiteness in an Ethiopian's teeth, nor for a short while, as a blush arising from shame, nor of low degree, as the heat normally found in water. Finally, something can be denominated from what does not inhere in it even though it depends on or had some ordination to that thing, as an agent from the action that is in the patient, and what is contained from the container. But enough of these three topics; now we proceed to the topic of the efficient cause.

Chap. 15. The nature and kinds of efficient cause

Just as the force and power of efficient causes is the greatest in nature and in art, so is their use most frequent among writers. Thus we must explain this topic with care, using the same method as for the others. First we state what an efficient cause is. [351] An efficient cause, from Aristotle, is that whatever is the first beginning of change or of rest,[52] or that from which an operation first begins; or, according to Agricola, it is anything that offers the energy for making a thing, that truly produces an effect by its power, as the sun light, and fire heating.[53] It seems obvious, therefore, what we should understand by efficient cause.

Efficient causes are divided in various ways. One kind is natural, in the way in which fire is the cause of heating; another is artificial, in the way in which the medical art is the cause of health; so we say that some things come to be by nature, others by art.[54] Again, among efficient causes some act by themselves and need no extrinsic help for operating; in this way, though God alone operates perfectly, there are also agents that can produce an effect without external help. In this way intelligences and the human mind effect operations. Other causes must be helped, as the architect, who needs many workmen to construct a house, and the political art, to administer a city, and others of that kind.[55] Again, some efficient causes are constant and stable, as [352] are agents that always attain a proposed end by their own power and produce their effect; in this way the sun always illuminates the entire hemisphere. Others can be impeded and so act contingently; in this group are found many natural causes and agents that act from deliberation. Again, some produce an effect that cannot be produced by another cause, as virtue a happy life, and the sun the day; others are sufficient to produce an effect, but this could result from another cause. In this way the drinking of hemlock is the cause of death. Again, there are some agents that produce an effect and conserve it, as the sun light in the atmosphere; others produce it but do not conserve it, as a father a son; others that conserve it only, as food an animal; and yet others that destroy. Here are pertinent the songs of Ovid.[56]

Again, some causes operate necessarily by their nature, as a stone moves in a downward direction. Others are carried by an extrinsic force, as an arrow tends to the target [353] and a stone moves upward, and heated water produces heat. Others again operate neither from the impulse of nature nor from extrinsic violence. Again, some act from knowledge, as do animals that have use of sense and intelligence; others act without any knowledge, as do those that lack sense. Again, other causes act from deliberation and counsel, as does a nature capable of reason; others act without any deliberation, as do brute animals, in which, despite what some have written,[57] there is neither reason nor counsel, but what they do they do by nature. Again, some causes are essential, and these attain their effect by their own power, the way fire effects heating; others are accidental, as those that may be conjoined with a cause that is operating essentially but help it in no way, as music with the medical art. Yet again, some causes are efficient in act, others are efficient only in potency. Again, some causes are sufficient and suitable for producing an effect, others are not suitable; this is described in a verse from Ovid.[58] And finally, some causes are proximate, others remote from their effect; others prevent an effect, which follows when that cause has been removed;[59] in this way the removal of a beam is the cause that explains why the stone [350] resting on it falls downward. Of this kind of cause one may interpret a saying of Horace.[60]

These are the principal modes of efficient cause that should be known for arguing correctly, for praising, and for ornamenting. And, that we may grasp all the force of an efficient cause, by 'efficient' we may understand any cause, whether it attains an effect or not, as long as it is related in some way to producing an effect, either by counseling, or by providing an occasion, or by not preventing, either essentially or accidentally (in the way that truth gives birth to hatred), either proximately or remotely. From this it follows that instrumental causes are also included here, as a pen used as an instrument in writing. To the topic of efficient cause some writers reduce place, time, custom, occasion, will, power, fortune, and chance—of which matters we treat elsewhere. But enough for divisions; now we turn to different modes of arguing and the use of this topic.

Chap. 16. The ways of arguing from an efficient cause and the use of this topic

[355] Among the modes of arguing four are the most important. These are taken from a cause operating necessarily, from a sufficient cause, and from a cause that operates actually or potentially, to which is added the mode of arguing from properties of the efficient cause to the effect. The first mode is from a cause producing to its effect necessarily: the sun has risen, therefore it is day; the earth has come between the sun and the moon, therefore the moon is eclipsed; and for refuting, the sun is not over the hemisphere, therefore it is not yet day; the sun is not on the equator, therefore there is no equinox. The common topics: a necessary cause being posited, the effect is posited; the same taken away, there is no effect. The second mode is from a sufficient cause to an effect, and this is used only for proving: he was strangled or drank hemlock, therefore he died; there is fire, therefore heat. But if one were to say, he was not strangled therefore he did not die, one would establish nothing, since death could arise from another cause. The common topic: a sufficient cause posited, the effect is placed. Third, from a cause actually operating to its effect, which can be used for proving and disproving: he is reading, therefore there is a lesson; [356] he is not reading, therefore there is no lesson. The common topic: when the cause is operating, the effect is present; when not operating, the effect is not. Fourth, from a cause that can operate we conclude that the effect can come to be. There is a reader, therefore there can be a lesson. If, apart from the efficient cause it is necessary to have other requisites, they also should be posited. The common topic: posited a cause that can operate, with other requisites, the effect can be present.

Note that no argument can be drawn necessarily from an accidental cause. For people are not to be condemned for the fact that they offer an occasion for sinning,[61] nor is truth to be hidden for the fact that it might lead to hatred.[62] Theologians reduce a meritorious cause to the efficient cause, whence they take the following argument: "Only one who has fought the fight will gain the crown."[63] From the attributes of causes we sometimes dispute necessarily, sometimes probably, in this way: the world was created by a good God, therefore it is good. Matrimony was instituted by Christ; therefore it is appropriate for Christians; therefore it is to be regarded as holy. The book was written by Cicero, therefore it is elegant; he was taught by the best teacher, therefore he is expert. On this account attributes that are present in efficient causes are attributed to their effects, since causes of this kind tend to produce effects similar to themselves.

For a [357] yet fuller explanation, we add other examples taken from various modes of efficient causes. An example from Virgil is taken from a solitary and principal cause.[64] Here Nisus blames every defect in himself on Euryalo, claiming that he alone was the author of the carnage. From a helping cause an ample topic is found in the oration for M. Marcellus, for warlike praises occasion some to amplify words and take them away from leaders, so as to communicate with many, lest such words be thought proper to emperors alone. And similarly in arms and things that follow on them. From an instrumental cause, which is like a helping cause, there is the argumentation in Virgil of Menalcas against Dalmeta.[65] From the same topic Epicurus tried to prove that God is not the maker of the world, since there were no iron tools, or bars, or machines by which such a product could be fabricated.

The argument in Cicero against Laelio is from an essentially efficient cause.[66] Since virtue attracts friendship, [358] as was said above, if this meaning of virtue may be elucidated when one applies and joins oneself to a similar soul, in such circumstances love will follow. From the removal of a cause, this example from the same author in the same book. For, since opinion was the reconciler of the virtue of friendship, it is difficult for friendship to remain if one falls from virtue. And in the oration *Pro Murenam* there was no cause that could provoke Murena to dance—neither a banquet, nor love, nor gluttony, nor libido, nor gain; therefore she would not dance. Jurisprudents consider a cause operating through another, when they say that whoever does something through another actually does it himself. Also, whoever provides the cause of the harm is responsible for the harm itself. From the attributes of the producing cause Moses urged the Israelite people on when he said: "Is this what you, a stupid and foolish people, render to the Lord? Is he not your very father, who possessed you, and made you, and created you?"[67] An example from the removal of an efficient cause is this from St. Paul: "How shall they hear without a preacher?"[68] Again, fish do not breathe, for they lack lungs. From a conserving cause: an animal lives longer the better its protective covering; [359] one lives longer in Venice, since that city has a healthy climate. From a destroying cause: "Every kingdom divided against itself will fall."[69] Dissension is rife among the citizens, therefore the city will be destroyed. An example found in Virgil is from a natural cause.[70]

In addition to these examples, we must say something about the use of this cause, although from the foregoing its quality and quantity should be sufficiently apparent. Poets take descriptions of day and night from this topic; they also use it to describe the unerring stars. Whence Statius[71] and Pontanus.[72] From this same topic poets and astrologers attempt to make conjectures concerning the affairs of men from the various arrangements of the stars, though in our judgment they do so foolishly. He was born, they might say, under the star Mars, therefore he has a propensity for war; under Mercury, therefore he is suited for eloquence. Among the same writers, as also among jurisprudents, [360] a probable argument for some fact is often taken from this topic: since any factor can induce one to do something, they offer it as the cause. Whence this example taken from Terence: "Nearness enables me to warn you daringly and familiarly";[73] and another from Ovid.[74] Among these same writers, when a fact has some appearance of ugliness, a cause for excusing or exonerating is rejected in favor of necessity, chance, fortune, violence, ignorance, or the fault or attempt of another. Here is pertinent the excuse offered by Aeneas.[75] Moreover, great use is made of this topic in blaming and praising. From it Cicero often praised philosophy, stating that it is a certain gift given by the immortal gods to humankind; from it Menalcas also offered his toasts.[76] From it Dido attempted to vituperate Aeneas when he said that he was born, not of Venus and Anchises, but of the hard rocks of the Caucasus and nourished by Hyrcane tigers.[77] From it one frequently considers the agents who might have done a particular thing, either God, or [361] man, or someone expert in an art, or prudent and knowing, or acting on one's own or with the advice of another.

Consideration of this cause is very necessary in the deliberative genus, since such cases look to our powers and those of others. They deliberate over helps and requisites, and show them to be present or absent. In judgments, finally, one considers will, power, occasion, and cause generally: from these are taken reasons for condemning or acquiting or for seeking a greater or lesser punishment. Thus one may gather that not only in natural philosophy, in which the efficient cause is most investigated, but also in the science of morals knowledge of the efficient cause is of the greatest use. To this topic some reduce the topic from corruption and generation, concerning which we will treat separately at a later time. But now we must put an end to this chapter and turn to explaining the final cause.

Chap. 17. The topic of end, its nature and kinds

Since we have already treated three of the four causes, the fourth remains to be explained, the final cause. Concerning this, first what it is; then how it is divided; after that, the modes of arguing it provides; and [362] lastly, its use. As an aid to perceiving what an end is and why it has the power of a cause, note that anything has the formality of an end insofar as it is good or perfect.

A thing is said to be good because it has in itself something that makes it desirable, or because it is able to be perfected.[78] It is not necessary, for something to be proposed as good, that it be truly good; it suffices that it be included under the formality of good even though in actual fact it is not so. For this reason if one errs in comprehending, one will also err in executing. And since no agent is moved to action except to attain some known good, the result is that the end is a quasi-rule for things that are required for its attainment; and according to the variety of ends the variety of things that are ordered to ends should be judged. Whence it results that the end of human actions is said to be a principle or a beginning, since from knowledge of it the agent is moved to operation, and from it takes the formality of acting. Thus with reason is it called the cause of causes and a principle by philosophers, and much more so than things that are ordered to attaining the end.[79] From this is apparent why the end is said to be first in intention and [363] last in execution, since the agent is not moved to action except from knowledge of the end, which he later attains by acting through the means.

From this one may understand why those who begin the treatise on the end and on human actions first say something about the good,[80] and also discourse first about the end rather than about things that are ordered to the end. Every formality and division of end is to be sought from the good,[81] and the suitability of consequents and means from the end, since the end and the good are equivalent. The good thus is twofold: one of individual things, which is placed in some ultimate perfection that is necessary for each thing in its genus, as for fire to be intensely hot and dry, for man to be composed of mind and reason, or to live according to his nature, or to make himself an image of God, or to follow God, or finally, which is the same thing, to be aware of nothing in himself, according to the saying of the wise man in Ausonius.[82] The other good is common to any universe of things or persons, to which the good of individual things is referred, as the good of the parts to the good of the whole, and the good of the family to the good of the city. For the order of things is so constituted that [364] the inferior and less good are ordered to the superior and better; and the more common a good is the more perfect it is, and the more to be sought and conserved, as the Philosopher teaches.[83] For this reason we can discern in each thing a twofold end:[84] one common to all things, to which all things are ordered in an equal way, and this end is nothing more than the glory of the eternal Godhead;[85] the other private, of every thing whatever, to which each thing proximately aspires. Finally, there are some things that are called good because they are to be sought for themselves, as things that are supremely good and are not sought for the sake of other things. There are others that are thought to be good because they are desired for the sake of others, as are things that are not sought except insofar as they aid in attaining another good: for example, in human life food, clothing, money, and war for conserving the peace. The latter goods are spoken of as conferring and helping. From these few observations concerning the good one should be able to understand what we now say about the end.

The end, as one can gather from its definition, is that for the sake of which all things act;[86] or, on account of which something is done; or, that to which the use of a thing looks. It is [365] a certain good proposed by nature or by reason, by which an efficient cause is moved to action, and to which, as to a target, everything is ordered, whence it provides a norm for action. End is twofold: one is highest or ultimate and perfect; the other is directed, that is, non-ultimate, but ordered to another.[87] The former is either the highest and ultimate of all things absolutely to which everything is ordered, and this is God the Best and Greatest. Just as he is the maker and perfecter of all things, so he is their ultimate and absolute end. Or it is ultimate and perfect in its genus, as is that on which the best and perfect state of any thing proximately depends. Thus the end of man is a happy life; of studies, erudition, or a correct judgment of things human and divine; of rhetoric, persuasion; and of war, peace. A directed end is that which is ordered to attaining a supreme end, such as are food, clothing, and wealth, which are ordered to maintaining life, and virtues, which are ordered to living a good life. Of directed goods, some are more important and the better; others are in turn ordered to them. Thus the end of the art that makes bridles is ordered to the equestrian art, the equestrian to the military, and the military to the civil. From this one may gather another distinction of ends, [366] that one type is sought for itself and in no way for another, as is that which is absolutely highest; another type is sought only for another, as food for maintaining life; yet another type, which indeed can be ordered to another but which, even if not so ordered, would still be sought for itself, as are virtue and a good life, which would be sought for themselves even if happiness were not attained through them. Again, among ends, one kind is of the work, to which the work by its na-

ture is ordered, as of war, peace, of studies, erudition; another kind is of
the agent, which the one who acts proposes for himself, as of war, a voluptuous or glorious life, and of studies, gain or honors. Whence one may
gather another division of end, that one kind is proper and internal, the
other improper and external.

Finally, Aristotle in more than one place divides end into "of which"
(*cuius*) and "for which" (*cui*):[88] an end "of which" is that thing for the sake
of which something is done, as money is the end of the labors of an avaricious person; an end "for which" is that thing for which something is
sought, as in the example proposed, the avaricious person himself. For this
reason, not only God, but also other men, and even we ourselves, are ends.
For, as in the proverb, "Man is God to man," since God, compared to man,
is the end "of which," since we seek glory and honor for him, and also the
end "for which," since we wish to enjoy all things as God. [367] To this
may be added another formality of end whereby something is said to be an
end "by which" (*quo*), namely, the fruition, or attaining, or use of the end.
In this way Aristotle said that the end of man is the knowledge of God
and of intelligences. And thus much concerning the division of end; now
we turn to its mode of arguing and its use.

Chap. 18. The ways of arguing from the final cause, and the use of this topic

What should be said about the ways of arguing and the use of this topic
can be covered in a few words. The first mode of arguing: from an end already taken to the one directed, or to the means through which the end is
acquired. The man is learned, therefore he completed his work in letters.
He took the victory or the palm, therefore [he performed the required
task].[89]

Secondly, from an end not attained: he did not taste the victory, therefore he did not run in the stadium, or not properly. To this is related the
vain,[90] namely, when an agent operates and is frustrated from his end,
when he did not accomplish the things necessary for attaining it.

Third, from a desire for an end, [368] or an appetite, to the use of the
means. You wish to enter into life, therefore obey the commandments. If
you wish to enjoy peace, you must wage war. You wish to grasp eternal
goods, therefore contemn earthly ones. This is what Horace means in the
sentence with which he urged us to the attainment of heavenly wisdom.[91]
Again, the same author.[92] And a bit later.[93]

The fourth way: from the end to the removal of the means that are
contrary or are not compatible with the end. You wish to become happy,
then flee vice; you choose health, therefore avoid harmful foods; you wish

to be learned, flee laziness, [369] spurn the voluptuous. You aspire to erudition and eloquence,[94] then for you sensory appetites are to be curbed
and the search for pleasure set aside: games, jokes, banquets, talk about almost all vulgar things are to be given up. One must despair of salvation for
the one whose ears, says Cicero, have been closed to the truth, who is unable to hear the truth from a friend. "Who is the man who wishes life, who
loves to see good days,"[95] that is, to live long and to enjoy those things with
which a life is made happy and blessed; "Keep your tongue from evil, and
do not let your lips speak harm," says the prophet. From this consideration
of the end it is possible to take innumerable ways of refuting arguments,
since equally innumerable are the things in every genus that are not conducive to the attainment of a proposed end.

The fifth way: from the attributes or from the quality of the end to the
means. A happy life is good, therefore so is the virtue by which we achieve
a happy life; to live is good, therefore so is food; it is good to recover and
guard health, therefore medicine is good also; to procreate children is
from a law of nature, therefore so is the marriage of man and woman; if
adultery is bad, so is it bad to solicit a married woman;[96] it is evil to kill,
therefore so is it evil to prepare ambushes. The common topic: if the end
is good or best, or bad, so are the means good, or [370] bad. But note here
that the end should be taken to mean that to which something is ordered
by its very nature, for otherwise a bad argument might be made. Examples:
to give alms is good, therefore it is good to steal so as to be able to give
alms; it is good to preserve the life of a man, therefore it is good to lie to
preserve it; for theft, by its nature, is not ordered to almsgiving, nor is lying to saving life.

The sixth way: from the removal of the end, which, taken away, also
takes away what is done on account of the end. They were not being carried for love of glory, says Cicero, because of the fact that, where honor is
not present publicly, there cannot be love of glory.

The last way: from the quality of the end to the quality of the other
causes, since, as was said above, the end is the reason and a certain measure and rule of all the other causes. If the sword is to cut, it should be
sharp, therefore made of a hard material. You wish your son to be well educated, then give him over to a moderate and learned teacher for instruction. Marriage was instituted for the procreation and education of children, therefore man and wife should follow a monogamous way of life.[97]

For a fuller explanation of this topic other examples may be added.
From the end "to which" the argument is drawn as follows: all [371] creatures were made for the use of men; we therefore are the end of all
things.[98] Here the saying of the Apostle applies: "I put up with all things
for the sake of the elect." God made all things for himself, therefore he did

not make sin. "You wish to be perfect, go and sell all that you have." All things are to be done for the glory of God, therefore it is not right to blaspheme God. From the end "of which," in this way: "You have made us, O Lord," says Augustine, "for yourself, and our heart is restless till it rests in thee";[99] you wish to build a tower, then think first of the cost. From the attainment, or the use, of the end: you wish to see God, then be clean of heart.[100] From a useless end, for the sake of which one works in vain, is a saying of Horace directed to the avaricious man.[101] To this topic some reduce the topic "from use," from the fact that the use is the end of the work or of the instrument. Others think that this rather pertains to the topic "from effects," of which we treat below.

But before we end this chapter, let us add to what has already been said about this topic. First, among jurisprudents a knowledge of this cause is most useful and necessary,[102] as they themselves affirm in many places, for inflicting just punishments, [372] for reconciling rights, which they say sometimes are to be seen as a principle, sometimes as a means for explaining laws correctly, since no law can be correctly explained if one does not understand for what it was intended. Natural philosophers see this cause as the most powerful in the works of nature, and from it they measure the others. Those who treat ethics must especially have this cause in view, since the species of human acts are taken from the end, and the end is the beginning and the terminus of all our actions. Orators make conjectures in judgments from this cause: in consultations, what they see can be done; what they understand to be expedient and not expedient; what they know to be useful and harmful. And there is nothing that is more conducive for persuasion than a treatment of the end, since men desire or flee from all things from the projected appearance of good or evil; in praising, since the use of the final cause is great here, for one looks not so much at what is done as at why it was done and came about. And finally, to conclude, since every art, method, action, and choice seeks some good,[103] the consideration of the end will be directly useful in every science and art, seeing that no art can be well constituted or treated, unless, [373] as Galen prudently taught, from its known and proposed end one is able to foresee the things that are necessary for it and for what end its instruments should be used.

BOOK FIVE

Chap. 11. The different uses of the topics by orators and by dialecticians

[595] Since in this work we have treated of oratorical and dialectical invention and in [596] our other book *De arte dicendi* we have distinguished between these two kinds of invention, it will not be without value to indicate briefly how much the dialecticians' use of the topics for arguments differs from that of orators. For since it is the goal of the dialectician to generate a rather firm opinion, as close as possible to scientific knowledge in agreeing with things themselves, whereas that of the orator is to attract popular opinion in a way agreeable with the human senses—since these two arts have different ends they should use their instruments in different ways so as to achieve their respective goals.

Thus it happens that the dialectician employs perfect definitions in his proofs, he seeks complete divisions and enumerations, proper and proximate causes, effects that are connected with and known with their causes, signs that are necessary rather than verisimilar, and preferably argues from things that are conjunct rather than adjunct to the matter at hand. On the other hand, if one studies with care the writings of orators, one will find in them definitions or rather descriptions that are not completely exact and from which a dialectician would not be able to deduce a conclusion, as, for example, descriptions from contraries, from resemblances, from effects, those by analogy, by negation, and similar kinds that are not proper to the subject. [597] They frequently include comparisons that are imperfect and employ causes that are trivial, frivolous, and remote, and this in all kinds of cause including efficient causes. And in place of necessary causes they oftentimes use those with hardly any force, and even, when they employ necessary causes, do not grasp their necessity. It is not unusual that they base a judgment on events rather than causes, and they do not always comprehend properly the events on which they think they are making the judgment. Their divisions are rarely complete and integral, and occasionally are redundant, as when they say, for example, that there are two things that impel men to vice, ambition and avarice, whereas there are many other motivations for this. They do not trace effects to their proper causes, and they call things effects when there is no cause to which they can be assigned. Meanwhile I omit that they employ topics not for establishing a proof but for amplifying and embellishing so as to seduce or to move their hearers by delighting them. For this reason they pursue not so much the truth as verisimilitude, not so much things themselves as what people say and want to hear, and make use of topics far different from those of the dialectician. Add to this that they regard as their most important topics those that dialecticians [598] would regard as the weakest and most inconclusive.

From this one can clearly gather how much in error are those authorities who claim that the treatment and art of inventing topics belong to the dialectician alone, against which position we have argued in our *De arte dicendi* in the third disputation. We do not deny, of course, that when the case and the topic require this, orators also employ necessary arguments, since it pertains to them to dispute on any problem proposed and to do so everywhere, as Hermogenes rightly taught. But these notes are sufficient for briefly indicating the different practices in these two disciplines when treating of invention. Now, since arguments and topics once invented are of no value for persuasion unless they are put into an argumentation, for the perfect use of topics we say a few things in the last part of our work about the judicative part, as required for our purposes. . . .

ENDNOTES

BOOK ONE

1. Numbers inserted in the translated text in square brackets are the page numbers in the original Latin version.
2. Cicero, lib. I, *De inven.*
3. Cicero, lib. *De oratore*
4. Lib. 2, *De arte dicendi,* disput. 9
5. Arist., lib. I *Topicorum,* cap. 2
6. Cicero, *De partitione oratoria*
7. Here he cites Virgil: Ille regit dictis animos, et pectora mulcet—*Aeneids,* lib. I.
8. *De partitione*
9. *De arte dicendi,* lib. 2, disput. 3
10. I.e., in Book II of *De arte dicendi.*
11. Lib. 2, cap. 6
12. Doctores Lovanienses
13. In schol. Agricola. lib. 2, cap. 6; Doctores Lovanienses in suo Actuario
14. Agricola
15. Doctores Lovanienses
16. Cicero, *De officiis,* lib. I
17. Lib. 2, c. [?]
18. Aristotle, *Posterior Analytics,* lib. 2, cap. I
19. Cicero, Perionius
20. Agricola, lib. 2, cap. 6
21. Aristotle, *Topics,* lib. I
22. Cicero in *De partitione*
23. Cicero in *De partitione*
24. *Topics,* lib.I, cap. 2 [our chap. 4]
25. Porphyry, cap. de genere
26. Porphyry, cap. de specie
27. Porphyry, cap. de differentia
28. Porphyry, cap. de proprio
29. Porphyry, cap. de accidente
30. Cicero
31. Lib. 2 infra, in principio
32. *Topics,* lib. I, c. 2 [our chap. 4]
33. Perionius
34. Agricola, Peter Ramus
35. Quintilian, lib. 3, c. 6
36. Aristotle, *Categories,* chapter on substance
37. Aristotle, *De anima,* lib. 2, cap. I
38. Aristotle, *Categories,* cap. de quantitate
39. Aristotle, *Categories,* cap. de qualitate

40. Lib. 2

41. Aristotle, *Categories,* cap. de relatione

42. Gilbertus Porrectanus, cap. de actione

43. Aristotle, *Ethics,* lib. 1, cap. 1

44. Aristotle in the postpredicaments

45. St. Thomas, Prima secundae, quest. 1, art. 1

46. Aristotle, *Physics,* lib. 6, tex. 6

47. Aristotle, *Ethics,* lib. 3, cap. 1

48. Gilbertus Porrectanus, cap. de ubi

49. Aristotle, *Physics,* lib. 4; Virgil, lib. *Georg.,* Plutarch, *Opusculum de hac re*

50. Gilbertus Porrectanus, cap. de quando

51. Aristotle, *Physics,* lib. 4

52. Lib. 3, cap. 6

53. Pronaque cum spectent animalia cetera terram, / Os homini sublime dedid, caelumque videre, / Iussit, etc —Ovid, *Metamorphoses,* lib. 1

54. Alexander of Aphrodisias

55. Cicero, *In partitione*

56. Lib. 2, cap. 10

57. *Perihermenias,* lib. 1

58. Perionius

59. Strebeus

60. Et semel emissum volat irrevocabile verbum—Horace, Epist. 8, lib. 1; Sed tibi claudetur rapidae vox nunciamentis—Iuvenalis

61. Lib. 2, cap. 12

62. Urbs antiqua fuit, Tyrii tenuere coloni, / Carthago, Italiam contra, Tyberinaque longe. / Ostia dives opum, studiisque; asperima belli, / Quam Iuno fertur terris magis omnibus unam, / Post habit coluisse Samo, etc.—Aeneid, lib. 1

63. . . . Me ne incepto desistere victam? / Nec posse Italia Teucrorum avertere regem? / Quippe vector fatis: Pallas exurere classem / Argivum, atque ipsos potuit submergere ponto, / Unius ob noxam, et furias Aiacis Oilei? / Ipsa Iovis rapidum, etc.—Aeneid, lib. 1

64. *In partitione*

65. *Aeneid,* lib. 4

66. Cicero, *In partitione*

67. Lib. 1, cap. 2

68. *De arte dicendi,* lib. 1, q. 8

69. Disp. 8

70. [In our *Introductio in logicam*].

71. Cap. 1

72. Lib. 1, cap. 2

73. *De partitione,* lib. 5, cap. 10

74. *In topicis*

75. Quintilian

76. *Rhetoric,* lib. 1, cap. ult.

77. Franciscus Toletus

78. Aristotle, *Prior Analytics,* lib. 2, cap. 1

79. *De arte dicendi,* lib. 2, disp. 3

80. Aristotle, *Rhetoric,* lib. 1, cap. 15

81. Lib. [?]

82. Aristotle, *Posterior Analytics,* lib. 2

83. M. Ioan. Merc.

84. *Institutiones,* lib. 1, tit. 2

85. Ioan. Dadr., Ludovicus Granatus, Polyanth.

86. Strebeus in *Orat.*

87. Cicero, *Pro Archia*

88. Aristotle, *Topics,* lib. 1

89. Cicero, *De partitione*

90. Quintilian

BOOK THREE

1. Cornelius Ultraiect., Agricola

2. Doctores Lovanienses

3. Felix qui potuit rerum cognoscere causas—Virgil, *Georgics,* lib. 2

4. Discite nunc miseri, et causas cognoscite rerum—Persius

5. Est mihi disparibus septem compacta cicutis fistula—Virgil, *Ecloga* 2

6. *Institutiones,* lib. 1, tit. 2

7. Sumite materiam vestris, qui scribitis aquam viribus—*Ars poetica*

8. Aristotle, *Physics,* lib. 1

9. Acts, 8

10. *Institutiones,* lib. 2, tit. 1

11. Illi robur, et aes triplex / Circa pectus erat, qui fragilem truci / Commisit pellago ratem / Primus—Horace, *Odes,* lib. 1, 3

12. Ventris onus misero, nec te pudet auro: / Bassa bibis vitro, carius ergo cacas.

13. Aristotle, *De anima,* lib. 1, cap. 1

14. Protinus aerii mellis caelistia dona / Exequar.—*Georgica,* lib. 4

15. *Bellum civile,* lib. 1

16. Regia solis erat sublimibus alta columnis, / Clara, micante auro, flammaque imitante / pyropo: / Cuius ebur nitidum fastigia summa tenebat: / Argenti bifores radiabant lumine valuae.—*Metamorphoses,* lib. 2

17. Lib. 2, ser. 8

18. Cicero, *De officiis,* lib. 1

19. . . . formam populabitur aetas, / Et placidus rugis vultus aratus erit.—Ovid, *Medicamina Faciei*

20. Ut alta Sylvas forma vernantes alit, / Quas nemore nudo, primus investit tepor, etc.—*Hercules Oetaeus*

21. Claudius Min.

22. Aristotle, *De anima,* lib. 2

23. Cicero, Timaeus Locrus

24. Aristotle, *Physics,* lib. 2

25. Aristotle, *De anima,* lib.2

26. *Institutiones,* lib. 2, tit. 1 §sacrae

27. Cicero, *Paradoxa,* 1

28. Mat.

29. Lenta quibus torno facili superaddita vitis, / Diffusos hedera vestit pallente corymbos. / In medio duo signa, Conon, et, quis fuit alter? / Descripsit radio totum qui gentibus orbem.—Virgil, *Eclogae,* 3

30. . . . aspice, ut antum / Sylvestris raris sparsit labrusca racemis—*Eclogae,* 5

31. Est in secessu longo locus: insula portum / Efficit obiectu laterum: quibus omnis ab alto / Frangitur inque sinus scindit sese unda reductos, etc.—*Aeneid,* lib. 1

32. *Institutiones,* lib. 2, tit. 9, §Alia

33. Pronaque cum spectent animalia cetera terram, / Os homini sublime dedit, caelumque videre, / Insit, et erectos ad sydera tollere vultus.—Ovid, *Metamorphoses,* lib. 1, Sallust, Solinus

34. *Aeneid,* lib. 1

35. Nec cum adeo informis: nuper me in littore vidi, / Cum placidum ventis staret mare—Lege Aul. Gellium, lib.5, c. 11

36. *De anima,* lib. 2

37. Gen. 9

38. Matt. 5

39. *Institutiones,* lib. 1, tit. 11, §Minorem

40. . . . componitur orbis / Regis ad exemplum: nec inflectere sensus. / Humanos edicta valent, quam vita regentis. / Mobile mutatur semper cum Principe vulgus.—De quarto Honorii

41. Agricola, lib. 1, c. 13

42. Cicero

43. *Institutiones,* lib. 2, tit. 4, §finitur

44. Virgil, *Aeneid,* lib. 4

45. *Institutiones,* lib. 1,tit. 5, §iisdem

46. *De lege agraria*

47. Audax omnia perpeti / Gens humana ruitper vetitum nefas. / Audax Iapeti genus / Ignem fraudemala gentibus intulit.

48. Psal. 111

49. Psal. 7

50. Paul, *To the Romans*

51. Aristotle, *Topics,* lib. 2, cap. 1

52. Aristotle, *Physics,* lib. 2

53. Lib. 1, cap. 14

54. Aristotle, *Physics,* lib. 2, tex. 1

55. Cicero, *De partitione oratoria*

56. Ergo ubi visus eris nostra medicabilis arte, / Fac monitis fugias otia prima meis. / Haec ut ames faciunt, haec quae fecere iuventur. / Haec sunt iucundi causa cibusque mali.—*Remedia amoris,* lib. 1

57. Plutarch, *Opusculum de hac re*

58. . . . male quaeritur herbis, / Moribus et forma conciliandus amor.—*Epistulae Hyp.*

59. Aristotle, *Physics,* lib. 2

60. quod si / Frigida curarum fomenta relinquere posses:/ Quo te coelestis sapientia duceret, ires.—*Epist.* 3, lib. 1

61. Theodoretus, lib. 12

62. Terentius

63. 2 Tim., 2

64. Me, me: adsum, qui feci: in me convertite ferrum, / O Rutili: me fraus omnis: nihil iste, nec ausus, / Nec potuit.—*Aeneid,* lib. 9

65. Cantando tu illum? aut unquam tibi fistula cera / Iuncta fuit?—*Eclogae,* 3

66. Cicero, *De natura deorum,* lib. 1

67. Deut. 32

68. Rom. 11

69. Luc.11

70. Incubuere mari, totumque a sedibus imis, / Una Eurusque, Notusque ruunt, creberque procellis / Africus, et vastos tollunt ad littora fluctus.—*Aeneid,* lib. 1

71. arcanae moderatrix Cynthia noctis.—*Thebais,* lib. 10

72. Sidereis nocturna umbris Latonia gaudet.

73. Vicinitas facit ut te audacter moneam, et familiter—*In Eauton.*

74. Quaeritur, Egistus quare sit factus adulter? / In promptu causa est, desidiosus erat.

75. Me, si fata meis paterentur ducere vitam / Auspiciis, et sponte mea componere curas.—*Aeneid,* lib. 4

76. Fagina caelitum divini opus Alcimedontis—Virgil, *Eclogae,* 2

77. *Aeneid,* lib. 4

78. Aristotle, *Physics,* lib. 2

79. Aristotle, *Ethics,* lib. 1

80. Aristotle, *Ethics,* lib. 1, c. 1

81. Cicero

82. Quaenam summa boni? Mens quae sibi conscia recti.—Ausonius, *De 7 sap.*

83. Aristotle, *Ethics,* lib. 2, c. 2

84. Agricola, lib. 1, c. 15

85. Psal. 18

86. Cicero, *De finibus*

87. Aristotle, *Ethics,* lib. 2, c. 1

88. *De anima,* lib. 2

89. Multa tulit, fecitque puer sudavit, et alsit—Horace

90. Aristotle, *Physics,* lib. 2

91. Hoc opus, hoc studium parvi properemus et ampli: / Si partriae volumus, si nobis vivere cari.—*Epist.* 3, lib.1

92. Quaere fugam morbi: Vis recte vivere? quis non? / Si virtus hoc una potest dare: fortis omissis / Hoc age delitiis. virtutem verb putas, ut / Lucum ligna?—*Epist.* 6, lib. 1

93. Si fortunatum species et gratia praestat, / Mercemur servum, qui dictetomnia: lae-

vum / Qui fodiat latus: et cogat trans pondera dextram / Porrigere.

94. Cicero, *Pro M. Caelio*

95. Psal. 33

96. *Institutiones,* lib. 1, tit. 2

97. *Institutiones,* lib. 1, tit. 9

98. Aristotle, *Physics,* lib. 2, and Cicero

99. *Confessions,* lib. 1, cap. 1

100. Matt. 5

101. Quid iuvat immensum te argenti pondus, et auri, / Furtim defossa timidum deponere terra?—*Satirae,* lib. 1, ser. 1

102. Nicolaus Everar., loco a veritate finis

103. Aristotle, *Ethics,* lib. 1, cap. 1

Ludovico Carbone's
On Divine Rhetoric

DIVINUS ORATOR
VEL DE
RHETORICA DIVINA
LIBRI SEPTEM

In quibus bene dicendi recteque concionandi doctrina
ex divinis Scriptoribus collecta,
et ad facilem absolutamque artis methodum redacta continetur

Atque eloquentiae comparandae, observandae, et ad usum
traducendae perspicua traditur ratio:

Opus a multis olim desideratum, et omnibus divini verbi Ministris,
sacraeque doctrinae, atque bonarum literarum studiosis
apprime utile et necessarium

Auctore
Ludovico Carbone a Costaciaro
Academico Parthenio, et sacrae Theologiae in almo
Gymnasio Perusino olim publico Magistro

Cum Quadruplici Indice
et Privilegio

VENETIIS: Apud Societatem Minimam

MDXCV

THE DIVINE ORATOR
OR ON
DIVINE RHETORIC
SEVEN BOOKS

*In which a teaching about the art of speaking well or of preaching
drawn from the Scriptures is contained and an
easy method of acquiring it explained*

*And a clear way is given for comparing, observing, and
putting to use various forms of eloquence*

*A work long desired by many, and especially useful and necessary
for all ministers of the divine word and of sacred doctrine,
and for those desirous of good learning*

by
Ludovico Carbone of Costaciaro
Parthenian Academic, one time public
Master of Sacred Theology
in our Gymnasium at Perugia

With Four Indexes and
With Privilege

VENICE: From the Press of the Society of Minims

1595

Ludovico Carbone on Divine Rhetoric

This work of Carbone, *Divinus Orator, vel de rhetorica divina libri septem* (The divine orator, or seven books on divine rhetoric), applies his vast knowledge of rhetorical theory to the art of preaching. It seems to be the most original, and certainly the most elaborate, of his writings on rhetoric.[1] As a teacher of oratory, both secular and sacred, of philosophy, and theology, and as a priest, he combined the activities of *docens* and *utens.* He declares in the preface that the divine orator would profit from knowledge of his other writings on rhetoric and that, in turn, secular orators should also find this book useful in mundane affairs. This marks a break with the more common attitude of clerics to look upon profane rhetoric with some disdain. Marc Fumaroli in his magisterial treatment of rhetoric of the Renaissance finds Carbone's stance toward the two registers of rhetoric remarkable, saying that this is the first time he has seen a work on ecclesiastical rhetoric treat sacred and profane rhetoric on much the same level.[2]

Carbone draws heavily upon his secular rhetorical teachings throughout the seven books of this work, especially in books two, three, and five, but he turns the lore in these to the uses of divine oratory. The remainder of the books address divine oratory directly, as can be seen in the table of contents translated below.

We have selected materials for translation from the books that treat the special concerns of the preacher. These include, besides the table of contents, dedication, and excerpts from the preface, the following: three chapters from book one, wherein Carbone defines divine rhetoric and examines the qualifications of preachers; the first three chapters of book two, in which he treats invention in relation to the genera of sacred rhetoric, the kind of questions in its purview, and the applicability of status; five chapters from book four, where Carbone examines emotions, the wisdom of moving them and how the preacher can do that prudentially; and finally, from book five, four chapters from Carbone's discussion of the fine points of style especially related to preaching. Not included in the translations are book six, in which Carbone takes up delivery and memory, or book seven where he describes the practical uses of divine rhetoric, how it can be acquired and how discovered in sacred writings.

---

1. The significance of Carbone's book on preaching in relation to recent accounts of the genre is discussed in Moss, "Sacred Rhetoric and Appeals to the Passions: A Northern Italian View," in *Perspectives on Early Modern and Modern Intellectual History. A Festschrift for Nancy Struever,* ed. Joseph Marino and Melinda Schlitt (Rochester, N.Y.: The University of Rochester Press, 2000), 375–400.

2. Marc Fumaroli in *L'Âge de L'Éloquence,* 184, n. 288.

Carbone's approach to sacred oratory provides a subtle variation in the Renaissance reshaping of the art of preaching. In the previous century, many preachers had begun to shift from reliance on the formulaic handbooks of the *artes praedicandi* to embrace a more flexible humanistic approach. The thematic sermon or "university sermon," organized around the scriptural text or theme, followed by a protheme to pique the listeners' attention, a restatement of the theme, its tripartite division, and definitions and distinctions, was designed for audiences trained in universities and used to disputations. It had grown out of the culture of the medieval university and in some areas it endured well into the Renaissance.[3] The newer style, popular in Italy, arrived on the crest of the humanist wave of appreciation for the more eloquent, more literary forms of expression to be found in Ciceronian oratory. That form could move both learned and common audiences. John O'Malley has described the way in which humanism affected sermons at the papal court, and his observations about that venue can also be applied more widely.[4] Epideictic or demonstrative rhetoric, the rhetoric of praise and blame, was carried to its most fulsome level in the period, and for preachers at the papal court that genus best suited their purposes—praising God, his nature, benevolence, deeds, creation. The freedom that immersion in this genre of rhetoric evoked can be seen in the form of preaching, where the concern was no longer to teach by analyzing a text, supplying proofs with painstaking care, but to persuade by creating an artistic rhetorical discourse whose parts were organized around a central point, amplified, and expressed in a graceful, poetic style.

Erasmus was to capture the new "ecclesiastical" oratory in his *Ecclesiastes sive de ratione concionandi* (1535). This handbook argues for the suitability of rhetoric to Christian oratory, treats the requisite moral character of the preacher, and suggests elements of classical rhetoric appropriate to the subject matter. The new ecclesiastical rhetoric embraced the Ciceronian offices of rhetoric—to teach, to charm, and to move, but differences arose over which of the three genres should be used in preaching. Erasmus thought that the deliberative mode—persuading or dissuading—was the primary resource, whereas Melanchthon desired a new genre altogether to express the preacher's teaching office, the didactic, *genus didaskalikon*. In addition, he disliked the excesses he found in the epideictic mode, preferred by papal preachers. For Erasmus, too, florid rhetoric was inappropriate for

---

3. James J. Murphy describes the *artes praedicandi* in his *Rhetoric in the Middle Ages* (Berkeley: University of California Press, 1974). He notes that the form survived in England into the Reformation.

4. John W. O'Malley, *Praise and Blame in Renaissance Rome: Rhetoric, Doctrine and Reform in the Sacred Orators of the Papal Court, c. 1450–1521* (Durham, N.C., Duke University Press, 1979).

the preacher. For his part, Carbone thought the demonstrative mode effective for arousing the affections, found the deliberative the most frequently used, and even recommended the judicial for certain purposes of the preacher. For Carbone the three classical genres sufficed, since he regarded teaching as part of the demonstrative genre.[5]

The significance of Carbone's work lies in the fact that the seeds for it must have been sown when Carbone was a student at the Jesuits' Collegio Romano, and so it can be seen as part of the campaign by the Order to respond to the call of the Council of Trent for zealous preaching by a clergy well trained in theology. The Council had recommended a reformed art of preaching based on the Fathers of the Church, and it recognized the power of oratory to counter the inroads of heresy. The *De doctrina Christiana* of St. Augustine provided guidance and inspiration.[6] At the same time, the Collegio, as we have seen, embraced the *studia humanitatis,* giving students broad training in the classics, including the Greek and Roman rhetorical classics. From these two streams, the Collegio inspired in Carbone the development of what Fumaroli has called "a Christian esthetic" for his teachings on oratory.[7] Both lay and clerical registers of oratory in Carbone's view should be characterized by a sober perspicuity. They should deploy the artifices of style expertly and in a manner consonant with Christian aims.

Carbone begins *Divine Orator* by stressing that preaching must be based on the Divine Word, the eloquence of the prophets, evangelists, and canonical writers who are "the messengers of God Almighty." He insists that, in this, his book differs from others that are more broadly concerned with sacred oratory. The title *Divine Orator* is meant to emphasize that difference. The aim of preaching is to unfold the revelation of Scripture, but first preachers must understand the remarkable eloquence contained in it before they can move hearers to take the message to heart. Using his favorite method of teaching in book one, Carbone employs a graceful humanized form of disputation to refute those who have contended that Scripture lacks eloquence.

Carbone reminds his readers that, while preachers should be called, they should also be examined and approved by the ecclesiastical authorities, as the Council recommended. His contribution to the Council's di-

5. For an excellent account of sacred rhetoric in the period, whose coverage extends beyond its parochial title to treat Continental works as well, see Debra K. Shuger, *Sacred Rhetoric: The Christian Grand Style in the English Renaissance* (Princeton: Princeton University Press, 1988).

6. While the first complete edition of *De doctrina Christiana* was published in 1465 in Italy, the most influential edition was that of Frobenius published in Basle (1528–1529), as Fumaroli notes, 70. It was this edition that Erasmus used in writing his *Ecclesiastes,* an amplification of the fourth book of *De doctrina.* See Fumaroli, *L'Âge de L'Éloquence,* 71, 109–110.

7. Fumaroli, *L'Âge de L'Éloquence,* 186.

rectives is to guide the focus of the preacher and equip him with the means of developing sermons appropriate to the tasks demanded by his calling: teaching, correcting, and consoling in response to his congregation's needs.

Carbone does not want his *Divine Orator* to be seen simply as a tool for seminarians trained by the Jesuits, even though he has extolled their teachings and commended his earlier books to their use. This book is dedicated to the Master General of the Dominicans, the Order of Preachers, Hippolyte Maria Beccaria. Carbone asks that the volume be promoted by the Dominican Order, not only because the Order is dedicated to training great preachers, but also because it commands positions of authority in the Vatican and can, through its endorsement, spread his teachings more widely. Carbone has chosen a kairotic moment for his dedication, in that the Dominicans will be holding the meeting of their General Chapter in Venice as his book is being published there.

The most interesting of the seven books is the fourth, dealing with amplification and the emotions. Carbone follows Aristotle's treatment of the powers of the soul as developed by Thomas Aquinas in the *Summa theologiae* (First Part of the Second Part, questions 22–23).[8] (A helpful diagram of the powers is included on p. 51 above.)

Aquinas had recognized a rational and an irrational nature in man, each of which has knowing and affective powers. The inferior kind of knowing and desiring is shared with animals, but the superior kind of cognitive power in mankind seeks truth, and its appetitive power can choose good and flee evil. The knowing powers also contain a kind of appetition in that they desire truth, thirst for knowledge. The term rational appetite was used by Aristotle; later philosophers termed it the will. The powers Carbone describes are not the compartmentalized faculties delineated by seventeenth- and eighteenth-century faculty psychology. They are free powers that can be elicited externally and controlled by the rational appetite that is seeking perfection. The task of the preacher is to move the emotions of its congregation to seek good and avoid evil.

Carbone defines and enumerates the emotions, eleven in all: six appetitive or concupiscent—love, desire, joy, hatred, aversion, grief; and five, contending or irascible—hope, courage, despair, fear, anger.[9] The Chris-

---

8. Carbone himself published an abridgement of St. Thomas's *Summa* entitled *Compendium absolutissimum totius Summae Thelogicae D. Thomae Aquinatis* (1587). Fumaroli mentions the work in *L'Âge de L'Éloquence*, 183, n. 284.

9. Shuger has noted the contribution of Hellenistic rhetoric to the writings of sixteenth-century sacred oratory. She notes that Carbone draws on Hermogenes in his discussion of style and its relation to the emotions. Shuger finds Carbone's treatment "confused," a point I have discussed in the article mentioned in note 1. She finds him guilty of crossing boundaries, mixing emotions with spiritual matters. An examination of his treatment of the powers of the soul,

tian orator in his roles as judge, teacher, father, and God's representative seeks to stir various levels of intensity through use of the common and special topics. In this he follows the lead of Soarez's *De arte rhetorica,* in which sixteen chapters are devoted to the emotions. The Spanish Jesuit had explained that the rhetorical topics can be used to stimulate the emotions. (See Carbone's summary of the work in the *Tabulae,* translated in the second section.) But Carbone goes far beyond this elementary discussion of Soarez in his philosophical analysis of the power of the common topics to tap both the appetitive and irascible emotions. He also explains how the special topics of theology can move levels of emotion. Milder emotions are touched in conciliating, consoling, inculcating virtue and in admonishing friends and in speaking of lighter things. Vehement emotions are stirred to incite and inflame hearers to avoid sin and strive for salvation. Carbone advises preachers to draw on Scripture or on the Church Fathers, but the material needs to be exaggerated and amplified, he says, in order to make a strong impression. He suggests, in the spirit of Augustine, that the best means of moving the audience is to pray fervently so as to be moved by the spirit himself.

Ignatius Loyola's *Spiritual Excercises* appear to be the inspiration for Carbone's advice that preachers employ memory, imagination, and the will to summon up the vivid, concrete details that stir emotions. Various occasions of sin are to be imagined by the sinner and the effects of these on his friends, siblings, parents, teachers. He should look upon them as one would who has betrayed his country, or has trampled on Christ's blood, or fouled and profaned the temple of God. His sorrow should mirror those who have lost all earthly goods so as to face eternal damnation. Such emotions should summon the will to repentance.

Stylistic devices are treated at length by Carbone in book five as further means of evoking the emotions. For each of the figures and schemes he provides illustrations from Scripture. He finds schemes particularly helpful, elaborating on thirty-one of them for stirring strong feelings. Among these are exclamation and apostrophe, which are effective in inducing sorrow and indignation. Following tradition he treats three levels of style, but employs many terms for describing each, as can be seen in our translation.[10] Agreeing with Augustine, Carbone advises orators to mix the three styles and not cling to one too long.

In the final book of the text, Carbone advises preachers to cultivate eloquence by reading Scripture and the Church Fathers and meditating on

---

however, shows that emotions are not compartmentalized into rational and emotional categories in the Thomistic understanding, but instead are acts of a rational *appetite* that seeks perfection in God.

10. See the translation of Bk. 5, chap. 25, below.

these. He provides advice on the correct way to imitate divine orators and how these accord with Hermogenes' seven ideas of style.[11] At the end of the work, he offers seven examples of analysis and explication of Scriptural passages for the edification of novice preachers.

Carbone's fear expressed in the preface—that his break with tradition in turning to Sacred Scripture to find the principles of eloquence might initially cause readers to question his wisdom—must surely have been groundless, given the extensive corroboration he brings to his argument.

The book proved to be popular, rivaling another important Tridentine rhetoric, that of the Spanish Dominican Luis de Granada, *Ecclesiastica rhetorica* (1576). Carbone mentions that his own book differs from Granada's in basing rhetorical principles on Scripture and also turning to it for oratorical models. The two books are similar in their coverage of the elements of rhetoric, although Granada omits memory, and Carbone provides a more philosophical analysis of the emotions and does so in much fuller detail. Surely Carbone must, in fact, have had reason to think that, rather than offend his Dominican readers, his privileging of scriptural sources might recommend his book to them as a valuable supplement to their own Granada's. One may also speculate as to whether Carbone thought that his book, emanating from Italian soil, might be more attractive to the Italian Master General, given recent Spanish-Italian conflicts within the Order.

Our translations here, as in previous sections, are given in idiomatic English and generally adhere closely to the text. Here also, as in section five, we have removed the citation of Carbone's sources and references from the text and provide their essential content in endnotes as "Glosses and Notes."

---

11. These "ideas" are not included in our translation but appear in *Divine Orator* in chapter 12 of book seven. Translated by Shuger the ideas are clarity *(saphenia)*, grandeur *(megethos)*, beauty *(kallos)*, speed *(gorgotes)*, character *(ethos)*, verity *(aletheia)*, and gravity *(deinotes)*. See *Sacred Rhetoric*, appendix, 259.

TABLE OF CONTENTS

*The Divine Orator, or On Divine Rhetoric, Seven Books
by Ludovico Carbone of Costaciaro*

BOOK I
*In which the nature of divine rhetoric and the functions and
qualifications of the divine orator are explained.*

BOOK II
In which invention is treated.

BOOK III
In which is treated arrangement (dispositio), *or the parts of the oration, both in general and in particular.*

BOOK IV
In which is treated amplification, or on moving the emotions.

BOOK V
In which is treated style and of the decorous and appropriate way of speaking.

BOOK VI

In which are treated delivery and memory.

BOOK VII

In which is taught how eloquence can be acquired, put into use, and observed in divine letters.

DEDICATION TO
HIPPOLYTE MARIA BECCARIA,
MASTER GENERAL OF THE ORDER
OF PREACHERS

Since the Dominicans are having their General Chapter here in Venice, and I have always been impressed by their teaching and morals, I want to show my admiration and respect for them in a special way. It happens at this moment that I have just finished my book *On Divine Rhetoric,* and so I have decided to dedicate the book to you, one and all, for several reasons. First to you, who are an excellent preacher yourself and the leader of the whole order, which is an Order of Preachers. I trust that you will find the work worthy of praise, for you know much about the subject and will understand what I have written—and should there be mistakes in it, you will be able to correct them. Finally, you are in a better position to defend me against calumniators, who are always to be expected with a work of this kind. Another thought that prompts me is that many members of your order, and especially those who have administrative positions in the Vatican, will have read the book and will be in a position to approve and endorse it—for several of them have encouraged me to write it. And lest I give too many reasons, my principal motive is the affection I have for your religious family, whose good works and virtues are known far and wide, and this at a time when religious observance has slackened generally. So I offer this little book to you and hope that you will accept it, so that the entire Order of Preachers, and indeed all who are concerned with preaching or who delight in the art of speaking well, moved by your example, will put it to good use. My only intention is that the ministry of the divine word will flourish from our labors, for both the immortal glory of God and the utility of the Church. That can be done, as I point out in the Preface to the Reader, if we use the eloquence and the art we find in the Scriptures themselves as a means of teaching divine truths. First you, most reverend Father, and then all the members of the family of Preachers, accept this work about preaching the divine word from Sacred Scripture. You Dominicans, I say, who have been especially entrusted with teaching and defending the truths of Christianity, not only in word but in the example of your lives. I hope that I will share in your prayers and in the good works of the Order, which you have the faculty of conferring on me, and should you do that in exchange for my little gift, I will be forever in your debt. At Venice.

THE AUTHOR'S PREFACE
TO THE READER

Excerpts:

[Bottom of second page:]

Moreover, I trust that you will not regard as useless, or not wish to thank me for what I have tried to do, what learned and pious men long ago have indicated and some have desired to do at various times, namely, that the art and the eloquence of speaking that is used in the Sacred Scriptures, which many say does not even exist, may be clearly shown to be there. Whether or not I have succeeded in what I have tried to do others will have to be the judge. . . .

[Bottom of third page:]

I offer this work *On the Divine Orator* not without fear. . . . In putting it together, some will say that I have written at too great length on the subject, which they would not say if they knew the extent and the depth of eloquence, on which I have published twenty-three works, which I have often cited in this book, and still I have not said all that could be said on this matter.

Therefore, dear reader, here you have a work on divine rhetoric prepared for the glory of God. . . .

BOOK ONE

Chap. 1. Is there such a thing as divine rhetoric?

[1] Before writing on divine rhetoric I need to explain a controversy that has been a source of worry for some authors, namely, whether there is any such thing as divine rhetoric. I do this so that having clarified this question, which is the entire focus of this work, we can proceed to develop the art more fully. And, lest one think that what we propose to explore is a simple matter, I show that it is not without its problems and I offer arguments on both sides of the controversy to demonstrate that the subject requires discussion. But first, so that the state of the question may be understood, I explain precisely what is meant by saying that a kind of rhetoric is divine.

By the term divine rhetoric or divine eloquence, therefore, I mean the kind of discourse that has been employed by men as God's messengers or delegates for making the divine will and teaching [2] clear to the human race in speech and writing, as was the case with prophets, evangelists, and those we call canonical writers. The following arguments may be advanced to demonstrate that there actually is no rhetoric or special dignity of discourse in the writings of these men.

First, if there is any form of eloquence and power in a sacred writer it will be found particularly in one whom God has elected by a personal and wonderful revelation to proclaim his name among all nations. I mean Saint Paul, whom God wanted to be his special messenger. But in Paul, as he himself testifies, there was no cultivation or sublimity of speech. Therefore there is no rhetoric in sacred writings. . . .[1]

And although these texts seem to indicate very clearly that there was no enhancement of rhetoric in St. Paul, we may confirm that there is not from the testimony of the ancient Fathers. . . .[2]

[3] Moses, who was the first writer and who composed a good many of the sacred books, stated very clearly that he was not eloquent and that it was God himself who was speaking. The same could be said of Jeremiah and other sacred writers. . . .[3]

To this could be added the authority of many other Fathers who, writing against those who attacked the sacred law, sought to defend its simplicity and rough character. They would not have been able to do this if they had made use of rhetoric and refined speech. . . .[4]

394

To the contrary, the fact that the canonical writers did use rhetoric can be easily demonstrated from their having used all the tropes, figures, and ornaments, as has often been observed. Consult, for example, Augustine, Cassiodorus, Bede, and others; likewise Job, Isaiah, and especially David. And in Paul the loftiness of subject matters and the splendor of his figures and artifices are most admirable.

What we are stating here has been taught openly by many Fathers, so it suffices to cite any one of them. . . .[5]

[4] First thesis: In the divine books there is much rhetoric of subject matter. I explain: practically all rhetoricians divide rhetoric into two parts, one of which they locate in the importance, dignity, and certainty of the subject matter, the other in the splendor, composition, and smoothness of the words. . . .[6]

Second thesis: The rhetoric of words, which they call phrasing and elegance and is seen partly in single, partly in conjoined words, is not found in some divine writers and it is not desired in others. This is to be understood of the first writers, who cultivated divine letters when they were directly moved by the Holy Spirit. Some of these, such as Moses, Isaiah, and David, spoke not only wisely but also ornately and elegantly, as those who know Hebrew and the art of rhetoric are well aware. Others, such as Amos and those who were Jews but wrote in Greek, spoke less purely and so did not use single or conjoined words, though they did use proper language and some few idioms, which [5] no one can deny.

Third thesis: The part of rhetoric that is seen in apt translations and figures or schemes, both of terms and of sentences, is found in sacred writings, generally speaking, in ways that cannot be found in human writings. One can see that this is true from the fact that all figures and schemes thus far discovered in rhetorics and rhetoricians can be found in the sacred writings. This will be demonstrated most convincingly when we treat of divine rhetoric.

Fourth thesis: We must acknowledge that there is a certain kind of rhetoric that is above all human teachings and is proper to God himself. This position is conceded as beyond controversy not only by Christian rhetoricians but also by those outside the Church.[7] All have thought that eloquence is a divine work and one of the greatest gifts that the giver of all good things has conferred on the human race. So it requires little confirmation. . . .[8]

[6] Fifth thesis: When speaking of this divine kind of rhetoric, we should say that each and every sacred writer has used it in writing and handing over divine mysteries, and has so written that, considering all matters, persons, times, and other circumstances, he could not have written more appropriately. Thus all sacred writers should be regarded as having written rhetorically, that is, eloquently and aptly. This should equally

be recognized as communicated by God to his ministers and so present in all sacred letters. . . .[9]

[7] Last thesis: A lesser care for the use of words, which human rhetoric would not permit, is not to be disparaged in sacred writers. On this account, a simple style less cultivated than the human art and used by the Church Fathers against profane and impious men can be defended. Such was used by Clement of Alexandria, Origen, Arnobius, Theodoretus, and many others. . . .[10]

[8] From all this one can gather in what sense the Church Fathers should be understood when they say that no rhetoric is used in the divine Scriptures. Here they are speaking of a purely human rhetoric affected with some diligence, not with what was suitable for such writers and the subject matters they had to treat. That is enough for the problem at this point. It will be clarified considerably by what we shall state in the following chapter.

Chap. 2. Should the divine preacher use rhetoric?

Since some, noting the phrasing of sacred writers and statements of the Church Fathers, think that a divine preacher's use of rhetoric is to be looked down upon, or not to be made much of, this offers us the occasion to take up the implied objection, which seems to be favored by the authority of the following most respected Doctors of the Church: [9] Clement of Alexandria, Cyril of Jerusalem, Athanasius, Basil, Gregory Nazianzen, Theodoretus, and Irenaeus. . . .[11]

To these authorities I would add arguments from reason. [10] The first is that those who try to speak ornately and compositely impede or hold back the force of the Holy Spirit, since, when they try to follow what they have skillfully put together, they do not allow the Spirit to move them. Then again, the entire notion of preaching correctly, as I shall explain below, seems to be located in a certain Spirit, which does not wait for, not does it expect, those who prepare themselves to speak rhetorically. Whence it happens, as a certain holy man once said, that one who sometimes prepares himself a little too carefully will find that his speech is lacking in something that otherwise is found abundantly in others who come unprepared in this way. And so Christ told his apostles, *"Do not worry about how or what you shall say, for in that hour will be given to you what you should say. For it is not you who speaks, but the Spirit of your Father, who speaks in you."*[12]

So it is that some think that rhetoric is not to be used by the Catholic preacher, as it is used most effectively by enemies of the faith, lest the cross of Christ be set aside. Which side should be held and practiced by the divine orator I propose with the following theses.

First thesis: the study and use of rhetoric is not to be denied to the sacred orator. This position I now propose to demonstrate in a general way, and later I shall explain in particular what kind of rhetoric is to be meant. So it is licit for the preacher to use eloquence in presenting divine cases. This is confirmed by the following arguments. First, from the authority of Scripture . . . .[13] Then, from the example of those whom God has chosen as his delegates and orators. . . .[14] [11] Moreover, the same is confirmed by the opinions of the Fathers. . . .[15] Finally, certain other opinions could be taken from the fourth book of St. Augustine's *De doctrina Christiana,* should one wish. . . .[16]

[12] To these authorities and examples, reasoning can be added. If sacred theology, which is concerned with knowledge, can make use of human sciences such as dialectics, physics, ethics, and other disciplines, why cannot disciplines that are concerned with human action, such as teaching and persuading through the art of rhetoric, also be used, since God does not destroy nature but rather perfects it, and uses means he has put into nature in caring for humans? God could divide the seas without using the wind, and convert bitter water into sweet without using wood, and bring forth water from a rock without striking it with a rod. If he wished to use an instrument in doing these things, why should he deny to human nature the assistance of an art of speaking that is so suited to it?

Second thesis: it is never right for the sacred writer or orator to use rhetoric that is counterfeit, harmful, immoderate, or forensic. This, I think, is the kind of rhetoric that was condemned by the Fathers of the Church, and particularly Jerome, in his introduction to the Epistle to the Galatians. . . . [13] Also what Ezechiel says in Chap. 33 can be applied to our times.

Third thesis: the eloquence that is sought in the sacred preacher should be serious, sober, modest, full of native and candid flavor, colorful, and in good form, as is suited to the matters being treated, the goal, the circumstances, and the person of the preacher. Examples of this will be found in Scripture. . . .[17]

Fourth thesis: the art of human rhetoric should not be condemned when used by the divine orator or legate, and from it should be taken anything that perfects divine rhetoric and is necessary for its proper use. For, if little things can be said simply for the purpose of amusement, why cannot the art of rhetoric, which is not amusement but is directed to explaining the truth suitably and correctly, also be used? If through its use speech will become more useful for its hearers, [14] it should not be rejected simply because enjoyment can be added to its utility. Indeed, compared to nature, the more delightfully, distinctly, properly, and clearly anything is said, the more will it delight. But anything said roughly, uncouthly, and in a disorganized way, and beyond that, whatever is hateful and harsh to the ears, will not bear fruit. It will not be received, or admired, or understood, nor will people try to understand things that are said ineptly and with obscurity of words and sentences.

Anyone who seeks an example to illustrate what I am teaching should read what the scholastic doctors have taught about the ornamentation of women, suitably transposed to our subject, as, for example, St. Thomas Aquinas and Alexander of Hales. . . . [15] The same applies to the ornamentation of the Church, making it pleasing to the senses, and thereby adorning and illustrating the divine mysteries.

At one time it was proper and indeed necessary that the Church be founded on a greater simplicity of words so that the force of the divine message might be more easily shown. At that time, I say, when there was need for miracles, when many charisms and *gratiae gratis datae* abounded in the Church, when men were infused by the Holy Spirit and spoke with various tongues. But now, miracles are not expected, and human care has to be joined to God's help. Languages have to be learned, and sermons prepared, and what to say has to be thought out and carefully weighed.

As to objections that have been raised about the use of rhetoric, I offer a few common solutions that serve to resolve them fairly easily. When the Fathers seem not to approve or not to require rhetoric in the Christian writer or orator, they should be understood as referring to an excessive, superfluous, or sophistic use of rhetoric; or they should be understood comparatively, in the sense that they more approve a certain true simplicity than adornment without any subject matter; or they are condemning [16] those who delight in embellishment and vainglory or care more for ornamentation than for moral integrity; or they are concerned more with words than with what they are saying, particularly when such things can be taught plainly and succinctly. Let me not omit that some speak so as to excuse themselves. But, I say, as to those who put their efforts into advancing the glory of God and the salvation of men, they should not be censured in any way. . . . [17] . . .

Chap. 3. Granted that a certain kind of rhetoric may be used, some examples are given.[18]

. . . .

Chap. 4. What is divine rhetoric, and how does it differ from human rhetoric?

[24] Since we have already explored whether there is a type of eloquence that might be termed divine, and that sacred orators are not forbidden from using this type of rhetoric under the impulse of the same Spirit that authored the eloquence contained in Scripture, we move now to treat of divine eloquence and the divine orator. To make clear what we are to teach, first we will set out the proposed scope of the entire work and its major parts; then, what divine eloquence and the divine orator are, what the latter's function and goal are, and the virtues that are desired in him. After that we explain the other parts of the work in their respective order.

Concerning the scope, the goal proposed for us is to show what constitutes divine eloquence by drawing the art of speaking well from sacred writings, just as Hermogenes demonstrated Demosthenes' way of speaking from an analysis of the latter's orations. In that way we identify the orator who may be called divine but who is called by others the ecclesiastical orator. To accomplish this, having shown the dignity and the difficulty of this art in the first book, we explain the qualifications that are desired in such an orator. In the second book [25] we take up the subject matter or the questions that concern the preacher, along with the topics required for explaining them, and in this way we cover invention. In the third book we treat the way of organizing the sermon, that is, its arrangement, both in general and in detail. In the fourth we consider amplification and how to move the emotions. In the fifth book we take up eloquence, that is, everything required for speaking fitly and aptly, including appropriate words, sentences, figures, and ornaments. In the sixth we treat delivery and memory. And in the seventh, the manner of acquiring eloquence and making proper use of it.

Again, the entire work can be divided into two parts, the first of which treats the nature of this art and the qualifications pertaining to the person who would use it. This part the Greeks refer to as *paedia*. In the second part the subject matter is explained and its precepts given. The first part is treated in the first book, the rest in the remaining books, following the order already given. And, although there are many arguable points about divine rhetoric, since many of these are found also in the human art of speaking, and we have already treated these extensively in our other books on rhetoric, we say little about them in this work. Matters that are required for instructing the divine orator, and that are proper to him, we explain in somewhat more detail.

Taking up the first point, we describe divine rhetoric as follows. Divine rhetoric is a doctrine or faculty of speaking well about divine matters, drawn from sacred writings, and directed to the salvation of individuals or to the constitution and perfection of the Church. It is said to be a doctrine by reason of the precepts contained within it, which are taken from sacred writers. It is said to be a faculty on the part of the person who uses this art, in whom is required not only the manner of speaking well but also knowledge of things to be said. From this arises a power of being able to discourse on or speak about divine matters correctly. It is said to be from sacred writings to make clear its origin and its difference from human rhetoric, which is drawn from humane letters. It is said to be for the salvation of individuals to show its goal, to which all of the divine orator's speech is ultimately directed. And from the description brought together in this way, even though we have not thought to define precepts that are to be followed religiously, we may gather the various causes from which this art is constituted.

The *matter* it teaches and explains are the precepts themselves for speaking well or for elegant and ornamented speech. The matter with which it is concerned and which it treats are divine things and whatever pertains to the salvation of humans.

[26] The *form* is the doctrine or the art resulting from a certain method, or a particular way of speaking, that is ordered to attaining a certain end or goal.

The *efficient cause* is partly God himself, the primary author of the sacred books from which it is drawn, along with the sacred writers whose art of speaking the Holy Spirit used, and partly the identification and gathering together of precepts. On this account, the divine teaching for speaking well that is contained in the divine oracles depends not only on divine power but also in some way on human effort, in such a way that human modes of writing have helped in constructing this art. In this way we have gathered the techniques of invention and elocution from sacred writings and sermons, but have taken the form of constructing this art from human reason and human teachers.

The *end* or goal of this art is to persuade to things conducive to attaining beatitude. The goal of the person who uses the art is the glory of God, who wishes all men to be saved, and so for God's glory, since it was for this reason that God, whose divine person gave being to the orator, wrote the Scriptures.

What we have just said briefly about the causes of rhetoric we shall explain at greater length in what follows.

The divine orator, whom one of the prophets[19] would call an "angel of the Lord," is a man adorned with Christian virtues and endowed with the science and art of speaking well on divine things. We shall expand on this description later on, when we make clear the qualifications desired in him. His task is to speak appropriately so as to persuade hearers toward things necessary for them to attain salvation. Or, toward perfecting the body of Christ, which is the Church.[20] Or again, to discover, arrange, speak, and say memorably whatever is appropriate for attaining his goal. Or yet again, to teach, to delight, and to move. His goal, as we have just said, is to persuade to the glory of God, and we fill this out more accurately below.

From the foregoing one may gather how divine and humane rhetorics, and celestial and political orators, are different. They differ first in the *matter* about which these faculties speak, because the one is concerned with human affairs, the other with divine matters or with human affairs as ordered to the divine. Then they differ in *form*, for they teach techniques of composing orations that are not completely the same, because the one is human, the other for the most part divine. They differ on the part of the *efficient cause*, for, as already said, these causes are not the same in the two cases. And finally, omitting other differences, they are distinguished by their *end* or goal, as is apparent from the above.

With regard to the persons who use these arts, [27] they also are differentiated in many ways that need not be listed here. They can be gathered partly from the foregoing, partly from what is to be said later about the virtues of the good preacher.

One may inquire at this point how the rhetoric we call divine differs from what others call ecclesiastical rhetoric, since they have the same subject matter, the same end, and other characteristics as well. First I would say that they differ in no way with regard to substance, and in this sense what others have written may be called divine and ours ecclesiastical. In like way, the ecclesiastic orator would be the same as the divine orator. But I would add that our rhetoric differs from what others have written in that others have not constructed their art of speaking well from sacred writings, nor do they offer illustrations from the sacred books, which we have done. We have taken all of our faculty of invention and speech from divine sermons, whereas they have taken theirs partly from the documents of ancient Fathers, partly from profane authors. But let others be the judge in comparing their efforts with ours.[21] This is all I would say, that in some matters they leave things to be desired, compared to one who demonstrates the art of preaching from sacred letters.

That is what we have proposed to do, and others will judge whether or not we have succeeded. If our effort is useful for those who wish to be well versed in the divine office of preaching, let this be referred directly to God. With these preliminaries about divine rhetoric aside, we move on to explaining the topic we have proposed for the second place.

BOOK TWO

Chap. 1. What are the number and kinds of subjects for preaching, and what kinds of oratory are available to the preacher?

[69] Since we have explained in the first book the qualifications desirable in the Christian orator, in the following books we shall attempt to show how sermons can be constructed properly. We have already published many books on the correct manner of speaking and could easily reduce the ecclesiastical message to matters we have already taught, seeing that the preacher has a great affinity to the political orator as treated in our previous books. Nonetheless we feel that a special treatise taken from sacred sources is needed, since the preacher does differ in important respects from the political orator. Many authors have written extensively in this field, and so we have composed ours as briefly as possible, treating only matters that are useful and necessary. We have also drawn on whatever is worthwhile in what others have written and have added new material as well.[22]

Since the subject matter cannot be understood unless its subject genus and causes are known, [70] we first explain the various kinds and causes of sermons or orations.

Following the teaching of rhetoricians, those who write on the correct manner of preaching reduce all sermons to three kinds. These are the demonstrative, that of praise; the deliberative, that of deliberation; and the judicial, that of accusation.[23] Of the first kind the common and principal parts are praise and blame; the time, present and past; the goal, good and evil; and the emotion, love or joy and hate. The objects of praise are either persons or things or deeds, as will be explained more fully later. Of the second kind the parts are persuasion and dissuasion; the time, future; the goal, the useful and the useless; and the emotion, hope and fear or despair. Under this kind falls everything that pertains to human beings and what they can do. Of the third kind the parts are accusation and defense; the time, present and past; the goal, the just and the unjust; and the emotion, clemency and severity.

Other authors, not content with these three kinds, add a fourth, called in Greek *didiscalicon* or *didacticon,* and in Latin, *doctrinale.* Its proximate end is the knowledge of truth and the refutation of falsehood. As we have taught in our treatises on rhetoric, this kind should not be differentiated from the other three but should be located under the demonstrative.[24]

Still others, thinking that yet more should be treated by the Christian preacher, take from St. Paul additional kinds of speech: the didactic, the refutative, the formative (*institutivum*), the corrective, and the consolatory. The first kind teaches the truth; the second refutes false teachings; the third forms character and shows how one should act; the fourth corrects bad deeds and reprimands; and the last consoles the afflicted, lifts them up, and offers them hope. Yet another kind is the mixed, composed from two or more kinds, as when the subject matter is partly didactic, partly formative. One of these is always the principal kind, namely, that with which the major part of the sermon is concerned and to which the other parts can be referred. Preferably, one should hold that all these kinds are contained under the three first named, as we have taught in our rhetorical treatises, for they are really only subdivisions. . . . [71] . . .

[72] One more thing should be noted. In no way do I approve of those who wish to restrict the Christian orator to one kind alone, the deliberative or persuasive.[25] Nor do I approve removing the judicial kind completely, as some do, since it treats some matters of justice, even though it does not take place in the forum.[26] I would say, along with others, that all three kinds are the preacher's proper subject matter, but he is more concerned with the deliberative kind than with the other two, and is involved more frequently with praise than with blame.[27]

Chap. 2. The various kinds of questions

We have taught above that anyone wishing to teach another to preach properly should pose him a particular question. On this account something should be said about various kinds of questions, for these are like different subject matters for invention. A question is nothing more than an interrogation in a loud voice: *Why this tumult among nations, among peoples this useless murmuring? What is truth? Is it licit to give tribute to Caesar?* Questions can be divided in many different ways, but we prefer divisions that are more adapted to our usual teaching.

First, among questions on which one can preach, some have to do with knowledge, their goal being knowledge of the truth. For example, *Is the Son equal to the Father? Is God everywhere? Which virtue is more powerful, charity or justice?*[28] Others are questions of action, inquiring how to live correctly and act religiously, as, for example, *If a person strikes one cheek, should we turn the other? Is it right to adore sacred images?* People need such instruction for their salvation.

Some questions are said to be infinite, in Greek *theses,* that is, positions or propositions that inquire about some matter universally, without regard to circumstances of persons, places, and times, as: *Is it better to live a life of chastity than to be joined in matrimony? Is it better to renounce all things than to possess any?* Others are finite questions, those contracted to definite persons, times, and places. The Greeks called these *hypotheses,* as if to say "contained under theses"; the Latins called them *caussae,* for causes or cases. For example, *Did John think it better to follow Christ than to be joined in marriage? Was it right for Peter to defend Christ with the sword? Is it right for a man to cure on the Sabbath?* Again, following Cicero, we can add [73] another division, one in which a question relating to action is further refined to one relating to an office, as *Should children hate their parents for Christ?* or to a question about how souls can be moved. The last includes exhortations, incitements, complaints, and commiserations, and indeed any speech thata arouses or suppresses the emotions.[29]

Some questions are absolute, others compared. The absolute question inquires about a thing considered in itself, as *Is charity a virtue? Must a person have charity to be saved?* The compared question asks about something compared to others, as *Is charity greater than other virtues? Is the person who speaks with tongues greater than one who prophesies? Which prophet was the greater, Moses or David?*

Among questions or propositions some are simple, as when an argument is proposed about faith, or charity, or Christ, or the four last things. Others are complex, such as *Was Christ the Son of God? Did Christ have two wills? Are the pains of hell everlasting?*

Going further, should we wish to reduce this variety of questions so that they can be better understood and explained, we can have recourse to the teaching of Aristotle, who reduced them all to four headings.[30] One heading is the question of genus, which contains under it the question of difference and species, namely, when it investigates a thing's difference, or species. For example, *Is matrimony a sacrament? Is matrimony a sign that falls under the senses? Was Christ a true man or not?* Another heading is that of definition, which inquires into the nature of a thing and is explained through the genus and the difference, or through properties. Pertinent here is the question of the meaning of a word, and how it differs from related terms. For example, *Is faith the substance of things to be hoped for, an argument for things that appear not? Is approbation the same as justification?*[31] *Is the baptism of John the same as the baptism of Christ?* A question of property would be: *Is faith alone able to justify? Is it appropriate for Christians to love their enemies? Can God alone be good, or a teacher? Was it right for Christ to speak in parables?* The question of accident inquires about something that is not necessary for a thing, either absolutely, such as, *Can there be prophecy without charity? Can grace once lost be regained?* or comparatively, such as *Which law is better, the old or the new?* Note that a question of accident cannot be asked about it unless it is about an effect he produces in creatures and by which he is extrinsically denominated as creator, mover, [74] administrator, etc.

Yet again, all questions can be reduced to the ten categories, such as those of substance, quantity, quality, and so forth. And if one wishes to know the type of question, one should direct one's thought to the subject's attribute, for if this is something intrinsic and common, it will be a question of genus; if a definition, that of definition, and so on.[32]

Why are we offering all of these divisions of questions? First, to make clear that not all matters are to be treated by the same method, as explained below; second, that the same topics are not always to be invoked; and finally, that we may teach how one form can be reduced to another. Thus the finite can be reduced to the infinite, so that whatever is being said can be said definitely, such as, whatever is said about Paul as a virgin may be said about virginity in general. Similarly, the infinite can be reduced to the finite. This latter is especially appropriate for the preacher by reason both of his end, which is the good life of his hearers, and of his office, which is to root out vice and inculcate virtue. He can never reach this goal, nor can he fulfill his office, if he does not move souls by personal appeals, and this much more than the civil orator. Thus, what he says universally he should try as much as possible to translate and adapt to individual cases. In this way his office is, as already said, to speak so as to persuade, and his goal, as just explained, actual persuasion. Hence it follows that he should teach, move the emotions, and produce joy; he should invent, arrange, be eloquent, commit to memory, and deliver; and all of this is acquired partly from nature, partly from art, partly from practice and imitation. The instrument he should use to attain this end is the sermon, not any type whatever, but the work of the careful composer, whose use is threefold. The first is simply to narrate and expose; the second, to argue and convince or refute; and the third, to amplify and expand. It is one thing to narrate, another to prove, another to amplify and to polish, each of which will be covered in its place.

Chap. 3. Of the nature and number of status questions that enter into preaching.

[75]
Since all the artifices that enter into speaking also apply to preaching, and these are usually reduced to certain queries that are called status questions, we must now treat these.

We should do so, first, for the sake of the preacher we are instructing, so that, knowing these he will fulfill his office properly and attain his proposed goal more easily. Those who are versed in preaching can omit it completely. Then, we do this for the sake of those who interpret Sacred Scripture, which is an office the preacher must also fill. For one who cannot find the status question when explaining a book or part of a book or particular place will never be able to explain it correctly. I refer especially to places in which a controversy is being treated. On this account, those who do not perceive the status or the aim of the sermons of the prophets, or of Paul's epistles, or David's psalms, and lastly of Christ's discourses and sermons will never be able to explain them properly. Knowledge of statuses is thus necessary. We shall treat them here briefly; those who seek more details should read our rhetorical treatises.[33]

A status is nothing other than a heading, or a summary cause, or goal, to which an entire oration and every disputation and argument is directed. Or we might say that a status is a question that arises from the contention of parties who are adversaries. For example, Saul says of David that he is seeking to be king; David, denying this, says that he does not seek to be king; and from this conflict there arises the question or status, *Did David seek Saul's kingship?* This cause or case is treated by David himself. The lying and indecent old men accuse Susanna,[34] charging her: *You have committed adultery.* Susanna replies by challenging the fact: *I have not committed adultery.* Whence the question arises, *Did she commit adultery?* Daniel, filled with the Holy Spirit, answered this question himself. Thus what is treated is called a question, a status, or a constitution, and in this the entire cause or case consists.

Status is threefold. The first kind is one in which the query is whether something exists (*an res sit*), and this is called conjectural, because it is generally investigated by conjectures as to whether something exists or is a fact. For example, *Is the Messiah yet to come? Does God punish children for the sins of their parents?* The prophet treats these questions in great detail. Questions of the past pertain to this state, [76] and so also those of the present and the future, such as *Is there a place where souls are purged from their sins? Is Antichrist yet to come? Will human bodies one day be raised from the dead?*

The second kind is a status in which one investigates what a thing is (*quid res sit*), and this is called definitive, or "of a definition," since its explanation depends on a definition. Examples are: *Are the gods of the Gentiles demons? Is faith a virtue? Is holy water a sacrament? Can Christ be called the Son of God?* The latter question Christ himself put to the Jews; Paul treats it in detail in his letter to the Hebrews, and John answers it in his gospel. *Should the Virgin Mary be called the Mother of God? What is truth?*—the question Pilate asked of Truth Itself.

Third, a status in which one inquires what kind of thing something is (*qualis res sit*). This is called a status of quality and of consequence, wherein one inquires about something consequent on a thing's nature. For example, *Was it right for Moses to kill the man in Egypt?*[35] *Is it right to cure a man on the Sabbath? Is it proper for a woman to pray in Church with her head uncovered?*—a question Paul wisely heads off.[36] Arguments taken from tradition, which are crucial questions for the heretics, are of this type.

Philosophers add a fourth question with which they inquire why a thing is *(cur res sit)* or what is its cause. This question rhetoricians reduce to the first, just as they reduce questions relating to quantity and to number to the third. For example, *Do not three give testimony in heaven, the Father, Son, and Holy Spirit?*[37] The first two statuses are simple, whereas the third has parts which I list and explain later. Some writers add two more statuses to the traditional three: one they call the translative, the other, the legal.

The translative, or the status of translation, is one in which a controversy arises over a judge, an action, a time, a place, or other circumstance necessary for doing something correctly. Pertinent here is an example found in the book of Exodus, chap. 2. *Who made you king and judge over us?* Paul made use of this status when he appealed to Caesar. Since this takes away guilt from oneself or otherwise weakens a charge, it is said to be a status of translation. On this account Christ, who was the Son of God and so not subject to the law, could void any judgment; and yet he subjected himself to the law so that he might free those who were subject to it.

The legal or "legitimate" status is called such when a question arises from things written in the law, and to this are reduced all questions that arise from anything written or stated in any way whatever. This status has many parts, knowledge of which is useful for interpreting Scripture.[38] Indeed, the better teachers of speech reduce these last two statuses to the third status, and rightly so, since in both of them one is inquiring about the quality of a thing. . . .

BOOK FOUR

. . .

Chap. 4. What are emotions, how many kinds are there, and is it licit to move them?

[201] One cannot move the emotions without having at least some basic knowledge of them. This should be held for certain, following Plato, whatever teachers of speech may have held in this regard.[39] On this account, before discussing how they are aroused I shall briefly explain their nature.

There are in humans two parts, one capable of reason, the other not. The first is said to be superior, the second, inferior, and the first is proper to man whereas the second he shares with brutes. In both of these there are two powers, one whereby man knows, another whereby he desires. The power of knowing situated in the superior part has truth for its object, and it is moved by this object. The power of desiring seeks everything good and flees from everything evil. The power of knowing in the inferior part perceives only what conserves or destroys the nature. The power of desiring seeks only the kind of good that produces pleasure in the senses, and it has two parts. One bears on a good proposed that can be obtained without difficulty, and it is said to be concupiscible. The other bears on a good [202] that is difficult to obtain, and this is called irascible. And although there can be some type of appetition in both the superior and the inferior parts of the soul, properly speaking only movements that are accompanied by some bodily change in the sentient part are called emotions. So it is that by the term emotion we understand any change in the appetitive part that is aroused by an appearance perceived as good or bad by which a nature is moved from its state of rest.

The Stoics regarded such emotions as bad and thought that they should be completely suppressed. The Peripatetics, on the other hand, judged emotions as neither good nor bad and were content to say that they should be sufficiently restrained to be made obedient to reason. But some stupid men said that emotions are like demons that are affixed to human minds the way hairs are attached to the heads.[40] No less in error were those who said that every movement of the sentient soul arising in us against reason is a sin, as did Luther; yet nothing can be a sin if one does not give it the consent of reason. Thus are dispatched the Stoics, against whom Lactantius, Augustine, and many others disputed; and completely to be rejected are the heretics, whose opinions, should we follow them, would see every arousal of the emotions as illicit.

We say, therefore, following the common and true opinion of philosophers and theologians, that emotions called the passions are of themselves neither good nor bad, though they can become good or bad if they conform to reason or depart from it. Perhaps the Stoics thought only the latter to be bad, so that from the words they use to describe them one might gather that they defined an emotion as a perturbation, which they also called a passion, that is adverse to right reason and against the nature of the soul.[41] But we would prefer to describe it as follows: an emotion is an appetite of the sentient soul aroused by some thing that is regarded by nature as good or bad. So every emotion is caused by an object or thing that appears to be good or bad, either present or future, acquired easily or with difficulty, and indeed in three ways: either when we are inclined toward it, or when we pursue it, or when we have already grasped it.

Thus it is that eleven emotions are enumerated, six of which are in the part by which we are concupiscent, the remainder in that by which we are irascible. In the former, with regard to a good known through inclination there is *love*, through pursuit of an absent good, *desire*, and through the attainment of a present good, *joy* or *delight*. In the same part, with regard to something bad there are three contrary emotions, *hatred*, *aversion*, and *sadness*. In the irascible part, with regard to an arduous good that can be acquired there is *hope*; with one that cannot be acquired, [203] *despair*. With regard to an imminent arduous evil, if it is too strong to overcome there is *fear*; if not, there is *courage*. With regard to a good possessed in this part there is no emotion, because the difficulty is no longer present; with regard to an evil that is present there is *anger*.

There are some who enumerate only four genera of emotions and then put other species under them, as follows. From an absent good there arises *líbido* or *desiderium*, from a good as present, *laetitia*; from a future evil, *metus*, from one present, *aegritudo* or *tristitia*.[42] These genera are made up of many parts: for *laetitia*, *delectatio* and *iactatio*, and for joy over evil that hurts another, *malevolentia*. And then there are those similar to the others. To *líbido*: *ira*, *excandescentia*, *odium*, *inimicitia*, *desiderium*, *discordia*, and other emotions like these. To *metus*: *pigritia*, *pudor*, *terror*, *timor*, *pavor*, *examinatio*, *formido*. To *aegritudo*: *invidentia*, *aemulatio*, *obtrectatio*, *misericordia*, *angor*, *luctum*, *moeror*, *aerumna*, *dolor*, *lamentatio*, *solicitudo*, *molestia*, *afflictatio*, *desperatio*, and others of the same type. For those who have knowledge of these latter emotions, and particularly the first group, from which arise the definitions, causes, and effects of the others, note that they are much more suited for arousing the emotions. Those who desire to know about them should read our books on rhetoric.

Again, it is customary to divide emotions into major and minor, or milder and more vehement: the former are called *mores* (Gr. *ethe*), the latter, *perturbationes* (Gr. *pathe*). The former serve especially for conciliating, for seeking favor, for retaining hearers, and for pointing out the significance of character; the latter, for inciting and inflaming. The former are useful for admonitions and exhortations to familiars and in lighter matters; the latter we use for reproofs, censures, and in more serious matters, when dealing with religion, salvation, and the fleeing of vice.

In effecting emotional response the Christian orator has much more latitude that the civil orator, since the former comes to speak as a judge, teacher, father, and God's legate, and treats cases of greater moment. So he is used not only to warning mildly, beseeching, and giving precepts, but also to rebuking, upbraiding, and threatening. The civil orator acts in a more relaxed way and sometimes subjects himself to the judge, even flattering him. And since the Christian orator has a different subject matter and a different goal, he arouses private emotions and makes use of private topics to do so. This, universally speaking, is nothing more than a certain incitement of the mind, without which the speech of a preacher would be unpleasant and lacking in warmth. The human [204] orator incites more to indignation and commiseration under the appearance of honesty and utility. The divine orator incites to love of God, to desire for eternal salvation, to hope of obtaining pardon, and to fear of future judgment. He moves hearers to give thanks for benefits received, and finally he offers consolation to the afflicted. On this account, although it is sufficient for the civil orator to temper emotions when speaking, to do his work, and to exhort from turpitude to honor, this is not sufficient for the ecclesiastical orator. The latter should also direct the hearer to true praise of God and to the development of true and perfect virtues, as Lactantius says so well. For example, if the concupiscible power is directed to heaven, there arise laudable emotions that move us to perfect virtues, such as the tediousness of this life, the fear of future punishment, the desire for eternal happiness, the love of God, contempt for self, and feelings of this kind. And it teaches us that from the same root come pernicious and base emotions, if directed to earthly and human things. For the same reason, if the irascible power is lifted up, the result is the excitation and sustaining of that most outstanding emotion called zeal. Also aroused is correction, fortitude, perseverance, and other virtues proper for Christians.

But one might say, at this point, why is it so necessary for the Christian orator to arouse the emotions? When he is concerned with causes that are useful and necessary for his hearers, he is dealing with souls who are not opposed but rather are benevolent and disposed toward the goals to which he is persuading. This idea seems plausible enough to those who put little study into arousing the emotions and think that they have fulfilled their office well enough if they simply teach or amuse their hearers. But to answer this objection plainly, I first point out how much they are in error and distance themselves from the ideal of the preacher if they neglect this third task of the orator or fail to see its importance. Then I shall respond to the particular objection being proposed.

If it were not necessary for Christian orators to have the power of arousing the emotions, why would celestial orators and the writers of canonical epistles have written with so much feeling? Anyone who would not have recognized this in Isaiah, Jeremiah, Ezechiel, David, Paul, James, and others was simply stupid. Then, if it were not necessary when teaching to arouse the emotions, why would the preacher have said, *Cry, cease not, lift up thy voice like a trumpet?*[43] and, in another place, *Preach the word, be instant in season and out of season.*[44] Moreover, if there is no need to excite the emotions, there is no reason for a good many Christians to go to hear sermons. Since they already know practically everything, what more is there for them to do? And again, if it is not necessary to move the minds of the hearers, because it suffices for the hearer to know and to believe, this clashes with religion, for *only those can become just who not only hear the word but live by it,*[45] and *those are called blessed who hear the word and keep it.* If it is not necessary because, having heard, hearers of their own accord and without any other stimulation proceed to carry out the teaching, experience teaches that this too is false, since we see men who are not completely evil hearing sermons throughout the whole of Lent and yet making little progress in the spiritual life. Finally, lest I spend too much time proving the obvious, no one of sound mind would say that this task is no more necessary for the ecclesiastical orator than it is for the civil orator. If the latter does not move his auditors he is thought to be imperfect and useless; much more, therefore, will it be true of the former. On this account masters of speech have said well: To teach is necessary; to amuse is a gift; to move is the victory. In this one word a sermon becomes dominant: to arouse the emotions of the hearers by speech, both toward that to which he would attract them and away from that from which he deter them.

With regard to the difficulty proposed above, the hearer should be moved by the emotions because what he hears and knows he either does not do or does it coldly, negligently, and imperfectly. And thus he acts partly from fallen nature, partly from bad habits formed earlier, partly from the attacks of enemies, partly from depraved impulses, which in the end draw him away. Truly one can say, *The better things I see and approve, but the worse I follow.* From all this one can see how important it is to move the emotions. Anyone who is unable to move them, in my view, should not take on the task of preaching.

Chap. 5. Some admonitions to be observed for moving the emotions correctly

Just as the work of moving the emotions is absolutely necessary, so it is very difficult. On this account it will be useful and not alien to our treatment for us to indicate this by offering a few admonitions.

First: let no one shrink from this task because he [206] thinks it will be too difficult. Since the voices of women alone, without any serious subject matter, can move the emotions, why should a preacher endowed with wisdom and good rhetorical appeals not be able to do the same? If people who engage in histrionics and who tell fables and fabricate situations are able to excite the emotions of their hearers, why should the ecclesiastical orator, who treats of serious and true subject matters, not do so also?

Second: a person who wishes to arouse the emotions, using the gospel or other scriptural source, should take up materials that are most suited to arousing emotions, say, of fear, joy, sorrow, or hope. For there are some accounts, simply told or narrated, and particularly when told with a certain seriousness and sensitivity, that have the power to move people. I need only mention the story of Abraham and the sacrifice of his son, the patience of Job, the constancy and perseverance of Tobias, the courage of the Maccabees.

Third: in arousing emotions in oneself and in others it helps greatly if the preacher not only understands and commits to memory what he is to say, but also enters into the scene with his whole mind so as to make it present to the eye of the mind—forming a vivid phantasm, as the Greeks called it, of all of the emotional elements. Examples would be the horrible spectacle of the Last Judgment, the inexplicable joys of eternal beatitude, what Stephen saw when the heavens opened, the awful tragedy and betrayal of sin, and so on. . . .

[207] Fourth: when arousing the emotions it is not enough to conceive them intellectually. There must be brought to this a fervent and lively delivery, not one that is cold, languid, and bloodless but rather one that is inflamed and muscular, giving life to the situation being described.

Fifth: as all masters of rhetoric teach, the person who has already moved his own emotions will be in the best position to move the emotions of others. Examples may easily be found in Marcantonio and Cicero. . . .

[208] Sixth: also desired in one who wishes to arouse the emotions are vivid illustrations and examples, beyond the mere telling of the account, that make the emotional element readily discernible. The emotions are

aroused partly by the situation itself, partly by its graphic presence to the eye of the hearer. This type of amplification should be employed throughout. . . .

Seventh: The topic or cause that the preacher has at hand should be treated as something dear to him and requiring him to speak out, for things that we regard as in our own interest we generally treat more fully and more ardently than those that are not. . . .[46]

Eighth: The person who wishes to move effectively should take his materials, as much as possible, from the Scriptures or from the writings of the Church Fathers, and then [209] exaggerate and amplify them as may be necessary. For example, take the text, *The eye has not seen, nor the ear heard, nor has it entered into the heart of man to know what God has prepared for those who love him.* Less apt to move the emotions is material that takes nothing from the Scriptures or the Fathers or the Councils. Also, probity of life has great power to move one's hearers, for example moves better than words. As Quintilian puts it, "The person who seems bad when he speaks indeed speaks badly."

Finally, lest I make too many points, and there are indeed many, the preacher will be better prepared for arousing the emotions if he has prayed fervently to be moved by the Holy Spirit, which moves and reigns in the hearts of men. For it is that Spirit that opens the mouths of the mute and makes the tongues of infants wise, with whose help, without any art or careful preparation, hearts will be moved miraculously and efficaciously.

As to how and when to arouse the emotions, I say briefly that this is not advisable in all subject matters but only in those that are serious and of greater moment. In other cases it is sufficient to seek a mild movement, both when urging and admonishing, for love works better than fear and mildness achieves better results than harshness or asperity. Nor should the emotional appeal be made in all parts of a speech, but only in the exordium, the confirmation, and the peroration. In the exordium it should be less dominant, as also in [210] the narration, if there is any. In the confirmation it should be stronger, especially in the exaggeration of serious arguments and in any digression that requires amplification. And in the peroration it should be more ardent. Generally speaking, it should be used whenever the occasion presents itself. Emotion, like blood, should be diffused throughout the entire body, but its color should be more apparent in one part than another. . . .

Chap. 6. Topics for arousing the emotion of love toward God and neighbor, including one's enemies

[211] When Aristotle was explaining the arts that argue on either side of a question, he generally explained only a small number of topics. As he well knew, not everyone who dealt with these faculties would be able to put them to use and apply them to particular subject matters. For that reason he supplied in both the *Topics* and the *Rhetoric* various pronouncements, commonly called maxims, to open out fuller and ampler sources for more copious discourse. So we also, when instructing preachers, have been encouraged to do the same. Therefore, although all argumentation and amplification for teaching and moving the emotions may be taken from the common topics enumerated above, we now move on to more special topics that should help those less experienced in the art to arouse particular emotions.

Since every good emotion comes from the love of God and every evil arousal comes from love of self, we begin with topics with which the preacher can arouse the love of God in his hearers. Some of these are the following. Because God is good without limit, there are innumerable reasons why he should be loved and none why he should not; because he is infinitely beautiful and is beauty and majesty itself, and captures everyone with love and reverence; because he first loved us from all eternity, and cannot but be loved, since love is the magnet of love; because we have been made to his image and likeness, and he has given us the power to become his sons and daughters; because he has so loved us that he gave us his only-begotten Son; because he daily bestows on us innumerable benefits, raining them down on the just and the unjust; because he deals with us with mercy and clemency, not holding our sins against us, but overlooks our sins to move us lovingly to repentance; and so on. . . .

Since those who do not love their neighbor cannot love God, hearers should frequently be moved to love of neighbor. We should love our neighbor because he has the same nature as ourselves, because we have the same father in God, the same teacher, the Holy Spirit, the same mother, the Church, and so we are truly brothers; and we profess the same religion and receive the same sacraments. Also, this is the one precept God has given us. And finally, anyone in whom love is found, lives in God and God lives in him.

Since there is a particular difficulty that seems to be repugnant to our nature, that of loving our enemies, and since there are few who do not think they have enemies, we should move people to love their enemies. We should do so that we may be [213] sons and imitators of God, who loved sinners, who were his enemies, and who sacrificed his only Son for them. The good preacher should remind people that to condone injuries and love enemies is truly divine, since it is proper to God to show mercy and to spare. Moreover, there is no greater victory than that over oneself; whoever hurts his enemy hurts only himself; together with Christ and St. Stephen we should pray for our enemies; nothing is more inhuman than to hate one who is the image of God, a son and indeed a brother who has been redeemed by the blood of Christ. And finally, since there is no one who does not wish to be loved even by his enemies, every one of us, by a law of nature, is obliged to love others.

So as not to make my list too long, which I would do if I touched on every individual case, I now indicate only the types of love the preacher should seek to arouse. As the occasion offers itself, he should treat the subject of fraternal love, on which I have written an entire book.[47] He should treat of the love of parents for their children, and of children for their parents; of the mutual love of spouses; of love of country and especially of the Catholic Church, which is our mother and teacher; of love for the souls in Purgatory; of love for our rulers and prelates; of love for those subject to us and those entrusted to our care.

To conclude, the divine orator will best arouse his hearers to love of others if he is able to extinguish in them love of self—a vice that grows in the citizen of Babylon all the way to contempt of God himself.

Chap. 11. Topics for arousing sorrow over sin committed, and on the power of tears

[222] Since no one can come to fear of the Lord without having the greatest sorrow for sin, to which the good preacher will often move his hearers, we here note a few topics that are especially well adapted to effecting this sorrow.

Sorrow is nothing more than sadness over a present evil. Since any fault or sin alone deserves the name of evil (since all other things are good and are the source of joy, not sorrow), it follows that only sin should cause sorrow. But there is a virtue that removes it, namely, penance, without which no one can be saved. The law of the gospel takes its origin from penance, since John the Baptist, who prepared the way for the Lord, began his preaching by enjoining his hearers: *"Do penance."*

Penance itself is nothing more than voluntary sorrow over sin because it is an offense against God, with the firm intention of sinning no more. With the help of divine grace penance remits sin, opens the gates of paradise, heals the person who is sick, makes the sad rejoice, calls the dead back to life, restores one to a pristine state, reestablishes honor, and gives trust, strength, and grace. Penance is the mother of mercy, the teacher of the virtues. Its power is such that it frees the guilty, renovates the delinquent, lifts up the lapsed, and recreates the desperate.

The degree of the sorrow required for penance should be the greatest possible, and the following topics might be used to incite and augment it.

[223] Sorrow, which of its own power should be able to remove sin, should be as great as that of one who has fallen into the hands of his enemies and feels like a slave, vile and among the most abject of men, whom they insult and laugh at. As great as that of a person who is covered from head to foot with sores and sees himself swarming with hideous ulcers. As great as that of one whose hands have been bound by the executioner, one who has been put on a pile of wood, and sees himself about to be burned to death. (The executioner is the devil, the pile of wood the sins committed, the place of execution is hell, and the fire a flame never to be extinguished.) As great as that of one who is obsessed by one or more devils, who torture him day and night, never allow him to sleep or take food or drink, throw him first into water then into fire. As great as that of one whose body is afflicted by serious illnesses, such that he cannot move, or see, or hear, or experience sensation. As great as that of one who, suffering from all kinds of disease, is thrown into a foul and filthy prison. As great as that of one who recognizes that he knowingly has offended a friend, a brother, his parents, both spiritual and carnal, who gave him birth, raised him, educated him. As great as one who realizes that he has betrayed his country. As great, finally, as one who has trampled on the blood of Christ and has committed many crimes against the divine majesty, who has fouled and profaned the temple of God and the repository of the Holy Spirit, who recognizes that he has abandoned God, the spouse of his soul, and that he has committed adultery with the devil. To sum up, his sorrow should be that of one who has lost all of his goods present and future and has fallen into evils that must be endured perpetually. And just as there is nothing more evil than sin, so there should be no sorrow greater than that over sin, from which every other evil comes.

The following are a few things that might be said about the power of tears, about which we have written in our *De interiore homine*. Tears should accompany our mourning in penance: they wash away the sores of sins, suppress the flames of concupiscence, extinguish the fires of hell, and give joy to the soul. We should shed tears with Mary Magdalen, with Peter, with David so that we can say with him, *"Night after night I have washed my bed with tears,"* and finally with Christ, who wept for our [224] sins, and who experienced such great sorrow that the mere thought of them caused him to sweat blood. In this way we can make ourselves just through a just penance, having judged ourselves before we come to God's judgment. We can bring on ourselves a just sentence, before a most severe judge puts one on us. And we can deplore the sin, not the punishment. . . .

Chap. 14. On the variety of hearers and on knowing their characters.

[229] Since it is plain that the characters of men differ according to their various studies, arts, and ages, we must know these if we are to a rouse their emotions in the ways we have taught above. Thus it may help to reduce the variety of hearers to a few general types and then explain in general how their emotions can be aroused. That is what we propose to do in the present chapter.

Since, as St. Paul teaches, the Church is like the body of Christ in which there are many members, in different places, with different functions to perform, from whose ordering a perfect unity [230] is to be effected, so the preacher, whose task it is to move and direct this whole body by his preaching, should be aware of the power, the nature, and the functions of all its parts. He should be well versed in human affairs, so that he can direct all members to their ends and instruct them suitably in things that pertain to religion, which is like the soul of this body.

The members of this body, for our purposes, can be divided first by reason of sex into male and female. By reason of age, some are adolescents and youths, others are already adults at full strength, and others finally are old, it not being necessary to make further distinctions in this matter. Finally, by reason of states, arts, and studies, these can be considered either simply, as the states of widows and virgins, or comparatively, those of married people, princes, rulers, and others similar. And to speak generally, these constitute five kinds of hearers, namely, men, women, prelates, major superiors, and those who care for souls. The last can be broken down into priests, princes, magistrates, subjects, parents, sons, teachers, students, military leaders, soldiers, heads of families, servants, husbands, wives, widows, virgins, monks, nobles, rich people, those of low birth, poor people, farmers, and merchants. Although there are other classes of hearers, inclluding those that can be differentiated on the basis of arts and studies, if a preacher knows and understands the above and can speak to them aptly and decorously, which is the chief thing in the art of rhetoric, he should be well equipped to move the souls of his hearers.

The formality under which one should speak to different states is manifest in itself or is taught in this text of St. John: *"I write to you, little children, because your sins are forgiven you for his name's sake. I write to you, fathers, because you have known him from the beginning. I write to you, adolescents, because you have overcome the wicked one. I write to you, infants, because you have known the Father. I write to you, youths, because you are strong, and the word of God abides in you, and you have overcome the wicked one.*"⁴⁸ We refrain from indicating particular texts here, since those of average learning can locate them, particularly if they recall what we have already taught about locating texts. But to offer help for those who are less educated and less acquainted with the rhetorical art, I prepare the way by offering some admonitions.

First, one who wishes to arouse the emotions of different people should have a good idea of the power, nature, offices, [231] and functions of their respective states, and particularly the errors to which they are likely prone, that is, the sins that spouses, merchants, magistrates, and judges frequently commit.

Second, one should know what is convenient and inconvenient for the various states, how their burdens can be diminished or increased, and what is useful by way of amplification for encouraging or consoling them.

Third, one should be aware of their respective dignities, needs, and utilities in the common life, such as the need for merchandising, the dignity of agriculture, and so on.

Fourth, one should know the particular virtues that are to be commended and sought in each state, such as vigilance in bishops and those who care for souls, justice in the magistrate, trust in the merchant, modesty in a woman, and liberality in the prince.

Fifth, if the state is a related state such as that of husband and wife, of parents and children, one should teach how each should act, and comparatively, should urge each to fulfill his or her duties toward the other.

Sixth, of the many characters of the individual states, one should know what particular characters of youths, adults, and old people are good, and what bad. We have written much about this in the second book of our *De inventione*.

Seventh, since different things should be preached to those in particular states, such as youths and the elderly, one should see what in their particular characters should be restrained, as in youths, who are quick to condemn, in the elderly, who are greedy, and so on; similarly, what should be praised in them, as in the elderly prudence, in youths, liberality.⁴⁹ The former should be condemned, the latter commended, but always with an eye to good character traits that can be developed.

Eighth and last, hearers should be urged to remain in the vocation to which they have been called and not to look down upon their own particular state.⁵⁰ Many evils can arise from changing one's state, so one should strive to attain perfection by being zealous for the greater gifts; so beware of taking counsel from other than the Holy Spirit, lest one be deceived by the devil who changes himself into an angel of light.⁵¹ Much better, safer, and more desirable to remain in a lower state than in a higher, in being ruled than being a ruler. If one holds to these admonitions, it should be easy to locate topics that can move all hearers and so preach to them properly and decorously.

Should one wish to have more detail on particular states mentioned in the Scriptures, note what is said there about pastors, princes, spouses, [232] virgins, parents, children, and other groups. Also read what Antoninus of Florence, Denys the Carthusian, St. Thomas Aquinas, and others have written about states of life. For those who are eager to learn, simply indicating the sources ought to be sufficient.

BOOK FIVE

. . .

Chap. 25. Of the three styles of speaking universally

[345] The styles of speaking are said to be three in number, of which the first is called submissive (*summissum*), humble (*humile*), tenuous (*tenue*), slender (*gracile*), pressed (*pressum*), warm (*callidum*), plain (*enucleatum*), and pointed (*acutum*). The second is the contrary of this: sublime (*sublime*), serious (*grave*), grandiloquent (*grandiloquum*), full (*plenum*), copious (*copiosum*), ample (*amplum*), ardent (*ardens*), robust (*robustum*), vehement (*vehemens*), and sharp (*acre*). The third is medium, interjected, intermediate: suave (*suave*), tempered (*temperatum*), mediocre (*mediocre*), and equable (*equabile*). To the first kind is attributed comeliness (*venustas*), to the second, force (*vis*) and amplitude (*amplitudo*), to the third, suavity (*suavitas*). These ways of speaking, under the common name of forms, are said to be the characters or ideas of speeches, and Plutarch also calls them "plasms" (*plasmata*). Universally speaking, style is regarded in this way: the humble, subtly; the grand, seriously; and the mediocre, temperately, and each one has its proper decorum, which is always to be observed. . . .

Chap. 26. On the style of speaking submissively and humbly

[347] First to be explained is the nature of the styles, showing with what matters or sentences, and with what words or figures, and with what composition, they should be composed. The submissive and attenuated style requires sentences that are subtle and perspicuous, not rare, but learned and pointed and suitable for teaching, of the kind found in comedies, colloquia, and in common speech. The words ought to be humble, trite, but appropriate, not exquisite nor rare. . . .

This style is to be used in explaining partitions, divisions, definitions, descriptions, in the discussion of light matters, in narrations that are less serious, in arguments relating to subtle matters, and finally whenever anything is to be said simply. . . .

Chap. 27. On the sublime or grand style of speaking

[349] The grand style has as its subject great things, matters of great moment, and those which it is necessary to treat with contention, perturbation, and emotion, as are those which are treated in tragedies and more serious cases and where there is heavier persuasion. It takes words that are ample, magnificent, rare, ferocious, sharp, and significant epithets. Examples would be the terrifying punishments with which God threatened the Israelites if they did not obey his commands. . . .[52]

This style is used in great causes, in more serious exordiums, in the narration of brutal matters, in the treatment of stronger arguments, in epilogues, where there is need for indignation and complaint, in common topics, and in amplifications.

As to composition, this admits of long periods, as does the form of an oration, now quiet (cesa), now divided into periods, now full of turns and windings. As to their number there need not be great concern, particularly when it is a matter of arousing the emotions. Moses used this style when he inveighed against a people who were ungrateful for all God had done for them.[53] Read the prophets and also Paul, especially in Romans and in Hebrews. And John began in the grand style when he said "*In the beginning was the Word,* etc."

[350] The swollen and the inflated sin against this style, as do those who affect a certain counterfeit gravity, who use excessive ornamentation and prodigious metaphors, words that are hopelessly rare, and an improper style of speech, as did the Asiatics (*Asiatici*) at one time.

Chap. 28. On the style of speaking mediately and temperately, and the correct use of the three styles

This style is used in many exordiums, in prefaces, in narrations that are joyful and composed to delight; sometimes in confirmations, when arguments that are less urgent are explained; in stories and commentaries; in certain causes, and in letters, praises and blames, and writing on philosophy.

Not infrequently David uses this style in his Psalms, as when he sings the divine praises, gives thanks, and preaches divine providence. Paul does the same when he is exhorting. . . .

Before concluding, I now add a few counsels that I think are worthy of consideration.

First, it should be observed that people err when they think that great matters always require the grand style, for sometimes they should be explained more finely, as suited to the persons and circumstances involved. The same should be said of the other two styles.

Then, those also err who think that all matters are explicated, or should be explicated, with the same style. Nor should all letters be humble, nor all philosophical treatises tempered, nor all orations and epics delivered in the sublime style. On this account, when we say that any oration, or letter, or poem [351] should be written in a given form, this is to be understood by way of excellence, in the sense that this or that form should preferably be dominant in it.[54]

Moreover, one who wishes to delight, who seeks to flee from similarity as the mother of satiety, should mix the three styles together in an appropriate and apt way, and almost never stay in the same style for long. Of all styles, the more tolerable is the most submissive if it is long prolonged. This is as compared to the sublime and exaggerated style, in which one should not remain for any time, but should interrupt and vary it. Yet one might return to it, if able to interject some brief questionings that can be explained in a submissive way.[55] When the tempered style is taken on to delight, this should not be done by the preacher for that reason alone, since he has another goal than to appear eloquent, for he should be impelled to speak not so much to delight as to teach and move his hearers. What is most persuasive in the submissive style is the truth of what is being said. What is persuasive in the grand style is that people do what they already know should be done but are not doing it. What is persuasive in the tempered style is to speak beautifully and ornately, but, as we have said, persuasion does not stop there.

Thus it is of great importance that we temper our speech with the threefold variety of styles, for similitude is the parent of tedium and satiety, variety the parent of joy. On this account, granted that Augustine regards the tempered style as the lowest of all, for with it the speaker seems to do nothing more than speak beautifully and ornately rather than persuade, nonetheless it can be used for other reasons, so that we can make a smooth transition from the humblest style to the elation of the sublime. Contrary to what many say, read what Augustine has to say about the three styles in the text cited, for it is worth careful study.

ENDNOTES

1. Excerpts from Acts 1, Acts 14, 1 Corinth. 1; 2 Corinth. 2, 2 Corinth 11.

2. Cites Chrysostom, Basil, and Jerome.

3. Cites texts and their interpretation by Eusebius and Jerome.

4. Cites Origen, Theodoretus, and Gregory the Great.

5. Cites Augustine, Chrysostom on St. Paul, and Cassiodorus.

6. Cites Cicero, Horace, and Psalm 11.

7. A marginal note citing Hermagoras.

8. Cites various texts of Scripture, Origen, Augustine, and Cassiodorus.

9. Cites texts from the Book of Wisdom,

Psalms 1. 44. 67, and 80, Augustine's *De doctrina Christiana,* Theodoretus, and Dionysius Alexandrinus.

10. Explains why they did so, with added paragraphs on St. Paul and Moses.

11. Cites texts from these authorities.

12. Matth. 10.

13. Cites Proverbs 16 and 10, Wisdom 10.

14. Cites Moses, Aaron, Job, Isaiah, Jeremiah, Ezechiel, Paul, and Solomon.

15. Cites Chrysostom, Lactantius, Jerome, Justin, Tertullian, Arnobius, and Gregory Naziansen.

16. Again cites Chrysostom, Gregory, Basil, Jerome, and Cyprian.

17. Cites Esther 10 and Proverbs 19.

18. These examples are taken from the sayings of Christ and from John, Luke, Isaiah, Ezechiel, Job, and David, from the Psalms, and then from Cicero, Quintilian, and Paul.

19. Malac. 2.

20. 1 Cor. 12.

21. See Louis of Granada.

22. Cites the following authors: Ludovicus Granatus, Augustinus Valer., Thomas de Trugil., Franciscus Panicar., Didacus Stella, Lucas Ballionus, Laurentius a Villa Vicea, Alfonsus Zurilla, Trusignan, Jacobus Pares., Ambrosius Quis., and Didacus Vallades.

23. Cites Iul. Roger.

24. Lib. 2 *De quest. orat.*

25. Cites Antonio Riccobono.

26. Cites Luis of Granada.

27. Cites Augustinus Valerius and

Rogerius.

28. Refers the reader to his *De quest. orat.*

29. Refers the reader to Aristotle's *Topics.*

30. Refers the reader to the *Topics.*

31. See Heb. 11.

32. Cites his *Lib. De inventione dialectica et oratoria.*

33. Cites his *Lib. De questionibus oratoricis.*

34. Cites Dan.

35. Cites Exod. 2.

36. Cites 1 Cor. 11.

37. Cites 1 Ioan. 5.

38. Cites Lib. 2 of his *De quest. orat.*

39. Cites Trapezuntius.

40. Notes that this is found in Clement of Alexandria.

41. Cites Cicero, *Tusculan Disputations,* 5.

42. Cites Cicero, *Tusculan Disputations,* 4.

43. Cites Isaiah, 58.

44. Cites 2 Tim. 4.

45. Cites Rom. 2

46. Cites Cicero on Brutus.

47. *De amore et concordia fraterna* (1586)

48. Cites 1 Ioan. 2.

49. Marginal note to Book 2 of Aristotle's *Rhetoric.*

50. Cites 1 Cor. 7.

51. Cites 1 Cor. 12.

52. See Deuteronomy 32, Jeremiah, and the Psalms.

53. Cites Deut. 32.

54. Marginal note to Ioan. Mere.

55. Marginal note to Augustine.

Bibliography

Primary Sources

Albertus Magnus. *Omnia Opera,* ed. Auguste Borgnet. 38 vols. Paris: Ludovicus Vivès, 1890–99.

Arisotle. *Arisotle: Selected Works.* Trans. Hippocrates G. Apostle and Lloyd P. Gerson. Grinnell, Iowa: The Peripatetic Press, 1982.

———. *Aristotle "Topics": Books I and VIII with excerpts from related texts.* Translated with a Commentary by Robin Smith. Oxford: Clarendon Press, 1997.

———. *The "Art" of Rhetoric.* Trans. John Henry Freese. Loeb Classical Library. Cambridge: Harvard University Press, 1975.

———. *Topica.* Trans. E. S. Forster. Loeb Classical Library. Cambridge: Harvard University Press, 1976.

———. *Physics.* Translated with commentaries and glossary by Hippocrates G. Apostle. Grinnell, Iowa: The Peripatetic Press, 1980.

———. *Posterior Analytics.* Translated with commentaries and glossary by Hippocrates G. Apostle. Grinnell, Iowa: The Peripatetic Press, 1981.

Campanella, O.P., Thomas. *A Defense of Galileo, the Mathematician from Florence.* Translated, with an introduction and notes, by Richard J. Blackwell. Notre Dame, Ind.: University of Notre Dame Press, 1994.

Carbone, Ludovico. *Additamenta ad commentario D. Francisci Toleti in Logicam Aristotelis: Praeludia in libros Priores Analyticos; Tractatio de Syllogismo; de Instrumentis Sciendi; et de Praecognitionibus atque Praecognitis.* Venice: Apud Georgium Angellerium, 1597.

———. *De amore et concordia fraterna.* Venice: 1586.

———. *De arte dicendi libri duo.* Venice: Ex Officina Damiani Zenarij, 1589.

———. *De caussis eloquentiae libri iiii.* Venice: 1593.

———. *De dispositione oratoria, disputationes xxx.* Venice: 1590.

———. *De elocutione oratoria.* Venice: 1593.

———. *Della Ammaestramento de' Figliuoli nella Dottrina Christiana.* Venice: Giovanni Guerigli, 1596.

———. *De octo partium orationis constructione libellus.* Venice: 1592.

———. *De oratoria et dialectica inventione, vel de locis communibus, libri quinque.* Venice: Apud Damianum Zenarum, 1589.

———. *De pacificatione.* Florence: 1583.

———. *De praeceptis Ecclesiae opusculum utilissimum.* Venice: 1592.

———. *Divinus orator, vel de rhetorica divina, libri septem.* Venice: Apud Societatem Minimam, 1595.

———. *Fons vitae et sapientiae.* Venice:1588.

———. *Interior homo vel de suiipsius cognitione.* Venice, 1585.

———. *Introductio ad catechismum sive doctrinam Christianum.* Venice: 1596.

———. *Introductio in dialecticam Aristotelis per Magistrum Franciscum Toletum Sacerdotem Soci-*

etatis Iesu, Philosophiae in Romano Societatis Collegio Professorem. Venice: Apud Paulum Meiettum, 1588.

————. *Introductio in sacram theologiam sex comprehensa libris.* Venice: 1589

————. *Introductionis in logicam, sive totius logicae compendij absolutissimi libri sex.* Venice: Apud Ioannem Baptistam et Ioannem Bernardum Sessam, 1597.

————. *Introductionis in universam philosophiam libri quatuor.* Venice: Apud Marcum Antonium Zalterium, 1599.

————. *Summa summarum casuum conscientiae.* Venice: 1599.

————. *Tabulae Rhetoricae Cypriani Soarii S.I.* Venice: Ex Officina Damiani Zenarij, 1589.

————. *Vir iustus.* Venice: 1585.

Cicero. *De inventione.* Trans. H. M. Hubbell. Loeb Classical Library. Cambridge: Harvard University Press, 1949.

Cicero (Pseudo). *Ad Herennium.* Trans. Harry Caplan. Loeb Classical Library. Cambridge: Harvard University Press, 1981.

———— *De oratore.* Books I,II. Trans. E. W. Sutton and H. Rackham. Loeb Classical Library. Cambridge: Harvard University Press, 1948.

———— *Topica.* Trans. H. M. Hubbell. Loeb Classical Library. Cambridge: Harvard University Press, 1949.

Galilei, Galileo. *Dialogue Concerning the Two Chief World Systems.* Trans. Stillman Drake. Berkeley: University of California Press, 1953. Rev. ed., 1962.

————. *Galileo's Logical Treatises.* A Translation, with Notes and Commentary, of His Appropriated Latin Questions on Aristotle's *Posterior Analytics.* William A. Wallace, translator and editor. Boston Studies in the Philosophy of Science, Vol. 138. Dordrecht /Boston /London: Kluwer Academic Publishers, 1992.

————. *Le Opere di Galileo Galilei.* Ed. Antonio Favaro. 20 vols. in 21. Florence: G. Barbèra: 1890–1909, rpt. 1968.

————. *Sidereus nuncius or The Sidereal Messenger of Galileo Galilei.* Translated by Albert Van Helden. Chicago: University of Chicago Press, 1989.

————. *Tractatio de praecognitionibus et praecognitis* and *Tractatio de demonstratione.* Transcribed from the Latin autograph by William F. Edwards, with Notes and Commentary by William A. Wallace. Padua: Editrice Antenore, 1988.

Petrarch. *Epistola de rebus familiaribus et variis.* Edited by J. Fracasetti. 3 vols. Florence: 1859–1863.

Quintilian. *Institutio Oratoria.* Trans. H. E. Butler. Loeb Classical Library. Cambridge: Harvard University Press, 1980.

Riccobono, Antonio. *Aristotelis ars rhetorica . . . latine conversa.* Venice: Apud Paulum Meiettum, 1579.

————. *Aristotelis ars poetica ab eodem in latinam linquam versa. Cum eiusdem de re comica disputatione.* Venice: Apud Paulum Meiettum, 1579.

Soarez, Cypriano. *De arte rhetorica.* 2nd ed. 1568.

————. *The "De Arte Rhetorica" (1568).* Translation and commentary by Lawrence J. Flynn. Diss. University of Florida, 1955. Ann Arbor: University Microfilms, 16926.

Vallius, Paulus. *Logica Pauli Vallii Romani ex Societate Iesu.* 2 vols. Lyons: Sumptibus Ludovici Prost haeredibus Rouille, 1622.

Secondary Sources

Ashworth, Elizabeth J. "Traditional Logic." In *Cambridge History of Renaissance Philosophy*, ed. Charles B. Schmitt et al. Cambridge: Cambridge University Press, 1988.

Baron, Hans. *The Crisis of the Early Italian Renaissance: Civic Humanism and Republican Liberty in an Age of Classicism and Tyranny.* 2 vols. Princeton: Princeton University Press, 1955.

Berti, Enrico. "Ancient Greek Dialectic as Expression of Freedom of Thought and Speech." *Journal of the History of Ideas* 39 (1978): 347–370.

———. *Logica Aristotelica e Dialectica.* Bologna: L. Cappelli, 1983.

Bird, Otto. "The Tradition of the Logical Topics: Aristotle to Ockham." *Journal of the History of Ideas* 23.3 (1962): 307–323.

Black, Robert. "Italian Renaissance Education: Changing Perspectives and Continuing Controversies." *Journal of the History of Ideas* 52.2 (1991): 315–334.

Blackwell, Richard J. *Galileo, Bellarmine and the Bible.* Notre Dame, Ind.: University of Notre Dame Press, 1991.

Bonansea, Bernardino M. *Tomasso Campanella: Renaissance Pioneer of Modern Thought.* Washington, D.C.: The Catholic University of America Press, 1969.

Brandes, Paul D. *A History of Aristotle's Rhetoric with a Bibliography of Early Printings.* Metuchen, N.J. and London: The Scarecrow Press, 1989.

Camporeale, Salvatore. "Lorenzo Valla: The Transcending of Philosophy through Rhetoric," *Romance Notes* 30.3 (1990), 269–84.

———. *Lorenzo Valla: Umanesimo e Teologia.* Florence: Istituto Nazionale di Studi sul Rinascimento, 1972.

Carugo, Adriano, and Alistair Crombie. "The Jesuits and Galileo's Idea of Science and Nature." *Annali dell'Istituto e Museo di Storia della Scienza di Firenze* 8 (1983): 1–69.

Cassirer, Ernst, et al., eds. *The Renaissance Philosophy of Man.* Chicago: University of Chicago Press, 1983.

Clark, Donald Leman, ed. *Renaissance—Literary Theory and Practice: Classicism in the Rhetoric and Poetic of Italy, France, and England, 1400–1600.* New York: Columbia University Press, 1939.

Codina Mir, Gabriel. *Aux sources de la pédagogie des Jésuites. Le "Modus Parisiensis."* Rome: Institutum Historicum S. I., 1968.

Fantoli, Annibale. *Galileo for Copernicanism and for the Church.* George V. Coyne, trans., 2d ed. Studi Galileiani, vol. 3. Vatican City: Vatican Observatory Foundation, 1996.

Farrell, Allan P. *The Jesuit Code of Liberal Education. Development and Scope of the Ratio Studiorum.* Milwaukee: 1938.

Favaro, Antonio. *Galileo Galilei e lo Studio di Padova,* 2 vols. Padua: Editrice Antenore, 1966.

Feldhay, Rivka. "Knowledge and Salvation in Jesuit Culture." *Science in Context* 1.2 (1987): 195–213.

Finocchiaro, Maurice A. "Commentary: Dialectical Aspects of the Copernican Revolution." In *The Copernican Achievement,* ed. R. S. Westman. Berkeley: University of California Press, 1975, 204–212.

———. *The Galileo Affair: A Documentary History.* Berkeley: University of California Press, 1989.

Bibliography

——. *Galileo and the Art of Reasoning.* Boston Studies in the Philosophy of Science, Vol. 61. Dordrecht and Boston: Reidel, 1980.

——. "The Methodological Background to Galileo's Trial." In *Reinterpreting Galileo,* ed. William A. Wallace. Washington: The Catholic University of America Press, 1986, 241–272.

——. "Varieties of Rhetoric in Science." *History of the Human Sciences* 3.2 (1990): 177–193.

Flynn, Lawrence J. "The *De Arte Rhetorica* of Cyprian Soarez, S.J." *Quarterly Journal of Speech* 42 (Dec. 1956): 367–374.

——. "Sources and Influence of Soarez's De Arte Rhetorica." *Quarterly Journal of Speech* 43 (Oct. 1957): 257–265.

Fortenbaugh, William W. and David C. Mirhady, eds. *Peripatetic Rhetoric After Aristotle.* Rutgers University Studies in Classical Humanities, vol. 6. New Brunswick, N.J.: Transaction, 1994.

Fumaroli, Marc. *L'Age de L'Eloquence: Rhétorique et "res literaria" de la Renaissance au seuil de l'époque classique.* Geneva: Librairie Droz, 1980.

Funkenstein, Amos. "The Dialectical Preparation for Scientific Revolutions." In *The Copernican Achievement,* ed. R. S. Westman. Berkeley: University of California Press, 1975, 165–203.

Furley, David J., and Alexander Nehamas. *Aristotle's "Rhetoric": Philosophical Essays.* Princeton: Princeton University Press, 1994.

Garin, Eugenio. *Italian Humanism: Philosophy and Civic Life in the Renaissance.* Trans. Peter Munz. Oxford: Blackwell, 1965.

——. *Rinascite e rivoluzioni. Movimenti culturali dal XIV al XVIII secolo.* Bari: Laterza, 1976.

——. *Science and Civic Life in the Italian Renaissance.* Trans. Peter Munz. Garden City, N.Y.: Doubleday, 1969.

Gilbert, Neal. "The Italian Humanists and Disputation," In *Renaissance Essays in Honor of Hans Baron,* ed. A. Molho and H. A. Tedeschi. Florence: Sansoni, 1971, 203–226.

——. *Renaissance Concepts of Method.* New York: Columbia UP, 1960.

Grafton, Anthony and Lisa Jardine. *From Humanism to the Humanities: Education and the Liberal Arts in Fifteenth- and Sixteenth-Century Europe.* Cambridge: Harvard University Press, 1986.

Gray, Hanna. "Renaissance Humanism: The Pursuit of Eloquence." *Journal of the History of Ideas* 24 (1963): 497–514.

Green, Larry. "Aristotelian Rhetoric, Dialectic, and the Tradition of *Antistrophos.*" *Rhetorica* 8.1 (Winter 1990): 1–27.

——. "The Reception of Aristotle's Rhetoric in the Renaissance." In *Peripatetic Rhetoric After Aristotle,* ed. William W. Fortenbaugh and David C. Mirhady, Rutgers University Studies in Classical Humanities, vol. 6. New Brunswick, N.J.: Transaction, 1994, 320–348.

Green-Pedersen, Niels J. *The Tradition of the Topics in the Middle Ages.* Munich: Philosophia Verlag, 1984.

Grendler, Paul. *Schooling in Renaissance Italy: Literacy and Learning 1300–1600.* Baltimore: Johns Hopkins University Press, 1989.

——. *The Universities of the Italian Renaissance.* Baltimore & London: The Johns Hopkins University Press, 2002.

Grimaldi, William M. A. *Aristotle, Rhetoric I, II. A Commentary.* New York: Fordham University Press, 1980, 1988.

———. *Studies in the Philosophy of Aristotle's Rhetoric.* Wiesbaden: Franz Steiner, 1972.

Gross, Alan G., and Arthur E. Walzer, eds. *Rereading Aristotle's "Rhetoric."* Carbondale, Ill.: Southern Illinois University Press, 2000.

Hallyn, Fernand. "Dialectic et rhétorique devant la 'nouvelle science' du VIIe siècle." In *Histoire de la rhétorique dans l'Europe moderne 1450–1950.* Marc Fumaroli, ed. Paris: Presses universitaires de France, 1999, 601–28.

Hamlyn, D. W. "Aristotle on Dialectic," *Philosophy* 65:254 (Oct. 1970), 465–500.

Howell, Wilbur Samuel. *Logic and Rhetoric in England, 1500–1700.* Princeton: Princeton University Press, 1956.

Jardine, Lisa. "Humanistic Logic." In *The Cambridge History of Renaissance Philosophy,* ed. Charles B. Schmitt et al. Cambridge: Cambridge University Press, 1988, 173–198.

Kahn, Victoria. "The Rhetoric of Faith and the Use of Usage in Lorenzo Valla's *De libero arbitrio,*" *Journal of Medieval and Renaissance Studies* 13 (1983), 91–109.

Kennedy, George A. *Classical Rhetoric and Its Christian and Secular Tradition from Ancient to Modern Times.* Chapel Hill: University of North Carolina Press, 1999.

Kristeller, Paul Oskar. *Renaissance Thought I.* New York: Harper Torchbooks, 1961.

———. *Renaissance Thought and its Sources.* Ed. Michael Mooney. New York: Columbia University Press, 1979.

Kuhn, Thomas S. *The Copernican Revolution.* Cambridge: Harvard University Press, 1957.

Leff, Michael C. "The Topics of Argumentative Invention in Latin Rhetorical Theory from Cicero to Boethius." *Rhetorica* 1 (Spring 1983): 23–44.

Lohr, Charles H. "Jesuit Aristotelianism and Sixteenth-Century Metaphysics." *Paradosis* 32 (1976): 203–220.

———. *Latin Aristotle Commentaries, II. Renaissance Authors.* Florence: Olschki, 1988.

Mack, Peter. *Renaissance Argument: Valla and Agricola in the Traditions of Rhetoric and Dialectic.* Leiden: E. J. Brill, 1993.

Marsh, David. *The Quattrocento Dialogue.* Cambridge: Harvard University Press, 1980.

Miller, Carolyn. "Aristotle's 'Special Topics' in Rhetorical Practice and Pedagogy." *Rhetoric Society Quarterly* 17 (Winter 1987): 61–70.

Monfasani, John. "Lorenzo Valla and Rudolf Agricola," *Journal of the History of Philosophy* 28 (1990):181–199.

Moss, Jean Dietz. "Antistrophic Rhetoric: Aristotelian Rhetoric in Renaissance Rome and Padua." In *Philosophy in the Sixteenth and Seventeenth Centuries: Conversations with Aristotle,* ed. Constance Blackwell and Sachiko Kusukawa. Aldershot, Hampshire: Ashgate, 1999.

———. "Dialectics and Rhetoric: Questions and Answers in the Copernican Revolution." *Argumentation* 5 (1990): 17–37.

———. "Galileo's *Letter to Christina*: Some Rhetorical Considerations." *Renaissance Quarterly* 36.2 (Winter 1983): 547–576.

———. "The Interplay of Science and Rhetoric in Seventeenth-Century Italy," *Rhetorica* 7.1 (Winter 1989): 23–43.

———. "Ludovico Carbone on the Nature of Rhetoric," In *Rhetoric and Pedagogy: Its*

History, Philosophy, and Practice. Essays in Honor of James J. Murphy. ed. Winifred Bryan Horner and Michael Leff. Mahwah, N.J.: Lawrence Erlbaum Associates, 1995.

——. "Ludovico Carbone's Commentary on Aristotle's *De caelo*." In *Nature and Scientific Method,* ed. Daniel O. Dahlstrom. Washington, D.C.: The Catholic University of America Press, 1990, 169–192.

——. *Novelties in the Heavens: Rhetoric and Science in the Copernican Controversy.* Chicago: University of Chicago Press, 1993.

——, ed. *Rhetoric and Praxis. The Contribution of Classical Rhetoric to Practical Reasoning.* Washington, D.C.: The Catholic University of America Press, 1986.

——. "The Rhetoric Course at the Collegio Romano in the Latter Half of the Sixteenth Century." *Rhetorica* 4.2 (Spring 1986): 137–151.

——. "The Rhetoric of Proof in Galileo's Writings on the Copernican System." In *Reinterpreting Galileo,* ed. William A. Wallace. Washington, D.C.: The Catholic University of America Press, 1986, 179–204.

——. "Sacred Rhetoric and Appeals to the Passions: A Northern Italian View." In *Perspectives on Early Modern and Modern Intellectual History. A Festschrift for Nancy Struever,* ed. Joseph Marino and Melinda Schlitt. Rochester, N.Y.: The University of Rochester Press, 2000, 375–400.

Murphy, James J. *Rhetoric in the Middle Ages.* Berkeley: University of California Press, 1974.

——, ed. *Renaissance Eloquence.* Berkeley: University of California Press, 1983.

Nelson, Norman E. "Peter Ramus and the Confusion of Logic, Rhetoric, and Poetry," *Contributions in Modern Philology* 2 (April 1947), 1–22.

Olivieri, Luigi, ed. *Aristotelismo Veneto e Scienza Moderna.* 2 vols. Padua: Editrice Antenore, 1983.

O'Malley, John W. *Praise and Blame in Renaissance Rome: Rhetoric, Doctrine and Reform in the Sacred Orators of the Papal Court, c. 1450–1521.* Durham: University of North Carolina Press, 1979.

Ong, Walter J. *Ramus, Method, and the Decay of Dialogue.* Cambridge: Harvard University Press, 1958.

Pagano, Sergio M., ed. *I Documenti del Processo di Galileo Galilei.* Vatican City: Pontifical Academy of Sciences, 1984.

Rauh, Sister Miriam Joseph. *Shakespeare's Use of the Arts of Language.* New York: Columbia University Press, 1947, 1949. Abridged and reprinted as *Rhetoric in Shakespeare's Time.* New York: Harcourt, 1962.

Rorty, Amelie Oksenberg, ed. *Esssays on Aristotle's "Rhetoric."* Berkeley: University of California Press, 1996.

Santillana, Giorgio de. *The Crime of Galileo.* Chicago: University of Chicago Press, 1955.

Scaglione, Aldo. *The Liberal Arts and the Jesuit College System.* Amsterdam/Philadelphia: John Benjamins, 1986.

Schmitt, Charles B., Quentin Skinner, et al., eds. *The Cambridge History of Renaissance Philosophy.* Cambridge: Cambridge University Press, 1988.

Schneider, Bernhard, ed. *Aristoteles Latinus,* Vol. XXXI–2, *Rhetorica,* Translatio Anonyma sive Vetus et Translatio Guillelmi de Moerbeke. Leiden: E. J. Brill, 1978.

Seigel, Jerrold. *Rhetoric and Philosophy in Renaissance Humanism.* Princeton: Princeton University Press, 1968.

Solmsen, Friedrich. "The Aristotelian Tradition in Ancient Rhetoric." *American Journal of Philology* 62 (1941): 35–50.

Struever, Nancy S. *The Language of History in the Renaissance: Rhetoric and Historical Consciousness in Florentine Humanism.* Princeton: Princeton University Press, 1970.

———. "Lorenzo Valla: Humanist Rhetoric and the Critique of the Classical Languages of Morality." In *Renaissance Eloquence,* ed. James J. Murphy. Berkeley: University of California Press, 1983.

Stump, Eleonore. *Boethius's* De Topicis Differentiis. Ithaca: Cornell University Press, 1978.

———. *Boethius's* In Ciceronis Topica. Ithaca: Cornell University Press, 1988.

Trinkaus, Charles. "Italian Humanism and Scholastic Theology," in *Renaissance Humanism: Foundations, Forms and Legacy,* ed. Albert Rabill, Jr. Philadelphia: University of Pennsylvania Press, 1988, 327–348.

———. *Renaissance Transformations of Late Medieval Thought.* Variorum Collected Studies Series. Brookfield, Vt: Ashgate, 1999

Vasoli, Cesare. *La dialettica e la retorica dell'Umanismo.* Milan: Feltrinelli, 1968.

Vickers, Brian. "Epideictic Rhetoric in Galileo's *Dialogo.*" *Annali dell'Istituto e Museo di Storia della Scienza* 8 (1983): 69–102.

———. *In Defence of Rhetoric.* Oxford: Clarendon Press, 1988.

Villoslada, Riccardo G. *Storia del Collegio Romano dal suo inizio (1551) alla soppressione della Compagnia di Gesù (1773).* Rome: Gregorian University, 1954.

Von Gebler, Karl. *Galileo Galilei and the Roman Curia.* Trans. Mrs. George Sturge. London: C. K. Paul & Co., 1879.

Wallace, William A. "Albert the Great's Inventive Logic: His Exposition of the Topics of Aristotle. *American Catholic Philosophical Quarterly* 70 (1996): 1–39.

———. "Antonio Riccobono: The Teaching of Rhetoric in 16th-Century Padua." *Rhetoric and Pedagogy, Its History, Philosophy and Practice. Essays in Honor of James J. Murphy,* ed. Winifred Bryan Horner and Michael Leff. Mahwah, N.J.: Lawrence Erlbaum, 1995, 149–170.

———. "Aristotelian Influences on Galileo's Thought." In *Aristotelismo Veneto e Scienza Moderna,* ed. Luigi Olivieri. 2 vols. Padua: Antenore, 1983. I: 349–378.

———. *Causality and Scientific Explanation.* 2 vols. Ann Arbor: University of Michigan Press, 1972, 1974.

———. "The Certitude of Science in Late Medieval and Renaissance Thought." *History of Philosophy Quarterly* 3 (July 1986): 281–291.

———. *Galileo and His Sources: The Heritage of the Collegio Romano in Galileo's Science.* Princeton: Princeton University Press, 1984.

———. *Galileo, the Jesuits and the Medieval Aristotle.* Collected Studies Series no. 346. Hampshire, Great Britain: Variorum, 1991.

———. "Galileo's Early Arguments for Geocentrism and his Later Rejection of Them." In *Novità Celesti e Crisi del Sapere,* ed. Paolo Galluzzi. Florence: Istituto e Museo di Storia della Scienza, 1983, 31–40.

———. "Galileo's Jesuit Connections and Their Influence on His Science." In *Jesuit Science and the Republic of Letters,* ed. Mordechai Feingold. Cambridge, Mass. and London: The M.I.T. Press, 2003, 99–126.

———. *Galileo's Logic of Discovery and Proof. The Background, Content, and Use of His Appropriated Treatises on Aristotle's* Posterior Analytics. Boston Studies in the Philosophy of Science, Vol. 137. Dordrecht: Kluwer, 1992.

——. *Galileo's Logical Treatises. A Translation, with Notes and Commentary, of His Appropriated Latin Questions on Aristotle's* Posterior Analytics. Boston Studies in the Philosophy of Science, Vol. 138. Dordrecht: Kluwer, 1992.

——. "Galileo's Pisan Studies in Science and Philosophy. In *The Cambridge Companion to Galileo,* ed. Peter Machamer. Cambridge: Cambridge University Press, 1998, 27–52.

——. "Galileo's Science and the Trial of 1633." *The Wilson Quarterly* 7 (Summer 1983): 154–164.

——. "Galileo's Trial and Proof of the Earth's Motion," *Catholic Dossier* 1.2 (1995), 7–13.

——. *The Modeling of Nature: Philosophy of Science and Philosophy of Nature in Synthesis.* Washington, D.C.: The Catholic University of America Press, 1996.

——. "The Problem of Apodictic Proof in Early Seventeenth-Century Mechanics: Galileo, Guevara, and the Jesuits." *Science in Context* 3.1 (1989): 67–87.

——. "Randall *Redivivus*: Galileo and the Paduan Aristotelians." *Journal of the History of Ideas* 49 (1988): 133–149.

——. "Science." *Encyclopedia of the Renaissance.* 5: 427–29.

——. "Thomas Aquinas on Dialectics and Rhetoric," In *A Straight Path: Studies in Medieval Philosophy and Culture. A Festschrift in honor of Arthur Hyman,* ed. Ruth Link-Salinger. Washington, D.C.: The Catholic University of America Press, 1988, 244–254.

——, ed. *Reinterpreting Galileo.* Studies in Philosophy and the History of Philosophy, Vol. 15. Washington, D.C.: The Catholic University of America Press, 1986.

Weimar, W. "Science as a Rhetorical Transaction." *Philosophy and Rhetoric* 10 (1977): 1–29.

Weinberg, Bernard, *A History of Literary Criticism in the Italian Renaissance,* 2 vols. Chicago: The University of Chicago Press, 1961.

——, ed. *Trattati di poetica e retorica del cinquecento,* 4 vols. Scrittori d'Italia n. 253. Bari: Laterza, 1972.

Westfall, Richard S. *Essays on the Trial of Galileo.* Vatican City: The Vatican Observatory, 1989.

Westman, Robert S. "The Copernicans and the Churches." In *God and Nature,* ed. David C. Lindberg and Ronald L. Numbers. Berkeley: University of California Press, 1986, 76–113.

——. "Politics, Poetics, and Patronage." In *Reappraisals of the Scientific Revolution,* ed. David C. Lindberg and Robert S. Westman. Cambridge: Cambridge University Press, 1990, 167–205.

——. "The Reception of Galileo's *Dialogue.*" In *Novità Celesti e Crisi del Sapere,* ed. Paolo Galluzzi. Florence: Istituto e Museo di Storia della Scienza, 1983, 329–371.

——, ed. *The Copernican Achievement.* Berkeley: University of California Press, 1975.

Wyss-Morigi, Giovanna. *Contributo allo Studio del Dialogo all'Epoca dell' Umanismo e del Rinascimento.* Diss. University of Bern, 1947.

Index of Names

Index of Subjects by Author

Carbone

Art of Speaking

Introduction to Logic

On Invention

On Divine Rhetoric

Carbone-Soarez

Tables of Soarez's Rhetoric

Riccobono

On the Nature of Rhetoric

On the Nature of Oratorical Demonstration

The Nature of the Oration of Character

Rhetoric and Dialectic in the Time of Galileo was designed and composed in
Requiem by Kachergis Book Design, Pittsboro, North Carolina; and printed on
sixty-pound Sebago 2000 Eggshell and bound by The Maple-Vail Book
Manufacturing Group of York, Pennsylvania.